The Ironside Diaries

1937–1940

General Sir Edmund Ironside

TIME UNGUARDED

The Ironside Diaries
1937-1940

Edited by
Colonel Roderick Macleod, D.S.O., M.C.
and Denis Kelly

DAVID McKAY COMPANY, Inc.
NEW YORK

Printed in Great Britain by
T. and A. Constable Ltd
Hopetoun Street, Edinburgh

CONTENTS

Part One

TIME UNGUARDED: 1937–1939

Part Two

THE SECOND WORLD WAR

Part Three

SCANDINAVIA

Part Four

THE BATTLE OF FRANCE

Part Five

HOME DEFENCE

MAPS AND ILLUSTRATIONS

Maps

Illustrations

7

Maps and Illustrations

8

ACKNOWLEDGMENTS

THE editors' thanks are due to Mariot, Lady Ironside, for granting unrestricted access to the diaries of her late husband; to Brigadier and Mrs. W. E. Duncan for many months of hospitality and accommodation in their London home while this book was being completed; and to Ralph Arnold for much wise advice. The editors, however, bear sole responsibility for the present text.

Mr. J. F. Trotter drew the maps, and in the course of many re-drafts, over a million words were typed with patience and accuracy by Mrs. Kloegman.

Biographical notes on the principal personalities mentioned in the text have been included. These are of the briefest character and have been extracted mainly from past and present editions of *Who's Who*.

RODERICK MACLEOD
DENIS KELLY

LONDON
Ash Wednesday, 1962

PART ONE

TIME UNGUARDED: 1937-1939

CHAPTER I

The Man and the Diaries

IRONSIDE was Chief of the Imperial General Staff for the first nine months of the Second World War. On the eve of the evacuation of Dunkirk he was appointed Commander-in-Chief of the Home Forces of the United Kingdom, and on July 19, 1940, when a German invasion of England seemed imminent, he was succeeded by General Alan Brooke. He spent the rest of his life in retirement and died in Millbank Military Hospital on September 22, 1959. Six foot and four inches in height, and popularly known as "Tiny", he was an interpreter in several languages and the original of Richard Hannay of *The Thirty Nine Steps*, *Greenmantle* and *Mr. Standfast*. His life was almost as varied and romantic as John Buchan's soldier-hero.

William Edmund Ironside was born on May 6, 1880. His father, a Surgeon-Major of the Royal Horse Artillery, died when he was very young, and his mother, a Miss Emma Maria Richards, was a strong-minded lady who made many sacrifices to equip her only son for the Army. In those Victorian days it was cheaper to live abroad, and she eked out her widow's pension by much travel on the Continent. Thus, like Sir Anthony Eden, he began to learn foreign languages. When the time came for Ironside to go to school, he was sent to St. Andrews in Fife and to Tonbridge School in Kent. In 1897 he became an officer-cadet of the Royal Military Academy at Woolwich, and two years later he embarked for the South African war with the 44th Battery of the Royal

13

Field Artillery. He served throughout this melancholy struggle and at its conclusion he escorted the future Field-Marshal Smuts to the Peace Conference at Vereeniging.

Soon afterwards, disguised as a Boer transport driver, he accompanied the German military expedition to South-West Africa in order to gain information for the British Intelligence. His bulldog, with a collar labelled "Lt. Ironside, R.F.A.", went too. A German officer asked him how he had got the dog, and Ironside, stroking its neck to conceal the label, replied in Cape Dutch that he had stolen it from the British. He soon buried the collar, but narrowly escaped detection when beginning to answer back a bullying N.C.O. in pure German. Later on, when visiting a bank-manager's office, he overheard a German officer in the corridor giving a detailed description and enquiring for a British spy. The game was up, and Ironside had to escape.

Then followed service in India with "I" (Bull's) troop of the Royal Horse Artillery, and "Y" troop at Robert's Heights in South Africa. Two staff appointments with cavalry and infantry brigades gave him considerable knowledge of these arms, and in January 1913 he went as a student to the Staff College at Camberley.

He spent the whole of the First World War on the Western Front until his appointment in September 1918 as Brigadier General Staff to the Allied expedition in Archangel. His own account of this campaign has been published.[1] He took over command within a few days of his arrival, and under Lord Rawlinson was largely responsible for its successful withdrawal. In March 1920 he headed the British Military Mission to Hungary and helped the operations of Admiral Horthy and the drawing of the frontiers of that unhappy country. The summer found him in command of mixed Allied forces on the Ismid peninsula to the east of Constantinople and in the wild North Persian frontier against threatened Turkish and Bolshevik invasions. By now he was the youngest Major-General in the British Army. Ability as a commander and diligence in foreign languages had brought their reward.

[1] *Archangel 1918-19* (Constable)

14

In 1922 he was made Commandant of the Staff College at Camberley. There, and later in India, he taught tactics based not only on the weapons of the present but on those likely to appear in ten years' time. Forceful, outspoken, imaginative and unconventional, Ironside was not appreciated by certain of his superiors. He never intrigued and never refused a job, and after several years on half-pay, caused by his rapid promotion, found himself, somewhat disillusioned, General Officer Commanding the Eastern Command in England. The date was April 1936, and it is thirteen months later in his career that the present selection from his diaries begins.

"Diaries", said a famous statesman, "are tricky material to publish", and Ironside expressly forbade the publication of his own diaries in a will dated January 1, 1930. Between 1945, however, and his death in 1959 there appeared a number of factually misleading accounts of the opening months of the Second World War, and the senior editor of this book, Colonel Roderick Macleod, asked the Field-Marshal's permission to tell the truth. Macleod had been his friend and brother-officer for more than thirty years. Together they had been at the Staff College at Camberley, Macleod as pupil and Ironside as Commandant; they had served together in India; and when Ironside was appointed Chief of the Imperial General Staff on September 4, 1939, Macleod became his Military Assistant. He accompanied the Field-Marshal on nearly all his tours of the Front in France and to the Conferences at French Headquarters, and they remained in intimate contact until Ironside's death. Ironside agreed to Macleod writing an account of the period 1937–1940, and relented to the extent of encouraging him to illustrate this account with extracts from his diaries. Indeed he gave him *carte blanche* to quote what he chose. The Field-Marshal approved Macleod's first draft, but realized it was over-long. He died before the text could be shortened. The problem then arose: to shorten this existing draft, or to start afresh?

Ironside had played an important part in these critical years. He had met Hitler in September 1937 and attended the autumn

manœuvres of the German fighting services. As one of the most
senior generals of the British army he had a precise knowledge of
the nakedness of Great Britain and had watched with dismay her
slow, fumbling efforts to rearm. As Governor of Gibraltar in 1938
and 1939, when the Nazis were marching into Austria and
Czechoslovakia and Mussolini was busy in North Africa and
Abyssinia, he had perceived the crucial importance of the Middle
East in the coming war. As Chief of the Imperial General Staff
he had watched the Russo-German partition of Poland, the
German conquest of Scandinavia and of France. Finally, as
Commander-in-Chief Home Forces, he had witnessed the
expulsion of the British Expeditionary Force from the Continent of Europe, and had largely laid the plans and gathered
the troops to repel Hitler's expected invasion of the United
Kingdom. Throughout all this time he had kept a diary—
writing it up at the end of each day. With this material
in their hands it seemed to the editors of this book that
extracts from the relevant diaries would be of far more interest to
the general public and of far greater historical value than any
account based on the inevitable hindsight and second-thoughts of
twenty years after. In selecting the passages to publish they sought
to respect the well-established principal of English criminal law
that a witness may refresh his memory from notes written at the
time of an event, or immediately thereafter, but that anything in
the nature of subsequent written reflection or reminiscence is ex-
cluded. *L'esprit d'escalier* is not good evidence. This rule has been
departed from only in a few instances where Ironside's subsequent
non-diary comments, either volunteered, or elicited in reply to
enquiries put to him by Macleod, seemed to illuminate the story.
Diary entries are always prefaced by a date. Post-war reflections
are inset and clearly indicated. The editors' explanatory notes and
narration passages are again differentiated typographically and
have been kept as brief as possible. They are needed because the
diaries do not always tell a continuous story, and because in times
of especial stress Ironside had not always the time to write a full
account. Each night, however, he discussed the events of the day
with his military assistant, and the narrative is based on Macleod's

notes and recollections of these conversations, on what he saw and witnessed at the time, and on the official histories.

Ironside had kept a diary since his subaltern days in order, as he himself said, to clear his mind and crystallize his judgments of day-to-day events, and to refresh and correct his recollections of the past. Every night he wrote a page and sometimes several pages in his clear and characteristically bold hand, in brown, leather covered, foolscap-sized volumes, each about half-an-inch thick and bought from the Aldershot publishing company of Gale & Polden. Cartoons, press-cuttings, photographs, letters and, in at least one instance, an entire article from a magazine were pasted, with comments, into these diary volumes after the manner of a Victorian common-place book. Ironside wrote as the thoughts formed on his pen, and in all the twelve volumes, containing some 850,000 words from which the present selection is taken, the editors have been struck by the fact that there is not a single correction or interpolation. He never crossed out or altered a word, and since he only wrote in volumes which were already bound, it was impossible to substitute a page. The diaries may therefore be accepted as a genuine and spontaneous day-to-day composition. But spontaneous composition has its disadvantages. Ironside would occasionally start with a crucial subject, digress into other happenings of the day, and then revert, sometimes many paragraphs later, and often repetitively, to the topic with which he originally started. These distractions have been omitted in the version which is now presented, and their excision is indicated by dots. All other omissions are indicated in the same manner. These omissions are confined to entries dealing with Ironside's family and private life, to occasional over-harsh judgments on individuals, to repetitions, and to passages which have had to be sacrificed to produce a book of reasonable length. The general tenor of Ironside's judgments on individuals has, despite occasional suppressions, been preserved, and there is room to read between the lines. When Ironside has repeated himself, the editors have used their discretion, and as a general rule have preferred first thoughts to second thoughts. Hearsay—"met so-and-so who told me such-and-such"—has also led, in accordance with what lawyers term "the best evidence rule"—to more excisions and to more dots, and so too has speculation about the past or future, except where such hearsay and speculation appear to have influenced the diarist's conduct or judgments. Great care has been taken to ensure that, subject to these omissions, all of which are typographically indicated, the present text accords word for word with what Ironside originally wrote. Mariot, Lady Ironside, and the present Lord Ironside, have generously allowed the editors untrammelled access to the Field-Marshal's diaries. There has been no vetting or censorship by his family, and indeed no member of his family saw the present text before it was made public.

This, then, is what Ironside wrote at the time, day by day, under pressure of events, and with no thought of eventual publication. In the words of a famous author: "It is not history, but it may be judged a contribution to history." The full text of the diaries cannot be published for many years, but the editors earnestly hope that when the time comes for scholars and other serious enquirers to examine the original volumes, the present selection will be judged an honest one.

CHAPTER II

Eastern Command and the Meeting with Hitler

GREAT BRITAIN ended the First World War as one of the strongest Powers in the world. Her Fleets dominated the seas, her Air Force the skies, and her Armies were supreme in Europe and in the Middle East. When the Second World War started she was desperately weak on land, weak in the air, and not very strong at sea. This might not have happened if her Army, small though it was, had been equipped for modern warfare. But very little had been done.

In 1926 General Sir George Milne had become Chief of the Imperial General Staff and announced his intention of mechanizing the Army. An "Experimental Force", the forerunner of the modern armoured division, was formed. "It is enough for us", he told an assembly of senior officers, "that we have the means in the petrol engine of altering methods of warfare. Crowds of men on the battlefield are out of place when you have low-flying aeroplanes against them. Think of their communications and supplies. The hostile machine-gun takes away the tactical mobility of the infantryman, and we add to his difficulties by an enormous artillery preparation. Petrol mobility enables you to carry armour and to break through. Against the machine-gun the solution is the Armoured Fighting Vehicle. We shall also

□□ have Armoured Divisions." He acted swiftly, and on November 13 the new armoured and mechanized vehicles were demonstrated near Camberley to members of the British Cabinet and to various Dominion Prime Ministers who were attending an Imperial Conference. The latest tanks, "dragons" to pull guns, and cross-country carriers all made a deep impression on the assembled company.

But Parliament grudged the money and the Army reactionaries were hostile. In September 1928 the Secretary of State for War told the House of Commons that the Armoured Force would be dispersed, and the War Office would experiment on strengthening the infantry division with an infusion of armoured vehicles. It was not until 1937 that three armoured brigades were formed. By 1939 the Germans had six fully equipped armoured divisions, and Britain had only two. Even these were incomplete. Both the War Office and the Government had been tempted to reconstruct the new Army on the pattern of the First World War, no Government had decided what kind of Army was required, no one, until it was too late, would provide the money.

There were a number of excuses. The War Cabinet had ruled in 1919 that the Fighting Services should frame their estimates on the assumption that "the British Empire will not be engaged in any great war for the next ten years, *and that no Expeditionary Force will be required*". It was recognized that the Army might have to fight in places other than Europe, such as the Western Desert of Egypt, and it was admitted that Armoured Divisions would be desirable, but despite the urgings of the C.I.G.S., very few tanks were produced. The Army's task, so ran the official doctrine, was to defend the United Kingdom, police the Empire, guard our overseas possessions and ports, and deal with "a second-class Power in the Middle East"—meaning Italy. It was only to be trained and equipped for these functions, and there was no need for mechanization or for Armoured Divisions. Training for a European war was ruled out, and the Army was given no heavy equipment for fighting a first-class Power. Most of its weapons dated from 1918. "The British Army", said Mr. Duff Cooper, then (1933) Financial Secretary to the War Office, "is not designed for Continenta wars. The purpose of the British Army is to maintain order in the British Empire only." And later: "The Army is not likely to be used for a big war in Europe for many years to come." Next year he became Secretary of State for War. Such pronouncements and policy all depended on there being no world war in the foreseeable future.

In February 1937 a White Paper on Defence proclaimed a five-year plan of rearmament on a much bigger scale, and in the following May Mr. Neville Chamberlain succeeded Mr. Stanley Baldwin as Prime Minister. But the War Office still clung to a 1914-pattern Army with the addition of modern equipment; and the White Paper itself was vague as to how and when such equipment would be provided.

General Sir Edmund Ironside, General Officer Commanding-in-Chief Eastern Command,[1] with headquarters at the Horse Guards, noted in his diary: "The rôle of the Army has not yet been decided. They are all frightened to death at the prospect of our being ready to make an enormous Continental Army again. The cry is that we squandered men in the last war." After an interview with the then Chief of the Imperial General Staff, Sir Cyril Deverell, he wrote in his Diary:

May 13, 1937

The whole policy is once more to be reviewed. Whether we are to have an Army or not has been considered and reconsidered by the Committee of the Chiefs of Staff. They have unanimously

---

[1] Eastern Command then covered twelve counties—Norfolk, Suffolk, Essex, Kent, Sussex, Northampton, Bedford, Herts, Surrey, Middlesex, Cambridge and Huntingdon—and contained the 4th (Regular) Division, three Territorial Divisions, the 1st Anti-Aircraft (Territorial) Division, and some Coast Defence troops.

come to the conclusion that you cannot equate an Army and an Air Force. Neither can replace the other. They still adhere to the three duties of an Army:

    (i) Garrisons overseas.
    (ii) Home Defence and Security.
    (iii) An overseas force ready to go anywhere.

The strength of the Army at home is dictated by the strength of our overseas garrisons. This should then be organized in the most modern form.

These Chiefs of Staff gave it as their opinion that the German Army could not be stopped in its advance by an Air Force alone. We could not limit our help to an Air Force alone. That sooner or later we must be called upon to find an Army and that Army must be trained and given proper reserves. . . . Our Regular Army has no reserves. The difficulty is that no Chancellor can possibly keep up a Navy which has a recurring yearly budget of £100 millions, and an Air Force costing a like amount, and then an Army on top of that.

The question at the moment is quite different to 1914. Then, the Terrier [i.e. the Territorial Army] went off at once. Now it will be twelve months before any Terrier can be equipped and trained on a modern scale. The Army is trying to get this period reduced to four months, but that means that the Terrier Army must have modern weapons issued to it in peace. As we know, even the Regular Army has none.

To re-equip and put our Imperial Coast Defences in order will cost £204 millions. Deverell told us that he thought he had made an estimate upon which his successor might work. The new Terrier equipment would cost £9 millions. The question of equipment is by no means easy, because we had undertaken to re-arm both Egypt and Iraq. It was most urgent that we should not allow this trade to pass into the hands of Germany who, of course, would be most eager to take it on. Neither of these two countries would believe that we hadn't got all the necessary new equipment packed away somewhere. We had to make issues to them to keep them quiet. . . .

22

Once again I came home profoundly sad at the state to which the Army has been brought.

May 22

We have no more troops this year and I am afraid that our training is going to be just as poor this year as last. . . . Why cannot we make some attempt at reducing our overhead expenses? I cannot believe we are justified in keeping the Commands and staffs that we do. I have no experience of the War Office,[1] but I simply cannot believe that we are doing the right thing. . . . If I were called suddenly to be C.I.G.S. I should take a year at least to get down to things. We must have the men. Without them it would be better to close down half the regiments, instead of making more. . . . I quite understand that many of the officers at the War Office are kept as a reserve, but even then we must have too many. If we take the Intelligence Branch, I am sure that if we didn't have so many constant changes we should have better results. . . . In the Armies on the Continent the Intelligence officers make a profession of their branch and remain in it for years. They do not aspire to go out and command things. They remain as specialists.

May 23

The Recruiting campaign for the Regular Army is not going well. . . . What we want is a very definite statement from the Prime Minister that we need an Army. Then we can lay down what they want the Army for and how it is to be used. Then and then only shall we begin to get men of any sort.

A few days later Mr. Neville Chamberlain appointed Mr. Leslie Hore-Belisha Secretary of State for War. The Prime Minister doubtless hoped to raise the Army's prestige, and Hore-Belisha had proved a successful and popular Minister of Transport.

[1] Ironside had never served there in any capacity.

May 28

In the evening the new Cabinet is now out. Duff Cooper moves on to the Admiralty and we get Hore-Belisha. . . . He is a young man and has certainly had some bright ideas while he has been running the Ministry of Transport. I don't know him, and have only seen him a couple of times. Is it a good thing to change horses at this moment? Will Hore-Belisha be able to seize the reins quickly enough? He may be the very man we want.

May 29

I cannot say what Hore-Belisha will do or what I think of it. He is only 41 and full of energy. . . . We are at our lowest ebb in the Army and the Jew may resuscitate us. I hope that he hasn't been ordered to cut us down, and yet surely we can be cut down in our overhead expenses.

May 30

I lay awake in the morning and thought of Hore-Belisha. He will probably be our saving. He is ambitious and will not be lazy like some of the others were. He starts in when things are at their worst and will have to show results.

June 13

I sat thinking of our military position last night, and came to the conclusion that the absence of an Expeditionary Force at this moment is probably a godsend. Nobody can send off a force to the Continent. Our contribution would be derisory. I think that in the organization of this Expeditionary Force we have been thinking too much of the war in France. What we want to think of is a force capable of restoring our lost position in the Mediterranean. A much smaller and more mobile force than we imagine. Only light transport, since the Navy will supply most of the long-distance traffic. Landings of every sort and kind in all sorts of weathers. . . . We shall begin from the eastern end [of the Mediterranean] as much as from the western end—even more in all probability. We will use Iraq and Palestine as our jumping-off stations. We may have to send off troops *via* the Cape. Small fighting Brigades. We need not enter into land campaigns, such as we did against the Germans in German East Africa, and such as might occur to strategists in the future of Abyssinia. The settlement with Italy must come sooner or later. . . .

I think that if I were C.I.G.S. I should cease organizing an Expeditionary Force upon the French pattern except on paper. I should organize one in small compact brigades [each] of some 5,000 men in all. Lightly equipped and very handy. I should study to get our Brigadiers younger and more active. Far fewer office men.

June 26

Churchill urges Chamberlain to take a stronger line with Germany and Italy. The papers say that Chamberlain will be stronger than Baldwin. The real question to my mind is whether we can yet afford to be strong with anybody. Somebody might call our bluff and we should then be exposed. . . . I think that it is quite certain that it would be far too dangerous for our ships to think of going into the Mediterranean until we had cleared the air properly. . . . More and more air bases are being set up by Italy, not only in the Mediterranean but in the Red Sea.

June 27

We have nothing with which to fight—literally nothing—and will not have anything for two years.

> Mr. Hore-Belisha, in search of more soldiers, improved the conditions of service. Reservists were allowed to rejoin, thus increasing the peace-time strength of the Regular Army, but depleting its mobilization reserves. He also lowered the physical and mental standards for recruits.

August 7

Belisha has made a speech somewhere in Hampshire, saying that changes [will be made] in the terms of enlistment—the most drastic that have ever been made—and I suppose that it will be "long service being brought in". Anything to get men, but I am sure Privates of 40 or thereabouts are not much good for field service. A man in the ranks ages far more quickly than the officer does. The work he has to do is not work for a man of over 30.

August 8

The papers are full of Belisha's speech. Men in the Army are to have the same chance as those in the Navy of having long service. . . . The ramifications of the whole thing are incalculable. Still, anything to get the men before next year. . . .

August 11

The nation does not believe an Army is necessary and the Government, so democratic is it, will not make up the nation's mind for it.

September 17

The B.G.S. [Brigadier, General Staff] rang me up and told me that . . . Gort had been put in as Military Secretary. This was the best piece of news I had heard for many years. We shall now have one of the best officers we have in the Army, a man of human parts who is not finished as regards the Service. He will follow Caesar humanly. He will not deal with men as if they were so many pieces of paper with figures on them.

Such was the scene in England. Ironside was now to have a view of the enemy's preparations for war. In August 1937 he had been invited to attend the German Army manœuvres. He sailed from Harwich on the evening of September 21 and dined next night at the Baltic port of Warnemünde with General von Reichenau and Marshal Badoglio. He was briefed as to the course that the manœuvres would take. Next morning he was driven to a *rendez-vous* where he met Field-Marshal von Blomberg, the Director of the manœuvres, and General von Fritsch, the commander of one side. Von Blomberg was at this time in command of all the three German fighting services, von Reichenau was his second in command, and von Fritsch was Commander-in-Chief of the Army. He noted in his diary that he saw no signs of malnutrition among the German population, and made this observation about the German Army: "I am quite sure that they are nowhere near ready for war, even at the tempo they have been going. If I were to hazard a guess, I might say 1940. . . . When they have had several more manœuvres and exercises they may go a little quicker."

September 24 [Germany]

I am not sure whether the German may not become once again the seeker after world-power when he once more feels his feet. It is possible that the Junker feeling may come on once more, but it isn't here at the moment. I suggest that we study the post-Jena period once more to see how the symptoms fit. In those days things went slowly but now the tempo of everything is terribly fast. We must remember that when we try to compare things. . . . "Can a leopard change his spots?" But I don't think there is any immediate danger.

September 25 [Germany]

Last night I got [Generals] Richtman and Reichenau and Koch and got them drinking whisky. They were silly to think that they, who had never tasted it, could compete with an old Scotsman like me. I got them more than a little bit full and it was a question of "in vino veritas". In the end Reichenau wanted to drink to "brotherhood with England, but only for two years". Most amusing, and I don't think that any of the three villains saw any humour in their toast, which I drank enthusiastically. I wonder if there is anything prophetic in 1940 or 1941? There is no doubt that these people are not ready. Not for a big foe. I am sure of that. But will they try it out on the dog first?

To-day we had a devil of a day with the Navy. As our genial General Koch said "the Navy have produced all their trumps". Submarines attacking, smoke screens, aeroplane torpedo attacks, shelling and bombing of convoys, all very well shown. . . . The central direction of the three Services is now in the hands of von

Blomberg and is completely military. The central piece is the Army. They still believe in that. The other two Services must devote their energies to co-operating with the Army. . . . All are full of enthusiasm in working for one thing—the defence of Germany. We have nothing like it here in England. With their usual thoroughness they are working out a complete system for the defence—and for offence also, for they have not given up the idea of forestalling an enemy attack. . . .

All the minor nations are now terrified of [Germany]. We shall no doubt be faced with a *fait accompli* one of these days, and the little nation that has been raped will scream in vain. I hope we shall then be strong enough to look after ourselves. We want a great fright to make us realize that we are in danger and then a knock or two to unite us all firmly.

On the 26th, a Sunday, the show-piece of the manœuvres was staged—an attack by 800 tanks and 400 aircraft.

September 26

About 12 o'clock about 20 cars came up the road. In the leading one, an enormous open grey six-wheeler, sat the Führer in light brown—almost biscuit colour—with a cap with a brown leather peak. On his right was Mussolini in his greyish field kit, almost a light blue. His great black face and big jaw stuck out fiercely. Then he raised his hand in a Fascist salute as did Hitler with his. The German seems less theatrical. Mussolini gave one the impression of trying to look fierce. He stalked up the hill with the Führer almost hurrying beside him. Neither of them big men in size. . . .

The air attack and the tank attack was then launched with a lot of popping and banging. Rows and rows of them coming in waves. . . . It showed what a force Germany has created in such a short time, even though it is at the moment in many ways an experimental one. They still require a long time to perfect this great instrument of theirs.

Just after the attack commenced Goering came up in Air Force uniform and walked up the hill. A youngish but immensely fat man, with simply enormous legs. A fair unlined face, and a few longish hairs hanging down under his cap. I should say that his life is not a very good one, for he panted badly coming up the hill and was obviously distressed. He was surrounded by a small band of his party, all frightfully enthusiastic at being in the train of so great a man.

After the attack had been going along for nearly an hour, we, the British delegation, were ushered up towards the tent and introduced to the Führer. He came walking down to us in his long coat and I was at once struck by his vacuous-looking grin—one can hardly call it a smile—and his watery, weak-looking eye. . . . Reichenau told Hitler that I could speak German, and I chatted for a minute with him in German. He complimented me and told me I spoke it like a German.

The man struck me not at all. His voice was soft and his German of the south. He made no more impression on me than would have a somewhat mild professor whom I rather suspected of having a drop too much on occasions.

I must say that I was disappointed. The man must have the stuff in him, but he didn't make any impression upon me.

Then, a minute later, Goering came gracefully as an elephant down to us. . . . I thought Goering a nasty creature . . . a harsh and domineering voice.

One almost wishes that our rulers could have seen this show. They would have been impressed by the pace at which these people are working, by their obvious earnestness, their sincerity. The more I look at it the more do I think that they will pull off what they are after. The French want us to join with them in an offensive the minute that Germany turns eastwards and attacks her [i.e. France's] allies there. Can their Army carry out an offensive? I should much doubt if the French soldiers will fight an offensive battle in support of any Ally so far away. . . . An offensive against Germany from the West must penetrate very deeply and would be a question of an enormous invading force. It would mean something that France couldn't, in my opinion, sustain for a minute.

September 27 [Berlin]

I think that the German Army has developed in a marvellous way. It is madly enthusiastic and very efficient. . . . Everybody watching this effort is terrified, and I am sure nothing will stand up to it when the moment comes. . . . The German Army, Navy, and Air Force are all united and are working for one thing together. They have one direction and as far as I could see no jealousies. They have no watertight compartments. They have thus a great advantage over us, who have made no attempt even to lay down the duties of the various forces. No one will touch this thorny subject. . . .

There is no danger now but there will be in, say, five years. We want to get a move on pretty quickly to be sure.

On September 29, his last day in Berlin, Ironside watched a march-past of troops, and then lunched with the senior officers of the German Army. "The march-past", he wrote afterwards, "took place down the Unter den Linden. It gave us a good opportunity of seeing most of the old soldiers in the German Army and most of the principal Nazi leaders. Our seats were to be in the front row of the stand, immediately behind the saluting point. As we came up and stood in front of the stand to salute, all the old generals stood up to return the salute. The most conspicuous figure was Field-Marshal von Mackensen in his Hussar busby, with its regimental skull-and-crossbones badge. The sun was shining, and his long grey moustaches and his piercing blue eyes showed up very clearly.

"The first Nazi leader to arrive was Hess, Hitler's deputy. He gave the Nazi salute in front of the stand. All the generals, including ourselves, rose and answered him with a military salute. As I looked round I saw that many of the officers were looking away from Hess as he stood right in front of us. They looked uninterested and disgusted, and his bad reception was most marked. All sat down as quickly as they could.

"The next to arrive was Goering, in his Air Force kit. He made a more imposing figure, but he looked very young with his pink clean-shaven face. He gave the Hitler salute and repeated the words 'Heil Hitler', which drew a more or less reluctant military salute in return and no repetition of the 'Heil'. Goering's enormously fat body and legs seemed to be shaking like a jelly inside his light-coloured uniform. I gained the impression that he, too, was an unpopular man.

"Finally Hitler arrived with an A.D.C. He stood only a yard or two in front of us while he saluted stiffly. All the old generals gave him a very hearty reception. They all gave him the Hitler salute, and shouted out his name. As I watched them I got the impression that each general hoped that his arm and hand would be seen by the Führer among the many. His reception was quite tumultuous. It was evident that he was very much accepted as their leader."

September 29 [Berlin]

Lunch at the Continental with General von Fritsch. Some hundred of us. All the senior German generals of the Army. They are all pretty well chosen, I should say. All physically fit. . . . I sat next the Commander of the Armoured Division and he told me that they had copied us pretty religiously as regards tanks, even to the men's uniform. . . . They are probably more industrious than we are, but I am sure that they require all their rules to be there. . . . They shrink from improvisation. . . . One General said to me that he envied us our chance to serve out in the world. That he had noticed that you had only to put a Britisher in a difficult position and he at once took charge naturally. He seemed to wake up and do things whereas he had been asleep before. I thought to myself that he had judged us very well.

Immediately after his return from Berlin, Ironside noted the following impressions:

October 11

Looking back upon what I have said about the Germans and Hitler, it looks as if I thought Hitler would let loose a war for certain. Only the future can show whether he will do this or not. I think he won't be able to resist it. He is sitting on a safety valve and he probably knows it. It is all a matter of calculating the proper moment.

CHAPTER III

Mr. Winston Churchill and
Mr. Hore-Belisha

I̶N LONDON, Ironside still found little guidance on policy, strategy and training. "This Army Council", he wrote a few days later, "it an invertebrate way of governing the Army. The members never mix with the Army and are hardly ever to be seen out with the troops. They are swallowed up with routine and with the necessity of being present at all times to answer questions which are asked in Parliament. . . . I sent in a report on what I had seen at the German manœuvres. I understand that Belisha has read neither Deverell's report nor mine. War seems more certain to both of us. The Secretary of State has now been in office for four months and does not seem to realize what war means to an Army in the condition ours is in. I am the senior Commander-in-Chief and my advice was never sought after I had got back from Germany."

But Mr. Hore-Belisha was beginning to move.

October 26

I had Gort round to see me in the morning. He has been some three weeks as Military Secretary and I found him already almost prepared to give it up. He had been talking with the A.G. [Adjutant-General]. He was really very upset with the new Secretary of State. As he put it, he was in the bad position of

C   33

having to sell him unsound horses and Belisha was too clever to
buy duds. . . . Gort said that Belisha has refused to accept our
Candidate, [A], for the Mobile Division. This is one of our unsound horses. I am not sure that I don't think he is right. I think
that he [A] is too bull-headed.

October 27

We had a long day at the Selection Board. . . . The C.I.G.S.
[said that he] had put forward "A" for the Mobile Division after
consulting the Selection Board. Belisha had sent for "A" and after
5 minutes' conversation he had said that he would not accept him
under any circumstances . . . [he] could only slap his thigh and
shout. . . . Deverell then said that Belisha dabbled in every kind of
tactics and strategy far worse than Winston Churchill did at the
Admiralty. That Belisha had far less knowledge than Winston and
was far more rude and insulting. . . . I said to myself that I couldn't
see the thing lasting much longer. . . . Eventually we chose Alan
Brooke, now Director of Training at the War Office, for the
Mobile Division. . . .

Then came the case of "B", the Territorial Colonel, whom
Belisha wished to make a Major-General and put in to command
the A.A. Division. Here I felt that I was more mixed up in the
affair since I am responsible for the defence of London. I told
Deverell that here was a good case upon which to fight. It was
indefensible to put a man like this into such an appointment. . . .
We then chose the best man we could find, "C". I finished the day
with the feeling that a row is imminent. Anything may happen.

November 4

Belisha did not take our first recommendation for the A.A.
Division and went and offered it to the second string. This was
"D". "D" refused it, saying it was not in his line. . . . I am wonder-
ing what Belisha will do now. . . . All the jobs are being held up.

November 12

We have come to a point of great change in Army affairs.
Obviously we couldn't go on as we were going and it is right that

we should have had someone put in with courage sufficient to bring in the changes. Belisha will certainly do this and it is for the good of the Army that he should do.

November 16

I told Massingberd [C.I.G.S. 1933–36] that Belisha was merely baiting the Army Council and would get rid of them as soon as he could.

> On November 12 Ironside had sent in his annual training report. He made the following points: there was no tactical doctrine (i.e. there was no prescribed method of moving and fighting); it was essential to have tanks to work with the Infantry; too much imagination was needed in training owing to a lack of man-power; it was necessary to learn to exploit night and mist in the attack; there was too much movement of motor transport without protection; the new Field Drill should be adopted immediately (i.e. drilling and marching in threes instead of fours); ideas must be revised about dress; and "far too much time, energy and competition is spent on spit and polish".

November 21

I am still worrying about the troubles of the Army. Even if we have a Commission to discover what its rôle is to be, it will take months and even years to get an answer—an answer that can be translated into training and organization. The Committee of Imperial Defence might well be assembled for the special purpose, but it's against our nature to do anything in a hurry. We always seek for some compromise. Without some ruling from above we cannot very well get on with the making, or rather re-making, of the Army.... How are we to prepare any Force for Imperial commitments if it is not trained as a force of some size? Are we to cease thinking of European conditions when we may well have to fight European troops in conditions other than European? Above all, we don't want Belisha or any other politician to make a decision as to our future based upon insufficient evidence.

Mr. Hore-Belisha had made the conditions of service more attractive for all ranks, interesting himself in Army welfare, in improved pay, in terms of service, and better barracks. As a "reforming" Secretary of State for War he was at first welcomed both by senior and junior officers, though his dealings with senior commanders were too often conducted with a curious lack of tact. But he was little interested in formulating a policy for the Army, or in equipping and training it for a modern war. Ironside was yet to meet him.

November 29

I found everybody away in my office and I was just considering whether I was to get away or not when a nondescript looking clerk crept in and said "The Private Secretary to the Secretary of State would like you to call on the Secretary of State at 12.30 p.m." A curious method of being summoned to the presence of the All-Highest.

I duly went over some 4 minutes in front of time and was kept waiting until the exact hour had struck. I was then ushered in by the Secretary into the Presence. A short little man with a curious breed of grey felt topped boots with a zip up the inside. Why is it that one looks at people's feet first? French couldn't work with a man in Jemima boots. I haven't seen zip boots on a Secretary of State before. Fluffy grey hair over his ears. I found my chair well placed so that the light fell on my face and the shade on his. He smoked incessantly cigarettes and offered me some too. Also sent for cups of coffee. His manners are not good. He talked [on the telephone] to a man . . . about a paragraph in the *Evening Standard* saying that he had been newly appointed a member of White's Club. How he had been a member for many years. . . . He didn't mind but it was important to have things correct. I thought it was all rather to impress me.

He started off by saying "What do you think of the state of the Army?" How could one discuss such a thing in a few minutes? He said that he thought the whole Army machine very clumsy. Things went slower than they did in the other departments he had run. The Cabinet had not accepted the sending of another Army to the Continent. What did I think? . . . He finally finished up by saying "Come over and see me whenever you like." I explained to him that I couldn't do that under the circumstances, that the Army Council was responsible to him for all military matters. I told him that he didn't use his senior Generals enough and that there was no *Conseil Supérieur de Guerre* as they had in France.

The little man didn't strike me as being stuck-up or anything like that. Unconventional. But he doesn't have much dignity, I thought. To see people for a few minutes like he does doesn't seem very practical and he may think he can judge people, but I should call it all very sketchy. Practically the only thing which I thought was sound was his determination to abolish half-pay and to promote people into definite jobs. He hoped that the present Commission sitting on the retirement ages of the three Services would arrange the pensions of people more justly. He will do a lot of good if he does that.

December 1

Rung up by Deverell [the then C.I.G.S.] and went over to see him. I found him very much interested in what had happened in my interview with Belisha. He told me that he had no idea when people were summoned to see the Secretary of State. That Dill had rung up from Aldershot to say that he had been summoned to-day. I told him clearly what had transpired. Deverell said that Belisha didn't like Dill because he hadn't agreed with him. . . .

Deverell told me that they were all at the end of their tether and I think he was all agog to see if anything had been said about him (the C.I.G.S.). Obviously, he wanted to make sure if I had been approached as a suitable C.I.G.S. I think he quite expected that I had. I was able to reassure him that there was nothing like that. . . . Deverell then asked me if Belisha had mentioned the Expeditionary Force and I said that he had. That I had said it was a matter of policy and that we daren't say that we would not send one to France. That if we did say so, France would lie down and defend herself no more. That we shouldn't have a single friend in Europe.

He [Deverell] thought that the next war would be quite different from the last. That Germany would not go for France until she had a certainty. France in a rotten state internally. [He thought that the German attack would consist of] a mass of aeroplanes backing up the machines attacking the Maginot Line, followed by mechanized troops and lorried infantry. . . . He didn't think we could send [an Expeditionary] Force in time unless it went to France before war. That we must be ready to send it to carry out a counter-offensive. That training must be the same.

December 2

Fateful day. Down to the office where I was immediately met by a messenger [who said] that I was to go to see Belisha at 4 p.m. . . . I rang up the C.I.G.S. and . . . Deverell answered at once and said "I can tell you what it is for . . . I am going and Gort is to succeed me" . . . and then he added "And he is going to tell you that you are not going to get it." The whole thing was not a surprise. I knew Deverell was going. . . . I was not even much surprised by Gort being put in. A good choice I think, a man of great prestige in the Army who will enthuse life in the machine. A man of social position and strength of character. The Army will welcome the new C.I.G.S. with enthusiasm.

I was a few minutes early and so I went along to the C.I.G.S.'s Assistant's room and there I saw Gort. . . . I asked for the Field-Marshal [Deverell] and was told that he had gone for good. A somewhat awkward moment. I congratulated Gort. I told him that I was not so surprised, and that I was very glad and wished him well. The method of telling Deverell was not of the kindest, just a note to say that he had been suspended at once. It was apparently a bombshell to him [Gort] when he was asked to be C.I.G.S. . . . The first news that came in was that Adam had arrived from the Staff College as D.C.I.G.S. Gort didn't know then that he was to be C.I.G.S. [until told by Adam].

I saw Belisha and talked to him. Successful on the whole. The man is clever and courageous. He started by asking me if I had heard of the changes, and I said that I had seen Gort. I then told him that I thought he had chosen the right man and that the Army would be delighted. That I had never really pictured myself as C.I.G.S. and was in no way disappointed. He then most surprisingly said "God bless you. I cannot tell you how I appreciate that." He said that he had seen Dill who had taken things very well . . . [though] he said that he was disappointed he couldn't be C.I.G.S. I told him that I had never thought I would make a good C.I.G.S. Then he told me that he considered the halo which surrounded people at the War Office to be quite uncalled for. That he was reducing the authority of the War Office and increasing that of the Generals' outside. That he considered myself, Dill and Wavell as his Generals ready to go wherever they were required for operations. He was going to make a *Conseil Supérieur* and take the Generals into his confidence. I then let him have a few ideas upon what I thought of his plans.

December 4

I finished my preliminary paper upon the new idea of an Inspector-General[1] and gave it to Gort last night at dinner. It gives the framework of a system for training the Army.

> Shortly after Lord Gort's appointment as Chief of the Imperial General Staff, Sir Edmund and Lady Ironside went to stay at Houghton Hall with Lord and Lady Cholmondeley. Mr. Winston Churchill was also staying in the house, and had expressed a wish to see the General. "Winston and I", Ironside later wrote to a friend, "had been subalterns together in South Africa. I had known him all my life. I had served under his orders and instructions in many parts of the world. I had visited and stayed with him many times during his long sojourn in the wilderness. We had kept up a correspondence for many years."

December 6

We drove to Houghton near Fakenham [yesterday] where we found the Winston Churchills. He had said he wished to see me, and I thought that I ought not to miss the chance, even from the

[1] Appendix, page 391.

point of view of interest. Winston was most cordial and kept
reiterating that he must see that I was not done down. He was
horrified that Hore-Belisha had not seen me before he made his
decision to change to Gort. He talked about the *Conseil Supérieur*
and more than once said that he would see Belisha this next week
and impress upon him that I was not to be thrown over. He told
me that I should not go abroad and that I should resist being sent
because I was the man that would be called upon to lead the
Army were we unfortunate enough to have to go to war. I told
him that the whole future of the Army was in the melting pot.
That neither the Cabinet nor Belisha had any idea what the Army
was wanted for. That they were groping about for a solution and
hadn't even begun to formulate a policy. . . . He then told me the
story of Lord French. How he had had in view the chance of commanding the British Army in the field all his life. How he had
been thrown out at the critical moment over politics. Chiefly
Ulster. How he had come on the Admiralty yacht with Winston
a broken man. And within a fortnight he was the Commander-
in-Chief of the greatest Army we had ever put in the field. A
dramatic turn of fortune. He then agreed with me that things
were "written". They may or may not be "written" for you, he
said, but you must do nothing to prevent the fulfilment. I told
him that I had never influenced my career in one single way by
asking or intriguing for things. He told me that he had not either,
and added "I have had my ups and downs".

Winston loves to hold forth. We touched upon every kind of
subject. He told me that he was now more than profoundly upset
with things. He set forth the European situation from his view
with blistering clearness. Very pro-British and very pro-French
for our goodselves' interest. He thought the French Army an in-
comparable machine at the moment. It would be so during 1938
and 1939. Unassailable. But from then on he thought the Germans
would have caught up the French and distanced them. He catechized me over the Germans as to their lack of training, lack of
staff and lack of leading experience. An Army in the making. But
by 1940 the annual contingent in Germany would be double that
of France. He said that the power of France to defend herself was

terrific. . . . He was in agreement with me that 1940 was a very bad time for us.

I could get nothing out of him as to our need of sending an Army to France. He launched out into the action of the Air and the Navy. He said that the Navy was all right. Absolutely efficient. That a modern fleet was unassailable from the air. A floating movable dock that was guarded by anti-aircraft gunfire from hulks. A curtain of fire could be put up which would make it impossible for aeroplanes to come. He even thought Malta was unassailable. I simply couldn't agree. The Navy cannot mend ships in Malta and they would go away. I wasn't sure how the A.A. defences of Malta had progressed, so I didn't join issue; but I believed that we had done nothing.

The Far East he dealt with in a way that left me gasping, though I believe that he is right. He thought that we shouldn't have Hong-Kong very long. Declare war against Japan and retire to Singapore. . . . Don't send troops out there. No mention was once made of the U.S.A., and I had no time to bring in about Australia and New Zealand. After all, Japan is a long way from Australia, and our big Fleet should be able to compete with Japan. What about oil for the Japanese?

Then Mussolini. Winston thought that there was a good deal of bluff. That we had a good many cards in our hands. He pictured a very different picture to myself in the Mediterranean. He was definitely of opinion that we ought to have done with Mussolini before 1940; that it was very imperative to do so. The Germans wouldn't come in before 1940. He foresaw our Fleet paramount in the Mediterranean having dealt with the Italian Air and Submarine Forces. He saw the Italians in Libya and Abyssinia hopelessly cut off. He saw our Fleet bombarding the Italian coast ports. . . . He could not picture to me any Army landing, though he said it might be necessary. . . . He thought the time was not very far off when Mussolini must crash. . . .

I am afraid that I still think the situation in the Mediterranean most precarious. I am inclined to think that the British Navy is optimistic. Supposing Japan is at war with us, that Italy starts operations, and Germany asks questions. Have our political leaders the power to stop such a set of circumstances?

Winston then said that he was afraid of the R.A.F. expansion. That it was not going as well as it should. That it was behind-hand in many ways. . . .

He ought to be the Minister of Supply if we are in for a crisis. His energy and fiery brain seem unimpaired with age. He is certainly not dismayed by our difficulties. He says that our rulers are now beginning to get frightened. . . . He said that sometimes he couldn't sleep at night thinking of our dangers, how all this wonderful Empire which had been built up so slowly and so steadily might all be dissipated in a minute. He was just the stuff required in an emergency. The thing is to say when the emergency has arrived.

> "Both my wife and I", Ironside wrote to a friend, "were much exhilarated by his talk. It was a wonderful thing to have said to me by such a great man. It did something to dispel the anger and disgust which had invaded me at the way things were being mishandled. . . ."

December 29

The Cabinet, in a muddled kind of way, are terrified of making an Expeditionary Force. They reason that if they have such a Force they may be forced to send it to Europe once more. They dread a Continental commitment such as we had, and honoured, in 1914. I don't blame them, for France will scream louder than ever for help in the next crisis. Belgium will shout equally loudly. Once we are landed, our commitment is limitless. With our good faith it is always ahead of expectancy by our Ally. They only wish to get us committed, and we are then harnessed to the cart driven by them. Our contribution outside an Expeditionary Force, which is visible, is never even considered. Out of sight, out of mind, is particularly applicable to a people come to such straits as France to-day.

The Cabinet also thinks that the Air Force can finish a campaign. They are terrified now of a war being finished in a few weeks by the annihilation of Great Britain. They can see no other kind of danger than air attack and discount all other dangers. . . .

Imperial commitments absorb the Regular Army surprisingly quickly—with 30,000 men and 2,000 officers short—and there is no reserve. Imperially, the Air Force can do very little defence, and our men must be ready to meet the best kind of troops. At the moment our Regular Army is unorganized—one might even say disorganized—untrained and badly equipped. It is disheartened by all that is written and said about it by hack writers. It distrusts the politicians more than ever.

Belisha is playing with every sort of idea of change. I am told that he rushes from one idea to another—long service, short service, conscription, volunteer service and every variation of these. India and the Colonies all mixed up, and no plan coming out of it. It is exasperating that one cannot have some sort of general plan. . . . I feel it the more maddening because, if we have a crisis, I shall have handed over to me all the chaos that now exists—perhaps too late.

CHAPTER IV

Annus Horribilis: 1938

January 2

The newspapers try to say that 1938 gives more hope, and that Germany is more peaceful. I wish I thought that was anywhere near the truth.

January 7

A long document [from the War Office] on the world situation. . . . This is the beginning of letting C.-in-C.'s into the picture. . . . Germany is . . . pretty stable. There is a passionate belief in Hitler. The War Office believes that the German Army will put a brake on Hitler undertaking any foreign adventure until the armed forces are fit to deal with all eventualities. But even the Army might not be able to deter Hitler if the internal situation in Germany made it imperative for him to seek distraction elsewhere. . . . The German Army is not ready and doesn't want war at the moment. The War Office is not so strong upon this subject as I am. As regards Italy, it is clear that she has transferred her interest to the south—Libya and Sicily. . . . The W.O. make little of the Italian menace. I consider it pretty bad. Poland is a possible Spain, with a struggle between Fascism and Communism. This must mean a clash between Germany and Russia on Polish territory.

January 10

All my thoughts outside the tactical training of the Army are

44

always centred upon the Mediterranean. I cannot help believing
that we are taking Mussolini too lightly. Have we anybody who
has considered all the aspects of Defence in the Middle East? The
Mediterranean is a vital artery to us just as much as the Suez
Canal. The centre of gravity is continually changing and so, with
the quarrel with Italy, it has shifted again. I hope we are taking
stock of the fresh circumstances. The arrival of Italy in Abyssinia
and the strengthening of the Italian garrison in Libya have made
our position much more difficult.

The position of Italy is particularly difficult, and we must not
forget her difficulties. Italy, with her enormous force in Abyssinia,
needs the Suez Canal almost as much as we do. Even in the home
country she needs security on the sea, for she imports all of her
raw materials by sea and there seems to be no possibility of her
becoming self-supporting. She must import rubber, platinum,
tin, nickel, coal, copper, cotton, iron, lead . . . oil and wool. Not
an enviable position. The greater part of this trade comes through
the Straits of Gibraltar or the Suez Canal; but Turkey has
the power to shut off all the oil coming from Roumania or
Russia. . . .

For Italy to ease her position she must turn us out of the Mediterranean or else make friends with us. . . . Our Egyptian garrison
—now concentrating on the Canal—consists of two infantry
brigades, a mechanized cavalry brigade, two artillery brigades
and a tank battalion. Not a very formidable force. And it is as far
if not further from the Egyptian western frontier as are the
Italian troops in Libya. This frontier is now held by Egyptian
troops, and it cannot be denied that an Italian with his tail up is
quite a match for an Egyptian with his tail down. . . . [An Italian]
advance upon Egypt from Libya means some 200 miles of water-
less desert, but mechanization has altered the problem considerably. It isn't as hard as it looks at first sight.

Have we sufficient troops in the Egypt-Palestine area? Could
we reinforce from Europe? The answer to my mind is "no" in
each case. We ought to have more both in Egypt and Palestine.
There is no use in having surplus troops in England which cannot
be moved where we want them. If we have decided not to have a

Continental commitment, then we ought to act at once in re-adjusting our numbers in the Middle East. I wonder if the Imperial Defence Committee reasons in the same way?

In mid-January the Government at last reached certain decisions about the Army.

January 20

As far as one can see they [the new reorganizations] are all very sound:

(i) No foreign commitment. A force ready to be sent abroad of two divisions, complete in every way and under the command of a senior officer. This must, of course, be the man in command at Aldershot.[1] . . . It solves the difficulty of the Army ever being sent to France again. There isn't one to send. It means that the other Commands can be reduced very much in size and importance. The regulars they contain will be negligible in numbers.

(ii) They are to have four divisions of anti-aircraft troops and are to appoint a General to command them all. . . . It was even hinted that they are playing with the idea of a combined G.O.C.-in-C. in Great Britain of all the Army and Air. . . .

(iii) The Cabinet have decided behind closed doors that the Territorial Army is required to keep the peace in England and restore law and order in air raids. They daren't give this out because it would be unpopular and would result in the Terriers fading away.

(iv) The Staff College course is to be reduced to one year, and there are to be 120 let in. The Senior Officers' School is to be done away with. . . .

(v) Sandhurst is to revert to a Military College and there is not

[1] In 1937 General Dill had taken over the Aldershot Command, comprising the First and Second Divisions forming the First Corps, which was then regarded as the Expeditionary Force for Britain's overseas possessions.

46

to be so much University idea of a general education. Cadets are to be taught to be soldiers. Drill and Ceremonial is to be cut down to a minimum.

The Government also decided, as Ironside hoped, to reinforce the British garrisons in Egypt and Palestine. A meeting of Commanders-in-Chief was held at the War Office, which made him comment "I am more than glad that I didn't get put in as C.I.G.S." Ironside thought that the Navy and the Air were getting all the available money; and he predicted a war in the Mediterranean "within the next three years, and sooner rather than later".

February 3

The Air Defence of Great Britain is absorbing all the money which was intended for the Field Force. The Air Ministry dictates what it wants and the Army Estimates bear the cost. . . . We have no control financially. Then the Navy are calling for Coast Defence to be put in order. They call the tune there. It is not wonderful that we are reduced to:

1st Corps. Two divisions and a mobile division. Full-scale war reserves. Ready to embark in 21 days.
3rd and 4th Divisions. Half-scale war reserves. Ready to start embarking in 40 days.
All other units peace equipment only.
Pool of equipment so that the equivalent of two Regular or Territorial divisions are prepared to embark at about four months.
This is back to the South African War days. . . .

A few days later Hitler dismissed Blomberg and Fritsch and assumed command of the German Army himself.

February 5

I don't wonder that our Government is in a fluster over its military affairs after their years of neglect in the face of so much warning. . . . We have no Continental commitment now. I told the Commanders' Conference that our wretched little Corps of two divisions and a mobile division was unthinkable as a contribution to an Army in France. Nothing behind it either. Let us make Imperial plans only. After all, the politicians will be hard put to it to refuse to help France and Belgium when the 1914 show begins again. There won't be any doubt about the Germans occupying the Channel ports this time. . . . Belgium has once more declared her neutrality and has asked for protection from the Great Powers. I see that our people have been sitting in the Foreign Office discussing the situation for hours. They must all be in a terrible fright. . . .

I wonder what the reactions of the country will be when the storm bursts. . . . We all seem helpless. Shall I find myself sent out to command our nondescript forces in some chaotic situation? I feel that I shall find something like this if the storm breaks within the next three years. It is not a nice idea to contemplate, having had no say in the preparation and no responsibility for the position in which we find ourselves. . . . I still think that both the Admiralty and Air Ministry are very light-hearted about the situation, and they will not have the solid support of the War Office in the future, for the Army has sunk too low. All the old plans came down to guaranteeing success by the Army. If one investigated the plans of the other two Services they always depended upon the Army. Now they cannot.

February 6

Our Government now appears to recognize that if we again land an Army in France it must mean a repetition of the 1914–1918 struggle under more difficult circumstances. . . . This present Government has rightly made up its mind not to do this, even in the face of the danger that France may be overwhelmed and our position rendered more dangerous by the approach of enemy air bases to the United Kingdom. . . . The Army has heretofore been able to transfer the struggle away from home. Now it can no longer do this. . . . The Air Force takes over the defence of the United Kingdom assisted by as much A.A. defence as it can prepare.

On February 12 von Schuschnigg, the Chancellor of Austria, was summoned to Berlin and presented with an ultimatum.

February 16

Hitler has managed to coerce Schuschnigg in Austria and there is now a Nazi in control of all the Police and Defence services. Mussolini has done nothing. Is this the beginning of trouble in Europe? I take it that it means a pacific conquest of Austria and the next to be attacked will be Czechoslovakia. Does this mean that Hitler is squaring things behind him before he turns and makes his demands to France and ourselves? . . . I cannot see how war is to be avoided in the next two years.

February 18

Halifax said in the House of Lords last night that war was not "imminent". I remember the same thing from Lord Haldane in 1914, who said that the relations between ourselves and Germany were never better. . . .

On the night of March 11, 1938, Germany invaded Austria, and on the 13th, abetted by Mussolini, Hitler announced the dissolution of the Austrian Republic and its annexation to the German Reich.

March 13

The moral for us is that force is the only thing which tells with these two gangsters. If we are not ready to meet this force, then we shall go under. We have had ample warning. . . . The earnestness of these Germans is awe-inspiring. Can any system of easy-going democracy compete with the solid and ruthless rule of such a thing as Germany? . . . One hopes that the [National] Government will not now wait for "democratic mandates" and that they will leave no stone unturned to prepare the country.

March 15

We had our Commanders' meeting this morning. Pownall, the Director of Military Operations and Intelligence, was brought in to make a statement to us upon the European situation. I thought he did it exceedingly well.

He described most dramatically the scene in the ante-room at Berchtesgaden, when Schuschnigg was summoned to meet Hitler. Apparently, the Austrian Chancellor was kept waiting an hour. During this time he was left in full view of a map showing the disposition of the German troops in South Germany. All the time he was waiting German Generals came in and loudly reported that their various commands were ready to march. Everything was done to intimidate Schuschnigg.

When Hitler eventually received Schuschnigg he [Hitler] was in a highly neurotic and excited state. He raved at Schuschnigg and talked about the German people in Austria. Schuschnigg stood up very well to the tirade, but gave in to the show of force.

Italy undoubtedly knew that this meeting was to take place, but did not know what ultimatum was being delivered. Our Ambassador, Henderson, saw Hitler and was treated to a diatribe upon the behaviour of the British Press. Hitler told Henderson that Germany would act like lightning and that Germany would know how to fight. . . .

The result of this capture of Austria is to open the very heart of Czechoslovakia, which has no fortifications against Austria. All is open for an *attaque brusquée* [blitzkrieg] from Austria. The Czechs . . . could not stand up long against Germany. Hitler is an opportunist. Even he may not know what his next move is, but everything seems to point to Prague being the next objective, Hungary being taken in by being promised their lost Slovak provinces. Hitler goes one bite at a time, feeling his way carefully. . . .

The French have reiterated their decision to fight if Czechoslovakia is assailed. Personally, I cannot see that they can get their Army to advance into Germany. They have prepared their Maginot Line for a strategic defensive and it seems to me doubtful if they will get their men to take the offensive for anything so far off as Czechoslovakia. . . . France and then ourselves will be the final objective, and if we allow disunion we shall be attacked in turn. Winston Churchill has made a great speech calling upon all to combine the elements of democracy against Germany. If we allow the smaller [nations] to be eaten up in turn we shall be destroyed in the end. I must say I agree with him. . . . Time will not be in our favour if we allow the lesser democracies to be destroyed, even if it allows us to get stronger. Chamberlain has called upon the people to make an effort, but has specified nothing whatever. . . .

March 22

There is no Army and there cannot be an Army, even on the scale of four divisions and a mobile division until the end of 1940. . . . I feel inexpressibly weary and disgusted with it all. I never in my worst fits of pessimism thought we should come to such a pass.

March 25

Winston Churchill argued . . . [for] an immediate and close military alliance with France. Personally, I cannot see that we could ally ourselves blindly with France. We have many common interests, but we have many which are not common. . . . We must have a little more patience. We are not ready and we will not be ready till 1940, even if we continue to go at the pace we are keeping at this moment. . . . The French have much more definite problems to solve than we have. They love order in their plans, [which] . . . often become inhuman and impracticable in consequence. We cannot make hypothetical plans to meet uncertain circumstances. We are arch-improvisers. We hate jumping fences before there is any necessity. Our problems are so vague that we must keep our plans liquid. . . .

I should sum up the German character best by saying that they are the best of losers and the worst of winners. They are wonderful stout and stubborn soldiers, but they become bullies if they achieve any success. They believe in their racial superiority and have a contempt for all others. Physically a very fine race. Orderly and happy at grinding work. . . . They loathe any kind of improvising. . . . Their capacity for work is enormous.

Ironside's personal fortunes and prospects had meanwhile been placed in the melting-pot. On January 29 he received a letter from General Brownrigg, the Military Secretary. It was surprisingly dated the 29th of May and offered him the Governorship of Gibraltar for five years at £6,000 a year. The offer puzzled him. His appointment as G.O.C.-in-C. Eastern Command had another two years to run. He had never been sounded about this new post. Gibraltar was usually given to a distinguished soldier at the end of his career and, since the fortress had been so long neglected, the appointment had come to be regarded almost as a sinecure.

Ironside at this time was the only general in the British Army who had commanded more than a battalion on active service. He spoke German and French and knew many of the leaders on both sides. He had travelled in Bohemia, Slovakia, Ruthenia, Poland and Lithuania. He knew Horthy, the Regent of Hungary, and Sirovy, the Czech Chief of Staff.

January 29

My mail this morning contained the offer of the Governorship of Gibraltar. I think I was a little surprised, but my main feeling was one of relief. It is the end of any soldiering and of ever being a Field-Marshal, but then I never expected very much after the advent of Belisha and his *coup*. It means six more years of a well-paid job, which will see me a good way through my son's education. That's where the relief came in. . . . I think I have made up my mind to accept the thing without any further trouble. I am really jumping at it. I haven't had to ask for it which is a mercy. I should have hated to tempt Fate in that way. A thing I have never done. I am devilish lucky and I realize it thoroughly. . . . Things may happen in the Mediterranean after all. . . .

"I have", he wrote in his diary on February 1, "taken the plunge and accepted the Governorship of Gibraltar. Belisha put it to me that we must have a C.-in-C. in the Mediterranean and he wanted me there. I must say that I hardly believed him, but I couldn't refuse the offer. . . ." The pay was later reduced by £500 a year and the tenure to three years, but Ironside nevertheless stuck to his decision.

March 29

I went in to see Belisha at 12 noon. . . . He wanted to ask me if I really wanted to go to Gibraltar. He had doubts if I wanted to go. I told him that I had accepted and so meant to do my job. He then talked of how the Dictator Powers were getting what they wanted and we could do nothing. That Franco was winning and that it would be bad for the British Empire. That the British Army might well be employed in Spain, the most likely place in fact. That I would be on the spot.

"This last statement", he wrote in a later letter, "seemed so preposterous that I was left speechless. I asked him whether he had been told that by his military advisers, but he did not answer. This meeting left me somewhat shaken. The man felt lonely and isolated. He wasn't satisfied with his advisers and turned to me. He had no plan and was for ever flying off at a tangent."

On April 1 the announcement appeared that Ironside would take over Gibraltar in September. He was inundated with more than a thousand letters. Most of them said they were horrified at his leaving the country. To cap all, when he asked the War Office for information about Gibraltar he received the following communication from an officer who shall be nameless:

"I am sending you a few notes on Gibraltar, which will be all you will want, *as there are no outstanding questions at the moment.*"

March 29 (continued)

The paper on our rearmament has come in. It is truly the most appalling reading. How we can have come to this state is beyond believing:

Present Situation (March 1938)

(i) We can put into the field two divisions only, with an incomplete quota of Corps troops, and deficient of many types of equipment essential for warfare under modern conditions.

(ii) The main deficiencies are:

Cavalry

Mechanized Division. Cavalry regiments are not yet equipped or trained.

Artillery

Field Artillery. We have 18-pdrs. and 4·5 hows. only, with maximum ranges of 9,000 and 6,000 yards respectively; the German 33-pdr. field artillery is reported to have a max. range of 17,000 yds.

Medium Artillery. We have 60-pdrs. and 6-inch hows. with maximum ranges of 15,000 and 10,000 yards respectively; the corresponding German weapons have ranges of 21,700 and 16,700 yards.

Anti-tank Artillery. The delivery of 2-pdr. guns is only just beginning.

A.A. Artillery. One A.A. brigade only available. All 3-inch guns.

Infantry

No Bren guns.

No armoured carriers.

75% deficiency of anti-tank rifles.

No 2-inch mortars.

75% deficiency in 3-inch mortars.

A.F.V.s

Obsolete medium tanks.

No cruiser tanks.

No "I" [Infantry] tanks.

Obsolete armoured cars.

No light tanks (we have one unit now in Egypt).

Miscellaneous

Considerable deficiencies in up-to-date engineer and signal equipment.

And this is the state of our Army after two years' warning. No foreign nation would believe it if they were told it.

April 8

We had our Commanders' conference yesterday. . . . Gort gave us a small dissertation upon the *attaque brusquée.*

"He delivered it well," Ironside wrote later, "but it did not seem to fit in with anything we were doing or were likely to be doing. Training for war was missed out.

"He then let out that there was going to be a reduction of 1,500 officers in the establishment of the Army. It was Belisha's way of filling a gap. He was going to replace them (he had not got them) by Warrant Officers Class III. This he had done arbitrarily, without reference to the Army Council or the Commanders-in-Chief.

"To me this appeared a most serious step in the wrong direction. Warrant Officers, however good, can never replace commissioned officers. Later in the day when Belisha came strolling in I tackled him on this matter. He drew a pyramid with a pencil on a paper. The position of junior officers had long been an unfair one in his opinion. They were at the base of the pyramid and very few had any chance of reaching the summit of the pyramid, where sat the Field-Marshal. He now proposed to lessen the numbers of subalterns in the base and give them all a better chance of reaching the top. He seemed like a boy with a new idea. He could not understand that if the pyramid did not have a strong base it would collapse. He did not seem to realize that there were many kinds of casualties amongst the subalterns before they reached the rank of Captain. Many were retired. Some retired on their own. Some were killed or maimed. He also could not understand that the new Warrant Officers would not be able to pay[1] or to punish their men in a platoon. They could never replace young officers.

"Gort finally disclosed to us that he thought the Cabinet was slowly coming round to the view that a B.E.F. must be sent to France in case of war with Germany.

"This statement was received in complete silence."

[1] Only officers were entitled to issue pay to the troops.

April 21

I now have our deficiencies and the recruiting statement for the year. We are truly in an appalling state whatever Belisha may say. We have to make up just over 53,000 men, and during this last year Belisha got in 26,000 men by the most intense effort. Such a deficiency—all calculated upon a reduction of establishment of well over 100 men per battalion—is so terrific that one cannot contemplate it with complacency. A battalion of Infantry is now to have 28 officers and 763 men. The deficiencies in the 4th Division show what these mean to the training of a Regular battalion.[1]

Belisha's method of getting men is to say that there is a continual improvement over the year before. He thinks that this is the psychological method of inducing more men to come in. . . . But you are kidding the people of the country all the time and lulling them into [false] security. In the end, by saying that things are all right, you will yourself begin to believe that they are. Even the reduced mental and physical standard has failed to produce more men. The introduction of 3,000 reservists has reduced the Reserve by that number. . . .

I have been going into the training of the 4th Division. There is no good concealing the thing from oneself. With no artillery and insufficient men to make up one brigade of infantry I simply haven't the heart to push these people too hard. They cannot imagine Bren guns and armoured carriers. They have never seen them. . . .

Somebody asked me the other day whether I didn't think the Army ought to have its own Air Arm. I told him that I always had thought that it should. That what we had now was a hopeless compromise but that the moment was inopportune to attempt any change. That we had no combined training between the Services must mean that other countries with a common direction must defeat us. . . . These services—reconnaissance, spotting and air transport—are just as much part of the Army as the Artillery or Engineers.

[1] Some battalions had an average strength of 5 officers and about 300 men.

Meanwhile, the Nazi party in the Sudetenland, led by
Henlein, were beginning to demand autonomy. The newspapers at the end of April were full of the Anglo-French
Entente and the future of Czechoslovakia. Ironside saw it as a
complete deadlock. The demands of the Sudeten Germans
were evidently backed by Hitler, and were clearly unacceptable to the Czechs. On the night of May 20 Czechoslovakia
began to mobilize, and on the 23rd Hitler ordered an attack
on her to be prepared.

May 24

A meeting of the C's.-in-C.
We had in the Director of Military Operations, Pownall, who
gave us the story of what had been happening with the Czechs.
It all worked up on the Friday and came to a head on the Saturday. . . . Most of our news had come from the Czech General
Staff, who asserted that the German troops were moving up to the
Czech frontier all round the country. . . .
We are in no state to go to war. . . . I can see the Field Army
receding more and more into the far distance. There are no men
and there is no money for [their] equipment and there is no will
amongst the Cabinet Ministers to want an Army.

May 25

Thinking things over, I think that there must have been a very
near thing over the Czech show. Goering was pushing Hitler to
make a move and couldn't get him to decide under the menace of
the British protest. The [German] Army, as usual, was against
movement. They are not ready—and they always want to be
absolutely ready to the last gaiter button with their methodical
minds. It means that Goering will try again, and probably pretty
soon. . . . The great struggle between ourselves and Germany is
coming. Will we be ready in time? Surely our diplomats are
cunning enough to arrange the Balance of Power, now that the
wretched League of Nations is no more in action.

May 29

I have been turning over in my mind our Army position and

the picture becomes clearer and clearer. The decision to form six A.A. divisions seals the fate of the Territorial Army as an Army able to go into the field. . . . All our guns and money and energy will be expended in making these divisions. . . . We ought to have done it before. There were two main causes for preventing us from doing this. First, the fact that the R.A.F. and the Air Ministry refused to believe that there was any efficacy in passive defence. They not only didn't believe that guns could hit hostile planes, but they advocated an immediate air offensive—bombing of the enemy—and no fighting planes at home to intercept hostile bombers. That was called "defensive action" and was deplored. This attitude has been defeated and the A.A. Defence has been taken out of the hands of the Air Ministry and has been forced along by the War Office. Secondly, the General Staff, typified by Deverell, were afraid that the growth of the A.A. Defence would absorb all the money available for the Army. They combated the idea that no Expeditionary Force was necessary. The War Office under Belisha has forced this principle upon the General Staff and we now have no Army fit to send abroad to our foreign stations, but we have swallowed up our Reserve. . . .

Never again shall we even contemplate a Force for a foreign country. Our contribution is to be the Navy and the R.A.F.

On June 18 Hitler had issued his final directive for the attack on Czechoslovakia. Six days earlier, Daladier, the French Premier, had renewed his predecessor's pledge that France would honour her treaty with the Czechs. These were empty words. On the 26th the British Government decided to send Lord Runciman to Prague to try to find a compromise between the Czech Government and Henlein.

August 12

The Czech situation remains the main important business in Europe. This Runciman Mission is a last despairing attempt to arrive at a compromise—and we are the champion compromisers of the world. I suppose that any time gained is a good thing, but I cannot see that we can gain much time by our methods. . . . The

Germans are against any form of compromise. I think that the
Germans will take action in their own time. . . . Hitler may
detonate at any moment. . . . The German Army is really big.
They have 48 divisions, including 5 armoured, 3 mountain and
2 light divisions. They then have 20 reserve divisions and 36
Landwehr divisions. When one thinks that we have not got even
2 divisions it shows what a puny Army contribution we can make
to any European war. The Czech Army . . . can produce 21
divisions. . . . The reserves come to another 21 divisions. . . .
Germany is merely waiting for a favourable opportunity. That
she will march in the east seems certain.

August 15

This morning's *Daily Telegraph* shows what the German plan
is. A display of her strength in such a way that she is ready at a
moment's notice to enforce her will in Czechoslovakia. . . . She
stands there with a hammer in her hands and says "I am ready to
negotiate, but if you don't do what I want I am ready to knock
you into submission." . . . Germany has called up 750,000 reservists and is to have manœuvres for ten weeks. . . . A clever
move, and as good as a declaration of war. . . . We are impotent.
Made so by all these cranks and peace-mongers.

August 27

The news from Czechoslovakia is about as bad as it well can be
this morning. The Nazis there are talking of "one last effort",
"now or never", and the Czechs are talking of disciplinary action
against the Nazis. Chamberlain and Halifax are having daily meetings about the situation and they are all very worried indeed.
Runciman is reported as coming home to consult with the Government. It seems to be leading straight to a crisis. The German Army
must be ready to march, and will remain so till the hour has come.
Then Hitler will say that the situation forced him to move.

August 29

In my talks with Gort I could see that he hasn't a proper grip
of the situation. He has taken no steps for having a war H.Q. for

the Army. None whatever. When I told him that I proposed to clear the White City he seemed surprised that I had done anything. . . . I could get little or nothing out of Gort as to Government plans except that he had told the Prime Minister at a Committee of Imperial Defence meeting that we had no Army to send abroad. When I told him that it was the P.M.'s definite policy never again to send an Army to France he seemed surprised. He seemed out of his depth completely. I asked him where he thought that we should start reasserting ourselves in the Mediterranean and he didn't know. . . . It was all hopelessly vague. . . . I saw myself involved in one more gigantic improvisation. . . .

Gort told me that it was only a year ago that the orders were given for the 3·7-inch [anti-aircraft] guns. How could Deverell have delayed? He seems to have been obsessed with the idea of maintaining the Expeditionary Force with his limited money and to have neglected the A.A. Defence. Meanwhile, the Germans had carte blanche. You must make your fortress secure before you think of issuing from it. What an eye-opener we shall all get.

September 3

I saw the remnants of the 12th Dover Brigade—two battalions of a total of 320 men. This is all there is from a Brigade. Two batteries of Artillery totalling five guns. . . . Perfectly scandalous. Belisha going about saying all is well. . . . I feel very desperate about it all. That I should possibly have to go on active service with such an Army at the end of my long service seems almost tragic to me. No Army, no tactical doctrine, and no co-operation with the R.A.F., no material, and hopeless confusion as to A.A. Defence in England.

September 14

Late in the evening came the news that the P.M. had wired to Hitler that he wished to come over and see him. . . . The result is that he leaves for Berlin at 8.30 a.m. to-morrow. . . . A veritable messenger of peace. . . . It never entered my head that he would do a thing like that. . . . Will his gentlemanly calmness and sangfroid have any effect upon the Führer?

On the morning of September 15 Henlein fled to Germany, where he demanded for the first time the annexation of the Sudetenland to the Greater Reich.

September 16

Things look very bad. The P.M. is unexpectedly coming back [from Berchtesgaden]. He has evidently met with a stiff refusal. . . . It looks very like the disintegration of Czechoslovakia. . . . Runciman is returning to this country and there are to be conferences and Cabinet-meetings. . . . My own opinion is that . . . it would be madness to expose ourselves to annihilation for the sake of the Czechs.

Mr. Chamberlain returned to London two days later, convinced that only the cession of the Sudetenland to Germany could now prevent the invasion of Czechoslovakia; and convinced, also, that France would not fight to save the Czech Republic. On September 19 Anglo-French proposals, envisaging the cession of Sudetenland to the Reich, were handed to the German Government.

September 19

I see in the papers this morning that there has been "complete agreement" between France and ourselves over a scheme for Czechoslovakia. This means that the Czechs are to be sacrificed. I suppose one cannot blame the two Great Powers for doing this. They made this ramshackle country and presumably they can unmake it. . . .

I am now told that all the authorities have insisted upon the parcelling out of troops all over London during air raids. . . . It all seems perfectly puerile. . . . They want the sight of uniforms to quieten the people. . . . It is a curious ending to a Field Army and it seems stupid that we should go through the motions of training these men for anything other than these new police-duties. For these we are completely untrained.

September 20

This morning the Czechs have asked for forty-eight hours to

consider their partition. The Czech Cabinet must be writhing at their treatment. Sold in the cause of peace. . . . To dismember Czechoslovakia . . . can only be called "Peace without Honour". That must lower the prestige of the British Government. Chamberlain must be well aware of the results of giving in now and yet he must give in, for he isn't ready to enter the ring against Hitler. It would be madness to do so in our present state of unpreparedness. And we prepare so dreadfully slowly in these democratic days. . . .

> On September 21 the Czechoslovak Government sub-
> mitted and resigned. They were succeeded by a non-party
> administration under General Sirovy, who had commanded
> the Czech troops in Siberia during the First World War.

September 22

We have had an exciting few days and have ended with one of the greatest humiliations we could have suffered. Chamberlain is, of course, right. We have not the means of defending ourselves and he knows it. He is a realist, and any plan he could devise was better than war. One hopes that this will be a lesson to the people to get their defence in order. If it does not then it will all have been in vain. . . . Winston Churchill words his protest as follows:

> "It is necessary that the nation should realize the magnitude
> of the disaster into which we are being led. The partition of
> Czechoslovakia under Anglo-French pressure amounts to a
> complete surrender by the Western democracies to the Nazi
> threat of force. . . . The idea that safety can be purchased by
> throwing a small state to the wolves is a fatal delusion. . . ."

All very true, but *we cannot expose ourselves now to a German attack. We simply commit suicide if we do.* That is the fallacy of his argument. At no time could we stand up against German air bombing. Chamberlain knows this. He dare not say it to the people. What a mess we are in.

> On September 22 Mr. Chamberlain flew to Godesberg for
> a second interview with Hitler, taking with him the details

of the Anglo-French proposals. These, to his surprise, were rejected by Hitler, who said that unless Czechoslovakia accepted his demands before September 28 he would order his troops to cross the frontier. War was now very near.

September 24

I got back [from an afternoon's shooting in Norfolk on September 23] to find a telephone message telling me that Adam [Deputy C.I.G.S.] had rung up to say that I might be wanted in a hurry, and they wanted to know where I was. This seemed to me to be such enormous nonsense that I decided to send for my car and go up to London that night. . . . Is the thing serious? Is it real? One would hardly believe that we were not playing a game of marionettes. Incorrigible. And then the same old further improvisations. This time, the worst there have ever been. . . .

We heard the evening broadcast and things began to be a little clearer. Evidently Chamberlain had been met with a proper facer from Hitler at his first meeting on Thursday evening. It seemed to be that Hitler had not only demanded the cession of the Sudeten territory, but he had demanded complete power over the whole Czech State. He must have told Chamberlain of all the horrors going on in Sudetenland and have told him that he couldn't keep out any longer. This frightened Chamberlain, who wrote him a letter asking him to keep out whilst the negotiations were going on. Hitler replied evasively and they did not meet again till nearly midnight on Friday. As we came into London they were selling copies of the *Daily Express* saying that the Germans had already marched in.

In any case, troop-movements through Southern Germany seem to be going on day and night, all going eastward. The Czechs have mobilized and Sirovy has taken over the Government. Sirovy is a stout one-eyed man of about 56 or so. I have known him as a determined man in war and peace for many years. He is now a Dictator in whom the Czechs place complete trust, and of course the outcry in Germany has become more severe than ever. Actual bridges leading into Czech territory have been blown up and the Czechs are evidently in no state to surrender. One can imagine this. To have achieved their liberty for twenty years after being Slav and German for so many years, is something important to them. They aren't going to give it up for nothing. One of the extraordinary things to me is how we, with calculated cynicism, sign away the liberty of 9,000,000 people as if they had no feelings. People in this country forget that the Czechs have feelings and are civilized people. We think that they are pawns.

Actually, control of Czechoslovakia and economic alliance with Hungary and Poland certainly gives Germany that self-sufficiency and stability she has been seeking so long. The effect of this must mean that she is immensely strengthened in her final struggle against democratic government. It makes our problem much more difficult. But I am still of opinion that our defences are so bad that we should go to any length to put off the struggle; so long, always, that we start in at full speed at once. . . .

At 12 o'clock I was asked to go over to see Gort and he said at once "How would you look upon going to the Middle East?" He then said that he thought that Mussolini must be our trouble and that all the German troops had been withdrawn from the Italian frontier and Mussolini had taken his line. I told Gort that I was ready to go anywhere he wanted me. . . . He said that a new brigade had arrived [in the Middle East] from England and a brigade was just arriving from India. He finished up by saying "You will be cut off from us and will have military charge of the whole of the Middle East. We shall expect you to win the war for us out there."

He then said that my appointment[1] would go to the Cabinet at 5 p.m. and that I must be prepared to go on Tuesday morning, flying to Marseilles and then in one hop to Cairo. I have never een a man in a big show before who talked so much of smaller things. . . . He finished by saying that if nothing came of all this they could easily say that I had been out on a tour of inspection.

Of course when I looked this all over it was the biggest job that a man could well be given. Complete responsibility and

[1] i.e. as Commander-in-Chief designate for the Middle East, which Ironside was to hold at the same time as Governor of Gibraltar.

freedom of action, cut off from the Government with all the armed forces of the Empire coming in as they could be got ready. Will it come to anything? That is the question. Personally I think that things will drift on in an extraordinary way. We are not allied to the Czechs, though the French and Russians are. Our problem is Italy, and we have to face her. . . .

If Italy is against us I presume that we shall lose the Mediterranean for six months to a year, despite the shoutings of the Navy.

After Mr. Chamberlain's return to London on September 24, the Cabinet decided that the terms put forward by Hitler at Godesberg were unacceptable. The Czechs had a million and a half men behind a very strong defensive line, and France had partially mobilized. War was now nearer still, and Ironside was despatched to Egypt. On the 27th Chamberlain broadcast to the nation. "How horrible, fantastic, incredible it is, that we should be digging trenches and trying on gas-masks because of a quarrel in a far away country between people of whom we know nothing . . . but war is a fearful thing, and we must be very clear, before we embark on it, that it is really the great issues that are at stake." He had not yet abandoned hope of a compromise solution.

On the morning of the 28th the British Fleet was mobilized. At 3 p.m. that afternoon messages arrived for Chamberlain and for Daladier, inviting them, with Mussolini, to a conference with Hitler on the following day. The four leaders duly assembled at Munich, and, in essentials, accepted Hitler's ultimatum. Czech evacuation of the Sudetenland, with all its well-prepared defences, was to begin on October 1. "I believe", said Mr. Chamberlain on his return to London, "it is peace in our time." He based this hopeful forecast on a declaration of pacific intentions which Hitler had signed.

Ironside had meanwhile departed for the Middle East. He visited Palestine, Egypt and the Western Desert, and the following extracts from his diary summarize his judgments on the situation.

October 2 [Palestine]

I have always thought that the Mediterranean was now much more vulnerable than the Navy will ever admit. They think so much in terms of the Fleet and not in terms of traffic. For the Fleet only exists for the traffic. If that ceases the Fleet has no *raison d'être* until it has re-established the traffic. . . . None of our Imperial stations such as Gibraltar, Malta, Cyprus, Alexandria and Haifa is safe—or shall I say immune?—from heavy air attack in the early stages of a war with Italy and Germany. And no ships can lie in a harbour liable to air attack.

But we cannot afford to give up this Mediterranean route. We need it as an Imperial artery. We must be ready to re-establish it from either end the minute that it has been stopped. Stoppage must be temporary only. The use of the Cape line is always there but it must be a secondary thing. . . .

At this end it means the holding of Palestine, with the ever-increasing importance of the land route across from Baghdad. In fact, it is essential to build an *"auto-strasse"* across here. The holding of the Canal and if possible Egypt, despite treaties and talk. At the western end the problem is more difficult if Spain is hostile.

October 10 [on board S.S. *Otranto*]

I think that we shall have to institute a stronger defence of the Middle East. You must have the troops on the ground to secure the population. With the Air alone you cannot control the people. We must get the road across from Basra or Baghdad properly made to Jerusalem. A road rather than a railway which would be so much more vulnerable. . . . This modern security is so much a matter of communications that it is essential that we should see to them. I must rub this into the authorities. . . .

I shall write a general report:

(i) They must listen more to what the G.O.C.-in-C. in Egypt says. They must keep far more in touch with him over policy. They must send him constant letters or high officers from the War Office.

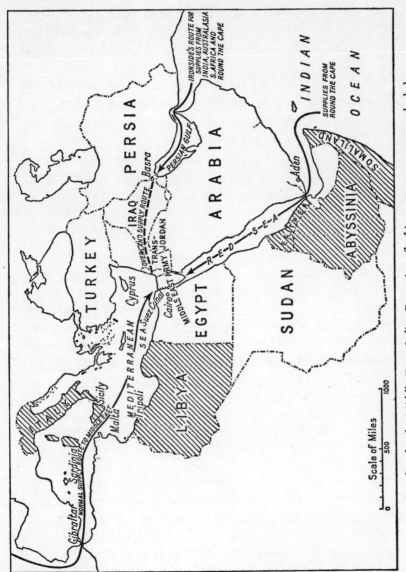

Supplies for the Middle East: Italian Possessions flanking our sea-routes are shaded.

(ii) The need for a C.-in-C. Middle East is established, but I cannot see that he can be sent there in a hurry at the last moment. It would be preferable to make the G.O.C.-in-C. in Egypt the C.-in-C. designate. If they were to make him a first class Command in peace it would make things easier.

(iii) There should be a proper reserve of stores in the Middle East. Nothing can get through in times of tension. . . .

(v) There should be a proper understanding with India as to reserves of men and material.

(vi) There should be a proper plan of action. . . .

(vii) There should be one commander of both Army and Air. The present position is anomalous and futile.

October 16 [London]

Gort says that it has been mentioned in Parliament that I am going to Gibraltar to be C.-in-C. [designate] Mediterranean and that people seem pleased about it. How do they propose to implement such an appointment? I shall be Governor of Gibraltar and unable to leave without losing that job, for I cannot be off the Rock for more than a few days at a time. It is all eyewash, for the C.-in-C. should be making plans at once. And these plans will take some making. . . .

I wonder what Chamberlain will do now towards getting on with his turning out of guns. Manufacture seems so hopelessly slow, but I suppose that we were so late in giving the orders that we cannot catch up. It goes back to the time of Baldwin, who wouldn't give the order to arm. . . .

What am I going to do at Gibraltar? Shall I be able to contain myself there while the world is crumbling under our feet? I feel as if I could get things going and I have no part in the work. . . . I see all this blundering with despair. . . . I find it hard to keep my patience. I know that that is my worse fault. . . . I am not thinking of myself but of the Empire. I shall [soon] be the senior General in the Army and the only officer serving who has ever led an Army or even a division in the field. To such a state has the Army

been reduced by Milne and Massingberd. And now Belisha.
What a record.

October 17

At 3 p.m. I saw Gort in his office. I found him very sprightly
and well and I handed in my report. I then had half an hour's talk
and told him exactly what I thought [about Palestine]. . . . He
then asked me to see Belisha. I had half an hour with him. I found
him agreeably composed, but distinctly gloomy. . . . I could see
that they were both apprehensive of operations against Hitler very
shortly. . . .

Gort said to me that Gibraltar was only a "garage" as far as I
was concerned and it didn't matter in the least whether I went
there or not. I smiled to think what the Gibraltarians would say
to this if they knew.

October 21

I have written a letter to Gort inspired by all I have been thinking here. I have made two points:

(i) *Middle East Reserve*
He must get something like a division in the Middle East
as a reserve. It will be impossible to reinforce from elsewhere.

(ii) *Command*
The plans have to be made. Can they be made in time by
passing papers round? Can the C.-in-C. designate get there
from Gibraltar in time? Does the situation make it imperative to have a C.-in-C. on the spot now or sooner? Can
the Commissioner in Palestine be changed to the C.-in-C.
Designate?

I have told him that I am terribly afraid of what may happen
to the Empire if we are caught napping. . . . Is that sufficient
reason to move our statesmen? Have the War Office put it clearly
to the Committee of Imperial Defence and the Cabinet? Does the
Prime Minister think that war may come?

To me, now, it seems absolutely clear that I should be in the Middle East if I am to be the C.-in-C. Designate.

November 2

A most unsatisfactory statement by the Prime Minister as regards his Foreign Policy and Defence. He made it clear that our re-armament was not against Germany. No compulsion and no Ministry of Supply. Some very futile questions by Attlee and a few to Belisha. I am quite certain in my own mind that Chamberlain did the best thing possible. He had no means of doing otherwise. What I dislike is the unctuous speeches of men like Halifax trying to explain away our humiliation. They ought to tell the truth. Nobody can possibly say that there has been any self-determination in Czechoslovakia. This ramshackle state has been dismembered by force. We avoided war, but at the expense of handing over the Czechs to the Germans. Why didn't we tell the Czechs long ago that we would not fight for them? The French and ourselves are both to blame for not having warned the Czechs. We did practically the same thing with Haile Selassie. "Believe in us, we will help you," and then we threw them over. The whole thing goes back to our belief in the League of Nations and Collective Security . . . "You do it", "I'll stand by". That was our attitude. Words were enough to stop Germany. We thought that Germany would hate war as much as we did. We forgot that the German people knew nothing about it all.

We could not say "If you cross the Czech frontier we will fight." It was risking the Empire and unjustifiable.

The first thing is that we must be safe here in Great Britain against air attack. It is useless to argue whether the Germans could or would destroy us in a few weeks. We must be quite certain that they cannot. Otherwise we cannot follow any policy of strength in any field. Our Base must be secure. . . . It seems to me scandalous that any Government with complete power owing to its majority in the House should not act with more vigour. It has to be driven every step it takes. It has some wonderful lawyer-talkers in its ranks, but executive ability has been absent till Sir John Anderson came on the scene. Will he alter things?

November 4

I went to the War Office and saw Gort and said goodbye. I got very little out of him beyond the fact that Belisha's statement in the House had gone very well. Indeed, he made a clean breast of all the deficiencies in material and took the wind completely out of the sails of the Opposition. Sam Hoare was far more hauled over the coals than Belisha for his Air Raid Precautions deficiencies which of course affected the population more *and were really far less serious.*

CHAPTER V

Chief of the Imperial General Staff

O N NOVEMBER 5, 1938, Ironside sailed for Gibraltar, where he remained as Governor until the following May. While he did much to strengthen the defences of the Rock and to acquaint himself with French North Africa, the scene in Europe grew steadily darker. The German Army had now outstripped the French. The dismemberment of Czechoslovakia had cost the Allies the equivalent of 35 divisions, and it was clear that her absorption into the Third Reich would be followed by the encirclement of Poland. On March 23, 1939, German troops occupied Memel, and six days later the plan to double the Territorial Army was announced in the House of Commons. This would mean an increase, on paper, of 210,000 men. It was not clear where the equipment was coming from or how it would be effectively officered. On the 31st Mr. Chamberlain gave a guarantee to Poland. On April 3, as we now know, Germany began to prepare to attack her, on April 7 Italian troops invaded Albania, and on the 27th conscription was introduced in the United Kingdom. It applied only to men of 20 years of age. They had yet to be equipped and trained. This valuable gesture was nevertheless opposed by Labour and Liberal members in the House of Commons. Mr. Churchill warmly praised Mr. Hore-Belisha for risking his political reputation, but the Government seemed to be very nervous about the step it had taken. They

□□ sent Ironside a "personal and private" message, which was presumably addressed to all commanders abroad:

> You will read announcement made by Prime Minister this afternoon. It may be useful letting you know that measures now announced are NOT, repeat, NOT relating to an immediate military measure. Indeed, the military situation in Germany at present time is that the great majority [of] army formations have now returned to their peace situations. How long this relative quiet position will last one cannot foretell.

At the end of this same month, April 1939, Hitler denounced the Anglo-German Naval Agreement and the German-Polish Non-Aggression Pact.

The French, by this time thoroughly alarmed, sent a Military Mission to Britain to concert plans for defence and to persuade us, in the event of war, to send a Force, even if it were only a token Force, to the Continent. It was agreed that we would send our 1st Corps, comprising two divisions—the only divisions fit to take the field. It was suggested that they might be followed later by two other Regular infantry divisions, which were not yet fully equipped. The so-called Armoured Division was not ready, and would not be ready for some time, as it still lacked battle tanks. It would also be some considerable while before the Territorial divisions would be fit to go overseas. Thanks to the Secretary of State's policy of doubling the Territorial Army by making each division and unit throw off a similar division and unit, they were short of trained officers, men and equipment. Nevertheless, and for the first time, Britain had now committed herself to sending an Expeditionary Force to the Continent if war came. No general plan, and no strategy for the Empire as a whole, were formulated. Each problem was dealt with as it arose, and Ironside wrote these words in his diary for May 6: "There is an absolute failure on the part of the War Office to realize the importance of the Middle East. They are hypnotized by the position in Europe. Perhaps

⊡⊡ this is quite natural. Anyway, here I am shut up in Gibraltar, with little hope of any active command."

A dramatic change in his fortunes was just round the corner. A telegram arrived at Gibraltar from the Secretary of State for War offering him the appointment of Inspector-General of Overseas Forces. It was dated this same 6th of May, his fifty-ninth birthday, and it ran as follows:

I have His Majesty's approval to offer you the appointment of Inspector-General Overseas Forces. You would be responsible to the Army Council for higher training of troops under control of Home Government which would go with any Field Force proceeding abroad. You would also consult such foreign staffs as Council thought advisable, would inspect and report on overseas garrisons and be available for consultation on matters of higher arrangements with Indian Military authorities. You would have a seat on the Selection Board.

The appointment would be for one year certain. The Colonial Secretary is willing that you should vacate your Governorship in view of need for your services in a more purely military way.

The King has approved appointment of General Kirke to be Inspector-General Home Forces.

I would specially ask you to keep this offer quite secret as I wish to make this announcement simultaneously with some others.

To assist him there were to be Inspectors of the various specialist arms. General Kirke, as Inspector-General of Home Forces, was made responsible for training below brigade level, including Coast Defence Units, the co-ordination of Home Defence schemes, and co-operation with Civil Defence, while the Inspector-General of Overseas Forces was responsible for the higher training. It was generally understood, though there was nothing in writing, that Ironside would be Commander-in-Chief of the British Expeditionary Force if war came, and that General Kirke would be Commander-in-Chief, Home Forces.

It will be recalled that Ironside himself had recommended appointing an Inspector-General so as to relieve the C.I.G.S. of the responsibility of training, and enable him to concentrate on policy and strategy.

"I accepted at once," he wrote later. "I thought long over this telegram. What did it mean? It still savoured much of peace. If the appointments meant anything, then I was to be chosen as G.O.C.-in-C. B.E.F. should war come. The conditions were almost taken from the paper which I had written for Belisha. Why was there any delay at all? I thought of visiting foreign stations and staffs. To my mind there would be little time for such things. What about the higher training? Had there been any of it yet? What about the relations between the Inspector-General and the C.I.G.S.? It was a surprising turn of fortune. I felt that I could not waste another minute in Gibraltar with such a job in front of me."

May 7

It is practically the same job that French had in 1914 and means that one would be C.-in-C.—consultation with all foreign staffs, inspection and report upon overseas garrisons, and consultation with Indian Government upon matters affecting them. Naturally I should never think of refusing this. . . . It will mean travelling a good deal. . . . The job is for one year certain. One year ought to see us out [of] or in our trouble and there is no good looking further ahead than that.

Treasury difficulties delayed the announcement of the appointment, and Ironside became understandably impatient. Four days later he sent a signal to London. The appointment was eventually announced on May 31, and, after handing over to his successor in Gibraltar, Ironside arrived in London on July 1 and went straight to the War Office.

July 1

I saw Gort in his office and found him very cheery and certainly pleased to see me. I had had doubts. We went through the list of senior officers, and I found that we had much the same ideas on their characters. The only thing I found out was that the main reason of my coming home was to command [the B.E.F.] in case of war.

July 4

I am told that I may have to go off to Warsaw at once as Beck [the Polish Foreign Minister] is very secretive. The Poles have a plan for dealing with Danzig, but they won't divulge it. I and a French General are to go and deal direct with Smigly-Rydz [the Polish Commander-in-Chief] and find out what it is.

July 5

I still have no office, no staff, no clerks. . . . I am told that the main object of my coming back from Gibraltar is to be in the country in order to take command of the Expeditionary Force in case war breaks out.

July 7

An interview with Belisha at 3.30 p.m. He had a splitting headache, he said, but we talked for an hour and a half. He greeted me back warmly. He also complimented me upon Gibraltar. . . . He then told me that he was considering my charter [as Inspector-General, Overseas Forces] and was trying to see that there should be no friction.

He then asked me where the future Generals were coming from. He could see no talent. I told him that he had turned out good and bad together, and that we must go warily in future. He promised me not to make any changes in the B.E.F. without my knowledge. . . .

I was to meet the P.M. and [Lord] Halifax at 12 noon on Monday [10th] to receive my instructions [for my visit to Poland]. Belisha had only the haziest idea what was to happen if we started to carry out our guarantee to the Poles. . . .

Belisha told me that the French C.-in-C. would be Generalissimo [of the French and British Armies in France], but that the
British C.-in-C. would have the "right of appeal". I at once asked
him to whom the British C.-in-C. could "appeal"?—to the
Cabinet, the Prime Minister, the War Office or what? Belisha said
he didn't know. . . .

On March 23, as we have seen, German troops had occupied Memel, and on April 3 Hitler had approved a secret
directive setting out military preparations for the conquest
of Poland at any time "from September 1 onwards". On
June 10 Mr. Chamberlain had repeated his intention of standing by Poland, and two days later Mr. Strang of the Foreign
Office was sent as special envoy to Moscow. Ironside had
meanwhile been instructed to go to Poland and measure the
situation.

July 10

I duly presented myself at 10 Downing Street at 12 noon and
was ushered in to see Chamberlain sitting with Halifax. I must
say that Chamberlain looks very young for his years, plenty of
hair with very little grey at the temples. He talked quietly and
easily and without hurry. . . . He told me that they had no idea
what the Poles were going to do and wanted me to go there to
find out. Beck had always put them off by saying that their action
was dependent upon the amount of provocation they got. I told
him that our chief card was that we had given a guarantee if
Poland felt her independence was menaced and that they must
therefore tell us what they intended to do. . . . Chamberlain said
that no undertakings by Hitler would be any use. We must have
some definite practical guarantee that with Danzig in the Reich,
Poland would have practical rights equal to those she had now. It
should not be beyond the brains of the Allies to devise some
guarantees that would bind Hitler. I must say that I was glad to
see that he had no belief in Hitler's promises. I told him that I had
seen and talked with Hitler and I told him that I was not sure
whether Hitler blew up spontaneously or whether he did it to

impress his listener. Chamberlain thought he did it spontaneously.
I said that if that were so there was more danger of war. He didn't
agree, but said that he agreed that something might always occur
to overbalance him. He thought that Hitler had an acute political
sense and didn't want war.

I told them that Hitler would present us with a *fait accompli* and
would then turn to us and say "Do you really want war over this
trivial matter?" They agreed, but said that we must settle Danzig
so that Hitler could not say that he had had a success through
threatening force.

Chamberlain asked me how long the Poles could stand up and
I told him that they must be overrun unless Hitler chose the wrong
moment. That you might take Poznania in a couple of months,
but that you couldn't overrun the whole country in a couple of
months. No one knew what a heavy air bombardment of Warsaw
might bring. I didn't think it would bring the Poles to their
knees. . . . They then told me that they had no answer from the
Poles as to my coming and were waiting that. My impression
was that they both thought that war was almost inevitable or
very nearly so. They did not express the optimism that Belisha
expressed. . . .

Chamberlain said that it seemed impossible to come to an
understanding with Russia. Did I think it was right? I told him
that though it was much against the grain, it was the only thing
we could do. Chamberlain ejaculated "The only thing we cannot
do." I told him that he must not expect too much from any
Russian advance, that the Russians had never done well outside
their own country, and that their Army must be very badly commanded. They had shot 80% of their officers over the rank of
Colonel in 1936 and couldn't have many left.

Ironside meanwhile continued to study the general European situation in preparation for his visit to Poland.

July 11

I examined the French plans and the only crumb of comfort is
that there is no hasty offensive to be seen against the Siegfried

Line. Gamelin told Gort that such an offensive would mean very careful preparation and [would take] some time. The British Expeditionary Force of two divisions is wanted over in France as a goodwill gesture, a definite indication that we are "all in" with France. They always have the idea that "*Perfide Albion*" might back out, and the B.E.F. is a *gage*.

The Siegfried Line is not such a line as the Maginot Line, which enables the French to economize in men, for it has to be held in depth. The Maginot Line, however, finishes on the Belgian frontier and does not turn westwards along that frontier. The French would like to continue their line north through Namur to Antwerp, but the Belgian authorities have refused to discuss any kind of defence. . . . If nothing can be done with the Belgians, we are to concentrate somewhere near Armentières on the Belgian frontier. I told Gort that this was the old game of pushing us too far forward, and that I considered that we should concentrate round Amiens. He is now going over to France, and said that he agreed and would get the French to agree.

Gort told me that all our ports of disembarkation were on the west coast of France and that even he did not know where they were. I told him that this wouldn't satisfy me, and that I must go into it. I then found that a new Section of the General Staff existed for the disembarkation plans and that they had been very fully discussed with the French. . . . I have told them that I must investigate this and go into it thoroughly with my Quarter-Master-General of the B.E.F., Lindsell. . . . The French were always very stingy over the room to be given us and I am quite sure that the plans must be overhauled. I am not prepared to take them for granted under the new conditions of air warfare.[1]

I then checked over the G.H.Q. staff and was relieved to see that it was very much smaller than in 1914. Many of the appointments have not yet been made, including the Chief of the General Staff. I wonder if I shall have any say in this. . . .

The French think that Hitler will go eastwards first, and have had conversations with the Poles for many years. They are almost futile in being able to do nothing much except take air-action

[1] On checking these plans later Ironside found them satisfactory.

against Germany, as I thought. The Poles are disappointed that the French do not go bald-headed for the Germans in the west, but the French stick to their plan.

The air-action to be taken is a matter of acute controversy, and the idea has been accepted of bombing only military objectives in Germany. If they think that this will induce the Germans to stick to the same thing in France and Great Britain they make a great mistake. Our R.A.F. are very anxious to bomb factories and oil installations. None of us want to have unlimited bombing and of course we shall not begin that ourselves. I am afraid that the Germans will be absolutely ruthless. . . .

In the evening I was suddenly summoned to see Belisha at the House of Commons. . . . We walked down to the Foreign Office and had an hour's talk with the Secretary of State. In the end I had to draft my own instructions [for my visit to Poland], which they signed. They are all dreamers and thinkers and cannot turn them into orders. Unpractical creatures. Not a good augury for war.

July 13

The Poles are convinced the Germans will concentrate against them and they admit that they must evacuate their western frontier. They think that they can maintain a front against Germany somewhere in Poland.[1] . . . The Germans will attack due south on Warsaw from East Prussia. They think that a Corps may be transported by sea from Hamburg to East Prussia. The Poles consider it impossible to hold the Corridor and Poznania. . . . They hope to keep a central reserve and to launch a counter-offensive. The Poles seem to have too low an opinion of the German Army's value. They consider that they are over-motorized. Apparently the war effort in Poland in the way of arms factories is incredible. . . .

The thing that emerges from a consideration of this subject is that we can do very little to help the Poles in a war that starts against them. An attack against the Siegfried Line will take a long time to develop and air attacks against Germany cannot reach as

[1] This was the line of the Vistula.

far as the German forces and bases operating against Poland.
Naturally, they demand immediate action, something that they
can see. It is difficult to know how we can realize this, despite our
guarantee to Poland. . . . I must get the Poles to realize that haste
is against them. We develop slowly and require warning if we are
to help Poland. We must therefore hope for a slowly developing
tension over Danzig and not a sudden *coup*.

On Monday, July 17, Ironside left London by air. It had
thus taken seven days to get him off to Warsaw. Nowhere
was there any sense of urgency. He was met by the Army
Inspector and by the Chief of Staff of the Polish Army, and
the Polish Air Force mounted a Guard of Honour. He dined
that evening at the flat of the British Military Attaché, where
General Carton de Wiart, who had made his home in
Poland, was a fellow-guest. "He was in good form," Ironside noted. "He told me that they hadn't had any proper
winter and snow for three years and that the whole country
was dried up. Unless they had rain, the German could go
anywhere with his mechanical vehicles. He was praying for
rain in case of war." Next day, Ironside had a conference
with Marshal Smigly-Rydz, the Polish Commander-in-
Chief.

July 18 [Warsaw]

I approached the question of Danzig, and found that neither
the Marshal nor Beck were opposed to negotiation over Danzig,
but they pointed out that Danzig was merely a pretext. That the
Germans were determined, if they decided upon war, to destroy
the Poles and then turn upon the other Powers opposing them. . . .
I have wired to the Government:

(i) That I am certain that the Poles will do nothing rash in a
military sense.
(ii) That the military effort they have made is little short of
prodigious.
(iii) That we ought not to make so many conditions to our
financial aid. That time is short.

(iv) That one of the ways of convincing Hitler that we are serious is by granting this monetary aid to Poland. . . .
(v) That the Poles are strong enough to resist.

The Poles, a poor nation, are straining their economy in order to arm.

It was evident that neither the Poles nor the Roumanians were anxious for Russian help; and the French had apparently told the Poles that if Poland was attacked they would start a counter-offensive in the west (this despite the fact that the French plan, as disclosed to Britain, was purely defensive).

On the two following days Ironside was shown something of the country and the Polish Army. He was impressed by the troops, but anxious about the plans. Smigly-Rydz had said that his main line of defence would be the River Vistula. He had three Armies: one in the north opposite East Prussia, one in the south on the Vistula south of Warsaw and opposite Czechoslovakia, and a third in the Posen Salient to the west. A gap was left on the Vistula for this Army to fill when it fell back. Ironside stressed the danger from the north and south to this Third Army, and suggested withdrawing it towards Warsaw and leaving only covering troops on the frontier west of Posen. But the Polish Commander-in-Chief maintained that there would be time enough to withdraw it when the situation developed. Ironside pointed out that communications were apt to break down under bombing and orders might not reach the Commander of the Third Army. Smigly-Rydz insisted on keeping to his plan. In the event, the order reached the Commander of the Third Army, but he refused to withdraw.

July 24 [London]

Up at 6 a.m. and down to the War Office. Here I saw Belisha . . . I had three-quarters of an hour with him. He asked whether I thought the world war was coming, and I told him that I thought it was. Was it coming this year? I said probably but that nobody could tell. He then pulled down the map of Europe and showed

the most amazing ignorance about Poland and what it was like. I
then suddenly realized that he and the C.I.G.S. and the D.C.I.G.S.
were all running off to a Committee of Imperial Defence meeting.
He was getting a few ideas out of me. When I thought of it, it
suddenly dawned on me that they were off to discuss Poland. I
had not sent in a report and none of them had had anything but
the haziest of conversations with me. It never dawned on any of
them that I ought to be there to tell them what I had learnt. . . .
Gort doesn't even begin to know how to run the bigger things.

July 25

I made a night of it with Winston Churchill at Chartwell. I
dined alone with him and then we sat talking till 5 a.m. this
morning.

What a man. . . . He remarked that he would have to pull in
his horns considerably if he ever took office, because he would
have to cease making money by writing. Last September, had
there been a war, he would have been given the Admiralty. Now
he might even be Prime Minister and perhaps the War Office.
He had made friends with Belisha because he says that it was
Belisha who got conscription through, "taking his life in his
hands". He nearly got the sack and acted with great courage. . . .

Neville Chamberlain is not a war Prime Minister. He is a pacifist
at heart. He has a firm belief that God has chosen him as an
instrument to prevent this threatened war. He can never get this
out of his mind. He is not against Winston, but he believes that
chances may still arrive for averting war, and he thinks that
Winston might be so strong in a Cabinet that he would be prevented from acting. . . . Winston thinks that Munich was a terrible
disgrace.

Winston considered that it was now too late for any appease-
ment. The deed was signed, and Hitler is going to make war. He
walked about in front of the map and demonstrated his ideas,
repeating, "You are destined to play a great part, you will be the
Commander-in-Chief. You must be clear on what is going to
happen:

(i) The crippling or annihilation of Poland.

(ii) The employment of Italy to create diversions. Mussolini had sold his country for his job.

(iii) The capture of Egypt, chiefly by Italian forces.

(iv) A pressing on to the Black Sea *via* Roumania.

(v) An alliance with Russia, when the latter sees how the land lies."

I told Winston that I was sure that we were in for a bad time and that we should have to have guts to withstand the first German and Italian rush. We had no considered plans; no plan to deal with the war in general. Even the hazy idea of attacking the Italians had not been put into even a framework. . . .

Winston then produced the idea of putting a squadron of battleships into the Baltic. It would paralyse the Germans and immobilize many German divisions. The submarine had been dealt with and would no longer be a menace. This idea of British ships in the Baltic was revolutionary, and I was very surprised at how Winston was so navally-minded. All his schemes came back to the use of the Navy. It ran through my head that here was a grand strategist imagining things, and the Navy itself making no plans whatever. Quite definitely, the man who is now First Sea Lord had no plan for his Mediterranean Fleet when he was in command of it. He could give me no idea of any offensive plan for dealing with Italy. I am sure there is none now.

July 26

I spent the morning in the War Office. I got the plan for our Expeditionary Force in France. We have tied ourselves to the French for six Regular divisions and the Air Striking Force. They are to go to France whatever happens, whether the Germans attack in the west or not. It is a token to the French that we are in the war with them. They cannot allow us not to give this pledge. A struggle is now going on as to the question of command. We send over our Corps from Aldershot and the Air Ministry sends over the Air Striking Force. No agreement has been reached as to the Air being under the Army Commander. It is now the intention to send over the eventual C.-in-C., who is presumably me, so that he can command them both. It seems pretty scandalous that this has not already been done.

Gamelin has arranged to disembark the British at St. Nazaire, Brest and Cherbourg. The reason for this is that the air and submarine menace makes it necessary to do this in the early days, perhaps shifting back to Havre and the other northern ones later. We then concentrate at Le Mans and move up to Amiens and finally Armentières on the Belgian frontier. The French plan is *purely* defensive. There is no sign of an offensive either against the Siegfried Line or against the Italian frontier in the south. No offensive can be undertaken without careful preparation. The French have lied to the Poles in saying that they are going to attack. There is no idea of it.

July 26 (continued)

I was so impressed by our lack of plan that I got in to see Belisha at 5 p.m. I told him the story of what I had discovered. I told him what the Germans could do to knock out Poland and Roumania. How we were not hurrying in getting in Russia, and we talked about an "Eastern Front" when it did not exist beyond the thought. I told him that the French did not mean to take any offensive, and that no plans for anything existed to deal any blow at either the Germans or Italians. The Navy had no plan and intended to act "according to the circumstances" and not in unison with any of the other arms. Everything was hopelessly defensive everywhere. Meanwhile our "Eastern Front" myth was being exploded. We should find the Poles destroyed and the Germans overrunning Roumania and on the Black Sea. We were doing absolutely nothing to stop it. Why were we not collecting an Army in Egypt at once, stripping India at once, to carry out an offensive against the Italians? Belisha said that he had been thinking about all this for a long time and had an uneasy suspicion that I was right. He told me to come in and see him again. . . .

I go to bed profoundly depressed at our Government's lack of decision. How have we got into this state of affairs? I have to go to see the King to-morrow. What shall I tell him?

July 27

I keep thinking of Winston Churchill down at Westerham, full of patriotism and ideas for saving the Empire. A man who knows that you must act to win. You cannot remain supine and allow yourself to be hit indefinitely. Winston must be chafing at the inaction. I keep thinking of him walking up and down the room.

July 28

At long last my Instructions as Inspector-General of the Overseas Forces have come in. . . . It is made quite clear that we report to the Army Council. . . . I must now collect the various Inspectors and have a talk with them. The only Corps which is functioning is the Aldershot one and we must take the training of that as the basis of the rest of the Army. . . . I sent over my Staff Officer to the War Office to find out when the Inspectors who were coming under me were to come over to Thames House. I then discovered that more than three-quarters of them had not been appointed, including all the Infantry Inspectors. . . . One might think that I was living in a madhouse, with the war perhaps upon us. . . . In fact I find that I shall be absolutely single-handed till October, all through this present training.

July 31

I found out a little more about the Command in France to-day. The Air Ministry have apparently agreed to the Air Striking Force being put under G.H.Q. in France. This means that a C.-in-C. has to go across immediately.

August 3

I have sent my G.S.O.(I.) [General Staff Officer, Grade One] over to the War Office to find out exactly what they want me to do with the coming manœuvres. Am I to run them? . . . Am I to lead the criticism at the end? Do I submit what I am going to say to the C.I.G.S.? The whole thing is most unsatisfactory. . . . If war comes I shall take over the Army having had little to do with the commanding of it. . . . There wasn't any urgency in bringing me home for such a job. The only necessity was to have me home to be given the command in case of war.

August 11

I have been thinking over the words of my Instructions. It is to supervise "the higher training" of the Army. . . . The War Office have no idea of the importance of this training. They have simply played at it all.

August 16

The 1st Corps can be assembled overseas in Z+24 days. *The remainder is all in the air.* But by September 1 we can have a further modified two divisions by Z+33 days.

Then in Z+4 months we can have two T.A. divisions to complete these two corps to three divisions each.

In Z+5 months we can have a further four T.A. divisions.

This is a terrible result after all these years of preparation. We have indeed to look to a long war. . . .

The recruiting is going steadily up. We have 744 men in July to 366 in 1938 and 199 in 1937. But we have a deficit in the Regular Army of 1,316 officers and 41,704 men. The militia called up by August 1 are only 34,498 out of 200,000 available.

August 18

I spent the day watching the training of the 1st Guards Brigade. I wandered about talking to various lots of men and found it a pleasure to be back with men again. . . . We saw the 2nd Brigade after a night operation. . . . So far I have seen an improvement in tactics, but there are still made the simplest of mistakes by young officers. None of the preliminary training has been thorough enough owing to the lack of equipment. . . . If we are allowed the September manœuvres we shall get the 1st Corps in good order. . . . Tactics amuse me still and I have jotted down a few notes that have come into my head after these exercises:

Continuity

No disconnected strategy or tactics ever lead to anything. . . . You must exploit your successes. . . . This means that you must

have a plan which enables you to exploit immediately. . . .
Advance to the Battlefield
. . . Troops moving up must do so in artillery formations. . . .
Columns within aeroplane range of a battlefield . . . may be
very dangerous. . . .
Reconnaissance
This must be continuous. . . . Once touch is gained it must be
maintained.
Troops in Defence
It is essential not to keep all men in action. . . . Men not
working should be rested. . . .
Training
If . . . a leader has made bad use of ground . . . stop the
operations and . . . re-enact the movement . . . taking the leaders
who have been at fault over to the other side. . . .
Security
. . . The adoption at all times of suitable formations. . . .
Observation. . . . A constant inquisitiveness by patrolling.
Headquarters
At all times concealed . . . from the ground and from the
air. . . . In no case located at cross roads.
Infiltration
. . . The only method which can be successful in close
country. . . . A steady exploitation of success in any direction.
. . . An early deployment of artillery. . . . Control of deployed
artillery. . . .
Air Attack against Troops
. . . Air attacks can occur at any time . . . and suddenly. . . .
Essential to adopt fighting formations always in the battle area.

August 20

Halifax has been back at the Foreign Office studying the latest
reports in the place. The Prime Minister remains fishing in Scotland. Parliament remains on holiday. There is nothing to do but
wait the desire of Hitler. He keeps the whole of Europe on tenter-
hooks in his nerve-campaigning. A dreadful state of affairs.

August 22

The news this morning must be flabbergasting the politicians. Germany and Russia are supposed to be signing a non-aggression pact. . . . War seems absolutely certain now. . . . One can hardly credit it and yet I have known it was coming for years. . . .

Lunch at the Carlton with Belisha, Gort and Pownall there. He was having a Cabinet Meeting in the afternoon and I have never met a man more unprepared strategically to meet any questions being asked. He was continually asking how many divisions the Poles had—and getting it wrong each time—and could not get down to what we ought to do. Neither Gort nor Pownall seem to have forced on him—if that was necessary—any *aide mémoire*. All Belisha could say was that we were in a bad way. And we are.

On August 23, following talks between Ribbentrop and Stalin, Soviet Russia signed a non-aggression pact with Germany, destroying in one stroke the dream of an "Eastern Front" to support Poland and Roumania. Two days later Great Britain confirmed her treaty with Poland, reiterating the guarantees we had already given.

August 23

This morning I get a message from the War Office to attend a conference for Commanders "to discuss the present emergency". It makes one quite sick. Why cannot the C.I.G.S. take charge of things and issue instructions? I told Belisha yesterday that he ought to mobilize. . . . We have absolutely no direction from above and no signs of anybody with personality enough to direct. Pitiable at a moment like this. . . . I have not been officially nominated as the C.-in-C. in France and I am wondering when they will make that appointment.

August 24

Belisha had apparently asked for mobilization of the Regular and Territorial Armies and had been refused. It would not be in accordance with the speech Chamberlain intends to make this afternoon. Gort led the wretched conference badly. . . . The

C.I.G.S. worrying himself about little details instead of thinking of the big things. . . . Manœuvres are definitely off.

August 27

Down to Chartwell for lunch yesterday. . . . Winston was full of Georges,[1] whom he had seen over in France. I found that he had become very French in his outlook and had a wonderful opinion of the whole thing he saw. He had General Spears with him. The burden of his song was that we must have a great Army in France, that we couldn't depend upon the French to do our effort for us. That we must get twenty Divisions by Christmas. I told him that we had no such plans in being. He showed me how the French were going to attack Italy and how they held the high ground round the Mont Cenis and looked down upon the Italians below them. I told him that the French had told him far more than they had told our General Staff, that I had been unable, as C.-in-C. designate, to get any clear plan out of things. Winston said that we were trying to get as much control in the conduct of affairs as if we had an Army of one and a half millions. This we couldn't have. . . . I rang up Macleod[2] and he had been to the War Office where they said that news was difficult to get through, but as far as could be ascertained no big movement of the Germans had taken place. They expected them to begin tomorrow.

August 28

Back to the Office where I found nothing. . . . Macleod was at the War Office and tells me that my name will be submitted to the Government when the time comes as C.-in-C.

Ironside had meanwhile moved his office from Thames House to the Horse Guards. On September 1 Mr. Churchill rang up to say that Hitler was moving his troops and that Warsaw and Cracow had been bombed at dawn. He seemed to know more than the War Office. At 2 p.m. the War

[1] The French Commander-in-Chief for North-Eastern France from Switzerland to the sea.
[2] Lt.-Col. (later Col.) R. Macleod, G.S.O.(I) to Ironside.

Office ordered mobilization. Chamberlain set up a War Cabinet, which Churchill agreed to join as First Lord of the Admiralty. The Prime Minister's hope of including Labour and Liberal representatives was not fulfilled. At 9.30 p.m. a British ultimatum, but not the final ultimatum, was delivered to Germany. A Commander-in-Chief and a G.H.Q. Staff for the B.E.F. had not yet been appointed.

September 1

A fateful day. I got to the Horse Guards as 10 a.m. was striking and was immediately rung up by Winston from Westerham who said "They've started. Warsaw and Cracow are being bombed now." I rang up Gort at the War Office who said that he was off to a meeting. [He] didn't believe it. I urged him to tell Belisha. He did and Belisha was seen rushing off to Downing Street. I rang Winston again and he said he had the news definitely from the Polish Ambassador, who had told him 1½ hours ago. . . . How could the War Office possibly be ignorant of this?

The German dispositions are now clear. They have 78 divisions in line with 10 in the centre of Germany and 18 in all on the Western Front. There are thus 50 divisions and all the air force massed on the Polish frontier. The main attack of 31 divisions is coming up from Slovakia on Silesia. The Poles cannot withstand anything like this for long. . . .

Mobilization was ordered at 2 p.m. today.[1] . . . Macleod was told that it was "practically certain" that I would be C.-in-C. and that I would be flying over very soon to France with the Chief of the General Staff and Deputy C.G.S. Naturally these things have to be done in order and there must be a Cabinet signature to the thing. . . .

September 2

Dinner at the Club [last night] where I saw Kennedy who told me that I had not [yet] been appointed to the B.E.F. That my

[1] Ironside, expecting to be Commander-in-Chief, sent his staff down to Aldershot to mobilize G.H.Q., but himself remained in London to receive his instructions.

name had been sent forward and that it was 10 to 1 that I should be appointed. . . .

Lunch [today] at the Club and Amery came up to me and said that he took it for granted I was to command the B.E.F. I told him that practically everybody did, but that although the papers had been sent to the Prime Minister days ago, he had not signed them. . . . My staff have all gone off to Aldershot and I am left here with nothing whatever. I ought to be studying all the reports and plans and seeing the latest reports from the French. . . .

The [German] main attack of 31 divisions is coming from Slovakia, with 9 divisions in East Prussia. The remainder, 10 divisions, are opposite Poznania. There are 10 divisions in Central Germany and 18 divisions opposite the French in the west. They have certainly concentrated in proper strategical way at the most important points. . . .

I saw Kennedy who told me that the plan had now come into action. The bombers and advance parties of the Army had gone over to France, and yet the Prime Minister wouldn't move.

September 3

[Macleod] rang up from Aldershot and said that G.H.Q. staff was all herded together in a barracks at a danger spot. Too many eggs in one basket and I ordered them to disperse. [They had in fact already been distributed over Sandhurst and Camberley.]

Then to the Horse Guards where we listened at 11 a.m. to the Prime Minister speaking. He made a very fine speech, though his voice was obviously much affected. We were at war from 11 a.m. We had sent an ultimatum to the Germans and had received no answer.

Almost at 11.20 a.m., just as the P.M. had ceased talking, the air raid warning went and I seized my helmet and gas mask and went over to the strong-room at the War Office, our place of refuge. Here I found the whole War Office crowding downstairs, officers clerks and women. Quite good operation rooms, but the temperature very high. Gort and Belisha there and Lelong, the French Military attaché, all in one room. Parliament was to meet at 12 noon, and Belisha went off. We heard various bangings and were all sure that the noises were the guns firing. It seemed almost incredible that they could have begun so quickly. After 20 minutes the "all clear" went and we trooped off. . . . When I got over to the Horse Guards my servant was sitting in his car and told me that the whole raid had been a trial one. Not even the War Office knew about it. . . . So now we are at war, and I shall know now shortly if I am to be given the command or not. . . .

I was rung up by Macleod from Sandhurst where he has established himself and asked if I was coming down to-night. I told him that I had not been appointed C.-in-C. and there didn't seem any signs of my being appointed. . . .

Back to the Club, where I sat down to have a drink with Freddie Maitland. I was summoned to the telephone and was told by Roseway [private secretary to the Minister for War] that Belisha would probably want to see me during the night. A few minutes later I was told to go to the War Office at once. I was ushered in to Belisha and there he said to me at once "I want you to come as C.I.G.S." Pretty devastating. I said to him "Why do you want to do this?" He then said that there were no ideas in the War Office and that I took a broader view of the war than anybody else. I said that I would do as I was ordered. That it was war, and I never picked or chose and neither asked for a job nor refused one. He then said that he would like to be quite frank with me. That he had had a great fight in the new War Cabinet and had been backed up by Winston Churchill. That it had been said that I talked too much and was unreliable. I told him that it was a most scandalous lying accusation. That if he thought that, I had no intention of taking the job. He said that he had complete trust in me and was quite satisfied to place his confidence in me. He also said that the report was [that] the Chiefs of Staff Conferences would be completely upset if I were in them. That he didn't believe that. I again told him that if he had the slightest doubt I wouldn't come. That I always spoke the truth, perhaps brutally, but when once a decision was taken there was nobody more loyal than I was. I always carried out any decision as if it were my own. Belisha then asked me to dismiss the conversation from my mind.

The appointment of Gort was most dramatic. As soon as I had said that I would be C.I.G.S. Belisha got up and appeared most relieved. He opened the door of his private office and ushered Gort in with the words "And here is the Commander-in-Chief." This was the solution of my becoming C.I.G.S. I could hardly believe that I was hearing aright. I merely wondered if Gort had known all along. He was delighted, of course, at having been appointed, and pleased at the idea of getting away from Belisha. I can hardly believe that he was any more informed of what was impending than I was. Gort is too simple and straight not to have told me.

He then had Gort in and told him that he could have *carte blanche* as to officers for the B.E.F. [Gort asked for Pownall as C.G.S.] I then told him that we couldn't make that mistake. The war was being run from the War Office by the C.I.G.S. and we couldn't allow key positions to be mutilated.[1] Gort agreed, and I said that Belisha must leave me to settle that.

I am bitterly disappointed that I am not to command the Army in the field. My great ambition. I am not suited in temperament to such a job as C.I.G.S., nor have I prepared myself to be such. My whole life has been based upon doing what I was told, and there it is.

The disgust I feel that I was considered unreliable and difficult to get on with makes me feel angry. I am not one to mince my words, but war does not require the same characteristics as peace. I'll do my job to the best of my ability and honestly, but I confess I have misgivings.

---

[1] Nevertheless, Belisha appointed Pownall. Thus the two men who knew the plans, Gort the former C.I.G.S. and Pownall the Director of Military Operations, disappeared from the War Office.

PART TWO

THE SECOND WORLD WAR

CHAPTER VI

Organization and Plans

HITLER INVADED Poland at dawn on September 1, 1939. The campaign was soon over.

Before the war the Poles were certain that their 35 divisions could hold up a German invasion. They relied on horsed cavalry, and on their rivers, streams and marshes to delay the enemy, but the fine, warm summer, following dry winters, had ruined these natural obstacles, and their brave cavalry were no match for the German tanks. Their only hope was to hold the line of the Vistula, but the river was now fordable in many places and there was a large gap where the Polish Third Army should have been. Its commander had refused to retreat when ordered to do so, saying he was holding out successfully, and his troops were cut off and surrounded. "It is now realized", wrote Ironside on September 11, "that nothing can save the Poles, and that the only way of restoring them is to win the war."

The Polish Military Attaché visited the War Office with long lists of urgently needed equipment, stores and supplies. In particular he asked for fighter-aircraft and tanks, and Ironside had to explain that while we would do everything we could to help, the fighters could not reach Poland because their range was too short to fly direct from France, and that we ourselves were desperately short of armour. All we could send were some machine-guns and ammunition. By September 18 the Russians and Germans had joined hands at Brest-

The German Campaign in Poland.

□□ Litovsk. Warsaw fell, and on September 29 Soviet Russia and Nazi Germany signed a treaty which partitioned Poland. Thus ended the first and only German campaign of the year 1939.

Superficially, at any rate, the British War Office continued to follow its peace-time routine. The civilian staff went punctually home each night. The military officers and staff stayed on till their work was finished, but some still lived as far away as Brighton. Ironside remained at his post and made do with a bed in his office. The three directorates of Military Operations and Intelligence, Staff Duties, and Military Training were expanded to six, grouped in pairs under an Assistant C.I.G.S. In course of time, a Vice-C.I.G.S. was appointed and the diagramatic result was as follows:

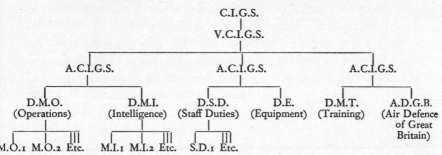

When things were reasonably quiet, Ironside rode in the Park from 8 to 9 each morning, breakfasted at the United Service Club, and was back in the War Office before 10 for the Chiefs of Staff Meeting at 10.30 and the War Cabinet an hour later. He usually had all his meals at his club, and in order to protect him from the many people who wanted to discuss the war or obtain preferment, two senior members, Admiral Wigram and Col. Freddie Maitland, were asked to keep him company.

It at once became clear that the Government intended to run the war through a War Cabinet, advised by a Committee of the three Chiefs of Staff. The War Cabinet, which included the Minister for the Co-ordination of Defence

□□ (Admiral Lord Chatfield) and the three Service Ministers, Mr. Churchill (Admiralty), Mr. Hore-Belisha (War Office) and Sir Kingsley Wood (Air), was regularly attended by the Chiefs of Staff. The Chiefs of Staff, sitting as a Committee, were expected to hear reports, measure the situation, make plans, decide day-to-day operational problems, and consider any matters specially remitted to them by the War Cabinet. In practice, the Chiefs of Staff Committee, which comprised Ironside, Admiral Pound and Air Chief Marshal Newall, became the professional advisers of the War Cabinet, and in due course sent instructions to commanders in the field.

Though forming a single Committee the three Chiefs of Staff bore quite different responsibilities, and their Services functioned in three separate fashions. The Army in France was under French command, and acted in accordance with French plans. The Air Force was directly under the War Cabinet, and the Navy followed a self-appointed course. Most of the strategy and planning carried out by the Chiefs of Staff Committee was therefore for the Army. In spite of the pre-war work of the Committee of Imperial Defence (now defunct), in spite of the Chiefs of Staff Committee, and in spite of the efforts of the War Cabinet, there was little co-ordination or co-operation between the fighting services. The Air thought they could win the war by bombing Germany, and built many large bombers which could only work well at night. Co-operation with the Army was regarded with little favour and suitable machines were scarce. The Navy thought of blockading Germany, and the Government hoped that victory could be won by bombing and blockade. Ironside maintained that Germany relied on her Army and, to win the war, this Army must be attacked and defeated on land, but until Churchill became Prime Minister in May 1940, no one could make all three Services work successfully to a common plan.

Then there were the Committees, nearly all of which Ironside had to attend. These included the Supreme War Council of the Allies, namely France and Britain; the War Cabinet;

the Chiefs of Staff Committee; the Military Co-ordination
Committee; the Land Forces Committee; the Priorities Committee, and the Army Council. The Army Council consisted
of the Secretary of State for War, Mr. Hore-Belisha, together
with three military and three civilian members: Ironside,
Chief of the Imperial General Staff, responsible for Imperial
Strategy, Plans, Operations, Intelligence, Staff Duties, Organization and Training; the Adjutant-General, Gordon-
Finlayson, responsible for recruiting, reinforcements, pay,
medical services, chaplains, discipline and morale; and the
Quarter-Master-General, Venning, responsible for food,
transport, clothing, equipment, petrol, ammunition, tools,
stores, depots, transport, billeting and quartering, docks, railways, shipping, and the supply services.

The three civilian members were the Parliamentary and
Permanent Under-Secretaries of State, and the Financial
Secretary.

No individual was responsible for the supply of arms and
equipment. This had once been the duty of the Master-
General of the Ordnance, but the post had been abolished.

The Council met whenever the Secretary of State considered necessary, and, though primarily charged with
administrative matters, also had the power to give orders to
the troops. Here was a fruitful source of conflict and confusion.

September 4

I had my first Chief of Staffs meeting at 10 a.m. in our battle
H.Q. Pound is very deaf and hardly says anything except on naval
subjects. Newall is quick and sketchy, I think. We got through
our work very quickly and I refused to have any endless talk.

Over to Paris by R.A.F. plane from Hendon. Landed at Le
Bourget and to Vincennes where we found Gamelin installed in
the old fortress in a war H.Q. A small, dapper little man with
dyed hair. . . . After some time I got Gamelin to explain his plan.
He [would have] finished mobilization [on the] 5th and was commencing his concentration at once. He intended to start at once—

if he had not done so already—to move up into the No Man's land between the Maginot and Siegfried lines. Still inside his own country in three salients from the N.E. corner to the Luxembourg frontier. He would squeeze out these pockets and by the 17th hoped to be facing the Siegfried line. He could then bring up his heavy artillery and try his experiments upon the line. All very steady and calm.

He reported German concentrations—he thought they were defensive—against the Luxembourg frontier. He hoped the Germans would attack him here. He was delighted at having completed mobilization without any bombing.

September 6

We are now in the soup and I feel that I have come in again at the last moment to try to do what I can. It really is a damnable show. Still I must put my back and brain into it. The worse things get perhaps the more control I shall get.

The French Staff is now working:

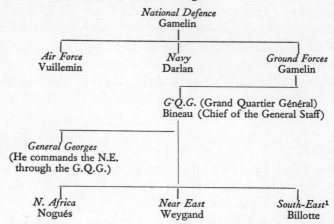

Again a day of meetings. I find the Chiefs of Staff agree well

As C.I.G.S., responsible for making plans for the Empire as a whole, Ironside's first action on entering the War Office

[1] South-East= the Swiss and Italian frontiers. North-East= from Switzerland to the Belgian coast.

□□ had been to find out what plans were in existence. He was surprised to find that the only firm plan was to send four divisions to France. There was no plan for the Empire as a whole. Nothing was said about the Armoured Division because its tanks were unfitted for war in Europe. He immediately protested to the Prime Minister. In the First World War the Empire had produced 95 divisions. The expansion of the R.A.F., the need for large Anti-Aircraft and Civil Defences at home, and the complicated modern weapons which required many men to make and maintain them, forced him to plan for a total of only 50 divisions. In addition, he needed supplies for another 10 divisions in case any of the Balkan States or Turkey came into the war, making a total of 60 divisions.

In general, his plan was:

1. At least 20 divisions from British and Canadian sources to be sent to *France.* He considered this contribution the minimum required to ensure the security of the Western Front.
2. Twelve divisions from the United Kingdom, India, Australia, New Zealand and South Africa for the *Middle East* with the task of securing our communications and seizing Italy's African possessions if Mussolini came into the war against us. They would be supplied, as far as possible, from local resources (which would be developed) and from countries east of Suez. An overland route from Basra to Palestine was to be developed.
3. Eighteen divisions in the United Kingdom as an Imperial Reserve, ready to go anywhere in the world and with equipment suitable for Europe, the tropics and the arctic.
4. Existing garrisons in the Far East to be concentrated at Hong Kong and Singapore in view of possible Japanese hostility.

Of these 50 divisions, 32 would come from Great Britain. Ironside put this plan on the War Cabinet agenda, but, though they passed a total of 55 divisions on September 19, they did not pass the plan. They would not listen to his strategy, and were immersed in trivial matters. Opposition also came from the other Services, the Navy because steel was scarce and many ships had to be built, and the Air Force because it would hamper their expansion.

September 7

It seems to me that if this war is to be won it must be won against the German Army and that means that an Army must be employed. We have not one at the moment. In the last war we tried to fight and make the Army from the beginning, and the consequence was that we never got it properly trained and the Army was not equal to its task. . . .

We know the demands for troops that were made in the last war. We actually sent overseas 74 divisions and the Dominions 14, with India 7, a total of 95 divisions. We cannot hope to reach this total now, owing to the size of the Air Force *and* its industry, plus casualties from enemy air action, and the Air Defence of Great Britain ground forces.

My calculations lead me to:

British troops in France	20 divs.
British troops in Middle East	12 divs.
Allies in Middle East (and possibly calls from elsewhere)	28 divs.[1]
	60 divs.

We must look to 60 divs. of equipment.

I have dictated a paper about our strategy in the Middle East. I have given it to my people as a *vade mecum*.

STRATEGY IN THE MIDDLE-EAST

At the moment we are committed to sending a Regular force of four divisions to France. This Field Force comes directly under

[1] This figure included an Imperial Reserve at home of 18 divisions and Allies 10 divisions.

French command. Later we are committed to sending two armoured divisions when they are able to go. There will undoubtedly be pressure put upon us to send more troops to France ... to take a large part in operations in France which are directly to be carried out by the French command. . . .

I wish it to be clear that our strategy in the Middle East must be Imperial strategy and it is important that it should never be subordinated to the French command. The Suez Canal is the centre of the British Empire. In the area comprising Iraq, Palestine and Egypt we can concentrate all the Regular forces which we may be able to strip from India and also any Australian, New Zealand and South African contingents which may come to our help.

There lies north of Syria—Turkey. The Turkish Army is a formidable body of troops. If Turkey comes in against the Germans there is no possibility of Turkey being overrun as there is in a country like Roumania. . . . I wish it to be borne in mind from a military point of view that we should develop our military strategy with Turkey if possible. . . .

When I interviewed General Gamelin in France he drew me a picture of General Weygand commanding in what he called the Levant. . . . I put in this warning because I foresee we may be led into a repetition of the unfortunate Salonika expedition of the late war.

7.9.39.   E. I.
                                                                    C.I.G.S.

September 8

I have a Secretary of State who knows nothing about military matters whatever and who is very jealous of Winston's interference. . . . I find Belisha cannot take in anything from reading it. He will not even begin to pick up the contents after having read it several times. He can only take a thing in orally and he will talk and argue over a subject with the object of getting his own ideas in order and maybe convincing himself.

I have had time to audit the Army in the few days in which I have been in power and my main job is to get across [to France] the contingents as envisaged. . . . Even this first contingent has deficiencies of a very serious nature. To the Ministers only yesterday I gave the details in full. Winston & Coy. were horrified when I produced the figures. . . . Winston was then for pushing more divisions forward even without the necessities which we lack. We could borrow from the French for the battle. All would be well.

Bodies are no use sent across in this way. They must have their proper equipment.

It was finally agreed that we should aim at the following:

(i) A war of three years' duration.
(ii) A total of 32 British divisions.
(iii) A total of 55 divisions in all to be equipped.
(iv) A total minimum of 20 divisions in one year.

Winston dissented and said that we should send 20 divisions in six months. I argued that these could not be equipped and could not be trained.

September 10

Yesterday was a fateful day and the British Government decided to prepare for a war of three years and more if necessary. When it was decided to dish this out to the papers the P.M. put his forehead down on the table and kept it there for nearly ten minutes. When he eventually looked up he looked more than ghastly. . . . When it was mentioned that the Chiefs of Staff were going to consider a recommendation of "gloves off" in an Air war, he shook his head in a dull way as if it were too much to consider. . . .

I had a farewell talk with Gort and Dill[1] . . . I told them all my strategical ideas, and I then made an appeal to them to see that their men and transport did not expose themselves to air attack. Anywhere behind the fighting line is the battle line. Nowhere is anybody safe. All must dig in and disperse themselves. This is particularly necessary amongst the Army Service Corps and the Army Ordnance Corps.

[1] Dill commanded the First Corps from Aldershot, consisting of the 1st and 2nd Divisions.

September 14

[General] Hotblack [our military attaché in France], back from the front. He gives a very dreary account of the French effort as it has now developed. At the bottom, the French believe that this struggle with Germany must happen in every century and probably more often. Their one desire is to emerge from the war with something of their manhood left. They are therefore going to do nothing until we are more in line. They do not want to fight in front of the Maginot Line and therefore they are not going to put too many men there with a possibility of not being able to withdraw them. They expect that the Germans will make an attack with some of the divisions which have not been engaged and they also expect some terrific attack by the German Air Force. . . .

It is a war of a Sea Empire against a Land Empire and at the moment the Sea Empire is at a disadvantage. Our criminal negligence in arming ourselves has brought us to this pitch. . . . It is no 4th Form schoolboy effort now and I cannot get people to understand that it is serious. The more I look into our strategical position the more serious does it seem.

On September 16 (a Saturday) Ironside wrote a paper on the strategic situation in Europe:

It seems to me that we must settle down to some sort of combined strategy in this war. We are now sitting and wondering what Hitler will do next and doing nothing ourselves.

The instrument which he [Hitler] has forged for his victory is the *German Army*. He will use this as his main weapon and all other arms will support it.

To defeat this German Army an Allied Army is required. The French Army is three-quarters the size of the German Army and we must supply the deficiency.

We cannot win the war without an army and it is important to examine the strategical conditions which it is possible to see even though dimly. . . .

General Gamelin has now definitely abandoned what little initiative he had seized and he is preparing for two things:

(i) A local counter-attack [by Germany] against the positions he has taken in between the Maginot and Siegfried Lines. . . . This counter-attack may come at any moment.

(ii) [A German] attack on a large scale through Belgium and Holland. . . .

Gamelin believes that it might be delivered about October 15. Personally I think this is a little early; it will not be possible before the end of October. . . .

The attitude of Italy is unknown. She may come in against us. If she does, then the practical result is to divide the Empire in two: the east and the west. . . .

If we cannot get Turkey in on our side, I think we should commence building a "Maginot Line" somewhere in Syria or Palestine as an essential defence against [an] . . . advance against the centre of the British Empire—the Suez Canal. The defence of Egypt . . . must be set in order at once. . . .

Ironside's idea for the coming battle in France was as follows. The traditional position of the British Army was on the left of the French, where it would probably go into the line. He was against the French proposal that it should, if a move into Belgium took place, take up a position on the Scheldt. "No dumps, no supplies, no line built, nothing; and only 35 miles from the sea", and very long lines of communication as the ports behind the line would be bombed out of existence. There must be no encounter battles in Belgium such as Mons and Le Cateau in the First World War. He thought that the Maginot Line could be extended to the left to Givet or Namur and then to the left flank, but the Belgians refused to discuss this or any other military proposals.

September 16

A better meeting this morning and I have fired off my effort. We are still fiddling away without any thought for the future. I hope the other Services will now put forward their ideas. It is terrifying, the complaisance of all these people.

September 18

I have several major questions for settlement and we don't seem any further than Committees:

(i) The main strategical plan for running the war, now that we have said it may last three years or more.

(ii) The Supply Department which is now making no attempt to get on with the manufacture of equipment.

(iii) The Master-General of the Ordnance's Department at the War Office which does not exist.[1]

(iv) The readjustment of the A.A. guns and [search-] light defence. Especially to cover industry and the British Army in the field rather than the so-called "morale" targets. . . .

We are to go to a Committee to-morrow afternoon to discuss the size of the Army which we are to maintain. The R.A.F. have put in a programme which they say precludes anything but a very small Army. They want all the men for industry in order to get the R.A.F armed. . . . I have tried to get the Committee to consider the matter from a strategic point of view and to decide what kind of an Army they want, then we can get down to details. I have sent in my strategic paper. . . .

We get no further with our strategy. I told the War Cabinet to-day that if the Germans advanced through Belgium and Holland we should bomb the advancing columns *à outrance* from the moment they crossed the frontier. Did the War Cabinet understand that? There must be no waiting for permission to bomb. It must begin at once and be carried out day and night to prevent the Germans setting up their stuff to attack us sitting in the trenches built by the French along the Franco-Belgian frontier. . . .

We have only had just under three weeks of war, but it seems truly terrible that we haven't yet made up our minds what Army we are to make. . . . The old gentlemen sitting here in London have no idea of the seriousness of the position. . . . We all seem to cower behind the French Army and the Maginot Line. How can we get a unified command of operations? How are we to stop

[1] The appointment of Master-General of the Ordnance had been abolished early in 1939.

those stupid conferences of Chiefs of the Staff and War Cabinets, discussing the little details of the nothings that have happened?

Gamelin [who had written Ironside a letter] is evidently convinced that he will be attacked. But I do not think he will be attacked this year.

CHAPTER VII

France

WHEN POLAND FELL, Ironside considered that there were four courses open to Hitler:

1. He might attack in the west.
2. He might go south-east in the Balkans, and thence either advance on Egypt, or against Turkey and Iraq and threaten India.
3. He might go east against Russia to obtain "Lebensraum", food and oil.
4. He might "sit tight" and defy us to do our worst.

Every effort was made to stop him if he went west or south-east. It was hoped to form a Balkan bloc of the small countries under the leadership of Turkey which would bar his advance to the south-east, and conversations were opened with each of the countries concerned. But one and all, owing to the little support Britain could give them, were so terrified of Hitler that they would do nothing to help themselves, or each other, and hoped by making no warlike preparations that Hitler would ignore them and that they might escape.

In the west we tried to induce Belgium and Holland at least to have staff conversations, but they both refused. The Cabinet could see no further than France. Even Mr. Winston Churchill wanted troops brought from India to England. But Ironside realized the importance of the Middle East, and started surreptitiously building up the Army there. He also, in his own words, "sneaked out" the Mounted Division to Palestine.

September 19

I had a great day at the War Council [Cabinet]. They were havering at the number of divisions they would make and I told them that Gamelin was terrified of a German attack. . . . It was electrifying. We got our orders to make 55 divisions. . . . I have told them that I will not agree to the British Army being put in the position of sitting on the Scheldt facing east. We got our 55 divisions settled in a few minutes and now we are able to make a programme and get on with it. Personally, I do not believe that the Germans will attack this winter; but he [Gamelin] is naturally up against it and fears it more, because he will have to bear the brunt of the attack.

September 20

There are certain facts to which we can adhere and develop as the situation becomes more clear. . . .

(i) Italy may come in at a later date. If she does, it will mean that the British Empire is divided in two.

(ii) The country that cannot be overrun by the Germans is Turkey. We must bank on her and prepare an entrance into Europe behind her.

(iii) We must get ourselves based strategically for supply. So much in the east and so much in the west.

The Turkish Military Attaché to see me. . . . Turkey wished to make friends with Russia and to prevent Germany from seizing anything in the Balkans. He was clear that Russia naturally wished both sides to fall down, but thought that Germany was the most immediate danger. Undoubtedly, the Germans were retreating in Poland in front of the Russians and were trying to avoid any fighting with them. I cannot think that the Germans have been able to bring across anything from the east to the west. I told the

Hitler and
Mussolini, with
Goering and General
von Fritsch in
the background

General Sir Cyril
Deverell, C.I.G.S.,
with Ironside and
von Ribbentrop

General von Reichenau

Marshal Badoglio, C.-in-C. Italian Forces

Turk that we wanted to make friends with them, and it was in
our mutual interests to be friends.

September 23

The French are pressing us more and more to send out all we
have to France [They were expecting an attack in three weeks'
time]. They appear to be adopting the usual attitude of all
politicians—forgetting what was agreed in peace. We agreed to
send four divisions and nothing more. Even that is not as well
trained as it should be. . . . We are now sending over to France all
we can scrape up to augment this force—which, by the way, only
has half its strength in France by to-morrow, the 24th. We are
actually sending at once six battalions of Regular infantry, two
machine-gun battalions and one regiment anti-aircraft artillery.

September 28

I have not been at all easy over the French project of our going
forward to the Scheldt and I have written a letter[1] to Gort telling
him to look into the matter. Even if we only go to the Scheldt, it
means coming out of our good prepared positions and going into
others which are quite unprepared.

September 29

We now have a flat refusal from the Belgians as to any staff
conversations. They say that there is no indication of any German
advance through Belgium. That the defences of Belgium are now
such that there is no fear of any of the troops of the guarantor
Powers being caught coming up to support the Belgians. Pious
hope, but we can now do no more.

We have practically been at war a month and nothing has
worked out as we thought it would. This wonderful Air Force of
ours has not been used at all. A few futile droppings of pamphlets
. . . a few bombings of "military objectives", a few reconnaissances
and nothing more. None of the long-distance bombers have been
used at all. The political creed is to remain "one behind the
Germans" in bombing factories and depots. . . . Militarily we

[1] Appendix, page 394.

ought to have gone all out against the German the minute he invaded Poland. . . . We did not. There were many reasons. We were to prepare for a long war. The French Air Force was so bad that it might be annihilated like the Polish Air Force. We were expanding rapidly in our industry. Our Air Force was not ready. Gamelin was mobilizing and concentrating. The British Army was crossing to France and passing up to the front. All was to our advantage to wait. And so we missed the strategical advantage of the Germans being engaged in the east. We thought completely defensively and of ourselves. We had to subordinate our strategy to that of the French and so didn't let our Air Force in. We missed a great opportunity.

September 17, the date on which Gamelin said he would bombard the Siegfried Line, had also passed without any action.

September 30

Daladier [the French Prime Minister] has been talking to the British Ambassador in Paris and telling him that the appearance of even one Regiment of British in the Maginot Line would hearten up the French and stop the [German] propaganda that the British are willing to fight to the last Frenchman. He says also that he wants more British fighters and bombers. . . .

As I wrote to Howard-Vyse [head of the British Military Mission with the French High Command], "We are . . . sending out ten Field Companies [of Engineers] and [mechanical] diggers, to make our line on the Franco-Belgian frontier secure. But it is not much use unless the French continue it either way."

October 2

I have had a review made of the situation after a month's war. It is not a very healthy picture. Largely is it one of equipment. We cannot get ready these extra Regular units without the equipment being taken away from the two Terrier divisions now training for war and being equipped—48th and 51st. It is all a vicious circle. In the middle of it all I am bombarded with demands for equipment for Turks and Dominions, Egyptians and Iraqians. . . .

A letter from Howard-Vyse telling me as follows:

(*a*) Gamelin thinks that the big attack will come against the Franco-Belgian frontier and not against the Saar.

(*b*) As to the nature of the land attack through the Low Countries they are unable to form any definite opinion. They, like me, do not exclude the possibility of its taking the form of a sudden long-distance night advance of mechanized formations.

(*c*) As regards the attack on the Saar, which they look upon as likely to be preliminary or subsidiary, they say that they are not at present able to say that there are sufficient indications of preparations to justify bombing. . . .

(*d*) Should this attack be made on a larger scale, I do not think they are frightened yet—as they intend to get back into the Maginot Line. . . .

Gamelin appears to be a man moved by his political superiors, for he changes his mind very much. His last letter indicated that the German attack was upon him, and now he says that he has not sufficient information of preparations to admit of his bombing. Also he is frightened of bringing on the German bombing.

October 4

There are now very definite signs that the Germans are arriving in greater numbers on the Western Front. Their total strength has gone up to 124 divisions in all. . . . I told the Cabinet this morning that there is no reason to believe that the Germans need leave 30 divisions, the number that Gamelin gave, in Poland. . . .

All the roads in the Duchy [of Luxembourg] leading to France come into the town of Luxembourg and lead from it. . . . If the Germans suddenly rush through the Duchy, are we to be ready to bomb them as they come through?

October 5

I was asked to go over to the Admiralty at 10 a.m. to see Winston. There I found Sir Roger Keyes, who is always in close touch with the Belgian Royal Family. . . . H.M. fully realized [our] difficulties [following] an invasion of Belgium, where he might call for help. But he thought that he must maintain his neutrality and must remain loyal to it. If he did not remain completely neutral he might well induce the Germans to invade his country at once. . . . While we were talking, messages began arriving from Belisha to come and see him at once. When I arrived I was told by the little devils outside that he was peeved at my going to see Winston. I found him quite amenable, but hurt at the method Winston had adopted in not asking him first. He thought that I ought to have refused to go. I explained that it might have been about some urgent military matter and that I could hardly have refused. I had him quietened down in a few minutes. These politicians are as jealous of each other as cats. Silly devils. They take up our time with their jealousies. They may think of the war, but not wholly as we do. . . .

I told Belisha that I should want to go from Paris to see Gort and would be back Sunday night. He held up his hands in horror and said: "What shall I do?" I explained that we were running a war, that it was probably the last time before I should see them, the men, in action. That I had to see Gort. Poor Belisha said he thought he might have to go too, and I told him there was no time for ceremonial visits. . . . Off by 3 p.m. by train from Charing Cross . . . an absolutely calm passage . . . and we bedded down at the Bristol [in Boulogne], the very hotel in which I started the 1914 war.

Ironside's Diary contains few references to these Allied meetings at which, during the early months of the war, decisions of the highest importance were taken, but his Military Assistant, Colonel Macleod, kept a full record of the proceedings, which was circulated through the War Office. The following account, without which many of the subsequent diary entries would be difficult to understand, is based on these notes which Macleod made at the time.

Ironside's visit to France had been prompted by Gamelin's fear of a German attack, and early in the morning of Friday, October 6, 1939, he and his Military Assistant arrived at Grand Quartier Général in the ancient fort of Vincennes.

⊡⊡ The conference was attended by Gamelin, General Georges,
Col. Petibon, the Chief of the Air Staff, Sir Cyril Newall,
and his assistant, Air Commodore (later Air Chief Marshal
Sir John) Slessor. General Gamelin was a small man, aged
about sixty-seven with a round face, fresh complexion, grey
hair, and very neatly dressed. He was frugal and abstemious.
He ate little and was a teetotaller and non-smoker. His staff
told us that he retired to his room punctually at 8 p.m. each
evening, and did not appear next day till 8 a.m., during which
time he was not to be disturbed, so he had a clear twelve
hours out of the twenty-four in which to think, plan and rest.
In times of crisis he appeared calm and composed. He was
always courteous and friendly.

He gave his "appreciation" clearly and well, but when he
came to his "plan" he was not quite so convincing. He probably did not want to trench on General Georges' preserve,
for Georges was the Commander of the crucial front from
Switzerland to the sea. At the same time Gamelin felt his
responsibility for the safety of France and the French Army.
Gamelin appeared to be the quiet intellectual type and a not
very decisive character, while Georges was the practical man
of action and decision.

Gamelin said that the chief lesson to be learnt from the
Polish campaign was the penetrative power of the speedy and
hard-hitting German armoured formations and the close co-
operation of their Air Force.

The French did not intend to carry out an offensive
because France could not stand the losses, but would fight
the Germans only in previously prepared positions. He hoped
that the German attack when it came would smash itself on
the strong Allied defences. When they were sufficiently
weakened, he would start a counter-offensive. The Maginot
Line was not continuous, but consisted of a series of forts
along the Franco-German frontier from Switzerland to the
neighbourhood of Longwy. From thence along the Belgian
frontier to the sea there were merely field defences and a
few block-houses. If the Germans attacked, their armoured

□□ columns might penetrate between two forts or positions. All posts were to hold firm, and infantry and transport following up the columns were to be stopped so that the German armour would receive no support or supplies, would run out of petrol, ammunition and food, would be brought to a standstill and rendered ripe for counter-attack. He would then launch his counter-attack. He was afraid the German Air Force might attack the counter-attack, and he requested that our Air Force should protect it.

He said that the Germans were keeping back 150 kilometres (about 100 miles) from the frontier, but might bring up their formations at the last minute. An attack was certainly coming. They would probably first push the French back to the Maginot Line. The French did not intend to fight in front of the Line, but would fall back on to it. The main attack might come through Switzerland and Italy, to the south of the Line, bringing the Italians in with it, or by Belgium and perhaps Holland to the north, but the Liège defences were strong. *He thought the main attack would be in the north.* It might either be a big sweep through Belgium, or a shorter move through Luxembourg and the Ardennes with their right on Valenciennes, outflanking the Maginot Line and turning south. Belgium was the more likely target because the Ardennes was not a good tank country and there were good defences behind Luxembourg. He stated quite clearly and emphatically that there was only one place where the decisive battle could be fought and that was on the plains of Belgium. It was the only place where the Germans could obtain decisive results. (This was an opinion he always held and never varied.) On other parts of the front it would take a long time.

The French plan was to hold a front line, with local reserves behind it to reinforce and counter-attack. In rear there was the general reserve around Paris, where, it was later explained, communications to any part of the front could best provide against an attack either from Switzerland and Italy or Belgium. The probable course of events would therefore be:

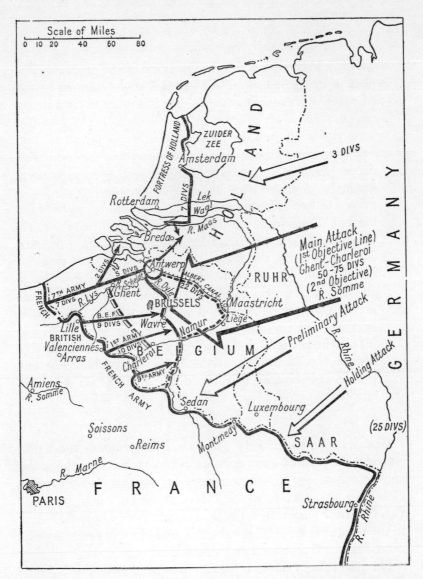

Scale of Miles

0 10 20 40 60 80

3 DIVS

ZUIDER ZEE

Amsterdam

FORTRESS OF HOLLAND

HOLLAND

Lek

Wal

Rotterdam

7 DIVS

R. Maas

Breda

RUHR

Main Attack
(1st Objective Line)
Ghent - Charleroi
50 - 75 DIVS
(2nd Objective)
R. Somme

Antwerp

2 DIVS

5 DIVS

ALBERT CANAL

7TH ARMY

FRENCH

7 DIVS

R. Scheldt

R. Dyle

22 DIVS

Maastricht

R. Lys

Ghent

GERMANY

R. Rhine

BRUSSELS

Liège

B.E.F.

9 DIVS

Wavre

Namur

Lille

BRITISH

1ST ARMY

Valenciennes

10 DIVS

Preliminary Attack

Arras

Charleroi

BELGIUM

Holding Attack

FRENCH ARMY

9TH ARMY

Amiens

R. Somme

Sedan

Luxembourg

Soissons

(25 DIVS)

Reims

Montmedy

SAAR

R. Marne

FRANCE

PARIS

Strasbourg

R. Rhine

Gamelin's Forecast.

119

1. A pinning attack on the Maginot Line, exploiting the Saar.
2. A preliminary attack by Luxembourg.
3. The main attack by Holland and Belgium.

This would be with tanks. An air attack would probably take place at the same time. The Germans might close up to the Maginot Line in about a week's time (October 13) and attack the Line itself in about a month (November 6). The date of a main attack through the Low Countries was uncertain, but by November 10 the principal threat would have passed. The danger was that an attack by fifty or seventy-five divisions might be mounted deep inside Germany and beyond the range of ground reconnaissance, and suddenly brought through. Ironside, unlike Gamelin, maintained that the main thrust would come through Luxembourg and the Ardennes and thence along the Franco-Belgian frontier, and that the Germans would use the Meuse to protect their right flank and hold off the Belgians. Could we not move into Belgium and hit them from the north while the reserve in Paris struck at them from the south?

Gamelin pressed us to send many more aircraft to France, because, if we were defeated there, the war would be lost, but Ironside emphasized that the defence of Britain was also essential.

October 6

Gamelin spoke with very great clarity, and again and again asked for the British fighter support. Newall was, I thought, weak and unconvincing. . . . It was decided eventually to send two Hurricane squadrons from the B.E.F. to the French and to have two Gladiator squadrons ready at short notice in England to send to the B.E.F. He would study the question of more flexibility and more bases in France for British squadrons.

He [Gamelin] reiterated again that he feared the "*attaque d'usure*" [i.e. a "wearing-down" attack] against his aviation by the German aviation and that he did not care much for anything that he could do after November 10.

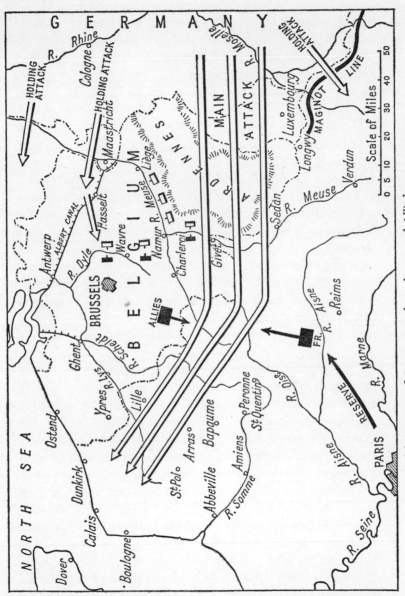

Ironside's Forecast of German attacks and proposed Allied counter-moves.

121

Newall insisted that I should say to Vuillemin, the head of the French Aviation, that we had had a proper scheme of Air Defence in England, whereas the French had not. This brought the somewhat tart rejoinder from Gamelin that they had concentrated on their Army. I nearly added that the British Air had been developed at the expense of the British Army. . . . I came away with the feeling that Newall could have done more if he had been cleverer.

If two French Armies and the B.E.F. could be safely moved into Belgium, both Ironside and Gamelin would be satisfied. If Ironside was right, and the Germans advanced by Luxembourg and the Ardennes, they could be encircled from north and south. If, on the other hand, as Gamelin expected, they attacked through Belgium, then the Allies could support the Belgians, add the Belgian Army to their total, occupy a shorter line, and be able to withdraw a large force into reserve for an eventual counter-offensive. If forced back, they could withdraw to the frontier defences. The original German plan followed the lines forecast by Gamelin, but, after this plan had been captured in January 1940, as will be described later, Hitler switched to the plan foretold by Ironside.

On Saturday, October 7, Ironside toured the front held by the British. The line taken over along the frontier near Lille consisted of a few block-houses every thousand yards along the front, and an anti-tank ditch which had been built by the French. The block-houses had to be altered to accommodate the British anti-tank guns, and extra works had to be constructed to give the position depth. The frontages were wide.

The area was well known to many officers from the First World War, and one claimed that in a moment of aberration he found himself writing to his old mother who had been dead some years.

General Sir John Dill, who was, however, sick at the time, commanded the First Corps, which consisted of the 1st Division under General Alexander and the 2nd Division under General Loyd. The country it occupied was low-lying with numerous farms, buildings, trees, small copses and hedges, all intersected by ditches and streams. The defences were well hidden.

The Second Corps under General Alan Brooke was on higher and more open ground, and its 3rd Division under General Montgomery had built a regular trench system, while the 4th Division was in Army reserve.

October 7

Gort took me up and showed me the line. A very curious position. Here we were in a foreign country, going in to occupy a line facing a neutral country, in absolute peace. Thousands of people live on one side of the frontier or the other, and cross to their work every day in the fields or the factories. Everything that we do or build must be reported to the Germans within a few hours. There can be no concealment. Everything will be pinpointed at once. . . . All the inhabitants are living right up to the frontier and the problem is to billet the men in houses and get them to their work. The French have done well. Most of the concrete has been put in during 1937 and it is curious to see the date in gold letters over the great concrete forts. The line follows the frontier fairly accurately and consists of a tank obstacle, which has been dug out by the big machines, built absolutely straight[1]. It is revetted with brushwood in places where it is very watery. The whole country in our sector round Lille is waterlogged in the winter. . . . Everywhere the trench turns to follow the contour or the frontier there is a concrete block-house. They are said to be proof even against a direct hit by a very big howitzer. . . . They are built to hold a couple of machine-guns and one or two anti-tank guns. They fire direct down the tank obstacle to the flank and are closed to the front where they are ramped up with earth. They have a good prism periscope sticking out of the top which gives an all-round view. The whole place is wired strongly with circles and circles of wire. . . . They are all built with water tanks and sleeping accom-

[1] The line was apparently drawn with no regard to the best tactical position. It seemed that the French did not mean to give up an inch of their country.

modation. It gave one a curious idea of a front line, just long lines of obstacle and barbed wire and great iron rails sticking up in places. Then one began to realize that in this very flat country artillery observation for accurate shooting upon these fortresses was next to impossible. Also, if the bombardment becomes very heavy the ground will become impossible for machines to move over. . . .

Gort and I discussed it and came to the conclusion that the key to the whole question was "ne pas bouger". The troops must be in position, not in a complete trench line. The fronts we have are too big for that. But in islands of defence, each defended by wire in circles. Each covering the country in between the front block-houses with fire. If the position is in sufficient depth there is no fear of the attacking infantry ever getting through. The tanks may get through and they may, as they did in Poland, push on till they can go no further, but the infantry cannot.

The only continuous things are the anti-tank obstacles. The rest are inconspicuous posts of machine-guns, anti-tank rifles, and guns. . . . Many of our gun positions and machine gun posts will have to be in the houses evacuated by the people. . . . Ammunition and stores are pouring up, but the Base is five hundred miles away and things go desperately slowly. One wants so much of everything. I think that people do not realize what it was to move an Army down to home ports, overseas as a tactical operation, and then land it and send it 500 miles inland. All this has been done without a casualty. A wonderful show.

October 11 [London]

The Germans seem to have some 68 divisions on the Western Front, some 49 on the Eastern Front and perhaps 9 or so in Central Germany. They show no more signs of an advance.

October 12

News this morning looks as if the Germans were really about to mount an attack through Luxembourg, and also along most of the front of the Maginot Line. Bridges of every sort are being put in over the Rhine. Reports are being circulated of a new gas in large quantities and the French are in a thoroughly nervous state. I wonder. I am like Gamelin: "Je me demande . . ."

I have been examining the situation and I still come to the general conclusion that the main German attack will come through Luxembourg and Belgium south of the Meuse. Holding attacks along the Liège–Namur line to block anybody coming south. . . .

I tried to show Belisha what I thought might happen. I left him after a bit at 7 p.m., absolutely exhausted and unable to take in anything I had said. He has been worked up to make his speech and is now non-compos. What can one do with a man like this? I shall just have to carry on in case of a war without him. He simply has no idea what the Army is doing, and one cannot get him to understand the simplest operation of war.

October 14

The Germans are building more bridges across the Saar—some nine in all—and the centre of the German activity has shifted to between Saarbrücken and the Luxembourg frontier. The concentration opposite the Luxembourg border . . . is a very heavy one. . . . The moment is arriving quickly and the Germans have very little time left of good weather.

October 15

At 10 p.m. in came a message from Swayne, who is with Georges, to say that an attack on France is expected to-morrow.[1]

October 16

One of the worst days we have had. I had two hours in the morning with the War Cabinet and the Chiefs of Staff. And then we had four and a half hours in the afternoon with the Army Council and the Air Conference. And then I had two hours with the Secretary of State from 11 till 1, having had from 9 till 11 with my own people. That is ten hours of talking and arguing and thinking.

[1] Nothing happened.

CHAPTER VIII

The Naked Army

IRONSIDE was, in his own words, "flabbergasted" when he first came to the War Office at the appalling deficiencies in the equipment of the Army, and at the very long time it would take to make them up. Not until April 1939 had the Government contemplated sending an Army to France, and even the Cabinet appeared to believe that it could be entirely equipped in a few months. We had then only engaged ourselves to send to France a total of four infantry divisions and two armoured divisions. On the outbreak of war only two infantry divisions had been complete, and only one armoured division was partially complete. The medium and heavy artillery all dated from the First World War, and were out-ranged by the new German guns.

Early in 1939 the post of Master-General of the Ordnance, who was a serving General and a member of the Army Council, had been abolished, but a Ministry of Supply, to which the Director-General of Munition Production and his staff were transferred, was not formed until a few months before the outbreak of hostilities. The whole of "Supply" was undertaken by this Ministry, and demands had to be put in to them. The one officer in the War Office left to do this was Colonel D. R. D. Fisher. The Ministry, not the Army, was responsible for the design of the weapons which the troops would use, and the soldiers had consequently little voice in

□□ the new arms with which they were expected to fight the
coming battle. The rules of procedure were so strict that the
Chief of the Imperial General Staff was not allowed to cor-
respond personally with the Minister of Supply, and when
Ironside complained, Mr. Hore–Belisha replied that it was like
ordering a motor-car: one merely asked for the equipment
for so many divisions and the Ministry of Supply sent it over
—in complete divisions. Ironside pointed out that so far from
being like ordering a motor-car it was like ordering all the
different pieces of the car and putting them together oneself.
It was the General Staff which must decide on the type, design
and number of weapons needed according to the war to be
fought, the tactics, and the topography of the theatre of war,
and he always maintained that the Ministry of Supply was
only suitable for producing standard equipment, like clothing
and boots, and not for designing new weapons, such as tanks.

"The Ministry of Supply", he noted, "has taken the bit
between its teeth and formed a Committee to decide on
making tanks to cross the Siegfried Line. But they are doing
this without consulting the General Staff. What are more
urgently needed are guns to beat off the impending German
attack in the west. There is not enough material and labour
to make both." Although we had the men for our 32
divisions, only two of the divisions were equipped with
modern weapons. The Ministry of Supply reckoned that at
the end of one year they could only provide equipment for
20 divisions, and it would take two years to equip 32, and
three years to equip 55.

The Ministry of Supply sent "forecasts" every month, bu
these were rarely fulfilled and some items fell far short. It was
thus exceedingly difficult to tell when a division would be
ready for active service. The manufacture of anti-aircraft
guns was far behind the forecasts, and led to great anxieties
over the defence of London and of our Army in France. Raw
materials were scarce because the Government had not laid
in enough stocks before the war, and all three Services were
competing for a limited quantity. A Priorities Committee

□□ was established, but the Army was seldom put first. Ironside sent agents throughout the country to report on the output of factories. They said that few were working all out, many only for eight hours out of the twenty-four, practically none worked at night, and there appeared to be no sense of urgency. The Ministry of Supply put out contracts for such large amounts at a time that small factories could not accept them, and in consequence many were idle.

Ironside tried all means to obtain arms from other countries. We were getting an infantry light anti-tank gun from the French, but most of these went to Turkey in the hope of persuading her to join the Allies. Italy had not yet entered the war, and it was thought that she would have much material lying idle in Abyssinia. Our secret requests to Italian officials were at first favourably received, but as soon as Mussolini got wind of them, he promptly stopped the negotiations. The one hopeful source was the United States. The American military attaché, General R. E. Lee, came several times to the War Office and said that President Roosevelt wanted to help, but would have first to educate the American public and he could only do this gradually. Ironside gave instructions to treat General Lee as if he were an ally, but Lease-Lend still lay in the future. Although we were at war, a peace mentality seemed to pervade all departments, including the Government itself. There were interminable delays in obtaining weapons, equipment and stores. The equipping of the Army fell badly behind programme. The scanty defences of London were further weakened since the Navy, which had said that it needed no A.A. defences because it could defend itself with its own A.A. ships, found that these were inadequate, and demanded A.A. guns and detachments to protect their bases at Scapa Flow and Rosyth.

Meanwhile it had been decided to adopt and order a Swedish A.A. gun, the Bofors, which, with its predictor and automatic laying, was reputed to be a "killer" of low-flying aircraft. One of these weapons was exhibited in the courtyard of the War Office, but on the outbreak of war, Sweden,

General Sir Edmund Ironside with the Secretary of State for War, Mr. Hore-Belisha

General Ironside with General Lord Gort

□□ frightened of Hitler, refused to supply us, and the British had
to make the guns themselves.

Taken by and large, our divisions in the field were better
equipped for war than the French divisions, particularly in
transport, which made us more mobile; but as the French
conception was purely defensive and a war of movement was
foreign to their current doctrine, they did not consider that
transport was so important.

As the Government had not foreseen the war, they had laid
in no large stocks of steel. There was a serious shortage, and a
system of priorities whereby the Navy came first and the
Army last.

The War Office organization was no doubt well adapted to
peace-time conditions where time was of little account and
the spending of every penny was carefully scrutinized in the
interests of national economy by a body of Civil Servants
under the Treasury. In war, speed in production is essential.
In April 1939, as soon as we had bound ourselves to fight on
the Continent, the General Staff urgently demanded 600,000
rounds of medium artillery ammunition. The Treasury representatives in the War Office raised doubts and queries and
passed the file backwards and forwards among themselves
and the military departments. It was "lost" beneath an influx
of new files at the bottom of an official's tray, and only discovered and rescued after three weeks by a Staff officer who
was anxiously trying to trace it. Not until a fortnight after
the war had started and nearly five months after the first
"urgent demand" had been made was Treasury sanction
given for this essential ammunition to be manufactured.

Ironside decided to organize a special department for
formulating demands for equipment, and proposed to do so
chiefly by withdrawing officers from other departments and
adding four more. This proposal was submitted to the
Treasury officials and there the matter rested for a considerable time. Ironside several times asked them to hurry, only
to be told that it was still under consideration as it had not

□□ been decided how many officers should be employed. Meanwhile the extra officers were receiving no pay. The C.I.G.S. asked that the new organization should be approved in principle if not in detail, but the Treasury representative in the War Office replied that no proposal could be sanctioned until the last final detail had been approved.

There were no battle tanks for our Armoured Division when the war started, and only two battalions of Army tanks for the infantry divisions. When the C.I.G.S. asked the Ministry of Supply what was being done to provide the Army with tanks, he was told that there were two committees, each working on a different design. One was the Stern Committee, of which Sir Albert Stern was the chairman, the other was under Sir Ernest Swinton, and each committee wanted the C.I.G.S. to order its particular model. He asked them to meet him and his own tank expert at the War Office. It then appeared that both committees were designing tanks without due regard for their use in the field and without settling the question of their armament or tactics. The Stern Committee was proposing to make a tank very like that produced by Sir Albert Stern in the First World War, slightly larger and more powerful, but with no turret with all-round traverse for its guns, and an out-of-date engine. The other committee, in view of the urgency of the hour, advocated a French tank which was already obsolete, under-armoured and under-gunned. Not the least surprising discovery was that there would be a delay of five months from the order being given for a tank and the signature of the contract to build it.

Ironside said he wanted two types of modern tank, a battle tank of about sixty tons and a cruiser tank of about thirty tons, and suggested that the two committees should be amalgamated and be joined by tank experts from the War Office. The Ministry agreed, but it was only in October 1939 that designs for a British battle tank were begun, and it was not until three years later, at the Battle of Alamein, that the new tanks went into action with our troops.

Nor was it easy to obtain a powerful enough engine for motor transport which had often to move across country and off main roads. The horsepower tax had compelled the motor-manufacturers to produce low-powered engines, and their factories were not equipped for a sudden change to more powerful types. Much of the Army's transport was consequently under-engined. Other problems were food, and military raw materials. Ironside sent his own representative, Sir Robert Waley-Cohen, to the Middle East to see if they could be obtained and manufactured on the spot. He received a favourable report on many items, but encountered two major difficulties. For a long time he received no answer from the Ministry of Supply, who hinted that the objection to building factories in the Middle East was that they might compete with our own when the war was over. Ironside pointed out that the first necessity was to win the war and that such problems could be dealt with afterwards. By making the Middle East self-supporting much shipping would be saved. Australian wool and Egyptian cotton were being sent home to be made into uniforms for our troops in the Middle East. The other difficulty was the Colonial Office, who maintained that manufacturing weapons and explosives in Palestine might put dangerous power into the wrong hands and lead to endless trouble after the war. Influential Jewish leaders, among them Dr. Weizmann, approached the C.I.G.S. with a request that a Jewish Army might be formed or, if not an Army, composite units from the Jewish population in Palestine. This appeared reasonable, and conformed with Ironside's idea of manning a Maginot Line in Palestine with a Jewish force, but the Colonial Office once more objected that a Jewish Army, trained, disciplined and led by Jewish officers would be yet another source of trouble when the war was over.

October 17

We had the most dreadful scene at the Army Council. We spent over an hour discussing some very small things in the Press world, and there were half a dozen other silly things to be done before my main question, the fighting state of the Army, came up. Eventually I got my subject taken up and stated the position of the tanks. This is quite calamitous. As Belisha felt he was responsible for this, he started a tirade about the organization being wrong. Grigg, the Permanent Under Secretary, jumped in, and for nearly an hour we had a fight between Belisha and Grigg. No one else spoke.

October 18

We had another meeting of the Army Council last night and settled the final business of the Director of Staff Duties Department. I got what I wanted in the end, but Belisha spent the whole of his time scoring off Grigg. There were some ten items on the agenda. All of them minor except the organization, and Belisha so dragged things on that we never got to any of the other 9. . . .

Our strategic project for erecting factories in Palestine has been held up. The Ministry of Supply is putting in its toes and has appealed to the Colonial Office and the old question of Jew and Arab has come in again. Meanwhile nothing is done. . . . I told the Cabinet this morning . . . that the Germans were driving back the French from the German territory occupied by them in front of the Siegfried Line. . . . The Germans are preparing a big pincer attack against France through Belgium and Holland on the right and Switzerland on the left. I personally thought it was too late in the winter to make such a big attack.

October 21

I had a long talk with [Admiral] Sir Roger Keyes [Britain's private envoy to the Belgian Court]. He has just come back from seeing the King of the Belgians. He told him that we were having difficulty in getting definite news of the state of the Belgian defences. That the Belgians must play up if they wished to get the best out of us. It was no good saying that we must trust the Belgians to hold up the Germans for a certain length of time. . . . We were not going to venture out of our good defences to risk an encounter battle in the low lands of Belgium. Our Military

Attaché must be allowed to see what was going on. I should need a personal guarantee from the Military Attaché before I would allow the Army to go forward.

Then Blake, the Military Attaché, arrived. He told me that the Belgians had practically completed a line from Antwerp *via* Malines, Louvain, Wavre, Hal, Ninove to Antwerp again. He assured me that the Belgians were working all out on the line from Wavre to Namur, a distance of some thirty miles. They were erecting at some 300 metres a day a steel anti-tank obstacle. I offered to sell or lend some mechanical diggers to complete this line.

Keyes told us that the King wanted the matter kept absolutely in military hands and I gave my personal guarantee that it would be so kept. That the French had never ceased to press them and that he was terrified of being accused of violating his neutrality and being invaded by the Germans. . . . Finally, the King said that he didn't think that the Germans would try to carry out a big advance this winter.

October 23

I have a long letter from General Gamelin dated October 20. He says that the Germans can deploy some 160 divisions of which, say, 130 can be used on the Western Front. [They] can do this by the spring of 1940. [Gamelin] has already called upon the Army of the Alps and the Army of Africa to strengthen his forces [opposite Germany]. Of course the withdrawal depends upon the attitude of Italy. He can make some 10 new divisions. He can do no more. . . . He definitely asks us for two things:

(i) The speeding up of the initial programme.
(ii) The formation of additional units.

I cannot get Belisha to consider this even. . . .

I went into the tank situation. We found that we had 50 "I" tanks,[1] that is the tanks that we use to break the line. For 12 to 15 divisions we need 450 tanks in first line and have only 100 in all in sight by June. One can hardly believe that all we can do

[1] "Infantry" tanks.

133

between now and June—eight months—is 50 tanks. Where is all our boasted power of manufacture?

We had the most ridiculous Army Council taking two hours to discuss the most trivial matters. My report on the strategical aspect was never even reached. Belisha knows nothing and cares nothing of what is happening strategically. The wretched Army Council never has a chance to understand the war it is running.

October 24

We had a very painful Cabinet meeting in the morning. Belisha took it upon himself to read Gamelin's letter to the Cabinet. I had told him that it was very secret and he took no notice. Belisha was at once taken up by Winston over not putting enough men into France. He gave a long harangue about our duty to our gallant allies and even said that we ought not to hold back half-equipped units. This disconcerted our Belisha as he had not expected this. He was catechized over not having brought back from India the Regular troops in India as Kitchener had done. He [Winston] would listen to nothing as to the needs of India, the lack of equipment, and as to what we were doing. In the end, as usual with anything to do with the Army, the question was referred once more to the Land Forces Committee, where we have to justify our procedure. Neither the Air Force nor the Admiralty is ever asked to show what it is doing. Always, every civilian thinks he can run or even command an army. It takes up hours of our time and is most annoying. The P.M. was a very good Chairman again and backed us up in our behaviour. One could see that Belisha is not in very good favour. He insists upon starting these things himself and is then caught out by people who question him on details. . . . There are reports of deluges of rain in France and Flanders. I think that it would be folly to think that the Germans will try an advance.

I cannot get people down to realities here. We are going to produce some 12 to 15 divisions in the spring and no more, and we must prepare for this. What is the use looking for astronomical numbers like 55 divisions? It is all very well ordering the equipment for them, it is a matter of getting it. We have to withstand

an attack in the spring with what we have got and we must be
ready for it. . . . You can only make war with actual trained
divisions.

Another dreadful Army Council meeting this evening. . . . I
managed to get two important things done, but the rest of the
time we wrangled about Press matters that did not matter in the
least.

October 29

Dr. Weizmann, the Zionist, in to see me. He looked a big
edition of Lenin. Yellow complexion, slanting eyes and goatee
beard. He put to me three things:

1. The formation of Jewish units.
2. The making of trinitrotoluol.
3. The making of aeroplane petrol.

Weizmann is going out to Switzerland again to get in touch
with his scientist friends, then he goes to the U.S.A. He told me
that the war would finish in the Middle East. I told him that I
agreed with him.

October 31

Thinking things over, I tried to make myself an impression of
Weizmann. I never once saw any expression in his eyes, which
watched me carefully all the time. Never once did they answer to
anything that I said or stressed in my own eyes. I have never met
anybody before who would not answer to my expression. He
gave me the impression that he was watching me and sizing me
up as to what I might do to help him in his Zionism. For this was
his main thought. He told me that he believed that the Jews would
get back to Palestine and that they would get there under the
aegis of the British. "That will be good for the British Empire
and for the Jews." One had the impression that he merely regarded the British Empire as something likely to further his ends.
That he had no interest in keeping the British Empire going except
that. I expect that he treats everything and everybody in the same
way. He gave one an eerie sensation. . . . I had strongly a feeling

of half resentment that I was being "used" for somebody else's benefit. I have never felt that in my life before.

November 13

The position of the Supply Board is a difficult one. I have no control over it and have no means of ordering it to do anything. I can only keep in touch with it through my General Staff. I think myself that we ought to have a man on the Army Council who is responsible for all this Supply. This was the Master-General of the Ordnance. Now he has gone. Belisha began blackguarding the General Staff for not knowing that these deficiencies existed and I told him that they could not find them out till told by the new civilian, who is in touch with the Supply Board.

November 14

We had an important meeting to decide what we could put into France. The Ministry of Supply was horrified at the demands we made and could not hold out any possibility of getting what we wanted. . . .

I once more laid down my main ideas:

  (i) We should work to a basis of 20 divisions in France and 12 divisions in the Middle-East.
 (ii) We should work to 10 divisions being ready in France by next March, and 15 divisions in the first year—that is by September 1940.
(iii) Of the 15 divisions, one would be a Canadian division.
 (iv) In the Middle East we should have: 1 Cavalry division, 1 Indian division, 1 Australian division, 1 New Zealand division, 1 Indian division ear-marked in India. We have at the moment in the Middle East the equivalent of 3 divisions. We may expect to send out another 4 divisions.
  (v) It was important to see that the 15 divisions were up to full strength in equipment, buying such as could not be made from Italy. The U.S.A. cannot produce what we require as their war industry does not exist.
 (vi) Four "Swinger" [i.e. reserve] divisions in England.

We now have to get this programme into the Army Council and so into the War Cabinet. . . . I cannot see that we can produce more than 36 divisions in two years. We should consider working up to 55 divisions in the third year. . . .

I had in Weizmann. . . . I told him that we had a lot of trouble with the Colonial Office over the Jew question, but that they were now trying to form both Arab and Jew units and did not intend to mix them up. I asked him to have patience. . . . He was interesting in saying that he had two thousand years of patience and that it was written in the books that the Jews would get to Palestine. Of that he was quite sure. He didn't want small things to get in his way in his preaching in America, where he was going to see his people. The Jews cannot remain as dust. They must have a home after all this accumulation of tribulation.

I must say that I agreed with him completely. We are probably missing a chance to get the Jews on our side. . . . The complication of the war has upset things so much that it is difficult for us to do anything at the moment except mark time. The more tribulation we have the more will we be forced to arm the Jews.

Weizmann told me that Hitler was confused and did not know what to do. He did not want war and was afraid of it in his soul. But he agreed that the Nazi régime was done unless they could do something spectacular.

November 17

We had our Army Council and I put in my paper saying what I thought we ought to aim at as a practical proposition in the way of troops for France. There is no good concealing from oneself that it is now almost entirely a matter of equipment, not of men. We cannot send men to France unequipped. It is a purely feminine argument that the men would not be put in the front line if they were in France. They would have to be put in in a crisis. The French know this very well indeed. . . .

I do not believe that he [Mr. Leslie Burgin, Minister of Supply] is putting the energy into the Ministry of Supply which Lloyd George put in, and I do not know how I can make him do so. . . . It is only by putting in this energy that we can get the men over.

I am sure that there will be a devil of a row in the Cabinet over it all, but the real fact is that we did not decide to have any Army at all upon a Western scale until April. To my mind we have done very well to have the programme I have now suggested. All the Cabinet except Winston bear the responsibility for the decision they refused to take. Now these same men are shouting for us to make an effort. But the time for recrimination has gone by and we have to see what we can improvise.

CHAPTER IX

The Royal Air Force

IN THE FIRST WORLD WAR co-operation between the Air and the Army became close, intimate and effective. The Royal Flying Corps provided near and distant reconnaissances with photographs. They reported targets for the artillery and ranged guns on to them. They carried out strategic and tactical bombing, protected our own troops against German planes, attacked enemy infantry, machine-guns and sometimes even batteries, and indeed formed an integral part of the Army. Between the two World Wars the Air Force had become a separate service. It struck out a line of its own, and the close co-operation ceased. The Army was deprived of its eyes and of some of its hitting power. Ironside foresaw the danger and in the years before the war had strongly advocated an Army Air Arm, or, since efficient co-operation would take time and training, the permanent allocation of squadrons to the military forces. The Navy had its own Air Service. Why not the Army? But his contentions had been deprecated by those in authority. They had not wished to upset what they called "the present happy relations".

The opening stages of the Second World War, with German dive-bombers preparing the way for armoured columns, now proved Ironside right. He tried to build up an air service manned by the Army. He found that it would be possible to make a suitable machine, simple and easy to fly, in two years.

But the R.A.F. objected, and were upheld by the Government. The machine which the R.A.F. proposed would take three years to build. Thus, for a considerable time, the Army was in effect fighting with one hand tied behind its back.

September 19

Sam Hoare has a secretary called Moore-Brabazon who had a lot to do with the air. He is now at a plan to have hundreds of little aeroplanes under the Army, which would work with them. The Air Ministry is now working on a programme of big bombers costing £26,000 apiece and God knows how many man-hours to build. They are not able to work with the Army and are used for this long-distance bombing against industry. The R.A.F. think that they will win by themselves. I try to tell them that the Germans will use their army with their bombers to destroy the French Army, and if that goes, the whole edifice of our defence goes too.

September 26

Disgusted with the way in which the R.A.F. treat the co-operation of the Air Force with the Army, we have put in a paper asking for a special Air Arm for use with the Army. We are looking for a small machine in large numbers, produced by mass production and manned by Army personnel. When one thinks that no training of any sort has ever been carried out with the R.A.F. for either offensive or defensive bombing, I think we are quite justified in what we are asking for.

October 9

Lunch at Hore-Belisha's [at which the Secretary of State for Air, Kingsley Wood, and the Chief of the Air Staff, Air Chief Marshal Sir Cyril Newall, were present], where we discussed the question of a machine for training with the Army in a tactical fight. Quite a friendly chat between the two Secretaries of State and the C.A.S. [Chief of Air Staff] and myself. I told them:

(i) That we could not advance without our own Air Support. That if we did not have it by the time we were expected to advance we should have enormous casualties.

(ii) That we must have a proper machine. That the machine must be delivered in time to get the proper training.

(iii) That it was immaterial what the machine might be called upon to do elsewhere, so long as when the Army went, it had its proper Air close support.

(iv) That it must be clearly understood that the Army was to have the machines it needed or it couldn't attack.

(v) That I believed the struggle [i.e. the war] might be finished on the ground.

We have put in a paper, which has been handed to the Air Ministry and, though I should have liked to have put the position more strongly, I think it will serve to bring our needs forward.

A meeting was held at the Admiralty, with Mr. Churchill in the chair, to discuss a paper submitted by the Air Ministry. This paper laid down the principles to be followed in case of German air attacks. Although attacks on our shipping, ports and industry were dealt with, no mention was made of attacks against the French and British Armies.

October 13

When I reiterated what I have said so often, that the Germans intended to use the German Army to defeat us and that that Army had been trained to operate with a very large Air Force and would never operate without it, the Air once more did not agree. . . . Kingsley Wood [the Minister for Air] came across [to me afterwards] and said that he now realized that the Army wanted bombers trained to act with it and that we must cease building only for the R.A.F. and do something for the Army.

I wrote out for the Secretary of State to send to the Cabinet:

As regards direct support aircraft, I cannot conceal from my colleagues that I find the position most disquieting. A modern Army cannot deal with its two main tasks (attack and defence) without bombing machines and fighters trained to work in close co-operation with the Army, and directed by the Commander of the Army in the field.

Defence. In defence the duties of these machines will be to deal with all attackers in movement, so that they are broken up in their formations from the inception of their attack and are kept under continuous fire until they come to grips with the Army. They will also be required to carry out intensive attack against the enemy commands and communications with the object of weakening the control of the battle.

Attack. In attack they are required to co-operate with the advancing columns, isolate the enemy in his defensive positions, prevent his reinforcing his forward troops or counter-attacking our troops when they have gained their objectives.

The work which has been carried out in close co-operation with the Army up to date has been entirely exploratory. No comprehensive training has been carried out whereby the tactics for the employment of this arm with the Army have been evolved. The Army is, therefore, short of one essential arm which it needs to fit it to operate against a modern enemy.

I must urgently plead that this question should be thoroughly investigated at once. The situation admits of no delay.

The Air Ministry put forward the plea that no demand has ever been put forward for such an Air Arm. I think that there is truth in this. Each successive C.I.G.S. has funked tackling the Air Ministry. Probably he was downed by the Cabinet and many preferred peace to a struggle which would take years to finish. I have told them that we are now at war and there can be no delay. We cannot advance without this close support arm and must have it under our command.

October 14

We had a meeting all the morning and discussed the question of the bombing of the Ruhr. We regarded the Ruhr as a crippling blow if we could bomb it successfully. It is certainly well defended. The Air staff say that it might mean the loss of half our bombing strength. I wonder myself if we can do it successfully. We came to the conclusion that we should not "take the gloves off" first.

That we ought to regard the following as decisive blows and at once apply for Cabinet decisions:

(i) An invasion of Belgium.
(ii) A decisive attack against our combined Army in France, which would involve a loss of women and children as a consequence.
(iii) A decisive attack against our industry or commerce.

There was a good deal of argument as to the bombing of Belgium and Belgian towns if the Germans came through, and we thought it was better to bomb German civilians than Belgian civilians.

I noticed how relieved the Cabinet was at not being asked to make a decision. I am sure it will be a dreadful moment when they have to make a decision.

October 23

At 5 p.m. we had another meeting of the Land Forces Committee about the question of a Close-Support Arm for the Army. It ended not very much further on. The Committee was inclined to be with us. I told them that we might be called upon to attack in June 1940. That we should then have 12 to 15 divisions in the field and for that we should require some 250 machines in the air. That we might be asked to carry out an attack for four days, and that we might be asked to attack twice or three times in the summer. We now have to arrange with Moore-Brabazon what we want and are then to do two things: (i) see if we can get something like our requirements from the R.A.F. before June; (ii) see if we can get a machine built on mass production lines for future use.

I had to reiterate again and again that we had to do the training and have command of the force. I told the Committee that we had always had our tactics dictated to us by the R.A.F. and had been refused all facility for training. The fact of the matter was that it had only lately been decided to have a Continental Army, but that did not prevent the fact being recognized that we had to have it properly armed.

October 29

There have been letters from the Air Ministry refuting any putting of the R.A.F. under command of the Army. Belisha has the letters and is very excited about it all. He wishes to bring it up to the Cabinet at once.

The question of Air Action against the Ruhr and the Germans advancing through Belgium has become acute. I have written a paper showing how unsatisfactory it all is. . . . The Air Ministry are now hypnotized by action against morale and will hear of nothing else. Their big bombers have been built for this purpose and will be wasted if used for the smaller targets. They are afraid to use them against an advancing German Army for fear of all the A.A. defence they may meet. . . .

A real row has now developed over the Army and its Air Force. We have had various committees upon the subject and nothing has been done. Belisha is now going to bring it up to the Cabinet for decision. The Air Ministry say that they cannot allot any machines to the Army because they are short themselves. They do not argue the principle, but state the impossibility of supplying the machines. We are at a complete and absolute deadlock about it. It seems ridiculous that we should be fighting these quarrels internally just before we enter the worst battle of our history.

November 5

Our military machine of command is truly bad. In theory it is the War Cabinet which directs the strategy. Men like Chamberlain, Sam Hoare and Halifax, with Belisha and Kingsley Wood, have no military conception of any sort. They don't even have a general knowledge of how to fight a campaign. . . . Our Army is under French command and must conform to the French general idea. But the Air Force is not, and the Cabinet dearly love directing its operations, discussing its most minute operations. If a reconnaissance over Germany discloses nothing they at once think that the Germans will do nothing for weeks. They look upon the Chiefs of Staff Committee as a clog upon their energies. They are bitterly jealous of their constitutional power to run the strategy of the war, though their knowledge of war is nothing, and their ignorance of the administrative questions involved is still less, if that were possible.

Chatfield has been constituted as the Chairman of a fresh committee[1] consisting of the three Service Ministers—plus or minus the Chiefs of Staff should they so arrange. It makes them into a kind of civilian strategical committee ready to force some plan upon the Cabinet. . . . It is only in times of stress that civilian strategists are dangerous. They are impatient of delays due to administrative difficulties and they grasp at any mad idea in the hopes that they have discovered a golden road to victory. They may not be "timid" or "weak", but they are all acutely aware of the remarks of the Press, which often holds the power to dismiss them from office. Perhaps the Prime Minister is the only one of the Cabinet in office at the moment who is not afflicted in this way. He seems to be the strongest character of them all.

November 6

An interesting Cabinet meeting. Winston had come back from France. . . . His enthusiasm brings him forward without thinking of many difficulties. As a token we are to put divisions to train in France. We are to land the Canadians there instead of in England. Matters of schools of instruction in England and not in France are not thought of. Also the effect of allowing Canadians to visit England and their relations in England was passed over without a word.

We took the invasion of Holland and the Cabinet got thoroughly frightened. I told them that we had no agreed plan in case the Germans invaded Holland. We had no plan to occupy the islands at the mouth of the Scheldt. . . . The Dutch think that the Germans will never dare to invade them. They are conscious of having committed no crime and . . . believe that Germany will be deterred by public opinion in the United States.

[1] This was the Military Co-ordination Committee, designed "to keep under constant review on behalf of the War Cabinet the main factors in the strategical situation and the progress of operations, and to make recommendations from time to time to the War Cabinet as to the general conduct of the war".

November 7

I was relieved last night by a letter from Howard-Vyse saying that the French were now taking the question of the invasion of Holland seriously. . . . They are now arranging to occupy the islands north and south of the Scheldt. They are to do it with mechanized divisions and Coast troops. . . . At 10 p.m. Howard-Vyse telephoned over that General Gamelin wanted to see me and Newall on Thursday. . . .

The Air Force now admit openly that their big bomber force is not suitable for anything but bombing something like the Ruhr. It cannot be used against troops in the field because the machines are too big and the casualties likely to be suffered are too great for the effect produced. This at once limits the usefulness of the force they have made. Also, politically, it is very difficult to get permission to use it, because we do not want to be the first to "take the gloves off". Our Government and the French Government both want incontrovertible evidence that the Germans have used their instruments against civilians. The Air Force now bring forward the theory that we have justification enough after Poland, and that it was merely expediency which held us back—our crossing to France and the French mobilization and, in a way, our numerical inferiority *vis-à-vis* the Germans. They argue that if the Germans invade Belgium, we are approaching a decisive point in the war and that our big bombers should be brought into action against the Ruhr. They say that the psychological moment to do this is the moment the Germans cross the Belgian frontier. All military action should be co-ordinated, and the two classes of bombers, light and heavy, should each act at the same time. The light bombers should be used against the Germans as they advance towards us, and *à fond*.

The machinery for launching the bombing on the Ruhr is at the moment defective. We have to prove to the British Government that there is justification for using this method of war, and then the Government has to convince the French Government and get agreement with it. Then perhaps they might let this force go. It will no longer be the psychological moment.

We discussed the relative strength of our Air Force and that of the Germans *ad nauseam*. Kingsley Wood said that the only reason the Germans had been stopped from bombing our industry was that we had this large force of bombers ready to do the same (500). . . . I have been going into the Ruhr defences and I must say that the German defence is a fine one. They have 280 fighter machines, 600 high-fire guns and 2,500 low-flyer guns. A terrific armament. If we do attack the Ruhr we shall find that their defence is pretty good and our casualties ought to be very heavy. I understand that we are going to fly low and attack by day.

CHAPTER X

Plan D: The Advance into Belgium

THE CONFERENCE requested by General Gamelin was held on Thursday, November 9, at Grand Quartier Général at Vincennes. Once again Colonel Macleod, Ironside's Military Assistant, was in attendance and took detailed notes. General Georges was present, as were the British Chief of the Air Staff, Sir Cyril Newall, General Gort, Commander-in-Chief of the British Expeditionary Force, and Admiral Darlan and General Vuillemin, commanders of the French Navy and Air. The conference dealt mainly with the action to be taken:

1. If Germany attacked only Holland.
2. If a general attack was launched in the west.

Gamelin began by saying that he expected Hitler to do something during the winter, probably a *Blitzkrieg* against Holland. He was temperamentally incapable of remaining inactive, and would probably use the same methods as had been employed in Czechoslovakia and Poland—attacking one country at a time and using that country as a base from which to attack the next. Thus the Germans might first attack Holland; and once they had occupied Holland they might then, and not until then, launch an attack on Belgium.

Gamelin said that the Belgians asked what they should do if the Germans attacked Holland. Were they to remain

□□ neutral, or join in? And what did the French intend to do?
He had replied that he wished the Belgians to join in, but that
the French could not go to the help of the Dutch without
going across Belgian territory. This they would not do unless
the Belgians definitely invited them in, which he hoped they
would.

The Dutch plan of defence was based on two systems of
inundations, an outer system a short distance behind their
frontier, and an inner system, like a moat, protecting Amsterdam and Rotterdam—the "fortress of Holland". But these
defences reached no further south than the Meuse, leaving the
mouth of the River Scheldt uncovered. If the Allies were
called in, a French Army would advance at once on the left
of the British, and occupy it.

If we moved into Belgium, the need to occupy defensive
positions must be considered. There were several defensive
waterlines: the Lys, the Scheldt, the Meuse and the Albert
Canal; and there was a new system of fortifications covering
Brussels. But there was a gap of some thirty miles between
Wavre and Namur in which, as far as he knew, nothing had
yet been done. He intended to make use of all possible
obstacles such as small streams, and the railway across the
plateau from Wavre to Namur.

As for a general attack in the west, Gamelin thought that
the campaigning season was almost over. The autumn rains
would soon fill up the streams and dykes and much of the
country would become sodden. The Germans were more
likely to stage a major offensive in the spring of 1940, when
the country had dried up. They might then either make a wide
and powerful movement through Belgium and possibly Holland, and thence into northern France, with their right flank
on the sea—a sort of Schlieffen Plan on a bigger scale; or they
might strike down from the north behind the Maginot Line,
combined with an attack through the Saar where the French
defences were weak.

The Germans relied on their armoured formations to break
through. He was not therefore afraid of the Ardennes, which

□□ was not a tank country owing to its deep valleys and wooded heights, and was traversed by the Meuse which, with its precipitous banks, was the best anti-tank obstacle in Europe.

Eighteen French divisions were in general reserve around Paris, ready to move to any part of the front and counter-attack the Germans if they penetrated the defences. The railways and roads from Paris made this the best location for the reserve. Although it had not been possible to discuss plans with the Belgians, it had been ascertained that the main Belgian line of defence was the Albert Canal from Liège to Antwerp. South of Liège their covering troops on the frontier would fall back on a time programme over three days to the Meuse, which would be their main line as far south as Givet where it would join up with the French defences. The weakness of this position was that it extended in a great salient into what would be German-occupied country, and it had little depth.

Ironside remarked that the Belgians, unaided, would not be able to hold out for more than a fortnight, and the Dutch unaided for not more than five days. Gamelin thought that the Belgians would be able to hold up the Germans for at least a week on the Albert Canal, but Ironside's estimate was not more than three days. Should we move into Belgium? Gamelin argued that if the Germans invaded Holland and Belgium we must go to their assistance, otherwise they might be defeated in detail, and 22 Belgian and 5 Dutch divisions would be lost to the Allies. If we advanced, it would considerably shorten our front, but he did not propose to move forward except to a suitable line which had been prepared for defence, and unless we could reach it well before the Germans. There was to be no race against time. The advance would be methodical, but would be fast to the Scheldt. General Gort, being under General Georges, would advance within one hour of receiving orders from him, without awaiting orders from the British Government.

Air Chief Marshal Newall urged that we should occupy as much of Belgium as possible to prevent the Germans

⊡⊡ establishing airfields from which to attack England with
fighter cover for their bombers. It would also bring us near
to bombing the Ruhr.

How far into Belgium should we go? There were three
possible lines to which to move: the Scheldt, the Dendre,
and the Dyle. An advance to the Scheldt would not only
cover its own estuary but also the mouths of the Rhine, and
the Meuse. It could be reached in reasonable security before
the Germans; it provided an excellent anti-tank obstacle; but
it had serious disadvantages. Behind it and the sea there was
a corridor only thirty miles deep for all "the rear organizations". They would be bunched and crammed and, since our
communications would run parallel to our front, there would
be much congestion and good targets for bombing. A break
through by the Germans with armoured forces would easily
and quickly reach the sea and imperil the safety of all the
troops in Belgium. It would do little to support the Belgian
and Dutch armies fighting many miles to the east and north
and they might be destroyed in detail before the Germans
turned on us.

If we moved to the Scheldt, the left of the First French
Army would be on the river itself, the British Army would be
between the Scheldt and the Lys, and more French troops
would be on the left of the British. The strategic islands of
the river mouth would be seized by two French motorized
divisions. The whole operation would take two nights and
a day.

The possibility of advancing to the Dendre was mentioned,
but Ironside pointed out that in the summer it was scarcely
a tank obstacle. It was therefore ruled out as a serious line of
defence, but might be suitable as a delaying position. The
next was the line of the Dyle east of Brussels. This was a good
obstacle, but between it and the Meuse at Namur there was a
thirty-mile plateau which was well suited for tanks. However,
it had many advantages. It was close to the Belgians who
would be fighting on the Albert Canal and they could fall
back on it if forced to withdraw. On its left lay the fortress

⌑⌑ of Antwerp through which help could be sent to the Dutch or through which the Dutch might fall back. And it kept the German fighters out of range of England. Their bombers would have farther to fly and they would have to fly unescorted. It was therefore decided to advance to this line of the Dyle provided the following conditions were fulfilled:

1. The Belgians should fortify it in every way possible.[1] Their existing defences on the Dyle faced east towards Germany. Their defences to the south of Brussels, however, faced towards France. These, it was urged, should be swung on to the Wavre plateau, where they would also be facing Germany, and a strong anti-tank obstacle should be made across it. Reports said that 10,000 Belgians had been working on it for the past week, and the railway between Namur and Gembleux was a good tank obstacle.

2. The British and French must be able to reach it well before the Germans. It was hoped that the Belgians could hold them up on the Albert Canal for long enough.

Four Armies would move into Low Countries, the Ninth to the Meuse, south of Namur, the First to the line Namur–Wavre, and the B.E.F. in the centre round Brussels to the Dyle, linking up with the Antwerp defences. The French Seventh Army on the left would move through Antwerp and join hands with the Dutch at Breda, thus protecting the left flank of the B.E.F. Its two motorized divisions would seize Walcheren and the other islands at the mouth of the Scheldt, and if the Dutch were defeated it was hoped the Seventh Army would also make sure they got back through Antwerp to join the Allies.

The first step was to seize the line of the Scheldt. The British advance would be in three echelons, with the 12th

[1] It was decided to ask the Belgians through diplomatic channels and, discreetly, through our military attachés, to make the Dyle line, particularly across the plateau south of Wavre, as strong as possible. Requests were duly made, but by May 1940 the Belgians had done very little.

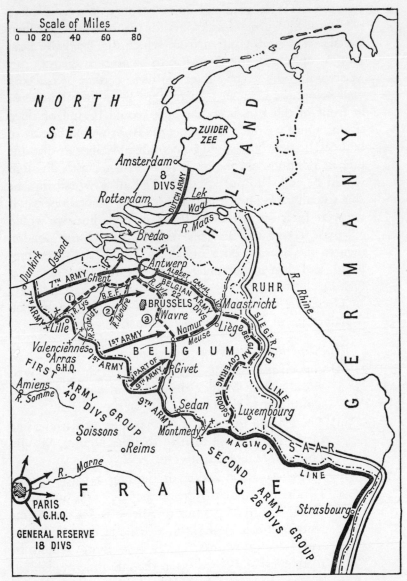

Scale of Miles

0 10 20 40 60 80

NORTH SEA

ZUIDER ZEE

HOLLAND

GERMANY

Amsterdam

8 DIVS

Rotterdam

DUTCH ARMY

Lek

Waal

R. Maas

Breda

Dunkirk

Ostend

7TH ARMY

Ghent

Antwerp

ALBERT CANAL

7TH ARMY

BELGIAN ARMY

RUHR

R. Rhine

① R. Lys

B.E.F.

R. Dyle 22

Maastricht

SIEGFRIED LINE

Lille

② R.Scheldt

R.Dendre

BRUSSELS

Wavre

Liège

BELGIAN COVERING LINE

③

1ST ARMY

Namur

Meuse

Valenciennes

Arras

G.H.Q.

1ST ARMY

BELGIUM

Amiens

R. Somme

FIRST

40

DIVS

ARMY

GROUP

PART OF

9TH ARMY

Givet

BELGIAN COVERING TROOPS

Soissons

9TH ARMY

Sedan

Luxembourg

Reims

Montmedy

MAGINOT

LINE

SAAR

R. Marne

SECOND

26

DIVS

GROUP

ARMY

PARIS

G.H.Q.

Strasbourg

GENERAL RESERVE

18 DIVS

FRANCE

French Plan "D".

153

⊡⊡ Lancers (armoured cars) going on to Brussels, and the British right on the main road and up to Malines. We would thus obtain the high ground and room for manœuvre. The Albert Canal was a weak position from which the Belgians might soon be dislodged. But there was to be no race against time. We would only occupy lines we were certain of reaching well before the Germans. There must be no bombing close in front of the British, as the area would be full of allied troops. Once we reached Malines the Ruhr would be easy to bomb. The new line would be considerably shorter than the present positions and the 22 Belgian and 5 Dutch divisions would be added to our strength. The allies would thus be able to pull back a much larger force into general reserve. If we were forced to withdraw from the Dyle line, we would fall back, taking the Belgians with us, first to the Dendre, then to the Scheldt, both of which would have been prepared, and then to our defences on the frontier. Such was Plan D.

"Georges", wrote Ironside, "then took up the word and explained his plan. It was in general this:

(i) A methodical advance into Belgium.

(ii) An advance to the line of the Scheldt as arranged already, from Maulde through Audenarde to Ghent, and thence to the Dutch coast on the Scheldt.

(iii) The sending forward of light troops, first to the line of the Dendre and then to the line Namur, Wavre, Louvain, Malines, Antwerp.

(iv) There was no question of fighting a battle on the Dendre. It must either be on the line of the Scheldt or on the line from Namur to Antwerp. He had no intention of being caught in a battle in the open as we had been at Mons. The whole thing would be methodical and based upon the safe time available.

(v) The occupation of the Dutch islands on the north and south of the mouth of the Scheldt. This was to be done by two motorized Divisions."

☐☐   Many French troops in the Maginot Line did not even know that there was a British army in France. To convince them of our presence, and to give our troops some fighting experience, it was arranged that brigade groups and then whole divisions should be sent in turn to the French sector about the Saar where there was patrol activity between the Maginot and Siegfried Lines.

Gamelin pressed for more British divisions to be sent to France, but Ironside refused to allow them to cross until they were fully equipped, saying it was useless to send unarmed men into a modern battle. There would be great loss of life and little gain. Gamelin then offered to disband ten of his Territorial divisions, send the men into the factories where they were urgently needed, and hand over their equipment to the British, but this was found to be so poor that Ironside refused the offer.

Much work had to be done during the winter on airfields and communications behind the line. The Auxiliary Military Pioneer Corps was organized and sent across, but even this was not enough, and eventually the political pressure became so insistent that Ironside was reluctantly forced to send the infantry of three divisions, the 12th, 23rd and 46th, for whom no equipment could be provided for several months, to do pioneer work in the rear areas on the distinct understanding that half their time should be devoted to training, and that they were not to be used in battle. In fact, they were soon engulfed.

Gamelin was concerned about the Air. The French, he said, were exceedingly short of aircraft. Nearly all their money had been spent on the Maginot Line and on their Army. They relied almost entirely on Britain for air support, and they wanted practically the whole of the R.A.F. to be concentrated in France. The British Chiefs pointed out that this could not be done because England had also to be defended. The French and British Armies were, therefore, only provided with a small number of squadrons in France to support them.

□□ Gamelin was rather nervous about air attacks on our advancing columns, and wanted us to bomb the Germans immediately they crossed the frontiers, but Air Chief Marshal Newall explained that we had no suitable aircraft. Our heavy bombers were too vulnerable and too valuable for attacks on troops, and anyway would have little effect. He proposed instead a heavy concentrated attack on the Ruhr which he claimed would have no immediate effect on the German advance, but a much greater effect on the war in the long run. Five out of the eight railways supplying the Germans in Belgium ran through the Ruhr, and if these were put out of action the Germans would find it difficult to keep their columns supplied and their advance would eventually be slowed down, pulled up, and become ripe for a counter-attack. Gamelin, however, thought it would be impossible to destroy all the railways. Attacking the Ruhr would, he said, have no direct effect on the main battle, because by then all the German forces would have passed beyond it.[1] It was indeed disappointing that the enemy columns could not be directly attacked, and he felt that an opportunity was being lost of damaging them.

He was not, however, in favour of attacking the Ruhr before the German offensive, because the enemy might retaliate by bombing French factories, and thus delay the equipping of the French armies. Only if the Germans started bombing French factories would he advocate bombing the Ruhr. By March the French would have several more fighter squadrons and their Air Force would be renewed. Three hundred to four hundred French bombers might then attack the Ruhr in combination with the British. Its complete destruction might have a decisive effect.

Finally, he was asked: "If the Germans attack Holland and Belgium, will you attack the Siegfried Line?" The answer was "No."

---

[1] In fact, the Germans built up huge dumps of materials on the west bank of the Rhine.

November 9

We came back by train and destroyer, reaching London at
9.10 p.m. Here I found a message saying that the Cabinet was
meeting at 9.30 p.m. . . . I found the Prime Minister was in bed
with gout. Simon in the chair. The Cabinet not so well run as
usual.

I explained what had happened and was at once asked if I
thought the British Army ought to advance. I had to remind them
twice that they had a C.-in-C. in France and that they had expressly put him under the orders of the French Commander. The
C.-in-C. had the right of protest to the Cabinet, but that until he
had protested—which he did not propose to do—they would be
very ill-advised to step in. Gort had agreed, and I had accepted the
advance. This quietened them down completely.

I told them that we still had no communication with the
Belgians and did not know what they were doing or when they
would call upon us. Eventually a strong wire was sent to Brussels
trying to get the Belgians to talk with us. . . .

Then we had a go at the Ruhr. Impassioned speeches from all.
The Supreme War Council is to go over to France and try and
make the French agree to the British bombing the Ruhr.

November 10

In the evening we had an Army Council meeting from 5.30 p.m.
till after 9 p.m. I at last got a chance to tell the Army Council what
was now happening in the war. Of doubtful utility because
Belisha suddenly started to give a dissertation upon the necessity
for moving the bases [in France] further north. This was very
badly done from what I had been trying to tell him some days
ago. He tried to impress the Army Council, but soon floundered
about and stopped. So much wasted time.

Then I took him over the [R.A.F.'s] proposed bombing plan of
the light bombers in case of a German advance. It is just so much
eye-wash. They have taken the map of Belgium, marked certain
roads coming in with great blue lines, have then ordered bombing
at certain points on these roads without any reference to whether

there are any Germans there or not. Just a pre-arranged programme without any reference to actual facts.

November 13

Gamelin has written to me upon the subject of the British Air
Forces in France. He is of the same opinion as I am—that no Air
Force operating in France can possibly be run from England. At
the moment, our B.E.F. is so small that it does not need the
services of the whole of the Air Striking Force. To put it under
the French Command would bring endless difficulties, since the
French Air Force is so very small and ineffective. Gamelin is very
insistent that no Air Force can be independent. It cannot just carry
out operations as it wishes on its own.

November 18

We are still haggling away over the question of how the R.A.F.
should bomb in front of the troops. The Air Ministry have put up
the most futile argument I can imagine. Everything must be on a
pre-arranged plan, exactly like a barrage. The troops are tied
down to a rigid timing which cannot be altered at all. With this
mechanized warfare it is essential that things should not be too
rigid. How the R.A.F. can think that it is possible to bomb in front
of advancing troops, or an enemy advancing against us, upon a
programme arranged in London I fail to understand. Two separate
lots of bombers arrive from London and Rheims and concentrate
by means of overhead telephones.[1] Anything more mad I cannot
conceive. What we want is proper reconnaissance and action upon
that reconnaissance. . . .

I am a little perturbed at the lack of plan that we have in the
Cabinet. It is all "wait and see" and a complete subservience to the
French point of view that all our effort should be made in France.
We have no plan for the Middle East, and nothing but long and
tedious discussions upon all and sundry. Chamberlain ends by
referring most things to a Committee. . . . He is just a weary,
tired old man, dominating at times all the other mediocrities who
bear the responsibility with him.

[1] I.e. telephone wires supported by posts on the ground.

I have just unearthed a paper by Chamberlain, dated December 11, 1936, when he was Chancellor of the Exchequer. Here he puts all the arguments he can against making an Army ready for war. He says we ought to concentrate upon an Air Force. He and all the rest of the Cabinet skate round the possibility of our having to send a large army to France. The very same men are now trying to hurry on the making of an Army in record time and are always disappointed that we can do no better than we are doing.

November 21

The struggle with the Air Force goes on and we seem a little nearer to getting control of the bomber planes to work in close support with our people. The Air Ministry are adepts at holding things up and drawing red herrings across the trail. Fighting like a fish at the end of a line. Chatfield . . . acts as a post-box. The difficulty is the moment. Swapping methods at the beginning of a campaign is dangerous. I would not ask for it unless the present method of using the bombers were not so bad. Nothing could be worse.

This damned struggle with the Air Ministry over the employment of bombers gets worse and worse. If we ever do get a proportion of the light bombers told off to us I shall have to get them trained, and that means that we have to keep these pilots handy to take on the job that they have been put to. The present system of using overhead telephones for orders is far too slow and machines would take hours getting to their destinations when the enemy have been discovered. They have no ideas of running communications in the R.A.F. between the Army and the machines. They have never practised it, and it would not function if a sudden crisis came upon us.

Later Ironside wrote:

We have advanced a bit over our Air Arm for the Army, and now have the chance of commanding some of our own aeroplanes. I am getting the training going.

CHAPTER XI

Friction with the Secretary of State

RELATIONS between the C.I.G.S. and the Secretary of State for War grew more strained as the result of two disputes. The first concerned the issue of orders.

On the night of October 30 a signal had reached the War Office suggesting that a German raiding force was on its way to East Anglia. Ironside warned General Kirke, the Commander-in-Chief, Home Forces, and ordered the division in reserve at Aldershot to move to East Anglia. The raid was a false alarm, and next morning, when Mr. Hore-Belisha saw the message, he told the C.I.G.S. that he was not authorized to send orders to Commanders-in-Chief. That was the prerogative of the Army Council. Ironside replied that the matter had appeared to be urgent, and the Secretary of State and other members of the Army Council were not in the War Office when the signal was received. Action had to be taken at once, and there was no time to wait for a Council meeting to be called. The Minister overruled him, and said that in future such orders must be issued by the Army Council. Soon afterwards, General Kirke complained that he had received an operation order which he could not understand. It was shown to Ironside, who found that it had been issued by the Secretary of State and signed by a secretary. It was now his turn, and indeed his duty, to tell Mr. Hore-Belisha that as he had had no staff training, and

□□ did not know how to write an operation order, he should desist from such activity.

Later on, Mr. Winston Churchill, then First Lord of the Admiralty, asked for a battalion to go to the Orkneys. It was urgently needed for the protection of the Fleet Base at Scapa, and Ironside at once sent the necessary orders to Scottish Command. They were cancelled on the instructions of the Secretary of State, but in fact were carried out, because the Scottish General ignored the cancellation.

The Army Council, which dealt principally with administration and not operations, seemed a somewhat unsuitable body for writing operation orders. In the First World War the C.I.G.S. had been authorized to issue orders to Commanders-in-Chief, and, now that there was a Chiefs of Staff Committee to decide the general line of action, it seemed to Ironside that the best procedure would be for each Chief to issue the detailed orders to his own Service. But this procedure was blocked by the fact that the Commanders-in-Chief were appointed either by the War Cabinet or by the Army Council and some were therefore under the authority of the Cabinet while others were under the Army Council. The C.I.G.S. could issue orders to those appointed by Army Council in the name of the Army Council, but what about those appointed by the War Cabinet?

During the course of the Finnish campaign, for example, the Army Council ordered the C.-in-C. of the B.E.F., Lord Gort, to withdraw the 5th Division from the line in France and prepare to embark it for Scandinavia. Gort said that while he would loyally comply with the order, he did so under protest. He had been appointed by the War Cabinet and he could not recognize the authority of the Army Council to give him orders. Future generations may find it surprising that so obvious a question as who should give orders to whom had not been resolved by the Committee of Imperial Defence in peace-time. Mr. Hore-Belisha had not been helpful in this procedural controversy.

The second dispute concerned the British Expeditionary

Force in France. The French still appeared to think that the British were dragging their feet about sending divisions to France, and Ironside, having obtained permission from the Cabinet, went over to explain the situation to Gamelin.

November 19

Down to Hendon aerodrome and over to France in a big twelve-seater machine. Quite a sunny day with lowish clouds and of course very bumpy. I must confess that I hate flying more and more every time I do it. I have a feeling of unease, and yet it is the only method by which one can get about and do all that one has to do. . . . I managed to get a meeting with Gamelin and his staff at 3.30 p.m. and there I told him the whole situation, showing him the state of our equipment and men. I also gave him a statement of our population.

Ironside said that when Reynaud was recently in England he had complained that whereas one man in eight was mobilized in France, only one in forty was mobilized in England; but, on going into his figures, it was found that Reynaud had included police, railway and dock workers, etc., in the French mobilization who were not included in the British figures. When these were eliminated, the proportions were much about the same. We now had five divisions in France, though the artillery of the fifth had not yet arrived. There would be ten in February and fifteen by September. If equipment could be turned out quicker by the Ministry of Supply, more divisions could be sent. The Armoured Division could arrive in March but it would not be complete in tanks, and their transport would be difficult owing to the number of ships needed. There would be three hundred tanks of which two-thirds would be cruisers.

The Germans, Gamelin said, generally attacked in March (Verdun in February was an exception), so he asked whether this would be too late. Ironside explained that in January we could decide whether to send it over incomplete or to wait longer till it was complete. Certain units and perhaps a brigade might be sent out sooner, beginning in January.

As regards the other four divisions not yet in France, they were not fully trained though two were more trained than the others. The question was, should they train in France or in England? Rennes, in France, was a worse training area than England, and if they remained in England there were schools for officers and N.C.O.s, to which it would be difficult to send them if the divisions were in France. Gamelin then agreed that they should complete their training in England. Ironside said that the politicians were always pressing him to accelerate the arrival of these divisions in France, possibly from the point of view of morale, but shipping was not easy. If it was a question of the morale of the French nation, General Gort could send troops to the fighting front in the Saar.

As for tanks, Gamelin suggested having a lower establishment in divisions and corps, and forming an Army pool. There was not the same danger of attacks by tanks in all sectors of the front, and divisions short of anti-tank guns could be sent to sectors where such attacks were unlikely.[1]

"It was", wrote Ironside that evening, "an interesting interview because I think I managed to dismiss all suspicion. They simply couldn't say that I was concealing anything. I told them that the men were there and we could only supply the equipment at a certain rate and no more. Either we could make divisions upon a lesser scale or we could reduce their size and the size of their transport which is terrific. Far too much."

But he still had to convince M. Paul Reynaud.

November 20

At 11.30 a.m. I went with Belisha to see M. Paul Reynaud, the Minister of Finance. I had quite a passage-of-arms with him when he repeated that we had one man in forty mobilized and France had one man in eight. I asked him where he got his information

[1] Gamelin considered that the Ardennes was one of these "unlikely" sectors for a tank-attack and his policy contributed to the French troops being overrun at Sedan in May 1940.

and he said it was well known. I told him that it was untrue and that I looked to him, a professed friend of England, not to repeat such obvious rot. We had the same argument as we had in the last war that France would be the target for the German attack. No thought of anything else. . . . His final statement about equipment was that the French could demobilize some of their divisions and give the stuff to ours. As if our men could go off five minutes later and fight with it.

While Ironside was in conference with the French, Mr. Hore-Belisha had been visiting the British Expeditionary Force. The Secretary of State's tour of the Front led directly to what became known as "The Pill-Box Row", and produced a controversy which not only smoulders to this day but may well have contributed to the War Minister's resignation six weeks later.

Before he left, Ironside had asked him whether he wanted to see the troops or the defences, as he would not have time for both in the two days he was to spend in France. Mr. Hore-Belisha had replied that he wished to see the troops and not the defences, and General Gort was thus informed so that he could plan his visit. On November 19 Ironside met Mr. Hore-Belisha in Paris. "I had a few words with Belisha," the C.I.G.S. noted, "and I gathered from him that he had had a wonderful trip. He glibly told me that he now had a grasp of things and had various ideas. He had been disappointed at the way the Sappers had failed to get a pattern of [i.e. a standard] pill-box and how Gort hadn't used all the extra sappers we had sent him. . . . I had to tell Belisha that he must be careful how he dealt with his C.-in-C. He was put in by the King and must not be monkeyed about."

On his return Mr. Hore-Belisha told the Cabinet *after Ironside had left the room* that he was not satisfied with the work the B.E.F. were putting in on their defences in France. In contrast, a French Brigade on the left of the British had done very good work.[1] He also stated that Gamelin had told him

[1] In fact, their defences had been made by the British.

that a concrete pill-box could be erected in three days, whereas the British took three weeks[1]. Apparently some Dominion Ministers who had served in France in the previous war and had toured the Front at much the same time had also commented to him about the seeming lack of defences, evidently expecting to see regular trench systems, and not realizing that tactics had changed. They were unaware of our well-concealed defences.

November 28

I have had what amounts to an attack on Gort over not having done enough work in the line. Our Belisha waited until I had left the Cabinet and then made a statement upon what he had seen in France. None of the Cabinet appears to have questioned what he said or to have thought of asking for professional advice. So I told Belisha that he must not lower the prestige of the C.-in-C. in the eyes of the Cabinet without telling him. I told him that I would go over to France at once and inspect the line thoroughly and make a report. I have only seen it once some weeks ago and I shall be able to see the difference.

At the end of an Army Council Meeting, which was attended by the Engineer-in-Chief in France, General Pakenham-Walsh, but at which the C.I.G.S. was not present, the Minister for War had also told the Engineer-in-Chief that he was to tell Gort he was not satisfied with the work the B.E.F. were doing on their defences in France. Pakenham-Walsh reported this to Gort. The Prime Minister told Ironside of the adverse criticisms that had been made. Ironside said that he must go to France and find out for himself. If the situation was as bad as Mr. Hore-Belisha had reported, it must be put right at once. Mr. Chamberlain agreed, and instructed Ironside to report to him on his return.

[1] Gamelin subsequently denied that he had said this. What he had said was that after the site had been prepared and all the material collected, the pill-box could be erected in three days with French quick-drying concrete, but the whole operation would take about twenty days.

November 29

We got started from Heston at 10 a.m. sharp and the pilot told us it was going to be bumpy. It was the worst crossing I have had anywhere. Fog and rain and low clouds. The pilot managed to strike Le Tréport, but at some feet below the top of the cliff. We then drove up the coast and finally up the Somme to Amiens as it was too foggy to go on to Douai. A hazardous journey. . . . I found all G.H.Q. in a devil of a rage over Gort's message that had been sent him by Belisha through his Engineer-in-Chief [General Pakenham-Walsh]. They showed me all the plans and maps and refuted utterly the strictures cast upon them by Belisha.

The Headquarters Staff of the B.E.F. had good reasons for their "rage". The War Minister had made no complaint to Gort during his visit to France and had appeared completely satisfied with all he saw. Having asked to see the troops and not the defences, he had not been shown the field-works. These were well concealed and camouflaged in houses, woods and hedges, and many could not have been visible when Mr. Hore-Belisha was inspecting the troops who, in several cases, had been formed up near roads to make inspection more easy. Nor did he seem to appreciate that as we intended to advance into Belgium in accordance with Plan D, it was not a front line but merely a jumping-off line, or a reserve position in case we fell back.

Next day, Ironside went round the 1st Corps front with Lord Gort in pouring rain, meeting the Corps, Divisional, Brigade and Battalion commanders.

November 30

I spent the most awful day in pouring rain going round the 1st Corps front. One and all were cursing Belisha for accusing them of not having done any work. . . .

I walked round the Front thoroughly and saw the enormous work that had been done and was being done. Over two hundred tons of cement being put in on the 1st Division front alone per day. Mud conditions were literally the worst I have ever seen. Simply impossible.

December 1

A much better day when I went round the 2nd Corps front [commanded by General Alan Brooke]. Brooke has done much more digging than 1st Corps, but his country was much more open. The men have worked marvellously well in bad conditions. Montgomery [commanding 3rd Division] told me that Belisha had thanked him for showing him round the men and not the fortifications, which did not interest him. . . . The whole Army knows that it has been accused of doing nothing and resents it. We have made up a long paper[1] [i.e. a Report on the defences] . . . and I now hear by telephone that I have been asked to see the Prime Minister at 12.30 p.m. on my return.

December 2

We came into Heston at 12.15 [delayed by bad weather]. I jumped into the car and reached Downing Street at 12.45, only to be told by a smiling secretary that they had thought I was coming back the night before and that I wasn't wanted. Then I went to the War Office and found Belisha. I told him how angry everybody was in the B.E.F. How Gort had resented the message he had received between him and Belisha through Pakenham-Walsh, his Engineer-in-Chief. Belisha was thoroughly upset and frightened. All out to show that he had cast no aspersions upon the Army. We both got a bit heated about it, and I was told that it was a matter of general knowledge that the Ministers from the Colonies had made a report to the Prime Minister.

December 4

A more successful Army Council in the evening. I managed to get my report listened to, so that they should all know what I thought the state of line occupied by the B.E.F. was. Belisha explaining why he wrote to Gort and did not do this or that. All trying to prove that he had not made a mistake in sending a message which Gort took as a censure.

[1] Appendix, page 395.

December 21

I had nearly an hour's talk with Belisha yesterday. He is evidently very perturbed at his position and was all out to be extra civil to me. He launched a tirade against Gort, who he said was "sulking". I told him that I didn't believe it. That he had been angry over the reports about the pill-boxes, and, in my opinion, with some justification. . . . I warned Belisha that any undermining of the C.-in-C. would be reflected at once in the B.E.F. That he couldn't start any intrigue against Gort. He denied any desire to do this. He then discussed various senior officers and I came to the conclusion that he only liked those who pleased him at the moment.

December 23

I had a talk with Hore-Belisha. . . . He told me that the P.M. had asked him whether he wished to make any change in France. That he was not to be afraid to ask if he wished to. Belisha had replied that he had complete confidence in Gort and wished for no change. . . . The P.M. had said to him on his return that he had complete confidence in him [Belisha]. That history would say what he had done for the Army and that the P.M. knew what he had done.

I wondered if this were true. Belisha said that it had made him ill thinking of it.

CHAPTER XII

The End of 1939

December 3

A curious commentary came to me yesterday when [General] Taylor and [Admiral] Brown, the soldier and sailor at the head of the Ministry of Supply, asked me to lunch with them each Saturday at the Senior [Club] in order to discuss things. This is the only means of liaison I apparently have with our people who supply things. We have nobody on the Army Council responsible, as we ought to have, owing to Belisha's split. Even Fortington, our statistician, says that we are running a great risk in sending the troops over with so few anti-tank guns and anti-aircraft guns against low-flying aeroplanes. I quite agree and I hope that my telegram from France[1] puts things clearly enough. It is for the Cabinet to decide. The same old Cabinet which would not have any armaments prepared. Now they are trying to escape by saying that the Ministry of Supply should make the things in a month.

There is a fresh development over the Middle East. Weygand has come home and Gamelin has asked that we should consider the question with him. Weygand is undoubtedly pushing for greater action in the Balkans and as far as I can see Gamelin wants our support to prevent him from commencing action that may lead to something bigger than is intended. No expedition ever gets smaller, but always grows and cannot be withdrawn in the

[1] See Appendix, page 399.

end. We have so many examples of this that I should have said that the truth requires no proof now.

The French High Command holds the view that the general course of events may render the actual presence of an Expeditionary Force in the Balkans necessary as early as next spring. . . . Here we have the beginning of a large Expeditionary Force, obviously to be commanded by a Frenchman, Weygand, and a larger commitment for the future. . . . The moment is not now. . . . We are not ready and have not the material ready to support our small friends [in the Balkans]. As in 1914–18 they may all be annihilated before we can prevent the Germans from getting at them. We are tied pretty solidly in Egypt by the possible action of Italy. Until Italy has declared herself, we cannot move troops.

December 6

We had a dreadfully futile meeting on munitions. Winston started off on a new method of computation, which meant the preparation of new graphs. A lot of old men sitting round a table juggling with numbers never come to any decision. I took half an hour to make them understand that I had to have delivery of the armament nearly one month ahead of the date troops were leaving for France. Even that date was little enough in the way of time to allow the units to settle down, despite the fact that they will have the training equipment in their hands for some time before that. We really got no way at all. We have all the statisticians we want and we are all agreed on the main shortages. It seems to me that what we want is a big industrialist in charge and not any odd politician, however clever he is.

December 7

The Cabinet considered the Near East and came to no decision. The Chiefs of Staff had come to the conclusion that it was a matter of policy as to whether we were to start anything in the Balkans or not. We feel that our disposition of troops is governed by the attitude of Italy. We do not want to irritate her into coming in against us. . . . If the Germans and Russians were to have a success in the Balkans she might well come in against us. At the moment we have enough on our hands. But the Germans and Russians acting in collusion may well begin a steady advance into the Balkans. The French have said that we must be ready by next spring. All this is a complete *volte-face* from what they have said so far—that Germany would attack with 160 divisions in France in the spring. I am sure that Germany cannot do both things—advance in east and west.

The French want us to make a study of what we can do in the Middle East. They feel they may be forced to send something to prevent the enemy getting the Straits and Salonika. We could back up Turkey and stand on the defensive, but no more. We have to go across to see Gamelin and find out what he really wants and then to report to the Cabinet. They will then know what the project really is and be able to decide upon the policy.

[General] Archie Wavell [C.-in-C. Middle East] in to a conference in the afternoon. He is a dour devil, but a good soldier with very great imagination. He is all for us preparing in the Middle East. He seems to be imbued with the firm idea that the Germans and Russians will come against the Balkans.

I can see an interesting conference with Gamelin and Weygand. We go over on Sunday afternoon.

December 11 [Vincennes]

It was interesting seeing and hearing Weygand. He is now seventy-two and seems as clear and vigorous as ever. He put the case of our going into the Balkans with great strength. Both he and Gamelin pointed to the peoples of the Balkans turning towards us. Weygand's simile was that we should not go in as if we were going to a death bed, but as a good doctor with a syringe of reinvigorating medicine.

December 12 [London]

At 7 p.m. I went over to see Winston Churchill at the Admiralty. He told me that he wanted to show me his "Cultivator". I found that he had invented and reduced to model a machine that would go through the earth at a good pace. He reasoned that, just as the man had had to go underground in the last war, so would the tank have to do so in this. The tank, which had solved the problem of machine-gun fire in the last war, could now no longer face the anti-tank fire. . . . I thought that we could make a great deal of these machines and they present the first of any possible offensive idea.

December 13

We must have a strategic plan and I wonder when we shall get it. The French are pushing us for a larger Army in France, and if we do not have it, the French Army may collapse and then all our Navies and Air Forces will not be of much good to us. We may think that we can retreat inside Great Britain and fight in the air, but we cannot do this. Our front line is in France and we must fight in France. We cannot escape that.

I am wondering if we have big enough men in the Government to make the proper decisions as to strategy? I haven't met them yet.

December 17

So far, I have failed to get out of Gamelin his idea as to a possible offensive. Perhaps it is probable that he has none. He is wondering and wracking his brains as to what may happen. He is in command, and he it is who will order any offensive, and he has the added burden of having supreme control over our troops. There is the difference to 1914. I wonder how the people will react when they know that their troops are subordinate to the French Government more than to their own? I don't suppose many know that there is a difference between now and 1914. I shall have to get from Gamelin what he expects from us in the way of an Army before he can consider an offensive. And when will he carry it out? He expects all he can get and will never be satisfied till he has the last man. We shall be less hardly put to it in that we shall have no side-shows—if I can prevent the starting of them. Side-shows ate up a great deal of strength in 1914–18 and took away a great deal of strength from France. Is France going to be the decisive front once more? Gamelin says that it is at the moment.

December 20

The Supreme War Council [in Paris on the 19th] lasted from 9 a.m. till after 1 p.m. Going all the time. All went well, but then there is no adversity to make the French more feminine than usual. It was interesting looking round at the faces at the table. Daladier sat hunched up in his chair. . . . He spoke clearly and well and much to the point. His two points were properly brought up and ably expressed. It so arose over the Military position on the Western Front, where the civilian mind sees a deadlock. Two Forces of equal strength and the one that attacks seeing such enormous casualties that it cannot move without endangering the continuation of the war or of the aftermath.

Then Daladier developed the "War Aim" theorem. He was afraid that we should be satisfied with the dismissal of Hitler, without security against one more war with Germany. . . . The talk became a little academic because we all felt that we hadn't won the war yet and that it had not even begun.

December 21

I had a long conference with the Supply people. Lord Woolton in too. I found that none of my letters about strategical location of factories had ever filtered down to his various departments. I found that financial sanction had not been given for such things as Eastern [i.e. tropical] clothing, which might be wanted by any division at short notice. It is really the fault of the head military man at the Ministry of Supply, who should have sent round the general information. The machine is so rotten that one finds holes in it every day.

December 30

I have had a first look at Gamelin's appreciation [of possible operations to be carried out in 1940] and I must say that I find it a very woolly piece of work. It shows very little desire to get a move on with the war. There is hardly anything but the most passive defensive, with a very hazy idea as to what the Germans may do. It gives Hitler almost complete liberty to do what he likes, and can suggest nothing better than to wait patiently till he does it. As usual, it is completely cynical as to the fate of small nations. . . .

Any question of Germany operating in Scandinavia and in the Balkans, besides being active on the Western Front, seems to me to be fantastic. The French have no intention of carrying out an offensive for years, if at all. There is none of that fire which animated them in 1914. . . . When one looks at all this it seems that Gamelin's attitude is governed by two things:

1. He believes that it is impossible for the Führer to remain in-active. He must do something for psychological reasons. If the Führer can only be induced to attack on the Western Front, he may be defeated militarily.
2. He believes that the internal situation in Germany will explode. The wish may be father to the thought.

The only place where he favours operations is in the Balkans. This is induced by the picture of saving 111 Divisions of Balkan troops from annihilation.

I have made an appreciation at the end of the year and have outlined a strategy that may help us to get out of this dreadful attitude of waiting. . . . The French argument against doing any-thing is always that we are too weak. Let sleeping dogs lie and do not start the German machine off until we are ready. But shall we ever be any better off in proportion if we wait? . . .

In this paper, which ran to several pages and was submitted to the Cabinet, Ironside summed up his ideas. They were much influenced by Russia's invasion of Finland which had begun in November 1939, and of which more hereafter. The following extracts may be deemed significant:

OUR WAR STRATEGY

In view of all the circumstances, I think the moment has arrived for some plan which will upset the German calculations,

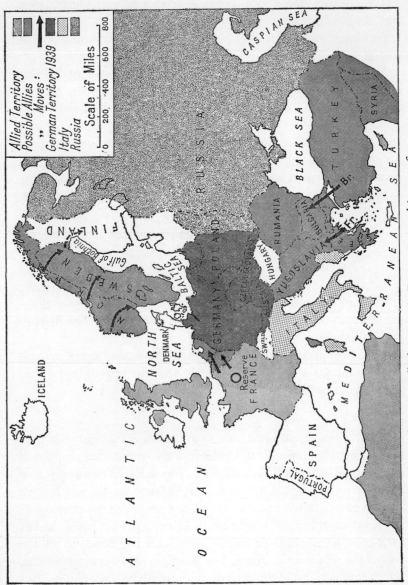

Some alternative Allied projects in Europe prepared in 1939 for 1940.

cause them to disperse their forces, confuse their curious leader, and escape from our position of passive waiting with all its alarms and doubtful advantages of increasing strength.

I outline a possible strategy, which I recommend should be presented to the French High Command. It is as follows:

A decision to put the Western Front in a proper state of defence, so that the present number of troops, or a less number, may be able to hold any German attack that may be launched against it. . . .

We should then lay ourselves out to attack the German directly and indirectly where we can, with the object of stopping his supplies and forcing him to disperse his forces and upsetting his plans. The German is a methodical creature and is not adaptable to improvization and we should try to take advantage of this fact.

I put forward the following strategical idea:

(i) An attempt to stop his supplies of iron-ore from Sweden. This plan has been put forward in detail by the Chiefs of Staff. It has many advantages and may be decisive. It will certainly make the Germans react immediately. It will make him disperse his forces and engage in overseas operations. . . . It will effectively prevent him from taking the offensive elsewhere.

(ii) This operation should be followed by an attempt to consolidate the Balkans, if possible with the help of Italy. This, again, will cause him to disperse still further.

December 31

What a year it has been, this 1939. I always thought that 1940 would be the time, and nothing very much has happened militarily. There is still 1940 to come. I wonder. We have got into this war unprepared. Our unmilitary leaders would not believe that preparations were necessary. They even called it warmongering to do anything that might excite Germany. I am frightened of their complete complacency. . . . They were frightened to tell the people the true state of affairs. The people were kept in ignorance, which is never a good thing to do with the British people. . . . But of this I am convinced. We must start a vigorous policy of forcing the Germans to disperse. We must not sit supine, hoping that something in our favour will come to pass. We cannot "convince the Germans that they cannot win" . . . by doing nothing.

These four months I have led at the War Office have been strenuous. Quite unlike anything I had imagined. . . . I find all this attending of Committees and endless discussions quite foreign to what I have ever had to do with. The lack of power to be able to decide a question and issue an order is deadening. . . . Perhaps the worst thing is to keep the Secretary of State in the picture of what we do at the Chiefs of Staff Committee when he will not give the time to listen. I get terribly tired of repeating to him and the Army Council and others what we have been doing. It seems such a waste of time. . . .

I wonder what the New Year will bring for us? Bad times, I fear. But we shall beat these swine. I shall have gone long before the end, and my second or third successor will bring in the victory. It is always like that in our wars. . . .

I believe that Hitler hoped against hope that we should never declare war to help Poland. He couldn't believe that we should risk so much for something which didn't touch us nearly. He has misunderstood us. He cannot understand how a nation can contemplate war in the unprepared state in which he thinks we are. Nobody could know the real truth but ourselves. After all, we do it every time.

When Hitler comes against us, he will be as ready as he can be. Curious that it may be two years from the '38 [actually '37] in which the Generals toasted me in the Adlon Hotel after the German manœuvres. The drunken aside of Reichenau. How long ago that seems, and how things have changed.

The one bright spot in all our efforts is the Navy and the Fighters of the R.A.F. Perhaps the most important things in our military forces.

PART THREE

SCANDINAVIA

CHAPTER XIII

Russia attacks Finland

INACTION was as displeasing to General Ironside as it was to Mr. Winston Churchill. While most of the Cabinet were inert, or content to follow the French policy of waiting to be attacked on the Western Front and pressing for more and more British troops to be sent to France, the First Lord of the Admiralty, like the C.I.G.S., was continually searching for some means of upsetting Hitler's plans, of defeating him instead of avoiding being defeated, and of staving off, or diverting, the attack which would surely come in the west. Scandinavia seemed the place to act.

Near a town in North Sweden called Gällivare was a large hill composed almost entirely of iron-ore. It was dug out and loaded direct into trucks, and it reached Germany by two main routes: in the summer it travelled from the port of Lulea at the northern end of the Gulf of Bothnia, and in winter, when the Gulf was frozen, from the ice-free port of Narvik, in Norway. To avoid a major industrial breakdown it was reckoned that Germany must import nine million tons of this high-grade ore in the first year of the war.

Mr. Churchill had called the attention of the Cabinet to this ore as early as September 19. On November 29 he sent a minute to the First Sea Lord about a proposal to stop it reaching Germany by laying mines off the Norwegian coast inside Norwegian territorial waters. He argued that if the

□□ traffic through Narvik could be blocked, Germany, by the end of April, would find herself short of a million tons of ore. If means could also be found of stopping the flow through Lulea in summer, German heavy industry might even be brought to a standstill. At the end of November, the Cabinet decided that the question of blocking the ore-traffic through Narvik should be examined from all military and economic angles, meaning: Should Britain stop it by force, or should she try to buy it? The Russian invasion of Finland on November 30 altered the entire situation.

His Non-Aggression pact with the Soviets had enabled Hitler to defeat the Poles, but Russia had soon shown that she was determined to look after her own interests. She had no intention of allowing Germany to seize the whole of Poland, and thus bring the German frontier nearer to the Russian homeland. Advancing into Poland herself, Russia had established her own frontier on the line she had held in 1920. Her attack on the Finns was launched in the hope of rectifying her northern boundary in the same fashion and stopping Germany using Finland as an offensive base.

Russia, however, encountered far stiffer resistance from the Finns than she had expected. She was severely defeated in the forests and her unprovoked attack produced a wave of sympathy for Finland. Demands reached the British and French Governments for immediate help. The only practicable route for supplies and troops was by the same iron-ore port of Narvik, and thence by rail through Sweden. A few guns and equipment were indeed sent, but neither Norway nor Sweden would allow formed bodies of troops to pass through their territories. Like Belgium, they were determined to cherish their neutrality.

Ironside was in a difficult position. He had sympathy and admiration for the Finns, but he never lost sight of the fact that Russia might one day become our ally, and he warned the Government against antagonizing the Soviets too much.

"The Germans and Russians", he declared privately, "are

Scandinavia.

183

⊡⊡ bound to fall out sooner or later." At the same time he ruled out as impractical many wild projects for sending British troops to Finland. One such notion, sponsored by a group in the House of Commons, envisaged demobilizing one of the British divisions in France, sending the men to Finland in civilian clothes, and remobilizing them on arrival.

Powerful and more sober elements in both Houses also urged that the two projects, namely interrupting the transit of iron-ore to Germany and helping Finland, should be combined, and by mid-December the Military Co-Ordination Committee were seriously considering Mr. Churchill's mine-laying proposal in conjunction with landing an Anglo-French force of three or four thousand men at Narvik and seizing the Gällivare ore-fields. Mr. Churchill welcomed the bracketing of these two projects. He favoured all possible help to the Finns, and was not unaware that this new and generous impulse might further the plan that was nearest to his heart, the mining of Norwegian territorial waters. He recognized that this might stir the Germans into invading Norway themselves, but he was inclined to regard with optimism the possibility of the war spreading into Scandinavia. The C.I.G.S., on the other hand, while most anxious to send such help as was possible to Finland, pointed out that there was no road and only a narrow-gauge railway from Narvik to Gällivare and thence into Finland. The transport and maintenance of any troops we sent would entirely depend on this railway, and the railway was Swedish. If, as seemed likely, the Swedes opposed the transit of our troops through their territory, the electric current might be cut off, the railway staff forbidden to co-operate, and the rolling stock removed. He emphasized that, in any case, a Brigade Group was the largest Force that could, under the most favourable conditions, be maintained in Finland. He was also inclined to mistrust the upshot of Mr. Churchill's "limited" mine-laying project, for he doubted whether it could, in fact, be limited. On the other hand he eagerly seized the chance afforded by "help for Finland" for intervening in Scandinavia, his purpose being either

□□ to forestall the Germans or, at the worst, to be there very soon after they had arrived, for he was fairly certain that they would invade either Sweden or Norway or both. He was also anxious to start some offensive operation which might upset the German war plan. But he insisted that any military intervention in Scandinavia should be undertaken on a proper scale and with sufficient troops, adequately trained and adequately equipped, and he emphasized that any such expedition would need the most careful planning and preparation and could not be hurried.

In private conversations with his Military Assistant Ironside said that we now seemed to have a chance of seizing the initiative from Hitler. The iron-ore field at Gällivare in Northern Sweden was vital to him, and if we could occupy this we would shorten the war and upset his plans in the west. We should go to help Finland by landing at Narvik and thence by the railway to Gällivare and Finland. While only one brigade group would enter Finland because the narrow-gauge railway could not support more, there would be four or five divisions on the lines of communication—including Gällivare. Once we were there it would be difficult to turn us out, and Hitler would be forced to attack us to regain his iron-ore. In such remote and forbidding country a very small force could hold up a large force. Any brigade that reached Finland would remain near the railway and the frontier so as to avoid either getting too close to the Russians, or being cut off by the Germans when the Gulf of Bothnia unfroze. Now was the time to go there while the Gulf was still frozen. It would not unfreeze till April, which would give us time to establish ourselves.

A detachment should also go to Lulea, the warm-weather port on the Gulf, and either deny it to the Germans or destroy it if forced to withdraw, and other detachments of about a brigade group each would seize the ports of Trondheim and Bergen from which railways ran inland to join up with the railway to Gällivare. Another group should seize the air field at Stavanger—"It's about the only decent airfield in Scandinavia"—to prevent the Germans using it, and give us an air base of our own. Before we started we should have to get the consent of the Swedes, because there was no road from Narvik to Gällivare—only their electric railway. "Winston Churchill", wrote Ironside on December 18, "is pushing for us to occupy Narvik in Norway and prevent all the iron-ore going to Germany. All his ideas are big if they are nothing else. He talks about occupying the islands and controlling the coast."

The whole matter was touched upon next day at the Supreme War Council in Paris, and Ironside made this comment in his Diary:

The Situation in Finland

The French thought that the Russians would continue into Sweden and Norway. The Swedes are much more frightened of the Russians than of the Germans. Both Russia and Germany might have their eyes upon the Swedish iron mines in the extreme north of Sweden. These mines are essential to the Germans. According to a paper made out by Fritz Thyssen, the great German industrialist, without the ore from Sweden it is possible to calculate the date upon which Germany must capitulate. Thyssen escaped from Germany and is now a refugee in Switzerland. The ore comes out through Narvik in Norway in winter and from Lulea, in the Gulf of Bothnia, in summer. How could we stop this? I said that if the ore is vital, then we ought to go all out to stop it. Unfortunately both Norway and Sweden are neutral and it would be an act of war to interfere without being asked.

Meanwhile, can Finland hold out against Russia?

December 21

We had a meeting of our Co-ordination Committee yesterday afternoon and discussed the question of the Swedish iron-ore. I told them that if the iron-ore was vital to Germany, then a small expedition to Northern Sweden would be more than desirable. It was quite possible and could be of limited scope. Winston was all out for it. I told them that here was a legitimate side-show,

unlike Salonika, Archangel and Mesopotamia. We could collect
the Force and the commander, and could limit his effort. This
portion of Northern Sweden was perhaps the most remote corner
of Europe imaginable. The man who was there was in a very
strong position and it would be very difficult to turn him out. I
have told people to get on with things, and I saw the head of the
Alpine Club with a view to collecting a lot of people able to run
on ski. Nobody is any use in such a country unless he can run on
ski in the winter, and a small body of skiers would be almost
unassailable.

On December 22, when the Finns were still holding the
Russians on the Mannherheim Line, Mr. Churchill's plan was
again considered by the Cabinet. No decision was taken, for
Norway and Sweden were still reluctant to hazard their
neutrality, but the Chiefs of Staff were instructed to consider
the implications of commitments on Scandinavian soil. They
were also instructed to plan for a landing at Narvik with a
view to rendering assistance to Finland; and to consider the
implications of a possible German occupation of Southern
Norway.

December 23

I have dictated a paper about the situation in Sweden. We must
look on the thing from its biggest aspect and have a definite plan
in front of us. There is no good in starting a line of action and then
being surprised by its implications. There is no good allowing one
Service to do something which will find the other napping. That
is what we tended to do in the last war. . . . Meanwhile the Finns
are doing well. They have even assumed the offensive. The
Russians will change their General and have another more careful go at them. . . .

Now we should be given time to see how things stand, and
perhaps the world will be given time to prepare a defence. It will
be pretty scandalous if they do nothing. It will be especially
scandalous if the U.S.A. does nothing after all their talk about
civilization and humanity.

December 24 [At Hingham in Norfolk]

I am wondering how the old Foreign Office intends to inveigle Sweden into taking part in the struggle. If she was terrified at the action Germany might take were she to let us have our peace-time contract of Bofors guns, surely she must be more terrified now. The temporary defeat of Russia by Finland may reduce the fear in Sweden for the moment. Only the very firmest and most definite offers of help will bring Sweden into the fold.

December 25

We should be able to look more into the future if we could find out what is going on between Hitler and Stalin. What are the real relations between Russia and Germany? Germany has probably always known the weakness of the Russian Army, but now the world knows it. Her prestige will have fallen considerably and the terror she inspires among the small nations must have lessened. Turkey cannot think that an attack through the Caucasus to be imminent. The solution rests with Finland. If we can keep Finland on her legs we shall certainly stop any combined advance in the Balkans. If we can transfer the scene of action to Scandinavia, then the Middle East will be quiet. We now have some months till the spring, and we ought to do something for Finland. . . . The offensive through Narvik to Lulea gives us the chance of getting a big return for very little expenditure. A chance to take the initiative and to throw a little confusion into the German councils. At the moment it is too easy for the Germans. We only parry each devilment which Hitler produces. Too easy for him.

December 26

I find the position of C.I.G.S. very much smaller than it was in the last war. Perhaps chiefly because we have the Committee of Chiefs of Staff with Newall, the airman, as Chairman by reason of his having been appointed last year, and I and the First Sea Lord are later than him. The War Cabinet deals strictly with the Committee. Also the Army is only just growing and has had no fighting to do. The other Services are already functioning. So there is little to ask the C.I.G.S. Later perhaps it will be different.

But when I think of the position occupied by Robertson and
Henry Wilson it seems to be very different. The Air Ministry
didn't exist and so there were only two strategists and not three as
now. Also the Cabinet is very much alive to the fact that they were
run more than they liked by the soldiers. They have now dug
themselves in constitutionally and have advice tendered to them
by the Chiefs of Staff Committee, which they read or do not read
according to their natures. This is all right now, but I wonder
what will happen when things become more hot. This coming
decision over the extension of the war to Sweden and Norway
may be an example. Are we going to drift into an invertebrate
show without realizing the consequences, or are we going straight
ahead with something vigorous? I believe that we have "stumbled"
on a means of upsetting the enemy. One can only call it "stumb-
ling", for we have had no steady thought. The Cabinet have at
least realized their impotence without an Army. The armament is
coming out so slowly that we cannot send any forces anywhere
in a hurry. We cannot arm any would-be allies. . . . Anything
which will get us out of this rut of passive defensive will clear the
minds of the people.

December 28

Winston Churchill rang me up [yesterday] and said that he
was in trouble over his Norwegian iron-ore. Would I come
back? . . . I came back to find that the Cabinet had made a decision
to allow Winston to do his show. I saw him at 7.30 p.m. We are
going to say to Norway and Sweden that we offer them protection against Russia. No mention of Germany. Then a few days
later they will go into Norwegian waters and interrupt the ships
carrying ore to Germany. Winston then said that Germany would
sit up and take notice. He didn't think that they could do anything against Norway and Sweden until May, and he flouted any
kind of landing in Southern Sweden in the winter. He might then
ask us to put a Force into Narvik and up to the iron fields. Down
to Lulea and then to be prepared to put up a show against a large
German Army coming in during May.

I wrote a paper once more on the Swedish position and put it in to Winston. A very small Force can grow into a large one, and one must be prepared to go all out without any stoppage when once one has decided upon a policy.

I believe that we have stumbled upon the one great stroke which is open to us to turn the tables upon the Russians and Germans. But we must play our cards very carefully. We must be able to act with surprise or we may be forestalled. For instance, unless we are prepared to go straight to Gällivare we may find the electric railway from Narvik out of order for several years at least. Without the railway we cannot go to Gällivare.

We have no war policy whatever. There is no plan to use the Navy, Army and Air Force together. The War Cabinet arrogates to itself the settling of combined strategy, and yet it produces no plan. It calls for a few straggling reports from the Chiefs of Staff as the situations arise, but it does nothing itself. The French are howling for a large Army to be developed in France—40 divisions —before anything can be done there. Is this the way to win the war? . . . The Germans are trying to make us disperse our forces and will doubtless get Russia to threaten us in the East. Now, we can make Germany disperse. It is opportunity itself to make Germany answer to our movement.

December 29

The first thing that we must consider is the attitude of Norway and Sweden. Any action *via* Narvik in the face of opposition by them is not feasible. We should have to prepare a landing, probably opposed, under severe climatic conditions. It would be a simple matter for the Norwegians and Swedes to render the railway running inland from Narvik useless to us, either by removal of rolling stock or the cutting off of electric power. *There is no road linking Narvik with Gällivare.*

Norwegian and Swedish co-operation is vital.

We must be absolutely clear that once we land a Force in Scandinavia we are committed to a war there. This war must be carried through to the end because we consider the iron-ore vital. There must be no holding back. It must be carried through despite all other demands made upon our troops and material. No half-

hearted measures will be any use. It will mean that both Norway
and Sweden will make large calls upon us for material. Our effort
will be a large one. The expedition itself may be small to begin
with, but it will grow to be a major effort.

December 30

Howard-Vyse has sent across to say that Gamelin has signified
that he is not in favour of the Narvik project. But in any case he
regards Scandinavia as a purely British sphere of interest. If they
agree to any operations there it will only be with extreme reluc-
tance. Gamelin's eyes are glued on the north-east frontier.

As regards the operations in Scandinavia, I am not frightened of
the *military* determination to carry out the operations. What I am
frightened of is the *political* determination. There will be so many
wires pulling in various directions. So many of the weak men in
the Cabinet will react to the screams of France. The French count
nothing as a British contribution which is not actually to be seen
in France. Nothing must diminish our military effort there, whatever the results of such action may be.

I must get the Cabinet to be clear upon the determination
which must be shown if we go into Scandinavia. If they all begin
their pet schemes, under the influence of the last persuasive man
they have met, we shall get undecided leading. So far, the Cabinet
has tried to keep the strategy of the war in their own hands—very
jealous of their own responsibility.

January 2, 1940

A long day. Actually $8\frac{1}{2}$ hours in Conferences and Meetings.
You cannot make war like that.

The Cabinet Meeting to consider the Scandinavian show
became a debating morning. They shied off the bigger issue and
took the smaller one of stopping the ore going to Germany.
Winston was all out to start at once without thinking much of the
consequences. He does not think that Germany will react strongly.
We, the Chiefs of Staff, thought that she would. Lord knows what
the consequences may be and we are not ready in the Army for
any hurried action. We have warned the Cabinet against this half-

cock scheme in Scandinavia. It is like putting a stick inside a hornets' nest without having provided yourself with a proper veil. It is the Dardanelles over again. Curious that Winston should have been the man who did that. It is so easy for ships to get up and start off, but when they use ports they always cry for the Army to come after them. This preliminary irritation is not the way to get the Norwegians and Swedes sweet to their allowing us to come into their country. Winston says that it will make them sweet. We are in actual fact seeking to extend the theatre of war to Scandinavia without being ready to do so. We are a couple of months behind. Maddening people, these politicians. Always snap decisions.

If Germany wishes to retaliate upon Norway, she can, in complete security from us, produce an armada at the mouth of the Oslo Fjord with the same sort of result as was produced by Italy against Albania. There is no Norwegian Defence Force. We cannot forestall the Germans in Oslo. . . .

I have sent to the Secretary of State:

> I think that the main argument against this project of the First Lord's is that it *may*, I think *will*, accelerate any contemplated German action in Scandinavia. We are not ready for this till the middle of March. Why do this for the sake of three-quarters of a million tons of ore?
>
> Landing soldiers in Norway *will* lead us still further. The occupation of Bergen means an occupation of the high ground in the snow above the town. It may mean the cutting of the railway and probably the feeding of the town by us.
>
> We must tell the French and they will be violently opposed to any acceleration of the French plans.

When I went in to see Belisha he hardly listened to the arguments. . . . In the Cabinet itself he then put up two proposals:

(i) That we should do the Narvik business and damn the consequences. All the occupation of Southern Norway by the Germans would not bother us.

(ii) That he would far rather we sent British troops to Finland.

Imperial War Museum

French concrete pill-box in the British sector on the Franco-Belgian frontier

Imperial War Museum

Some Dominion ministers inspecting a blockhouse in course of construction

Pill-box camouflaged as an extension to a barn at Mouchin

A camouflaged pill-box in France

Here I had to point out that the only way of reaching Finland was by occupying Petsamo, declaring war against the Russians and sending an unequipped expedition with no warm clothing to the Arctic regions. He is incapable of realizing the simplest problem. He does not read the papers sent to him and has them read to him a few minutes before he enters the Cabinet. . . . I cannot get him to consider the bigger questions. He did not read my paper on the strategy of the war and had no idea what I had said.

Winston of course was very persistent and the Cabinet was definitely in favour of carrying out this plan.

Dinner with Amery in the evening. . . . He had a fund of stories about Lloyd George and Henry Wilson and characters of the last war. Nobody now seemed to have the impetuous spirit that existed then. He told one of H. W.'s stories of a talk in the garden of 10 Downing Street. Something had gone wrong with the French and they had to be bucked up. Milner couldn't go and Lloyd George asked H. W. to go. He said that he would go that night. "Good Lord, that's not quick enough," said L. G. "Go yesterday."

There is so very little of the "Go yesterday" spirit now in the Cabinet. Of course, we haven't had any Blitzkrieg to ginger us up.

January 5

A very short Cabinet Meeting which was a welcome relief. We do talk a lot of nonsense these days. I have no further orders about our bigger expedition to Narvik, but the smaller one of stopping the iron-ore seems to be pretty well ready. It means that if Germany reacts violently to our stopping the ore and invades Norway we may have to send three battalions to Trondheim, Bergen and Stavanger. But I think that this is most unlikely. I think there will be a lot of chat, but you never know. It will attract attention to iron-ore in general and the mines at Gällivare in particular. All the preparations made by the Germans in the Baltic for embarking troops are undoubtedly for this. We should upset the Germans thoroughly if we pushed in a Brigade to Gällivare and occupied all Northern Sweden. . . . The effect will be electrical, but the Germans cannot do much till May in the Gulf of Bothnia. The difficult thing is to gauge the attitude of the Swedes and, in a lesser degree, of the Norwegians.

What a curious thing it is that we have no more strategic ideas than building up an enormous army in France, protecting England, and waiting to see what the Germans are going to do. A parlous state of affairs. The Army we have in France is really largely a militia. It is untrained. . . . Politicians think because we have the men we have a trained army.

January 6

At 8 p.m. last night when I went in to see Belisha's secretary I was told that Belisha had resigned. I had no inkling that it was coming. Changing horses in mid-stream is always a bad thing, but I must say that I had a feeling of intense relief on the whole. The man had failed utterly in war to run his show and we should have had a disaster. He is much better out of it. Oliver Stanley I just know . . . although I know nothing about his energy and determination. It will be much easier to get on with him.

The papers this morning are all headed with sensational lines: "Belisha and the Generals", "First Class Surprise", "Unaccountable" and so on. There has not been any cabal at all over Belisha. But both at the War Office and the G.H.Q. in France there will be intense relief over his going. Nobody had any confidence in him. Also the Secret Session must have shown the P.M. that the House was not in Belisha's favour. Now comes the question as to what I can do. Shall I be able to go over to France, because Stanley is in bed with 'flu? . . .

I have sent in a paper to the S. of S. [Oliver Stanley] upon this coming Narvik show.

With reference to this stopping of the Narvik ore by the Navy at an early date, the important facts to realize appear to be the following:

(i) The First Lord is anxious to carry out this project in order to do something definite, and he feels that this definite advantage may be lost in waiting for the greater project of seizing the Gällivare mines.

(ii) The Chiefs of Staff have recommended against this action because they feel it will gain little (at the maximum million tons of ore) and will jeopardize the larger project. The major project *may* be decisive, the Narvik ore stopping *will* not be so.

(iii) It is practically impossible to get ready for the major project till late March. Any hurried occupation of Narvik and Gällivare is bad strategy.

(iv) The consequences of stopping the Narvik ore have been pointed out by the Chiefs of Staff. It was the opinion of the Cabinet that the chance of Germany reacting as they thought possible was not great. But they still think that landings in a foreign country can seldom be easily liquidated.

On January 6 the Norwegian Government was informed that France and Britain would send warships into Norwegian territorial waters to stop Germany using the sea lanes, but the Norwegian protests were so violent that six days later the Cabinet decided to shelve Mr. Churchill's scheme for the present.

January 7

People were calling us up till late in the night to ask what Hore-Belisha's resignation meant. It all came as a surprise, and so people wondered.

The papers filled with the event, all the "gutter" press full of the "Belisha Scandal". One paper even said that Belisha had been turned out by the aristocratic Generals because he had tried to democratize the Army. Little do they know what a superficial creature he is. One always makes a hero of someone one doesn't know. I hope that the wretched thing will not have any repercussions upon the B.E.F. That is the main thing to remember.

We came across in *Codrington* in thick fog and comfortably up to Arras, to find Gort installed in his château. I found Gort worried as to how this resignation would affect us all. Apparently they were all certain here that Belisha would go. They were more in touch with the political situation than we were. Victor War-render, the Financial Secretary, who was staying here, told me that Belisha knew that he had to go at 3 p.m. on Thursday. He certainly showed no signs of it at the Army Council that we held at 5 p.m. that day. The P.M. had wished to announce it that day, but Belisha had insisted on waiting until 10 a.m. next day to consider the matter.

January 11

I take it that sooner or later there will be big changes in the Government. War Cabinets always change. It seems ridiculous that none of the Liberals are included, and above all, the Labour people. You cannot run a war, so largely a matter of material, without the active and willing co-operation of the men who make the material. Apparently Labour will not work with Chamberlain, and are remaining out of office till he goes. The people have great confidence in the P.M. and it will take a great revulsion of feeling to get him out.

As far as we are concerned, we have now the great difficulty of letting the people know the state of the Army. We have a shell, both in material and training, due to many of the things Belisha did. When it is discovered, there might be a row. The blame may well fall upon the soldiers, for the people will say that had Belisha remained, he would have seen that things were right. It depends upon how soon things get out. Soldiers may fall with the Governments. I realized that fully when I consented to take over the duties of C.I.G.S. I had no option but to take over.

January 12

My first day with the new Secretary of State . . . [Oliver] Stanley had already read up all the papers on Scandinavia and I had about half an hour with him. He was then able to take the thing at the War Cabinet without any further coaching.

Eventually, it was decided not to do the Narvik violation of Norwegian territorial waters, much to the disgust of Winston. Two factors turned the P.M. from the project. First the violent reaction of Sweden at the idea, and second a wire from Australia expressing mistrust in the advisability of doing anything so violent. . . .

In the afternoon Ling [the British Military Attaché] arrived from Finland with a letter from Mannerheim. We now have a good picture of what has happened and what his ideas are. They have done very well, but his men are getting very tired. He expects another attack during the next few weeks and then to be very hard pressed in May. He wants material now and men, up to 30,000 volunteers from all countries. The bombing of Finnish towns has been continuous, and though they have shot down some hundreds of bombers they cannot keep this up.

I wrote a note about the timing of all this Scandinavian show, which shows how difficult it all is. If we wait till May, we shall be too late in Gällivare and the Germans will have occupied it.

CHAPTER XIV

The Western Front

ON JANUARY 7 Ironside had travelled to France to be invested with the Grand Cross of the Legion of Honour. "Poor Gort", he wrote next day, "looked careworn and troubled over Belisha and the harm he could do to the B.E.F. Warrender said that he looked ten years older than he did four months ago. Of course it is worrying. Gort has never been alone before and he feels the isolation of high command. His staff are all very loyal to him and are devoted to him. I told him to come on leave as quickly as he could and go up to Holkham. There he would be away from all political troubles. Dill has been on leave and could easily take over from him for ten days."

January 8

We had the presentation of the Grand Cross of the Legion of Honour to myself and Gort. The French know how to run these shows so much better than we do. A company of Zouaves and a company of the Welsh Guards. It was curious to see the enormous Guardsmen filing past to the tune of *Pan, Pan*, a quickstep, many of the little Zouaves wearing the new Croix de Guerre.

The court, as it is called, was opened by Gamelin coming on parade, drawing his sword and raising it in the air and shouting "Ouvrez le ban". When finished, he shouted "Fermez le ban". He touched us twice on the shoulder and then gave the accolade.

As the French paper put it, "Alors, le géant anglais s'inclina pour rendre possible l'accolade".

It all went very well and all the sixty journalists of the B.E.F. were there to report and take photographs. I don't think that a British General could have done the thing gracefully. I know that I should have felt a fool.

In the evening Gamelin took Ironside by special train to Entzheim, near Strasbourg, which they reached at 8 a.m. next morning.

January 8

Here we were met by General Bourret, the Fifth Army commander. A short stout man with white hair and moustache. I thought that he was well up to his work though obviously well over 60. General Dentz, commander of the 12th Corps, was also there. A great big dark man, probably about 60 or slightly under. Very live and amusing. He told me that his father had left Alsace to avoid service in the German Army and had never gone back there. Dentz had gone back after 1918 and now found himself in command in Alsace. I thought him very well up to his job.

We were taken to Fort Hoche, south of Strasbourg, and here we put on French tin hats and had a look across the Rhine at the German casemates all along the right bank of the Rhine, many of them flooded. I thought this portion of the line unassailable. A great river and then dozens of streams running through bushy country, interlined with enormous barbed wire entanglements running in all directions. Unreconnoitrable and even difficult to photograph from the air. Concrete pill-boxes all over the place. The French had at least four lines of defence.

We then motored through Strasbourg. An extraordinary thing to see a town of 200,000 people evacuated to a man. Practically only a few gendarmes at the corners. I at once thought of homeless dogs and cats, but I am glad to say that I saw very few. No soldiers. An occasional woman coming back escorted by a gendarme or two with perhaps a handcart to fetch her things. I was told that there had been practically no robbery.

It gave one a feeling of sadness to see such a desert with many of the shop-windows containing women's hats and coats and shoes. All the foodstuffs had been taken away.

The Cathedral had been de-churched, or whatever the term is —secularized? We went in and found it a shell with the windows and statues all covered up. Some of the more precious glass had been taken away. I wondered what the effect of this would be on the Bosche. Would he refrain from bombing or shelling it? I doubted it, if the French used the roads, which they must do if they fight here. But the scene seemed peaceful and Kehl bridge still stood, neither side having attempted to cut it.

No aeroplanes flying about.

Dentz gave us lunch at his H.Q. A very good one. His A.D.C., a most attractive young Infantry Officer, stood up and recited us the menu and then wished us, "Bon appétit, messieurs". We could never have done that.

In fact, I saw a great change among the French Officers all through. They were all well-shaven in and out of the trenches. None of the two days' growth one saw so often in 1914–18. I saw some of the young men in the ranks growing a sort of Berber beard round the edge of their chins, with the rest clean shaven. Not attractive. But the French soldiers were all better looking in the way of fitness and cleanliness. The "poilu" has so far not appeared. They are all clean-shaven like our men.

We made an attempt to reach the great work in the Maginot Line of Hochwald, but failed. The roads were covered with ice. A thaw and then a frost had made them dangerous even with chains on the wheels and sand thrown on them. One car turned completely round and nearly crashed. "Ravitaillement" had practically ceased. So we left Pfaffenhofen by auto-rail and to our wagon-lits at Sarreunion for the night.

January 10

A long full day.

We were met in the morning by General Prételat, commanding the 2nd Group of Armies. A man of the Weygand type and resembling him very much. A man of 65 but very young and active and the best General I saw. Very well dressed. General Recuin, commanding the Fourth Army, looked thin and old on this bitterly cold day. He didn't strike me as being physically up to the standard of the others. . . .

The Fourth Army front is mostly inundations made by barraging the Saar south of Sarreguemines. There was more work going on here than in the other sectors. The pill-boxes were set in irregular lines and the enormous wire entanglements ran in all directions, dividing up the field of battle so that any advance would be confused as to direction. The fields of wire were all across open fields and I thought an attack very difficult.

After seeing a fort in the Maginot Line, typical of them all, though not so big as the Hochwald work, I came to the conclusion that the French would not construct a Maginot Line if they started again. It is necessary to have irregular field defences, and this the Maginot Line did not have. Had the Germans attacked immediately they would have found no defence in depth. This the French are putting in at top speed. They have had four months' respite and have done two things:

(i) Pushed out a forward defence in front of the Maginot Line.
(ii) Provided depth behind it.

I put it to Gamelin that the great difficulty in this coming war would be the assembling of a great army ready to assault. The Siegfried and Maginot Lines are at most places fourteen miles apart. Each side has troops pushed out some seven miles in front of their main line. Patrols move about long distances into the outpost line of the other. With the "air" alert, no preparations could be made for a surprise. It would be a matter of months and steady siege-work to bring up guns for bombardment. Nothing could be done in secret. An enormous system of trenches would inevitably grow up in front of each of the main lines and we should get back to the old trench warfare with an immensely strong main line behind.

The actual fort we saw was a marvel of engineering. It contained some five hundred men under an Infantry Captain. It provided about a battery of gun-fire and a company of Infantry fire with anti-tank guns. It had all kinds of packed ammunition underground and could best be described as an anchored man o' war. Gas-proof, and with immense power of resistance, it still seemed to me vulnerable in misty weather, where no observation could be obtained. It had to have its front defence well in front of it. Its cost seemed to me excessive for the security and the fire it offered. I think Gamelin agreed with me, though he wouldn't say so openly.

"To make each fort", wrote Ironside's military assistant soon afterwards, "the French had scooped out the inside of a hill and had made a concrete house of several storeys inside. There was a magazine for ammunition, store rooms, kitchen, dining-room, living-quarters, laundry, and, at the top, the levels from which the weapons were fired, all connected up by lifts and lighted by electricity made on the spot. Periscopes gave all-round fields of vision. At the very top was a disappearing field gun. It was pushed up to fire and brought down to load and lay, without a man exposing himself. The air pressure inside the fort was kept greater than that outside, so no gas could get in, and there were means of expelling the gases from the fort. The fort was ventilated and air-conditioned. Three forts could fire on one area so that if one fort was knocked out two others could still cover the ground. What was remarkable, however, was the small number of weapons in use for the large size of the garrison.

"Forts, accommodating from five hundred to one thousand men, varied in size according to the size of the hill. To keep the men fit and well trained, only one-third of the number was kept in the fort, the other two-thirds being outside exercising and training. They were active, fit and keen, and seemed more suitable for the field army than for fortress troops, who might well have been older and less fit men."

January 10 (continued)

The men seemed happy inside and were very keen on their fortress and took a pride in it. They didn't seem to suffer from being underground, and in this peace-time they were up for several hours for their exercise. The air seemed good and currents of air could be driven through it to purify it every now and then. The most elaborate arrangements had been made to catch all the fumes from the guns and ejected cartridges and to drive them outside. Food, water and sleeping arrangements were all good. Each fort came under the command of the Divisional Commander in the sector. Observation could be duplicated from other forts. Still, I thought these forts needed the field army to protect them more than ever.

We then went down to Kédange and visited the British Brigade under Gammell. The Norfolks, Borders and Royal Scots. A very good show. . . . We then went right up and had a look at the country in front of the outposts. One could see now there was a good chance of patrolling. The brigades only stay down a fortnight and it is too short a time for the study of the line and the ways of the enemy opposite them.[1] Each battalion has five days in the line. I was glad to see that they were keeping a careful account of what they did to hand on to the next brigade. All the French spoke well of the British and were loud in their praise of our equipment and transport. We do things on a much more lavish scale than the French and they must envy us all our comforts, rations and ration-cigarettes, not to speak of superior pay. . . .

I also saw General Condé, Commander of the Third Army, a tall bony man. A Gunner and more staid than some of the others. He seemed to be over 60, but strong and well. All the Generals treated Gamelin with respect, though they laughed and joked with him. They were certainly not overawed by him and I thought their relations with him very happy indeed.

I tried in my mind to sum up the state of the French Army and its fighting value. I must say that I saw nothing amiss with it on the surface. The Generals are all tried men, if a bit old from our view-point. None of them showed any lack of confidence. None of the liaison officers say that they have seen any lack of morale

---

[1] The idea was that as many brigades as possible should have a turn in the line, and then whole divisions should come in. The 51st Division was in when the Germans attacked in 1940.

after the long wait they have had, after the excitement of mobilization. I say to myself that we shall not know until the first clash comes. In 1914 there were many officers and men who failed, but old Joffre handled the situation with great firmness. Will the *Blitzkrieg*, when it comes, allow us to rectify things if they are the same? I must say I don't know. But I say to myself that we must have confidence in the French Army. It is the only thing in which we can have confidence. Our own Army is just a little one, and we are dependent upon the French. We have not even the same fine Army we had in 1914. All depends on the French Army and we can do nothing about it, but it is up to us to back it up and not to deny it. The only thing I can say is that the men are not doing the amount of work in digging-in which I should like to have seen. Gamelin is not downhearted and has breathed not one word of worry to me. I shouldn't have expected that he would. He is very anxious that the Bosches should attack and I think he would welcome a trial of strength. The French "air" is frightfully weak, and especially in fighter aircraft. Again we can do nothing about it.

Gort has given me no inkling that he finds anything serious amiss in the French Army. None of his staff have even whispered doubts. Gammell, the British brigadier I found in the French line, made no mention of any doubts. The issue is in the lap of the gods and we can do nothing to alter things. We must remain loyal to the French.

> On January 10, while Ironside was in France, a German aircraft made a forced landing in Belgium. Its pilot had been flying to Cologne and had lost his way. The other occupant of the plane was a German staff officer on whom was found a set of plans for an early German invasion of Belgium. He tried to burn them, but was not quick enough, and they were seized by the Belgian soldiers who arrested him. The Belgian Government took fright, and became convinced that a German invasion was imminent.

January 13 [London]

In the night we began to get news from Belgium that the Germans intended an attack through Holland and Belgium. . . .

It seems pretty definite. . . . We rang up the French, who reported that they were more sure than ever that something was about to be started.

I started thinking and came to the conclusion that things might be going to come. It is freezing hard and conditions are good for an advance through the Low Countries unless the thaw comes. It is possible to let the water away from the frozen dykes, so that the ice may crash under a weight, and tanks may well fall in. But I think that the limit of the advance should be north of the Meuse, for severe weather in the Ardennes might well make the roads impassable without a lot of work.

January 14 [Sunday]

At midnight last night our Ambassador in Brussels was asked to call on the Belgian Foreign Minister and was told that they expected to be attacked this morning. He said that "he expected H.M.'s Government and the French Government to give full support". I was woken up at 4 a.m. with the news and we set all our preparations in motion. Nothing happened.

The French and British Armies were alerted and closed up to the frontier ready at four hours' notice to put Plan D into effect. Ironside rang up the Prime Minister at Chequers (nearly all the Cabinet went to the country at week-ends) but was told that he was in bed, very tired, and could not be disturbed. Ironside rang up again later and said he had very important news and asked for the Cabinet to be summoned as soon as possible. A skeleton War Cabinet was ordered for 12.30, the earliest time at which these few members could be got together.

Meanwhile the French were on the telephone. Grand Quartier Général said they intended to move into Belgium at the request of the Belgians, but would not do so without the B.E.F. Would we give orders for the B.E.F. to move in with them? They were told that only the Cabinet could give permission, and that they were meeting at 12.30. The French seemed disappointed and said it was urgent. Gamelin, as

Supreme Commander, could order his troops to move without waiting for Government sanction, and they could not understand that the British C.I.G.S. had not the same authority. Ironside's diary continues:

I told Chatfield this morning that it was intolerable that the Belgians should treat us like this—refusing to have any conversations so that we can concert operations, and then screaming for help. There is no doubt that the Belgians thought they were going to be attacked, for they recalled 40,000 men from leave and various duties. I have sent a wire to Gamelin asking him to bring matters with the Belgians to a head.

We have to undertake a movement from a prepared position across a very flat plain to lines of obstacles which have in no way been prepared. All to help a country to resist invasion, and a country which is so terrified of infringing its own neutrality that it will make no preparations. We risk an encounter battle for the sake of Belgium. It is indeed to our advantage to save the Belgian divisions from being destroyed, so that we may incorporate them in our Army. And we keep the main force of the German Air Force away from possible aerodromes on the Dutch and Belgian coasts. . . .

The Germans have 44 divisions opposite Belgium and Luxembourg, and they undoubtedly have an attack mounted. Nobody can tell how the Belgian troops will stand up to a German attack or how long they would be able to resist. The weakest part of their line is the Albert Canal which faces Holland to the north. If this goes, then the whole of the back of the Liège and Meuse positions is exposed, and the Belgian defence collapses. . . . Unless we can come up pretty close behind the Belgians I cannot believe that they would stand any heavy bombardment. We must advance methodically.

I had a talk with Stanley this morning and found him very quiet and steady and ready to listen. . . . We had a War Cabinet at 12.30 p.m. and discussed for a long time the Belgian situation.

[Admiral] Keyes had reported that the King [of the Belgians] had said to him that he would consult his Cabinet as to the Allied

Army coming into Belgium. He thought that we must sign certain conditions:

(i) No separate peace.
(ii) No *pourparlers* without the co-operation of Belgium and the assurance that Belgium and her Colonies would be restored as they are now.
(iii) The financial and economic restoration of Belgium.

The P.M. reacted violently and said that the Belgians had no right to put such conditions under the stress of attack. That he thought the Belgians would never ask us in till they were actually attacked. . . .

> "The French", wrote Ironside's Military Assistant, "rang up about the result of the Cabinet meeting. They were told that the Cabinet had come to no decision, but that there was to be another meeting that evening. The wasted time and the possibility of losing this opportunity of going into Belgium made them extremely angry."

It was decided that I should talk with Gamelin at once. The Prime Minister was down at Chequers and telephoned a bit, but he did not seem taken with the military value of speed and wanted a full Cabinet to decide. They have always prated so much of a Cabinet being able to assemble so quickly that it disgusted me to find that it couldn't be assembled. Halifax doesn't reach London from his home till 8 p.m. and in this fog he will probably be late.

> The Cabinet met at 6 p.m., sat for some hours, and still came to no decision about a move into Belgium. Much of that night G.Q.G. were on the telephone. Gamelin himself came on the line and was almost speechless with rage that the great opportunity would be missed through the British Government's delay in letting the B.E.F. move in with the French Army. Next morning the Cabinet met yet again.

January 14 (continued)

We had another War Cabinet with the P.M. in the chair, and eventually sent off a telegram to the Belgians practically offering what they wanted with the full agreement of the French. The P.M. seemed to be of opinion that we should never be asked into Belgium until the last minute. I reiterated to Chamberlain the fact that if we could gain some hours on the Germans we should have a great advantage. He is most unmilitary. He wanted to know if Gamelin thought it was more advantageous to go forward at the risk of the Germans starting an attack to remaining where we were. Gamelin has replied that it is better for morale and militarily as well. I pointed out to him [the Prime Minister] that we ought not to risk another country being overrun. . . . Our troops are all tied up on the frontier ready to go at a moment's notice.

January 15

A quiet night and no German attack. The Belgians are still very nervous. . . . I am now busy putting Stanley in the picture. He picks it up quickly. . . . A wire in from Gamelin that we may miss a heaven-sent opportunity for improving our position militarily if we cannot get Belgium to let us in.

> Early on the 16th the Cabinet met again, and agreed to the B.E.F. advancing with the French into Belgium. G.Q.G. were at once informed by telephone. They replied that it was too late. The Belgians had just withdrawn their offer.

January 16

The Belgians have now answered "no" to our efforts to get into Belgium. It is not surprising as they know we shall make a supreme effort to get forward. The scare seems to have died away. Old Chamberlain may be a wise old thing, but he is not seized with the military position. He is never in close touch with his military advisers. Daladier is. All our troops are now back in their old places. . . .

The difference between Chamberlain and Churchill during this little crisis is most marked. Churchill, fully seized with the military value of going to Belgium, is enthusiastic and full of energy. Chamberlain negative and angry at Belgium making conditions.

Mr. Hore-Belisha with General Gort and General Brooke at the front

Mr. Hore-Belisha with the C.I.G.S. and the Army Council

General Ironside, Air Marshal Sir Cyril Newall and Admiral Sir Dudley Pound

CHAPTER XV

Cabinet Indecisions: The Collapse of Finland

January 17

We had a more interesting debate in the War Cabinet. Winston was most emphatic over this ore question. Ships were pouring down from Narvik and doubtless in May the port of Lulea will be opened. Neither Norway nor Sweden were taking any steps to prevent the ore leaving their country. They were thereby lengthening the war. . . . The Prime Minister also agreed, saying that he was desperately anxious to get hold of the Gällivare iron field. It would definitely tip the war over in our favour. I put the military situation to them again. Finland being overrun in May, the Germans advancing into Sweden to seize Gällivare, and we being unable to do anything. . . . Halifax is now going to meet the Swedish Minister and try and frighten him. Winston's suggestion that a very strong note be sent was turned down. We are now to consider a plan for helping Finland in the spring.

January 19

We had a poorish War Cabinet. Nobody will take the Scandinavian thing in its proper order. Geographical knowledge is sadly lacking. I cannot get anybody to understand that snow conditions stop the mobility of any man on foot and that snow conditions disappear very quickly with the coming of spring. We have to have two things before any action can be taken:

(i) Agreement with the French.

o   209

(ii) Conversations with the Swedes.

No one likes to face facts and it is the business of the Service Chiefs of Staff to represent these hard facts to the enthusiastic politicians. The civilian plan-maker is apt to brush aside any unfortunate difficulties.

January 25

The French observers in Finland seem to think that Mannerheim can last out a couple of months, but no longer. A little bit more pessimistic than we are.[1] Pure weight of shells and manpower must wear Mannerheim down. And here we are doing nothing very much. Talking and theorizing. . . .

We are going on preparing for intervention in Sweden, but I can see very little chance of the Scandinavian countries asking us to come in. Like all neutrals, they want to wait till the last minute. Sweden is much more terrified of Russia than of Germany and would prefer to call Germany in, were she to fall into danger.

> Ironside had by now earmarked the British troops for Norway: two Territorial divisions and the 5th Regular Division from France. He had sent a party of officers and men to Chamonix to be taught skiing, and had collected the necessary transport.

January 25 (continued)

We finished up the day with a Chiefs of Staff meeting which went on till 11.30 p.m. considering the Scandinavian business. I am afraid that we shall never get a chance of carrying it out. Our diplomats showed no signs of preparing the situation—the French talk of "making" an opportunity.

Our War Cabinet is quite incapable of running any strategy. None of them, except Winston, know anything about even elementary strategy. They are dilatory and will not take a decision. We want a War Cabinet of 3 or 4 at the most. I suppose it is the Prime Minister who is so unmilitary which is at the bottom of it all. . . .

[1] Finland surrendered to Russia on March 12.

The German Army is now concentrated in great strength in a central position, making it extremely difficult to attack. Every large detachment it can be induced to make will assist us when the time comes to make our decisive attack, without which the war is unlikely to end.

The Gällivare project presents the first chance of upsetting the German's plans and making him disperse. . . . An advance by us in Scandinavia, if it can be brought to pass, will create a great diversion of German force at small cost, prevent Germany from carrying out her preconceived plan and cause her to improvise, an art in which she does not excel.

January 27

There are collections of [German] ships in the Baltic for troops to go to Scandinavia. . . . We have been harried from pillar to post over this Scandinavian business and, as far as we can see, the diplomats have made very little effort to "make" an opportunity in Scandinavia. All the cards are against us in playing with these neutrals. Germany does not mean to respect them if it so suits her, and we must respect them. I have made out a final paper for the Supreme War Council which lays down the whole business for them. . . .

1. *Germany's Grand Strategy*

In considering the Scandinavian problem, it is first necessary to place ourselves, figuratively speaking, in the minds of the German High Command, and to attempt to get at what they are now thinking and how they are likely to fight this war.

The Germans are unlikely to launch a heavy attack on the Western Front until they have made sure of the two commodities vital to the prosecution of a major land and air offensive—namely, iron and oil. Germany may have decided to make certain of the first of these essentials by seizing the Gällivare iron-ore fields, as soon as the Baltic becomes free of ice, and to risk any temporary interruption of supplies that might ensue. Having done this, she may then turn to the southeast for her oil.

2. *British Policy*

We should not, if it can by any means be avoided, leave Germany undisturbed to carry out her long-term plans, which would enable her to build up her forces for an ultimate major offensive against Great Britain and France in the west. Intervention in Scandinavia is our first and best chance of wresting the initiative from her, and, in fact, of shortening the war. Our policy should be directed towards creating such an opportunity for intervention, and our military plans should include preparations to enable us to seize any such opportunity at once.

Equally, however, we must be prepared to intervene in the Balkans, in case the Germans should go that way. In other words, we must make preparations for operations both in Scandinavia and in the Balkans. It is not, of course, suggested that the Allies could operate substantial forces offensively in both areas simultaneously; but neither could Germany.

3. *German Air Threat against Scandinavia*

The air defences of Norway and Sweden are totally inadequate to meet the overwhelming scale of air attack which Germany could bring to bear on those countries. . . . The air forces which we could send to Southern Scandinavia would, owing to lack of operational facilities, be limited to a very small force of fighters. There remains the question of indirect assistance. As to this, attention should be invited to the possibility of making a declaration in advance that if Germany "took the gloves off" and bombed the cities of Scandinavia as she did those of Poland we should immediately retaliate on the cities of Germany.

4. *Finland*

The whole problem of a Scandinavian enterprise is closely linked up with the question of assistance to Finland. The fate of Finland is certainly a most important factor. . . .

Personally, I give ourselves practically no hope of getting Scandinavia in with us. That the same state of affairs will exist in

the winter of 1940–41 is hardly to be hoped for, and the war will
have continued for another year. I feel that now is the moment,
however ill-prepared we are in trained troops.

January 28

A long meeting of the Chiefs of Staff over Finland. . . . I had a
certain amount of difficulty in persuading the Inter-Allied Commission to go over to Paris the next day and get down to it. We
are the most unmilitary machine that can well be imagined. All
the Cabinet away for the week-end and very little of that quick
assembly that they talked of. . . . The stupid Cabinet is delaying
again and again our main "Strategy" paper and the aid in Scandinavia. They may have lots to do in other things, but a War
Cabinet should not have people on it cluttered up with the duties
of great departments.

January 29

Oliver Stanley is very good about reading papers and is very
understanding. He is quite ready to take responsibility and one
can trust him. . . .

The Cabinet has not taken the Scandinavian paper and I see no
likelihood of its being taken till Thursday or so. They are to have
a Supreme War Cabinet on the 5th, but I should like it before, so
as to follow quickly after on talks with the French staff. As
Daladier says, time is slipping on and we are doing nothing but
talk. . . . Winston is mad to start something. . . . I wish this
wretched Cabinet of ours to take my paper on Major Strategy
and look at each new idea from that point of view.

January 31

We met Gamelin, Darlan and Vuillemin at 10 a.m. at Vincennes.
After a long explanation of the points of view of both sides we
came to the conclusions [that] the direct support of Finland is most
desirable. . . . The French suggestion is a landing at Petsamo [in
the very North of Finland].

These operations do not involve the neutrality of Norway and
Sweden, but they do involve the danger of war with Russia with

all its complications. . . . [They] are no help to us in getting at the Gällivare ore-fields. They are directed against Russia and not against Germany. They involve the violation of Norwegian neutrality, in that a base must be established in some lonely Norwegian Fiord. . . . Would it not be more efficacious to demand from Norway and Sweden, in the name of the League of Nations, passage through Narvik to Lulea and Tornea? We should then ensure passage of troops and stores *via* the very place we wish to prevent the Germans taking—namely Gällivare.

February 1

We had a final meeting with the French. We now have a picture of the operations to show to the Cabinet. A military gamble without any political prize. That is how I should describe the thing. It is for the Cabinet to say whether it fills the bill. . . .

We had a War Cabinet at 5.30 p.m. where they decided to turn down the Petsamo project as we advised. They then came to the decision that we ought to do something, even if it were [only] to divert from ourselves the odium of having allowed Finland to be crushed. A demand is to be made to Norway and Sweden for permission under the League of Nations to pass troops through to the help of Finland. I think that we shall probably be refused, because there is so much terror over the action that Germany can take. We had one of the few effective debates I have yet seen in the Cabinet. Winston, for once, took our side and vetoed the Petsamo project.

We are all to go off to Paris again on Sunday, and I suppose back again on Wednesday. I wonder what attitude the French will take?

February 4

Flying was again impossible and so the whole party—Chamberlain, the three Service Ministers, and Halifax—came down by special train to Dover and over in the *Basilisk*. Almost a spring afternoon with the sun shining and quite calm. We discovered a great round mine with horns floating in front of us and this we eventually sank by gun fire, after having failed with a machine-gun. All the party were like school boys out on a trip instead of statesmen going to settle an important strategic move. We came into Paris about 5 p.m., having started at 10 a.m.—a loss of perhaps four and a half hours on the journey by air—and I found myself invited to dinner at the Embassy. All men and some twenty in all. Gamelin always refuses to dine out, and so we only had Darlan and Vuillemin there. A very good dinner and much too much to eat in consequence.

February 5

We started the Supreme War Council at 10 a.m. and took the Scandinavian and Finnish projects. Daladier with his foot in a special boot was very genial and amusing. We had come to the following conclusions in about one and a half hours. Everybody purring with pleasure. I wondered if we should all be in the same state if we had had a little adversity to touch us up. All is plain sailing. The French are handing an operation over to us and are sitting back pretty. But it couldn't well be otherwise because we know so much more about the North. We agreed:

   (i) That it would be a defeat for us to allow the Finns to be crushed.

   (ii) That we must do something as quickly as possible.

   (iii) That we must demand permission to enter Norway and Sweden to succour Finland.

   (iv) That if we couldn't gain the acquiescence of the Norwegians and Swedes we must try the Petsamo project.

The essence of the plan is to pass a strong force through Narvik and Trondheim. We are supplying two divisions and two strong brigades, while the French supply a brigade of Chasseurs Alpins, two battalions of the Légion and four battalions of Poles. This will all pass across the Narvik–Lulea line and we shall sit down in strength upon our L. of C., making sure of Gällivare and Boden. I can see a whole host of objections from the Scandinavians, but what I most fear is a passive resistance—a strike amongst the officials of the railway.

If we bring this off we shall have carried out a great *coup*, which will upset the even tenor of the German preparations. It may bring in Norway and Sweden. I don't doubt that it will have an electrifying effect upon the Germans. They will have to come out in the open and declare themselves for or against the Russians.

One is almost frightened at the boldness of the plan, knowing what slender means one has at the moment to carry it out. We must see that we are politically strong, and that we remain quite cynical about anything except stopping the iron-ore. I am sure that if France is secure—and I think she is—we could not possibly create a better diversion than this, and even if we were driven out we should not have been there in vain, for we should have prevented the Germans from getting any ore for a year.

I ratted from dinner at the Quai d'Orsay, having eaten and drunk far too much already. I had a quiet dinner of vegetables by myself at the Meurice, and thought of our successful day. May the operations come off and may they be as successful.

February 8 [London]

Reports are not so good from the Mannerheim Line in Finland. I am wondering what will happen if [it] bursts before the date upon which we can act. The Cabinet will try to rush me and I shall have to resist.

February 12

Snow again to-day and bitterly cold. . . . Meanwhile, the Swedes are getting more and more frightened of the coming of the Russians. The effect of our rash guarantee to the Poles shows itself in the fact that neutrals do not trust us. . . . The poor Finnish General Enskell with a fresh telegram from Mannerheim. They have no ammunition for their 76's and say that they must have some field guns and ammunition within a fortnight. We simply cannot send anything. Our training regiments are down to six training guns instead of twenty-four and the divisions get their service guns some three weeks only before going to France. I simply cannot strip them any more. We may be fighting hard in March. Enskell said that the Russians have given out that they intend to finish the campaign before April, cost what it may. These demands are heartbreaking to refuse.

February 15

We get closer and closer to this Finnish business and I can see nothing like permission from the Swedes to land. The old Foreign Office is as dilatory as ever. All perfect politeness and nothing done. We are now changing our Minister in Finland and have already changed the man in Sweden. But it is all too late to be much use to us.

Everybody knows that we are preparing, but I am hoping that it is being put down to Finland and that the method of our approach is not known. You cannot keep anything secret. I don't know whether the politicians or the Press are the worst. . . .

If the Finn field-guns had enough stuff to fire they could break up the Soviet attacks before they ever reached the lines. They are struggling to eke out their supply till the thaw comes. The U.S.A. has now hundreds of 75's parked in her old parks and not used in her Army. . . . These they will not allow to go to the Finns. It is difficult to follow such a mentality, but there it is clear enough. . . .

Hitler might, and I think would, react to our occupation of Gällivare and we might upset his manœuvres completely. . . . We have worked out our plans in very great detail and I am sure that we can do the landing.

February 16

I can find no reaction in Sweden to German movements to stop us going into Narvik. The whole project must be well known by this time. With the coast of North Germany iced up, she can do very little at the moment and must be watching us like a cat does a mouse. Our date is getting closer. We have to begin loading our stores on March 1 and the first troops sail on the 15th, under a month from now. All we can hope is that the frost will continue as long as possible and that the Finns will go on holding out, though the crisis remains. It may make the Swedes more terrified of the Russian advance when they know that the Germans cannot come to help them.

An interesting example of military timing. I think that we have it all worked out, but the weak link is the diplomatic pressure. I can see very little of that. . . .

I was strongly attacked this morning by Winston over the number of vehicles that we have put down for the expedition in Scandinavia. It works out as 100,000 men and 11,000 vehicles. I pointed out to him that the British Army was so organized and to alter the organization on the eve of departing upon an expedition was hazardous. I have ordered an analysis of what all these things are and I propose to send this in to the members of the Cabinet. It is really intolerable that such stupid things should come up at a War Cabinet. One cannot escape Winston's searchings. He cannot understand that a modern army requires much more ammunition for all its multitudinous weapons.

I was interested to see how not one single other member of the War Cabinet said a word. They sat quite glum while Winston let fly. He is such an impetuous creature that he is led away. Immediately after he had wanted to cut down our impedimenta he started a scheme for sending mines across the Swedish railways to the Gulf of Bothnia—with all the difficulties of finding men to unload the ships, the transport to take the mines to the railway, the loading and unloading at each end on the railway and finally the transference to the ships that go out to lay the mines. Somebody said the other day that Winston required a Man Friday to be with him always to check up his schemes. . . . I cannot get my big paper upon the strategy of the war brought before the War Cabinet. They all shy off it.

February 18

The Swedes have sent more A.A. guns and field-guns [to the Finns] and are now evidently terrified of what is going to happen if the Finns fall. They are terrified of the Germans attacking them, and I don't wonder, for we can give them so little help.

I find it very difficult making any coherent plans because we have mortgaged all our troops to France and have nothing left in England fit for fighting. All the disadvantages of not being ready. . . . All eyes are now fixed upon Scandinavia, and the two countries simply don't know which way to look.

On February 18 the Cabinet had discussed a joint report by the Foreign Office and the Chiefs of Staff on Scandinavia.

Troops could not be ready to land at Narvik until, at the earliest, March 20, and those for Stavanger, Bergen and Trondheim until February 28. It was agreed that the operation should begin as soon as possible. Consent to our landings by Norway and Sweden was now a matter of the greatest urgency. It was not granted. The forcible liberation of British prisoners from the German ship *Altmark* on February 17, when the Royal Navy boarded her in a Norwegian fiord, had produced a vehement protest from Norway, and Sweden had been no less indignant.

February 19

We had a quiet Cabinet meeting. Winston is now trying to lay minefields along the Norwegian waters used by the Germans. This will stop the traffic or drive the ships out into our hands. He proposes to link up the incapacity of the Norwegians to guard their neutrality in the case of the *Altmark* with anything fresh we may do.

As far as I see it, we cannot now hope for any willing co-operation from the Norwegians and Swedes, and must depend upon the Germans bursting out and violating Scandinavian neutrality. Otherwise our Narvik show is off.

So few of these men have any idea of the practical side of their decisions. Anything in the way of a gun that starts now will be a month, in good conditions, before it comes into action in Finland. So often they think that having given the order here the matter is done with. So many of them are tinged with the political aspect. To get an effect and show that they have the good will. . . .

I have wired to the U.S.A. to find out if the U.S. Army has a lot of 75's [75-millimetre field-guns] that they took home with them in 1918. They cannot be worth anything and would be of immense help to the Finns and perhaps even to us for training. I think that they could be pushed over the frontier to Canada as the aeroplanes are being handled.

I am terrified at our timing in this Scandinavian show being upset. If it comes off, the various parts all hang together, and any false advance may upset the whole scheme.

The thaw is now complete here and the streets filled with mud. I hear that it is still hard in N. Germany.

An Army Council which went very well under Oliver Stanley. Such a difference is hardly believable. No quarrels, no misunderstandings, and no reactions to the slightest little movement of the Press.

February 20

An unsatisfactory morning. I get such a feeling of futility with all our Committees. There is so much unreasonable discussion by people who are not up in their subject. The Committee of the three Chiefs of Staff is slow enough in all conscience, but when all their efforts have to be re-examined by another Committee, the pace at which we work becomes funereal. I feel that all this Scandinavian project has been on the stocks so long that it has almost become stale in waiting. . . .

I took the afternoon off and went up to my flat and spent four hours there. . . . It is an extraordinary life this running a war that isn't a war from the War Office. The only thing that consoles me is that every minute is of value. We were in such a state of unreadiness that we were not capable of doing anything. My fear at the moment is whether we are now making the best of our respite. There seems to be a kind of apathy amongst the senior officers, begat of not having sufficient equipment. Training has been much upset by the weather, but I hope we shall now get down to it.

I have been trying to get conversations with the Swedes over any possible help we may give them, and I have not had any very satisfactory replies. Baron Rosen, the Military Attaché here, says quite frankly: "One of the difficulties is to find a Swedish officer sufficiently senior and with a knowledge of the plans of the Swedish General Staff in whom complete and absolute confidence can be placed."

I have told our Cabinet that we can do nothing for certain without conversations with the Swedes. For instance, such a simple thing as the number of trucks and locomotives available on the railways cannot be guessed at any given moment.

I have also told the Cabinet that the one thing Finland does not want is to be attacked in rear by the Germans. I think that after the Gulf of Bothnia is free of ice it is certain that the Germans will dominate the sea and might at any moment land and occupy Gällivare. We none of us can say how close the alliance between Russia and Germany is, but we can be sure that they neither of them trust the other.

The Swedish M.A. here in London told me expressly that the French M.A. in Stockholm had told him that an Allied force meant to land at Narvik. You cannot keep anything secret with so many people with a finger in the pie. . . .

Both the Secretary of State and I think that this Scandinavian scheme is impossible unless Germany makes some false step.

By now Ironside had assembled the Expeditionary Force and the ships for Norway. Its Commander, General Mackesy, had been appointed. All that remained was for the Cabinet to reach a decision. About half the ministers seemed in favour of going ahead even if Norway refused to let us land, and half were against it. The debate vacillated with the latest diplomatic news.

There were signs that Hitler himself was preparing to invade Scandinavia. There was a constant movement of troops towards the North German ports, and night after night the R.A.F. saw and reported long columns of lorries moving towards these same ports with their lights full on. The R.A.F. asked permission to bomb them, but the Prime Minister refused, saying that he would not be responsible for dropping the first bomb of the war on a land target. Poland appeared to be forgotten.

In Stockholm some of the French diplomatic staff talked openly of the coming expedition to Scandinavia. This certainly gave Hitler an excuse for striking first. Ironside pressed the Cabinet for a decision. Finally it was agreed that some degree of force might be used to effect an entry of our troops into Norway, and the Prime Minister himself drafted an Instruction for the Commander of the Narvik force. This laid down that the Commander might attempt an opposed landing if the opposition were weak, but he was to break off if he came up against strong resistance.

Ironside refused to allow the Commander to be thus fettered. How, he asked, could he know in advance whether the opposition would be weak or strong? Once the battle started, it might be difficult to break it off, and anyway, resistance might be weak at first and then get stronger as reinforcements came up. The Commander would be in an impossible position, and would be blamed if anything went wrong.

February 24

Winston is now pressing for his laying of mines in neutral Norwegian waters as the only means of forcing the Germans to violate Scandinavia and so give us a chance of getting into Narvik. Otherwise I see no possible chance.

February 25

Ling has told Mannerheim of our plan and it has been agreed to. So much for Mannerheim refusing to have our aid for fear of Germany. The Russians have done little more since the Finns withdrew from their forward positions. Weather is bad and they have a good many preparations to make before they can start again.

Meanwhile the Swedes are in deep dejection. They realize the pressure that we and the French are putting on them and they already feel in the European war in reality. They cannot send any Regular units to Finland in consequence. The main point which has emerged is their lack of acquiescence over the Narvik landing. They have no illusions and are well aware that our landing there will mean war in Sweden. I cannot blame them.

Then Maisky [the Soviet Ambassador in London] has approached Halifax directly. He has been told to do so by his Government. Russia wants a peace patched up upon the terms offered before the war. That means that the Finnish defence will have brought them nothing. In fact, less—because Russia will not now give any compensation for the fortresses taken to protect

Leningrad. Maisky said that the Mannerheim Line had not been taken, but that it had been broken and the fate of Finland was certain. He said that Finland would be added to the diplomatic defeats of the Allies, such as Poland and Abyssinia. That it was impossible for the Allies to pierce the ring of neutrals. That Great Britain would be doing enough to incur the hatred of Russia for many years, but not enough to save Finland. That Russia had no wish to invade either Sweden or Norway and that she wished to remain friends with us. She had made a purely economic agreement with Germany and he could assure us that there was nothing military in it. Russia had been perturbed by the arrival of the Anzacs in Palestine and by the presence of a large French Army in Syria. Russia was now in process of fortifying the Caucasus.

Halifax does not seem to have told Maisky that it is exactly the economic agreement with Germany that she has made which has caused us to be angry.

The position is difficult. I shall be interested to see how the Cabinet reacts to this new situation. I know that Winston is all for forcing things on by laying minefields in Norwegian waters.

The French are urging us to push on with our preparations and not be so slow over sending the troops to Narvik. I do not think that they realize in the least how necessary it is to have the good-will of the Swedes in running the Narvik–Lulea railway. They brush aside all administrative difficulties. They will not be responsible for operations.

> In February the Cabinet had told the Swedish and Norwegian Governments that an Allied Force had been prepared to help the Finns, and that we would presently ask permission for it to land and for co-operation in its movement to the Finnish frontier. The Notes added that if this led to Germany attacking Norway and Sweden, we could give them considerable military assistance, but that prior staff conversations were essential.

March 2

We have apparently disclosed the whole of our plans to our Ministers in Stockholm and Oslo and cannot expect an answer from the Swedish and Norwegian Governments until to-night. As far as I can see there is no chance of their accepting our offer of help.

It was practically the opinion of the War Cabinet that we ought to let our Expedition for Narvik sail and even land at Narvik without the wish of the Norwegians. To do this unless the Norwegians actually prepared to fire at us. We could then go on talking about the use of the railway and stay in Narvik for some time. I could not get out of them whether they thought we ought to do the Stavanger, Bergen, Trondheim landings or not. The whole thing seemed rather nonsense to me, and I couldn't conceive what good we were doing, except to show the world that we had demanded passage to help Finland.

Then I rubbed in carefully to the Cabinet the fact that any troops sent south of the Tornea latitude[1] couldn't be withdrawn at will, and that they would be lost to the Allied cause the minute that the Germans could act in April or May when the Gulf of Bothnia unfroze. . . .

I believe that Hitler has three alternatives in his brain and that he is carrying out his plans quite methodically:

(i) To push for a patched-up peace at any moment that he sees a chance.

(ii) To carry out his economic warfare against shipping.

(iii) To attack as a final solution or after we have been weakened and confused by the first two alternatives.

At the moment intense pressure is being put upon the Finns to have an armistice:

(i) By the Germans because they want neither the Russians nor the Allies in Gällivare before the Gulf of Bothnia is clear of ice.

(ii) By the Russians because they have had enough embarrassment already and because they cannot satisfy the German demands for raw materials.

---

[1] Tornea is at the head of the Gulf of Bothnia. If our troops moved south of Tornea the Germans could land behind them and cut them off.

(iii) By the Swedes because they do not wish to become a bone
of contention and mixed up in the war.

Meanwhile we try to prolong the agony and keep everybody
looking to the north. . . .

Sweden and Norway now refused permission for the
Allies to land, and refused to hold any Staff conversations.

March 4

The Cabinet in the morning was more than exasperating. Nobody would get down to anything. . . . The Swedes are putting
the very strongest pressure they can on to the Finns to make terms
—regardless of what those terms are, so that they may not be
dragged into the war. They have even said that they will stop all
help now flowing into Finland if the Finns do not negotiate. The
Swedish Government had already stated, and now state again,
that they will never allow Allied troops through Sweden. The
Norwegians naturally follow suit. . . . Finally, a wire comes in
from Leger at the French Foreign Office saying that the Swedes
"expect to have their neutrality forced". That we ought to go on
with our expedition.

To try to get up the Narvik railway without any help from the
Swedish and Norwegian railway personnel is madness. . . . We
simply cannot do it. I must reiterate this to the Cabinet.

March 8

We are now threatened with a defeat. How we are to escape
from it I don't know. Our first defeat was the wiping out of
Poland. That took place in three weeks, far quicker than the
defeat of Tannenburg, and it was not complete defeat in the case
of Russia. We gave a guarantee to Poland. Doubtless that was a
political counter and was designed to stop Germany. Germany
counted the cost and carried on, knowing that the threat was
purely political and totally unmilitary. The collapse of Poland in
three weeks came as a great shock to everybody, even the French.
And so, instead of nearly three years to free herself of a two-
fronted war, Germany is freed in three weeks.

Now Germany—with Russia—is well on her way to establish herself actually or practically in Finland and Northern Scandinavia. She has subdued Czechoslovakia, Austria and Poland completely and is now keeping them in order with very few troops. She is watching the Finnish struggle with great interest. She will perhaps get her second victory without striking a blow. That is what Hitler likes in making war. A new technique which he seems to have mastered to the full. All the people expect it of him now.

March 11

Finland again this morning. . . . Corbin [The French Ambassador] came to see Halifax and said that Daladier would resign if we did not do more over Finland. That we made much of the difficulties in telegraphing to them. That people were beginning to doubt whether we were in earnest. As a matter of actual fact [the French] have been promising far more than they can ever carry out, and doing it very deliberately in order to force the Finns to ask for help. The French, who are not responsible for the military execution of the plan, put forward the most extravagant ideas. They are absolutely unscrupulous in everything.

The Cabinet decided this morning to go on with the Narvik plan at all costs and to arrive off the port and make a demand for passage through to Finland. We are now working away at this plan, which means that we must be prepared for some sort of an opposed landing. I can see our great big Scots Guards shouldering the sleepy Norwegians out of the way at 5 a.m. in the morning. It seems inconceivable that the Norwegians should put up any resistance if they are in any way surprised. Of course, we ran up against the Foreign Office, who wanted to protect themselves by giving notice to everyone, including the Americans, in order "to put ourselves right with the world". They live such a leisurely life that they cannot understand when there is a case for putting up a bluff. We are not good poker-players.

March 12

Chamberlain has made his speech in the House, more or less at the request of the French, saying that we are prepared with "all our resources". And yet we cannot even say that we have a sporting chance of getting to Finland. We gave a guarantee to the Poles which couldn't be implemented. . . .

We had a dreadful Cabinet. Everybody had a different idea upon how much force we would have to use at Narvik. In the end, the Prime Minister was persuaded to see the Admiral [Sir Edward Evans] and the General [Mackesy]—and he said he could see them to-morrow afternoon. When I explained to him that the men were commencing embarkation, they all seemed surprised. A more unmilitary show I have never seen. The Prime Minister began peering at a chart of Narvik and when he had finished he asked me what scale it was on. He asked what effect an 8-inch shell would have on a transport and finished up by saying that he was prepared to risk a 4-inch shell, but not an 8-inch shell. He then asked what the weight of the shells were. Chatfield, an Admiral of the Fleet, first said that we should not risk firing at the Norwegians, and then said that he thought we ought not to be bluffed by a mere Lieutenant in charge of a shore battery. The Cabinet presented the picture of a bewildered flock of sheep faced by a problem they have consistently refused to consider. Their favourite formula is that the case is hypothetical and then they shy off a decision.

I came away disgusted with them all.

I have actually taken my Instructions and ordered the General to start off. . . .

We finished up with a meeting in 10 Downing Street with the P.M., Halifax, Chatfield and Hankey to see the orders we had produced for the Narvik project. In the end, all we wanted was passed, but I think it showed me clearly that the P.M. was the biggest man there. He realized the position in which a General would be placed in an attempt like this. Halifax recoiled from any bloodshed and didn't want to try the thing. . . . If you send an Army it must not be tied down so that it loses its teeth. Chamberlain, despite his appallingly unmilitary brain, realized the position and was ready to back up the General upon whom he had put the responsibility. . . . Thanks to Chamberlain, we got things through.

The ostensible rôle of the expedition, as the Instructions show, was to help Finland, and to deny the Gällivare ore-fields to Germany and Russia. It was given three specific tasks: To establish itself at Narvik, to secure the railway into Sweden as quickly as possible, and to concentrate in Sweden for its principal rôle—aid to Finland. As the attitude of the Norwegians was in doubt, the commanders were instructed to land provided there was no serious fighting. The British had no intention of fighting their way through Norway and into Sweden. On the other hand, the commanders were not to be deterred by a show of resistance.

During the night of March 12 the Finns accepted the Russian terms. Our pretext for intervention had disappeared, and the expedition to Narvik was abandoned.

March 13

The papers are full of the peace having been signed between the Finns and Russians. And so all our weeks of work come to nothing. Our second defeat has come about and we must now look about for something else. I expect the Germans have heaved a sigh of relief. . . . If Mannerheim had been a younger man and if he hadn't gone down with influenza at the critical moment, perhaps things might have been different. Such small things often turn the scale one way or another.

March 14

We have held everything for Scandinavia up. Appropriate weather, for it is snowing hard, though the snow is not lying in the streets, it is still so warm. . . .

Winston has now suggested that we should occupy Narvik without the pretext of helping the Finns. I should say that the nearest we could go to this is to keep a Narvik force on ice in England. We should put ourselves diplomatically very much in the wrong were we to violate Norwegian territory. I can see that Winston wishes to ginger people up into doing something. What, he doesn't quite know.

This passage [from a report about the Red Army] struck me particularly:

"The Soviet Union is not a country which is working well within its capacity. It gives the impression of a country which is going all out the whole time, of a machine which is creaking and groaning but still with vast effort only just able to provide for the minimum needs of the population.

"The outstanding impression which is gained in the Soviet Union is one of inefficiency. Apart from the theatre and ballet, for which the Russians have a genius, it is difficult to find any single thing in the Soviet Union which is run efficiently."

. . . In the Cabinet there was rather a feeling of deflatedness after the Scandinavian failure. Tempers ran fairly high. Winston particularly annoying.

. . . I had an interesting wire from Helsinki telling me that the Finnish Army still has its tail up. That they regard this peace merely as a truce which will be broken at any moment. This is interesting because I have been thinking how I could keep alive the idea that we may still be called upon to save Scandinavia. When the ice has gone we may well find Germany stepping in— in her usual clumsy way—to secure the iron-ore. Russia may well overrun the north of Finland with a view to getting Narvik, a real warm-water port on the Atlantic.

> Ironside urged the Cabinet to keep the expeditionary force for Scandinavia in being, but after much debate the Prime Minister ordered it to disperse. Chamberlain argued that if Hitler got wind of its existence, it would give him an excuse for invading Scandinavia himself. The C.I.G.S. said that everyone knew that Hitler was determined to invade Scandinavia, and would need no excuses. But Ironside's protests were overruled, and the troops, which included a special Scots Guards battalion, trained to run on skis, were dispersed.

March 19

The Cabinet was more interesting. There was a long discussion over a paper put in by Corbin, the French Ambassador. He argued that we had suffered a defeat in the Finnish Peace and that it was necessary to recover our ground. The French urged us to occupy Norwegian ports, especially Narvik, and to keep in view the seizing of the Gällivare iron-ore fields. . . .

Winston put up three definite proposals, all of strength and possibility:

(i) *The stopping of the Norwegian neutral alleyway*
> This could be done navally and could not now affect the major project of Gällivare or Finland. We must stop the ore at all costs.

(ii) *The blocking of Lulea*
> This could be done by sinking a ship in the waterway to the harbour as a loss of mere sabotage, or it could be bombed from aircraft-carriers off the north coast of Norway using torpedoes.

(iii) *The mining of German inland waterways*
> This is already mounted. It would commence with floating mines down the Rhine and continue with aircraft-dropped mines all over Germany. . . .

Unfortunately the French have shied off this because of the fear of reprisals. The answer is that if they are not ready now they never will be.

CHAPTER XVI

The Lull

March 21 [*en route* to Paris]

The anniversary of the German attack in 1918 which so nearly succeeded against the Fifth Army. . . .

A special train to Paris in two hours with a good cold lunch on board and to the Meurice . . . and so to the Mission at Vincennes. As usual, Gamelin very calm and quiet and ready to talk. . . . The [new French] Cabinet came in with Reynaud at the head and Daladier as Defence.[1] . . . They seemed much calmer in Paris than we should have been, but that is because the usual life of a Cabinet is nine months in France. . . . I find that most of the French officers I have spoken to think that Reynaud's arrival is a good thing. They think that the Cabinet is too far to the Left. . . . The British Mission treated the whole thing as very ordinary.

March 22

We arrived at Verdun, having added to the time by halting for five hours, at 7.30 a.m. and away by motor. . . .

We then drove the whole day along the Luxembourg frontier to the Moselle. I have never seen such a difference in the French. The spring seemed to have made them start work, or perhaps the bad winter had paralysed them. Officers and men were working like beavers, and very intelligent. We all agreed that the Germans

[1] Daladier and his Cabinet had resigned on March 20 as a result of the Finnish "débâcle".

231

had missed their opportunity in not attacking when the French were concentrating. The Maginot Line had no depth whatever and that opposite Luxembourg was pretty sketchy. Now the depth was coming quickly. Condé and Huntziger both asked for two more months to get things right. There is no doubt in my mind that the French would not build the Maginot Line if they were going to start it now. Gamelin told me that as far back as 1930 he and Weygand had tried to get money for strong but smaller works. They had been consistently refused by Gillaumat, then the head of the Conseil Supérieur. The old ones were always looking for a field of fire, whereas he and Weygand were looking for obstacles. One can see now that Gillaumat was wrong. Without any depth, the Maginot Line might have been overrun easily. Now it cannot be with the depth achieved.

The first General we found was Huntziger, a little blond man, almost ginger, with a tiny clipped moustache. Gamelin told me that he was the best of his Generals after Georges, and I must say that he gave one the impression of being very much alive. Next to him was the old Gunner, Condé, a regular old type. Very badly dressed but working at everything himself. I was impressed at the way they answered Gamelin, and they all treated him with the greatest respect. I could see no ill-will or inclination to bad feeling. They put their opinions and then deferred to his expressed wish.

I saw no "*cafard*" among the men, who looked particularly bright and intelligent. Clean and well-shaven. The French are a practical people and they do not trouble much about uniformity of dress, especially when at liberty. They also bother very little about drill. The idea of "smartening up" their men after fighting or trench work appears to them—as it appears to me—as useless. We have so long smothered the intelligence of our men by "square" drill that we cannot be surprised that our men are stupid in war. It takes the insubordinate spirits—who are a nuisance to the ordinary peace-soldier-general—to shine in war. I am glad to say that our new drill has made things easier, but I believe that men will spring up once more to ruin our intelligence by drill. . . .

March 23

We had a good look at the Moselle, where the Luxembourg frontier ends, and could see Germany away in the distance. The most astonishing thing to me was that the whole gang of us— some fifty, including Gamelin, Condé and myself—drove down to our last work, where we came in full view of the German heights at 7,000 yards distance. There never had been any firing here, but there might be one day. And we stayed in full view on the road with maps out looking at things towards the bluff held by the French—the Stromberg. I was quite glad to come away because I thought it was so silly to tempt Providence in this way, quite apart from the chance of being knocked out oneself.

March 24

We are still in a state of doubt as to what will happen should the Germans invade Holland. A new enquiry has arrived from the Belgians: "Would we demand the right from the Belgians to march across their country to the help of Holland?" An answer to this is quite simple. We have not the least idea what the Dutch plan of defence is, and couldn't go to help them. At present they will have no communication with us and apparently are not in touch with the Belgians. It is of capital importance for us to get into Belgium so as to shorten our line and I think that the Belgians understand the importance of time. I told Gamelin that we ought to make no definite promise to go forward to the Albert Canal. That could be arranged on the day we get to the Namur–Antwerp line when we know what the Germans are doing. . . .

The French are regaining their confidence, but I have heard no voice raised for an offensive such as they tried in 1914. They all know what that means. But they are all confident of success and make no bones about there being no more war every twenty-five years. They say clearly that the Germans will only be beaten if their Army is knocked out. No mere change of Hitler for Goering, or Goering for someone seemingly more moderate, will suit them. They seem to think that Reynaud will push the war more determinedly, but I don't think that Gamelin has much faith in that idea. He said that if they want to do something they must form an assault-brigade from the deputies and start it off themselves.

March 26 [London]

Back again in the office. Apparently, they settled upon a Supreme War Council on Thursday and so we are in the middle of preparing it. I am told that Reynaud is coming across full of energy, to try to push the war on with more vigour. I hope he will not try to push something silly, merely for the sake of doing something spectacular merely to ensure his political future. . . .

We had one of the longest days we have had for a long time for my first day back to work:

9.30–10.15	Papers and telegrams
10.15–11.30	Chiefs of Staff Committee
11.30–1 p.m.	War Cabinet
2 p.m.–3.30	4 visitors
3.30–4.30	Secretary of State
5 p.m.–7.30	Army Council
9.30–12 Midnight	Chiefs of Staff
	Total 11 hours

And besides this a few odd things. I missed my ride and go to bed quite honestly tired. If one hadn't a good staff one's brain would stop.

M. Reynaud has issued the most extraordinary paper stating how he proposes to win the war. He says that so far nobody has done anything and he proposes to do it. I understand that when the P.M. read the paper he went through the ceiling. For it includes him amongst those who have so far failed. . . .

The leading sentence of the (very badly translated) French paper from the Prime Minister [M. Reynaud] is typical of the whole:

"The sudden outcome of the Finnish struggle has faced the Allies with a new and perhaps decisive situation. In order to seize again the initiative which they have lost, it is important that the two Governments, having learnt a lesson from recent events, should apply themselves without delay to draw from present circumstances all the possibilities of which an energetic and daring conduct of the war still allows them to take advantage."

This sentence made the Prime Minister very angry.

A useful principle if we can carry it out is:

"In the actual field of action of the Allies and of their collaboration, a revision of the methods of directing the war is certainly required, the procedure of discussion, in the course of which the necessary speed of decision is lost, must be modified, conception, preparation and execution of our plans must be assured so as to develop in such circumstances that they no longer expose us to discomfiture to which abstention would have been preferable."

March 27

I woke up at 5 o'clock, having had some four hours sleep, and then started thinking. What a mess our weakness has got us into. Here we are fighting for our lives and, although Ireland is presumably in the Empire, we cannot use her western harbours for our destroyers. They would save us 200 miles each way. Is there any other nation which would tolerate in a life-struggle being denied something vital? . . .

The new French direction of the war is to put an end to all this. What will Halifax say? It won't suit his upright nature. Perhaps Reynaud is right. The moment has arrived for us to be as brutal as the Germans. I shall be most interested to see the reaction of the various members. I expect they will all run true to their reputations. Better than betting on horses. . . .

The Cabinet brought forth a tirade from the P.M. about Reynaud. He was horrified when he saw the paper. It gave him the impression of a man who was rattled and who wished to make a splash to justify his position. He thought the projects put forward by him were of the crudest kind. That he should mention submarines going into the Black Sea without mentioning Turkey seemed fantastic.

Winston put up a plea for Reynaud, saying that he had not been taken into the confidence of Daladier—he had been told this by

Reynaud. Winston didn't seem to think that his adoption of Georges and Reynaud made it more difficult for Gamelin and Daladier. He cannot resist taking sides in other people's affairs.

The P.M. then said that the effect caused by Finland's collapse had largely died away and that perhaps the effect was greater in France than with us. But the appetite of the public for news and sensational news still existed and had to be taken into account. The P.M. said that he was in no way pleased with the way we handled our facts for propaganda.

I can see that we are not likely to have such a cordial meeting as we had with Daladier. The P.M. is already annoyed that he should be labelled as one of the men who failed in the last combination. . . .

Everybody expressed themselves in favour of a stronger policy, but nobody had the slightest idea of how this should be attained. I thought that the Germans were well on their way to settle all the neutrals by peaceful means. They would then be quite firm on the Western Front and sure "that they couldn't be beaten", and would then keep putting out peace proposals. I don't think that we shall ever get anything dramatic out of Chamberlain and Halifax. Both go calmly on.

I had a cup of Bovril and some sandwiches and then found my horse at the Duke of York's steps and an hour's ride and then to Victoria. The special train came in exactly to the minute at 2.50 p.m. and Gamelin and Darlan emerged with a good luncheon flush on their faces and quite pleased with themselves. They put up at the Hyde Park Hotel close to the French Embassy.

At 4 p.m. we had a very tedious conference, the six Chiefs of Staff. Everything through interpreters as I am the only one who can speak both languages fluently. I must say that I got terribly bored.

We tied Gamelin down to two facts:

1. That if the Germans invaded Holland and the Dutch asked us to help, we could not go through Belgium without having been so invited. That it was a vital military essential to get into Belgium.

2. That in the event of Germany invading Belgium Gamelin had no authority to go into Belgium without an invitation from the Belgians. This would come in the form of a request from the King of the Belgians to Gamelin.

We then discussed all the things like blocking the iron-ore from Narvik to sending submarines into the Black Sea and bombing Baku. The French had thought out nothing and put up the very vaguest things. *All of them to be executed by us with a little vague help from the French.*

The thing which emerged was that the French had not grasped the question of baiting Russia and Italy into war unnecessarily. I tackled Gamelin afterwards and he said rather bitterly that the "politicians" had not studied the results and consequences of any act. He asked me to see that our Government impressed this upon Reynaud. I told them that they need have no fear, our Government would do nothing for the sake of doing it only.

March 28

The Supreme War Council went far better than I expected. These old *rusés* politicians like Chamberlain have a strategy of their own and he certainly had a good one this time. He started off with a ninety minutes' monologue upon the general situation, apologizing every now and then for taking so long. He took all the thunder out of Reynaud's mouth and left him gasping with no electric power left. All the "projects" that Reynaud had to bring forward, Chamberlain took away. It was most masterly and very well done. Little Reynaud sat there with his head nodding in a sort of "tik", understanding it all, for he speaks English very well, and having to have it translated all over again for the benefit of the others. He was for all the world like a little marmoset.

The new Air Minister, Laurent d'Eynac, a little short immensely fat man with a beaky nose and dark hair. He had an enormous double chin, which seemed more marked when we came back in the afternoon after a lunch at the Carlton. He looked very like Stalin in a somnolent way. At the end, both he and Vuillemin, his Service Chief, were asleep. Vuillemin was what the French call an "as" [ace] of the last war. Not very intelligent.

Darlan, the French Admiral, smoked his pipe all the time and drew pictures on his bit of paper.

It was finally decided that we must treat the neutrals more strongly. That they could not maintain their neutrality by doing what Germany ordered out of fear. This was to apply to the Swedes and Norwegians with special reference to the iron-ore. A programme ran that we should send them an admonition and then wait a few days. It runs as follows:

April 1   Admonition to Scandinavia.
    „   4   Mines in the Rhine.
    „   5   Mines in Norwegian waters to stop the ore traffic to Narvik.[1]
    „ 15   Air magnetic mines in all the rivers and waterways of Germany.

All this can be said to be a reprisal for the way Germany has treated the neutral ships, but it may well start off some form of totalitarian war. . . . The whole War Council took in all five and a half hours and it was conducted completely from beginning to end by Chamberlain and Reynaud. A battle of wits, and I am quite sure that Chamberlain won. Nobody else said a single word. My admiration for the Prime Minister went up still more. Nothing vulgar. No excitement. And a clear exposition of the pros and cons of the various projects.

> On March 29 the Cabinet confirmed the decisions of the Supreme War Council. Mines should be laid in the coastal waters of Scandinavia and also in the Rhine. They "took note", as the officials put it, that a German reaction to these measures might offer the Allies an opportunity of landing troops in Norway with the acquiescence of the Norwegian Government. But it was not proposed to land in Norway unless and until the Germans made some move which would convert Scandinavia into a theatre of war.

[1] It was also agreed that the Lulea traffic should be interrupted by mines laid by aircraft later in the spring.

An incident now occurred which unquestionably harmed Ironside's popularity and standing with the Press. The Ministry of Information asked him to give an interview to an American newspaper correspondent so as to stimulate transatlantic appreciation of the Allied cause.

March 30

In the afternoon I had a visit from Frazier Hunt, one of the biggest journalists in America. A great big man who continually slapped his leg with the expression of: "Well now!" "You never said a truer word." "Just so." And the like. I had been told to impress him as much as I could and I think I did. No knowledge of war whatever. After all we are all pretty flummoxed ourselves. I asked him if he had thought of the moral aspect of this war and could anybody say that the Germans had any justification for what they had done? He seemed very certain of that. Then, he asked me whether I thought this war could not be fought without a great battle. I told him that it was conceivable but most unlikely. No one could say what might happen with a mad brain like Hitler's opposing us. I told him that I did not think that the German people had the same idea that they were right as they did in 1914. Now they had an uneasy conscience that what they had done was wrong. They held together because they were a disciplined people, and because they knew that the retribution coming to them, if they were defeated, would be something they wouldn't forget easily. Out of self-interest they remained together. But that I thought that the German nation was defeatist. At that the journalist ejaculated: "You have 'em licked, General," and slapped his thigh with enthusiasm.

This interview had a curious and unfortunate sequel. On April 5 Ironside wrote in his diary: "This American, Frazier Hunt, has published his interview with me in the *Daily Express*. I was asked to give it to him as he was so important in America. Apparently the *Daily Express* is in with the American papers, and so got the interview. It created a great deal of excitement, and all the other papers were telephoning

all night. The *Daily Mail* was particularly angry and demanded an interview with me at once. . . . All the other
papers complained bitterly at the *Daily Express* being favoured
above them. I had to go along to the Press Conference and
give them an impromptu talk on the same lines as I talked to
Frazier Hunt. A trying thing to have to do."

Unknown, apparently, to the Ministry of Information, an
arrangement existed under which Mr. Frazier Hunt's articles
were syndicated in the papers belonging to a British newspaper group. The C.I.G.S. had been under the impression
that he had been giving Mr. Hunt background information
which he would use for articles which would be published
only in the United States. At the express request of the
Ministry of Information he had given him as rosy a picture
as possible—rosier, possibly, than the situation warranted,
particularly as regards the prospects of the French Army on
the Western Front. But what had been intended as an in-
formal talk which would result in timely propaganda in the
United States was given the appearance in this country of an
official pronouncement by the Chief of the Imperial General
Staff. At the same time Ironside, through no fault of his own
and as a result, as it may be thought, of an oversight on the
part of the Ministry of Information, succeeded in annoying
the British Press and in creating to a certain extent a false
impression of his real views as to the course and prospects of
the war on the Western Front.

Ironside, in the meantime, crossed again to France.

March 31 [Paris]

The German rumours of attacks are being put out in great
strength once more. Goering has said that the war will finish on
the Western Front and when Hitler wishes to do so. The question
which comes into one's mind is "Why not begin at once?" That
the war will be waged in the most brutal way, without reference
to law or humanity. Gas and microbes will be used. It all seems
the same old story of talk to keep the people employed and away
from thinking of their troubles in war time. . . .

I asked Gamelin if he thought this inaction on the part of Hitler
on the Western Front was due to any rows with his General Staff.
He was still unable to give any reason for this inaction. He had
expected to be attacked. . . . He hopes that the Germans will
attack. He says that the French Army, despite all its deficiencies,
will fight. I believe it will and I cannot see that all this "peace in
war" has affected their morale. No one has even whispered this
to me. As far as I can judge they are all right, though short of so
much aircraft.

April 1

An absolutely gorgeous spring day. I walked out for a moment
in the Luxembourg Gardens and one hated to think that there was
a war on to upset everything. After all, we have all of us had an
easy time so far. There is no great difference from manœuvres.
The British Army is merely growing and training. I wish the
people at home had a better idea of work. So many of the senior
officers don't get about enough. With units that have been hastily
thrown together the only thing to do is to get about and see
things. The office can be run by the staff officers, and the General
can be met at any point he likes to sign papers. . . .

Down to Arras after lunch, where I found the military attaché
from Brussels [Colonel Blake] . . . Van Overstraten, the Belgian
Chief of Staff, told Blake that he was convinced that the French
would never come past the Namur–Wavre–Antwerp line and so
he would not deal with them.[1] I told Blake to say that Gamelin
and I had decided that we would have to be established on this line
before we went any further. That the Belgians had made so much
trouble about our reconnoitring the Wavre line [i.e. the line of
the River Dyle] that it had delayed negotiations. We now had no
idea what the Albert Canal line was like. That we most certainly
would not go to any line that we hadn't reconnoitred. Perhaps we
shall now get a look at this line. Blake said that the Belgians had
absolutely no touch with the Dutch and could not get any. I told

[1] This was the line of the River Dyle, which was in fact as far as the
Allies, under Plan D, intended to advance.

him to tell Overstraten that he could contrast our feelings with his own in like case. . . .

I found Jack Gort in good form, and the Chaplain-General visiting the troops. Jack has reduced the size of his Mess considerably, which is a good thing. Not so many people to worry him.

April 2

I looked over the repair shop at Arras and found the usual troubles which meet a Q.M.G. Having no Master-General of the Ordnance, owing to Belisha having abolished him, there is no master to look after the shops. The vehicles which come in for repair were all being cleaned by the trained mechanics. No untrained men to do this. . . . Gort could quite easily have set the first reinforcements on to this.

Dill was doing a manning exercise in his trenches and Gort was going up to see it. . . . He is much more interested in the little operations of platoons and the positions of machine-guns. It always makes me want to get back to the command of troops, which I can do so well. Still, that is the luck of the thing. . . .

I lay thinking of a great Bosche attack and all it would mean. I can see them tackling a big advance into Holland and Belgium, but not against the Anglo-French Army. . . . We start this war with many more men of experience than we had in 1914, but I am not sure if we have sufficient men habituated to "command" in peace. We have too many of the "staff officer" educated commander. . . . There was no doctrine for the training for twenty years and practically no manœuvres. Once more we enter the war with an Army which has no fundamental platoon training. The Regular Army, now being used to leaven the Territorials, is not too bad. [The Territorial Officers] do not take charge. They [the Territorial Divisions] are as bad or even worse, diluted as they were to make second-line divisions, than Kitchener's Army. . . . The French have so much better training in their "*sections de combat*" than we have with their three years of service. How am I to intensify this at home? I wish that our commanders had the terrific energy of McNaughton in the Canadians. Gort at least can try to put that right if he is allowed to have any men out of the line. The willingness of the men, especially of the young men of the obligatory service, is beyond praise, but they have to be led.

Perhaps the most dangerous thing of all is this idea amongst so many people that this war can be won without a battle and that we are not going to have any casualties. Are we going to win the war and destroy the Bosche power without fighting, just by proving to the Bosches that they cannot win? I very much doubt it, and it is going to be very hard for Gort to order his men to attack. This continual shouting about the "stupidity of the brass-hats" has been impregnated into the nation by the Press to such a degree that many people believe it. Nobody has dared to say that the Territorial Army is virtually untrained after seven months of training. It is untrained, and we don't seem to have made a very good show at it. There is a lack of leadership all through. One thing is certain and that is that we cannot attack until 1941, but shall we be given the time to train even for that?

At 4 o'clock I ran down to Vincennes and called on Gamelin. . . . He told me that their War Cabinet had assembled and that Daladier had gone completely against the project of putting mines in the Rhine. He had been for the project before, and apparently went against it this time because it had been arranged by Paul Reynaud and he merely wanted to put a spoke in his wheel. Lebrun, the President, stepped in and said he was responsible for the country and would not have it. Gamelin told the War Cabinet that if Germany wanted to bomb France she could do it at any moment. . . .

Nothing seems to have come of the Supreme War Council except the fact that some enemy may have got hold of a paper giving away all our projected operations. Perhaps it will serve as a nice little rumour, as we are not now going to carry them out. . . . How angry Winston will be after the show [Operation "Royal Marine"] was practically arranged.

It was most disappointing that, after they had accepted it at the Supreme War Council in London, Mr. Churchill's project for floating fluvial mines down the River Rhine, Operation "Royal Marine", was now rejected by the French.

□□ It would certainly have diverted German attention from the Norwegian theatre, and done much damage to the German Rhine communications. From Ironside's experience of these mines in the Northern Dwina in Russia, he thought that such an attack would be difficult to combat and should be employed to cover our impending action in Norway. A second wave of mines would then be let loose at the moment of the main German attack against the French line —the attack he thought was bound to come during 1940. But the French would not agree to the operation, being terrified of air reprisals against their industry.

CHAPTER XVII

Norway: The Landings

ON APRIL I, 1940, the British Cabinet approved the following proposals by the Chiefs of Staff: if, after we had
placed our mines in Norwegian territorial waters, the Germans either invaded Scandinavia or were clearly about to do
so, then we would: (1) despatch a force to Narvik to secure
the port and the railway as far as the Swedish frontier, thus
preparing the way to seize the Gällivare ore-fields; and (2)
despatch forces to Stavanger, Bergen and Trondheim, so as
to deny these ports and airfields to the Germans. But no
landings should be attempted unless the Norwegians were
prepared to co-operate.

The enemy also had a plan.

In October and again in December 1939 the German naval
chiefs suggested to Hitler that they should occupy submarine
bases in Norway. From there, they urged, they could attack
British shipping and block the trade routes to England. The
question of protecting the iron-ore field at Gällivare and the
supply route from Narvik to the Baltic had not yet arisen.

After Russia attacked the Finns, however, rumours reached
Hitler that the British intended to send them help, probably
through Narvik, and he began to be alarmed for his iron-ore.
In January 1940 he set his staff the problem of deciding how
far an occupation of Norway seemed feasible in relation to
Germany's Continental strategy. The General Staff did not

believe the war could be decided in the North. They were reluctant to start operations in Scandinavia; they maintained that in any case such a move should follow and not precede an attack in the west.

The boarding of the *Altmark* in February 1940 showed, however, that the Allies were quite prepared to disregard Norwegian neutrality, and rumours of Allied plans to land in Norway made the High Command fear that the enemy might get there first. They decided to occupy Norway themselves. By so doing they would not only be sure of getting the iron-ore, whether it came by the Baltic during the summer or down the Norwegian coast in winter, but they would also, in their own words, give their Navy and Air Force "a wider start line against Britain", and stop any danger of Germany being outflanked and attacked from the Scandinavian peninsula. The General Staff, however, refused to tie up strong forces in what they considered a minor theatre, and except for mountain divisions, they only allotted recently mobilized units. Nor did they make any plan for meeting a British landing.

The original British plan also assumed that German troops would not be met on landing. The sailing of the two expeditions at almost the same time was therefore coincidental, and neither side expected to meet the other.

April 5

We came to a decision at the War Cabinet this morning to go on with the Narvik mine-laying. It is to be done on Monday 8th.[1] I personally don't think very much will happen. Now that the French have ratted over the mines in the Rhine, all attention in Europe will be diverted to us, to our "brutal" violation of Norwegian neutrality. It might have been diverted if Germany had been kept busy on the Rhine. Winston flew over to Paris to try to get the French to agree, but he seems to have failed—even to have

[1] The delay of three days had been caused by a vain hope that the French might change their minds about permitting Operation "Royal Marine".

been converted. They say that there is an aviation *crise* in France
and that things will not be safe till June. Probably the French
terror of starting bombing is the real reason. "*Tout le monde est au
fond egoiste*" is as true now as ever it was.

April 6

A very quiet War Cabinet, and my Instructions[1] to the people
who may have to act in Norway if the German reacts [to the
mine-laying operation] went through without a comment.

Halifax reported that the Ministers had a difficult time handing
in their Notes [telling the Norwegian and Swedish Governments
that the Allies were about to lay mines] in Stockholm and Oslo.
The old Swede remarked: "Then our two countries are very near
to war." What that meant I don't know.

April 7

I cannot think that we have a War Cabinet fit to compete with
Hitler. Its decisions are so slow and cumbersome. We still refer
the smallest thing to a Committee. Halifax is much too good a
man to compete with a lot of knaves. The Prime Minister is hopelessly unmilitary. . . . Winston becomes a sort of Chairman of the
Co-ordination Committee.[2] We shall have more strength there
if he can be kept upon the proper lines. But the whole show is
ponderous and clumsy.

April 8

We laid the mines off Narvik without incident and broadcast it
to the world.

[1] These Instructions were similar to those issued to General Mackesy
shortly before the collapse of Finland save that the Narvik force was
not now to cross the Swedish frontier without further orders. As
before, it was not intended that the landings should be carried out
unless the Norwegians were prepared to co-operate, though "token"
resistance could be brushed aside.

[2] On April 3 Lord Chatfield had resigned his office as Minister of
Co-ordination of Defence. On the following day it was announced
that Mr. Churchill would preside over the Military Co-ordination
Committee. The office of Minister of Co-ordination of Defence was
left unfilled.

Then we had various air reconnaissances which showed a German fleet moving out of the Baltic. It looked as if it had a troop-ship with it. A report had come in from Copenhagen to say that the Germans, under order from Hitler, had started off to occupy Narvik. We had the *Renown* and the *Birmingham*, with twelve destroyers, just south of Narvik, and the Main Fleet moving over to the Norwegian coast. If the Germans were really off to Narvik they ought to be caught between these two Fleets. Three 8-inch cruisers were also ordered out of Rosyth to the Norwegian coast. It may all come to nothing and it may be another pocket-battleship trying to get out as a raider. We may hear something more to-day. . . .

Winston is back from France full of blood and we shall have far more co-ordination of effort. He was like a boy this morning describing what he had done to meet the Germans. His physique must be marvellous, but I cannot think he would make a good Prime Minister. He has not got the stability necessary for guiding the others.

On the morning of April 7 German warships were sighted moving north off the coast of Jutland. As the day wore on, further signals suggested that a substantial enemy fleet was steaming up the North Sea. That night, the Home Fleet and the Second Cruiser Squadron sailed to intercept them, while the First Cruiser Squadron, which had been embarking our troops for Bergen and Stavanger, was ordered to leave them behind and join in the chase. The escorts for the Narvik and Trondheim troopships were also ordered to sail with the rest of the fleet. A sneak-out into the Atlantic of the German Fleet was quite possible. In fact, all this was only to cover a full-scale invasion of Norway.

Between 4.30 and 5 a.m. on April 8 our minefield was laid off the port of Narvik. That afternoon, while protests were being drafted in Oslo for transmission to London, the British Admiralty informed the Norwegian Legation that German troopships had been sighted, apparently bound for Narvik. Denmark was overrun. That night, in the face of Norwegian

resistance, German troops landed near Oslo and at Kristian-
sand, Stavanger, Bergen, Trondheim and Narvik. At the
latter, throughout the previous week, apparently empty German ore-ships had been bringing in supplies and ammunition.
Within forty-eight hours all the main Norwegian ports were
in enemy hands.

April 9

At 6.30 a.m. we had a meeting of Chiefs of Staff and we then
learnt that the Germans had actually sent ships and troops which
had occupied Bergen and Trondheim. They appeared to get in
quite easily. It is a lamentable thing that we went on argle-
bargling and here we are with the Germans [actually in Norway].

The War Cabinet has no idea of time. They could not be
summoned till 8.30 a.m.—hours lost waiting. Then we had the
most dreadful exhibition of loose talk. No decisions on principle,
leaving the Service people to carry them out.

By midday we knew that Denmark had completely surrendered
and her administration had been taken over by the Germans. The
Norwegians had refused [to surrender] and the Government had
gone to central Norway.

The Germans have occupied Bergen, Trondheim and Narvik. A
good show for them. Now it is for us to mop them up here.

We ought to knock out some of their Navy. Reynaud and
Daladier are now coming over.

It seems to me that all this will be followed as soon as possible
by an advance upon the Western Front. Holland will be easily
overrun and Belgium as far as the point to which we arrive—
probably the line of the Dyle.

You cannot make war by referring everything to Committees
and sitting wobbling and havering.

The logical conclusion is an attack on the Western Front
against both Belgium and Holland. There is nothing more we can
do now. We have given the Third Corps to France and we have
one Regular Brigade and the 49th Division for Scandinavia. Nothing more. That cannot be said to be much with which to come
and go. They will be fateful days these next few.

Complete wireless silence in the Fleet gives us nothing to go on. Eventually late evening before we get news.

The Germans have scored another point. They have done something very bold indeed and have used their Navy to cover these landings in Norway with great success. The Navy could not have prevented the Oslo landing, but the Narvik one is inexcusable. The Admiral of the place must have allowed a ship to slip through. It will be interesting to see what the attitude of the Norwegians was when the German ship came in. They cannot have been a big party. These neutrals are all terrified of the Germans and their brutality. . . .

A Supreme War Council at 5 p.m. Daladier and Reynaud. As usual it went well. It was agreed to try against Narvik and Bergen and Trondheim. But here we are, the whole day gone and nothing but talk. You cannot make war like this. Sooner or later if we are to win the war we must have proper control. . . .

We went on till 11.30 p.m. with the Co-ordination Committee. Winston in the chair and behaving with monkeyish humour. How he could I do not know, because the situation is bad. He had said at the Supreme War Council that the operation against Narvik was easy. Now it appears that the Germans have some 4,000 men there. A frightful piece of carelessness on the part of the Navy. After laying their mines they stood off and allowed some six German destroyers, a submarine and ten other ships to slip in. The ore-ships being empties were being returned to Narvik. Apparently they had been working up the coast with the men cooped up inside them. No examination by the Norwegians. Not a word to anyone. They are now in Narvik and making themselves secure. They may be making a fortress out of Narvik, pill-boxes, guns and everything else.

Now we have to go and take this on. A poisonous proposition and something which cannot be done in a few minutes. Luck is so far against us and we have bungled badly.

On the morning of April 10 the Cabinet decided to try to expel the Germans from one lodgement at a time, and to make the first attempt at Narvik. It was resolved to establish an advanced base at nearby Harstad, on an island about thirty-three miles north-west of Narvik. Two battalions were immediately available, and six more would follow.

April 10

Yesterday was rather a bad day for us. The Navy didn't do too well owing to the bad weather and we have been thoroughly out-witted. The place stinking with Germans and we not being able to find out anything. The Norwegian authorities too terrified to do anything. A bad show.

We decided to make a plan to try and take back Narvik. We have nothing ready and have never even contemplated any op-posed landing upon such a large scale. We shall have to mount it at express speed because every day is now of interest. Any fight at Narvik will bring every German aeroplane to the place like a lot of bees or hornets.

None of our efforts yesterday seemed to do much, though the Navy are all out. The two big German ships are still in the un-known. So much for our command of the sea. The Air say that they have hit one cruiser in Bergen in the stern and also one cruiser in the North Sea. Things are not good and we have been caught badly.

The Cabinet was a ragged one. The naval story is not a good one. So few reports in and the weather bad. The Fleet has not got the command of the North Sea and German ships are running about freely. The Germans have acted very boldly and have risked their everything. The two pocket-battleships are some-where—in the *Ewigkeit* as far as our Navy is concerned. The Fleet has again gone back to Scapa.

I have told the Co-ordination Committee that if there are 5,000 Germans in Narvik it is a major operation to turn them out. We cannot be hurried. We must be assured of the following:

(i) That Narvik cannot be reinforced [by the enemy] from the sea any more.
(ii) That we will require an advanced base near Narvik for the marshalling of our forces.

(iii) That it would be of great value if we could seize the port of Tromsö to the north now, and establish an oiling base for our destroyers.

(iv) That I get some officers into the country to find out what forces there are in Narvik with some certainty, so that we may make a plan.

(v) That we be given sufficient time in which to make our plans and carry them out.

I have put my people on to studying the problem and have sent for the Generals to get them down to the plan. We are still a hopelessly slow and desultory machine. . . .

The naval attack on Narvik seems to have been better than was expected. Although we lost a couple of destroyers we seem to have sunk a German destroyer, blown up an ammunition ship and set three other destroyers on fire. The bad part of the show is that there are still German destroyers outside Narvik. I am telling them that this must cease and that the Fleet must ensure that we do not have any more Germans in Narvik. I am also going to ask for a battalion to be sent straight across to the fiords north of Narvik so that it can establish itself and if necessary get the reconnaissances made for an attack against Narvik. The collection of pack and wheel transport is also an essential to the start of any attack against the town.

The Navy have recovered themselves a little since their blob in letting the Germans in. . . .

We think we have discovered at Harstad north of Narvik some Norwegian troops and I hope to get a man over to this place to buck them up.

On April 11, at a meeting of the Military Co-ordination Committee, the Chief of the Air Staff raised the question of an operation against Trondheim or Bergen, after Narvik had been recaptured, and authority was given to the Chiefs of Staff to study this project, but not to prepare for it.

By the 12th the War Cabinet was being strongly pressed by the Norwegian Government to recapture Trondheim, the suggestion being that unless this was achieved Norway and

Sweden might capitulate. The Cabinet agreed that even small-scale landings on the Norwegian coast would be valuable from a political point of view, and the Military Co-ordination Committee ordered a plan to be prepared.

April 11

Things are clearing up a bit. The German Navy has suffered a pretty good knock from all accounts, especially at Narvik. Finally, a cruiser goes off to-day at 11 a.m. with General Mackesy with 250 men of the Scots Guards, and they should be able to gain touch with the Norwegians at Harstad. We want a bit of luck.

1 a.m. 12th

I really cannot go to bed without putting down my last conference. Over came the First Lord [Churchill], Pound, and little Phillips, the Deputy Chief of the Naval Staff, with Newall and Joubert de la Ferté. They wanted me to divert part of the force for Narvik to Namsos, with a view to "staking out a claim", as they put it, for Trondheim.[1] I told them my reasons for not thinking it possible, and then it came out that General Mackesy, instead of sailing at 11 a.m. [on the 11th] was to sail at 12 noon on the 12th —that is a delay of 24 hours. Nobody had said a word to me of this, though the Naval Staff knew this after lunch on the 11th. Then I found that they had had a destroyer into Namsos who made no touch with the people there, and that they knew it and said nothing.

Anything worse as staff work I have never heard. Maddening. I am afraid I lost my temper and banged the table. Only two days before I had asked the Admiralty and Air Ministry to see that information came to me. I shan't get much sleep to-night.

[1] It seems that the Admiralty were now contemplating sending the Fleet into Trondheim. Ironside was urged to land a force at Namsos, about a hundred miles by road further north, whence it would advance on Trondheim and co-operate with a naval attack from the sea. He refused because, as he wrote afterwards, "a convoy packed for one place is not suitable for landing at another".

□□ The convoy for Narvik, with General Mackesy at its head, duly sailed. Not until after the General left was Admiral of the Fleet Lord Cork and Orrery appointed to command the naval forces which were to co-operate with him. The General had had no opportunity of making a combined plan with the Admiral, and there was a further complication over their respective Instructions. The Admiralty, Mr. Churchill complains, were not informed of the Instructions given to the General. The War Office were certainly unaware of the Instructions given to Lord Cork, for they had never been put down on paper. The Admiral had, in fact, been told by Mr. Churchill and by Admiral Pound to take no undue risks, but to strike hard to seize Narvik. The substance of the Instructions given to General Mackesy was as follows:

"His Majesty's Government and the Government of France have decided to send a Field Force to initiate operations against Germany in Northern Norway. The object of the Force will be to eject the Germans from the Narvik area and to establish control of Narvik itself. . . . Your initial task will be to establish your Force at Harstad, ensure the co-operation of Norwegian Forces that may be there, and obtain the information necessary to enable you to plan your further operations. . . . It is not intended that you should land in the face of opposition. You may however be faced with opposition owing to mistaken identity; you will therefore take such steps as are suitable to establish the nationality of your Force before abandoning the attempt. The decision whether to land or not will be taken by the senior naval officer in consultation with you. If landing is impossible at Harstad, some other suitable locality should be tried. A landing must be carried out when you have sufficient troops. . . ."

The Instructions contained the following reference to bombardment: "It is clearly illegal to bombard a populated area in the hope of hitting a legitimate target which is known to be in the area but which cannot be precisely located and identified."

Ironside had supplemented these Instructions with a written message delivered by hand to General Mackesy. It included the injunction: "Latest information is that there are 3,000 Germans in Narvik. They must have been knocked about by naval action. . . . You may have a chance of taking advantage of naval action and you should do so if you can.

"Boldness is required."

April 12

We had a dreadful Co-ordination Meeting under Winston. . . . I couldn't get him to draft the orders under which we were to operate. Eventually we decided upon Namsos just north of Trondheim. Not before the 16th, four days from now. A meeting till midnight that could have been run in a few minutes if we had a man to give us our orders.

April 13

At the Cabinet we had the most extraordinary debate upon whether we ought to shift from Narvik to Trondheim. I am glad to say that Winston backed me up in saying that we must deal with Narvik first. If the Trondheim expedition is so important that we must go for it, then we must at least invest Narvik. My instructions from Winston last night were that Trondheim was to be a "diversion". Now in the eyes of the Cabinet it has become a "main operation", and all because of a wire that has come in from the Military Attaché at Stockholm.

I have therefore sent to Mackesy to tell him to curtail his wings after taking Narvik and to Carton de Wiart to open his wings a bit at Namsos.

Namsos, the small port about eighty miles north of Trondheim, had not been seized by the Germans. Ironside had decided to put Major-General Carton de Wiart in charge of the Allied troops who would land at Namsos and advance from there to Trondheim. He had summoned him on the night of April 11 to the War Office. The General arrived after a hazardous journey from the West Country and was ordered to go to Namsos as soon as possible, and there make everything ready for the troops which would follow.

April 13 (continued)

1 *a.m.* The Navy have had a very fine effort in Narvik, redeeming completely their mistake. They went right up the fiord with nine destroyers and the battleship *Warspite*. Not very much resistance was made and the result was the breaking up by heavy gun-fire of four German destroyers at the quayside in the town, and the driving up a fiord of three more and their total destruction there. One field howitzer was put out of action and the enemy appears to have evacuated the town. There may still be 3,000 Germans there, but their centre has now gone and there should not be so much difficulty in mopping up the remains of the force. We apparently lost two destroyers.

Bucked up by this brilliant effort the Navy now wish to repeat the process at Trondheim. They have put up a completely new plan—which has the disadvantage of taking some time to execute. I said that we must go on with our Namsos landing which can now be increased by one of the brigades from Narvik.

Up to this point the Military Co-ordination Committee had agreed that the seizure of Trondheim should be studied, but that no preparations should be made and no troops should be set aside to carry it out until it was known for certain how big a force would be needed to capture Narvik. Now, however, Trondheim became a most tempting target. It was the ancient capital of Norway. It had a large and excellent harbour, and a railway system connecting it with Gällivare in the north, and with Oslo and Stockholm in the south. Its liberation from Hitler would hearten the Norwegians and might even persuade the Swedes to make some sort of resistance. These and other factors now led to an incident which, though not directly mentioned in the diary which Ironside wrote at the time, is best described in an account which he approved some years afterwards, and which accords with the clear recollection of his Military Assistant with whom he discussed the matter next day.

At 2 a.m. on the morning of April 14, Mr. Churchill, accompanied only by the Deputy Chief of the Naval Staff, Admiral Tom Phillips, came to Ironside's room at the War Office. "Tiny, we are going for the wrong place. We should go for Trondheim," said the First Lord. "The Navy will make a direct attack on it and I want a small force of good troops, well led, to follow up the naval attack. I also want landings made north and south of Trondheim, one at Namsos and the other at Andalsnes, to co-operate with the assault when it comes off by a pincer movement on Trondheim." Mr. Churchill was unable to give any date for the naval attack.

Ironside protested that he had no troops available for Namsos until Narvik had been taken. Mr. Churchill then insisted that the rear half of the Narvik convoy, which was carrying the 146 Territorial Brigade, should be diverted to Namsos. Ironside again protested, this time with some heat, that Mr. Churchill at least should know from his own experience how impractical such a diversion would be. If half the Narvik force were removed, the Narvik operation would be ruined. The troops and their equipment had been loaded and the administration organized for a single operation, and everything would be upset if half the convoy was detached. There would be no commander for the rear half because the Brigadier, Phillips, had, quite correctly, been taken on ahead by General Mackesy. It would be better, said Ironside, to abandon Narvik altogether, or at most, to invest it. He was overruled.

"This change," as Ironside was to write some years later, "would make many difficulties. I turned these over in my head.

(i) Troops already embarked for Narvik would have been packed for a Narvik attack and might not suit the attack further south at Namsos. There was more ice and snow at

Narvik. Comparatively little at Namsos. It was always a risk to alter a destination for a force already embarked.

(ii) If the other half of the Narvik convoy were redirected to Namsos, it might be impossible to get in touch with them and give them their orders as Mackesy had received his.

(iii) The Narvik attempt would be ruined if half [the] troops [were] taken away. Better avoid Narvik, but [the] French were keen on this.

I asked the First Lord of the Admiralty if he were acting as chairman of the Military Co-ordination Committee and was told 'yes'. I did not like the scheme and protested."

Ironside elaborated on this in a letter describing a talk he had had with the author of the British Official History of the Campaign in Norway:

"I gave him the whole incident of how Winston came into my room with the Sub-Chief of the Naval Staff at 2 a.m. in the morning and ordered me to divert the rear half of the Narvik convoy to the Trondheim affair. I told him that I protested violently, telling Winston that he of all people knew that a convoy packed for one place would not fit another, and furthermore that all sorts of unforeseen happenings must take place. As we know, the after-half had no officer above the rank of Lt.-Col. in it and we did not even know the name of the Senior one."

It has been subsequently suggested that the decision to divert the rear half of the convoy was taken at a meeting of the Military Co-ordination Committee. This does not agree with Ironside's very clear recollection of the incident. The decision, which Ironside deplored, was taken, so he asserted, at this meeting of three people in room 209 at the War Office in the early hours of April 14. And it was taken on the insistence of Mr. Churchill.

Later that morning the C.I.G.S. took the new direction that 146 Brigade heading for Narvik should be diverted to Namsos to the Chiefs of Staff Committee. 146 Brigade would

□□ land at Namsos after the Naval and Marine parties; and there
would be a landing of another naval party at Andalsnes at the
same time. It was also agreed that, with the permission of the
French, the first demi-brigade of Chasseurs Alpins should be
transferred to reinforce the Namsos and not the Narvik force.

The C.I.G.S. was almost alone in refusing to regard the
Narvik operation as a "walk-over". 146 Brigade landed at
Namsos on April 16 and 17, without much of their equipment and without their commander, Brigadier Phillips. It
was also without its anti-aircraft artillery, which was in one
of the leading ships which went on to Narvik. Ironside, as
we shall see, accepted this last-minute change of plan with
very serious and well-founded misgivings.

The first set-back occurred at Narvik itself. The troops
ordered to capture it were, as already related, now at sea, and
heading under General Mackesy for the Norwegian coast.
Their destination was the small port of Harstad, situated not
on the mainland but on an island some thirty-three miles to
the seaward and northwesterly side of Narvik itself. Here
they would land, establish a base, and in due course carry
out the assault.

The naval commander, Admiral of the Fleet Lord Cork
and Orrery, had sailed not with this convoy but some twelve
hours later, intending to meet General Mackesy at Harstad
and there co-ordinate the final plan of attack. On the 14th,
while still at sea, Cork received a signal from Admiral Whitworth, whose fleet was already in the North, informing him
that all the German destroyers and supply-ships in Narvik
harbour had been destroyed by the naval action of the previous day (the impending naval action referred to in Ironside's
letter to Mackesy); and suggesting that Narvik could now be
taken by direct assault. Lord Cork thereupon altered course
and steered for Narvik. He tried to contact the *Southampton*,
in which Mackesy had sailed, in the hope of diverting him
and his troops from Harstad to Narvik itself. His signal failed
to reach Mackesy in time, the expedition continued on its
way, and on the morning of the 15th most of the troops

arrived, not as the Admiral hoped at Narvik, but at Harstad. The rear half of the convoy had already been diverted towards Namsos, and here also troubles were soon to arise.

April 14

One of the fallacies that Winston seems to have got into his head is that we can make improvised decisions to carry on the war by meeting at 5 p.m. each day. It is regardless of the enemy and decisions which have to be made at all hours of the day as the enemy reacts.

The S. of S. is going to see the Prime Minister to-day and tell him that war cannot be run by the Staffs sitting round a table arguing. We cannot have a man trying to supervise all military arrangements as if he were a company commander running a small operation to cross a bridge. How I have kept my temper so far I don't know. It seems incredible that these things should happen.

We are now getting frantic telegrams from various Commanders in Norway, including the so-called C.-in-C. All to the effect that we must capture Trondheim at once or Norway will collapse. Poor devils, one can imagine them framing their telegrams. Having refused to have any conversations with us so as to let us have any idea of their dispositions or ideas, they now expect us to be ready in a few hours. It is natural for all neutrals.

Anyway, the thing is pace, audacity and speed. We must take a chance. Any scheme which means delay must be rejected. We must take a very special chance. Our great handicap is that we have such untrained troops with which to deal. Presumably the Germans have not sent their worst troops to these ports. . . .

King-Salter [the British military attaché] has arrived with the Norwegians and wires that their "morale is deplorable", British landings are essential at Trondheim to save the day.

I have put down the orders that we must issue and I have the thing in my head. It now remains to see if we can get approval from this Co-ordination Committee which has usurped the functions of the General Staff.

A meeting of the Chiefs of Staff to decide upon the Namsos landing. That should take place to-morrow night. We have to get Carton de Wiart there in the night to meet the naval officer who is making the naval landing to-night. Every untoward business that can be imagined has dogged our efforts. This illustrates the difficulties of improvising these combined operations:

(i) Mackesy, thinking that he had control of Phillips as his second in command, took him off the ship with his troops and put him with the leading Brigade for Narvik. Therefore if we detach Phillip's Brigade we do it without its commander.

(ii) The Navy failed to try landings at Namsos last night and are landing to-night. We do not expect to hear that these landings have been effected till late this evening.

(iii) The Bofors guns going to Rosyth had a broken coupling on their train and were delayed four hours.

(iv) The confusion of the Co-ordination Committee and waiting for their decisions has made any decisions by the Chiefs of Staff impossible.

Combined operations require the most careful preparation of any operations. Only the pressing need for haste makes it necessary for us to run these risks—for risks they are. One link in the chain falling out and there may be long delay. . . .

Co-ordination Committee not too bad. Winston more reasonable because he has had some rest. A stream of wires coming in asking us to save Norway by attacking at once. . . .

Winston rang me up at 11 p.m. and began a long story about Mackesy having gone off to land his three hundred men at Salangen [near Narvik] "without consulting Lord Cork". I told him that the landing was in charge of Mackesy. If Lord Cork was going to make a naval attack, well and good, but even that should be in concert with the General. Lord Cork has no right to use any of the troops without concert with the General. I am waiting now to get the First Sea Lord to see that no naval signals are sent out that will upset the General's attack.

261

April 15

I managed to extract the First Sea Lord out of the First Lord's room and to get him to understand that it was fatal to start monkeying about from here with the General on the spot. I now understand that the C.-in-C. of the Navy has turned down entering Trondheim in the same way as they did Narvik. . . . The original plan of Namsos was in conjunction with a Trondheim attack. Change is vicious. . . .

Maddening thing that we cannot get the General[1] ashore at Namsos. Namsos and Bangsand are, I hear, very poor places for landing, and the General will have his work cut out getting any large force ashore there. Nothing can be done until he gets there and makes a plan. . . .

A very heavy day. Too many Committees and too little work at what is our job—the war. Explaining details to a lot of old gentlemen is weary work. . . .

A Chiefs of Staff Committee to consider the attack on Trondheim. We had been presented with a paper on how to attack the place by the Joint Planners.[2] This was not a helpful document, and Slessor, the Air Commodore, then produced the theory that if we took the place it would be no good to us because we couldn't use it. Owing to the air. I told him that he had argued the wrong way. We were considering how to attack it, not whether we should or not. That politically we had been ordered to attack it and that it was the only way to save Norway. He then said that he considered that we should be driven back on Narvik. . . .

At that very moment, a report came in that the Germans had been bombing the *Somali*, the destroyer in Namsos, and had

[1] Carton de Wiart was to have crossed on the 14th, but did not cross till the 15th owing to bad weather.
[2] The Joint Planners suggested that no attempt should be made to take Trondheim by a direct assault; but that the garrison should be isolated by converging advances from Namsos and Andalsnes (which was now preferred to Aalesund as a base). But neither the Chiefs of Staff nor, on the following day, the Co-ordination Committee, ruled out a direct assault. They stipulated that Regular troops should be employed with the direct assault.

dropped eighty-one bombs in two hours and had never had a bomb within two hundred yards. . . .

We then went on to make the plan: two landings north and south, and then at a suitable moment a dash up the fiord with a battleship as at Narvik. . . . I was pretty forceful in what I said and I forced the Committee to continue planning. We are now at the critical moment of the war from a morale point of view and we must expect to suffer casualties.

April 16

We finished up last night with dinner in the Admiralty with Winston Churchill, Oliver Stanley, the Deputy Chief of the Naval Staff Tom Phillips, and myself. Winston was in great form and had recovered some of his sleep. He is a curious creature of ups and downs. Very difficult to deal with when in his downs. He was full of confidence in the strategical error that Hitler had made in going into Scandinavia.

We have always pointed out that in modern war the man in possession has an advantage—so long as he can keep his maintenance going. Turning people out of a position is difficult. It requires time. In this case, Hitler has inserted himself by a bold *coup* right into the middle of Norway. He has succeeded in taking the Norwegians by surprise as much as he did us. But if the people are stout-hearted and can keep going it should be possible to reach them and help them. This takes time. At the moment, each of the authorities with which we are in touch is shouting for astronomical numbers of weapons and for help in a matter of hours rather than days.

The country is exceedingly difficult. And the thaw is just arriving, which has put a final touch to the badness of the communications. Added to that, conditions in the North Sea have been as bad as one can conceive. The only thing with which one ought to be able to strike quickly is the air, and the R.A.F. are now finding that Germany is better placed to work in Scandinavia than we are.

Carton de Wiart got over in his Sunderland flying-boat to Namsos. He must have had a hell of a rough passage and I was more than thankful that he had arrived. It was after 5 p.m. and I began to wonder whether I would have to get my replacement General ready. I had him in the picture already and he was prepared to go. Not only had Carton had a bad passage, but when he arrived at Namsos he could not transfer to the destroyer because she was being so heavily bombed.

The two leading battalions of Brigadier Phillips' 146 Brigade had by now landed at Namsos, but minus their Brigadier, who was at Harstad. Port facilities were poor, and there were four feet of snow. Carton de Wiart, anxious to reach Namsos as soon as possible, had left in advance of his staff, and to add to his troubles, he had to improvise one on the spot.

Ironside sent him the following signal:

Well done. Capture of Trondheim considered essential. Plan proposed is as follows. Intend landing 600 Marines at Andalsnes (not Aalesund) April 17 to be reinforced if possible at earliest opportunity. Propose you should exploit from Namsos while force from Andalsnes will also threaten Trondheim in conjunction with Norwegian forces. Meanwhile combined operation for direct attack on Trondheim will be timed to take advantage of your pressure. If exploitation from Namsos possible presume you will use Phillips' Brigade from Lillesjona. Suggest follow up with 3 battalions Chasseurs. In this event latter can be directed to Lillesjona to tranship and await your orders. Only troops available for reinforcing Andalsnes quickly are Morgan's brigade. Arrangements for command as follows. All troops operating from Namsos under your command. Troops operating from Andalsnes under independent command. Forces making direct attack on Trondheim under separate independent command. Adoption of plan outlined above would therefore involve removal of Morgan's brigade from your command and your views on this are particularly required.

The Germans, besides capturing the various ports, landed many men inland by parachute and glider. They had many casualties in crash landings, but succeeded in securing several important tactical points. The Norwegians seemed unable to deal with them.

April 16 (continued)

Chiefs of Staff [Meeting] 10.15 till 11.30. War Cabinet from 11.30 to 1.30 p.m. Execution of decisions 1.30 to 2.30 p.m. The decisions should have been made by the C.I.G.S. the night before, as they are what I proposed and have now been agreed to by first the Co-ordination Committee and then the same Committee with the Prime Minister sitting as chairman. It seems intolerable that little military decisions cannot be made by the Secretary of State upon the advice of his C.I.G.S.

I told Stanley that the Co-ordination Committee was all right for long-term policies, but for improvising day-to-day operations against an enemy it is too futile to be considered. Anyway, we now have things fairly in train, and I hope to be able to sleep at home to-night and get a little rest before we have more to do.

The Canadians have offered two battalions for operations in Scandinavia. Cut down to 500 strong each. They jumped at the offer and we shall get people capable of doing anything. . . . Meanwhile (4 p.m.) no signs from Narvik. We are having difficulty with Narvik signals.

April 17

Things began at 7 a.m. A meeting of the Chiefs of Staff to consider the position:

(i) *Narvik*

Mackesy has apparently been faced with very bad snow conditions and extreme cold at night (below zero) and land operations are not feasible for some time. A wire was sent to him to concert with the Admiral as to an immediate landing with the battleship *Warspite*, so as to capture and occupy the port and then to mop up the available Germans. These Germans are apparently Austrian or Bavarian ski troops. I hope this will come off.

(ii) *Namsos*

Carton de Wiart has got two battalions ashore and is in touch with the Norwegian commander. The Norwegians have control of Steinkjer, an arsenal, and have troops at Levanger, within fifteen miles of Trondheim. Troops are moving up to stiffen the Norwegians and get them to start guerrilla fighting. The French are to land at Namsos three battalions of Chasseurs Alpins and move inland at once so that immediate pressure can be put upon Trondheim from Levanger. A French General in command under Carton de Wiart. Pressure of a very definite sort should be exerted by the 21st.

(iii) *Trondheim*

We have a force under [Major-General] Hotblack which will be brought directly into the fiord with the Navy to capture Vaernes aerodrome and join with Carton de Wiart's force and mop up Trondheim. The numbers available are Berney-Ficklin's Regular [15th] Brigade of the 5th Division, 1,000 Canadians, and as a reserve Lammie's Brigade of Terriers.

(iv) *The Andalsnes Area*

The Navy failed to get its 600 men ashore owing to submarines. It is trying again to-day, followed immediately by Morgan's Territorial Brigade. They should move in to the junction at Dombas. . . .

Enemy bombing has been most persistent all along the Norwegian fiords, but most ineffective. At Harstad, near Narvik, nine planes bombed for five hours and hit no ship or even the town. No casualties. Carton de Wiart at Lillesjona and Namsos had some two hours with five planes on the *Empress of Australia*, then empty, without result. I have impressed upon all forces to push straight in from the sea and not to have any rendezvous and delay before [? after] they disembark. We must be bold and take some risk. . . .

I have just sent a memo to the D.C.I.G.S.[1] who will be going to
be C.-in-C. in Scandinavia. I have put down the lines:

(i) *Narvik*

Naval Base. Strongly defended A.A. and sea. Norwegian
troops with small British Garrison under British Commander. Traffic in iron-ore and mending of railway to
Sweden.

(ii) *Trondheim*

H.Q. of Army and probable H.Q. of Norwegian
Government.

(iii) *Norwegian Troops*

Some sort of Beresford as in Portugal. Perhaps Admiral
Evans and an Army Staff to reorganize the Norwegian
forces.

(iv) *Future Forces*

Armoured cars. Guerrilla troops. Arms and equipment.

. . . Massy said to-night that he thought our luck had changed.
I shall be more thankful when this Trondheim affair is over. It will
be a great feat of war if we bring it off. No news of any appreciation from Mackesy.

April 18

A disturbing wire from Mackesy at Narvik. He has apparently
pictured himself with French troops which have never been under
his command. I am afraid we have a *"coup manqué"* here. . . .

Carton de Wiart has his British Brigade ashore [at Namsos]
and the first lot of French ought to be there to-night and the
second [lot] the next night. We ought to get a definite success
here with luck. The Marines are ashore at Andalsnes and Morgan
should be ashore the next night pushing on to Dombas. . . .

The Narvik story will not be a good one. We started off with it
as the main objective. Then suddenly switched to Trondheim and
left the Narvik Expedition by itself. A Co-ordination Committee
under the P.M. We told him of the situation. . . .

[1] Major-General Massy had been appointed to command the Allied
Forces which would operate in Central Norway, but Narvik was not
to come under his command.

To cap all our troubles, Hotblack, the man told off as a Major-General to command the Trondheim main naval attack landing troops, was found in the night unconscious at the bottom of the Duke of York steps. He is now unconscious in Millbank Hospital. No sign of any wound on him. He may have fallen down or been knocked down. Nobody knows what happened.[1] . . .

Dinner at the Admiralty with Winston Churchill. He was very human. Told me that he had wired to Lord Cork to see if the situation could be cleared up. I told him I had also wired to Lord Cork. . . . I have come to the conclusion that I must send up another officer to investigate and if necessary take over from both Mackesy and Fraser. A man like Williams and a good Brigadier may perhaps see the situation through. It really is damnable.

April 19

We started at 8.30 a.m. and were out from the Co-ordination Committee, which I call the Decontamination Committee, by 11.30 a.m. The S. of S. then had to go off to the War Cabinet and I was not able to see him or talk to him for a minute. We are in a vicious circle. Whatever we do, we have to appear in front of Committees to justify the military recommendations we have made. Strategy is directed by odd people who collect odd bits of information. This is discussed quite casually by everyone. When the General Staff puts anything up it has to be justified in front of the wretched Decontamination Committee—composed of civilians, who will not listen to the military arguments, and then leave the details alone. It is a ridiculous situation. What ought to happen is that a C.-in-C. should be appointed at once to fight this battle for us. The War Office are doing it at the moment. The Naval C.-in-C. and the Army C.-in-C. are impossible to put in touch with each other. Therefore they cannot fight the battle.

If we appoint a C.-in-C. now, his staff are not ready to function yet and he is literally in no state to take over. The Cabinet is avid for news and would take up his time explaining what he is doing.

[1] General Hotblack had, in fact, had a stroke. Brigadier Berney-Ficklin was appointed to succeed him as commander of the troops which were to go into Trondheim with the Fleet.

I must try and get him going now. It is too late to send him in
after Trondheim has been captured.

At 1 p.m. in came a note asking for a Chief of Staff meeting
at 2 p.m. to decide whether we should go on feeding the two
forces on either side of Trondheim or to go on with the direct
attack on the port. That has apparently become more and more
inacceptable to the C.-in-C. Fleet and has already been put off till
the 25th and does not look like being possible before, or perhaps
even then. . . .

A wire from Mackesy who doesn't appear to be in the closest
liaison with Lord Cork. He appears to have failed utterly and to
be in a thoroughly disgruntled state. We shall have to liquidate
this affair of Narvik. . . .

Morgan has sent in a very good wire showing that he is *au fait*
with the situation and is in touch with the Norwegians.

At 3.30 p.m. came the news that Berney-Ficklin [who had replaced Hotblack in command of the Trondheim force] had
crashed with his staff. All knocked out though none killed. A
peculiar fatality over this wretched Trondheim attack. Two of
our best commanders knocked out as they had just got the plans.
Now we have to pick a third and get him into the picture.

A wire from the Military Attaché, Norway, King-Salter, saying that "he is taking" Morgan's Brigade[1] to the south as the
position is critical. He has no right to and the Brigade has neither
transport nor guns and would be in an impossible position.

But it is necessary to prop up the Norwegians as much as
possible. If they fall, our attack on Trondheim may be made
impossible.

The situation was now as follows. At Harstad Lord Cork
had urged General Mackesy to follow up the destruction of
the German shipping in Narvik by a direct assault, but the
General considered that such an attack, even if preceded by a
naval bombardment, was unlikely to succeed. The weather

[1] The Germans were advancing from the south very rapidly towards
Trondheim. It was necessary to hold them off if Trondheim was to be
captured.

□□ had worsened, and his troops were ill-equipped for Arctic conditions. 146 Brigade had been diverted to Namsos, and Mackesy had been informed that the Chasseurs Alpins would not now be sent to him. The military and naval commanders were thus at deadlock.

Four hundred miles to the south, trouble was also brewing. The opening moves in the attack on Trondheim had begun and were making progress. Carton de Wiart with 146 Brigade had landed at Namsos, and was about to advance on Trondheim from the north, and Brigadier Morgan with 148 Brigade had landed at Andalsnes whence, it was hoped, he would advance on Trondheim from the south. While the two forces thus converged, it was proposed to clinch their overland attack by a third, crucial move, namely a frontal assault on Trondheim from the sea, carried out by the Royal Navy, and followed through by 15 Brigade and the Canadians, with a second brigade in reserve.

But things had already gone wrong. Instead of marching northward on Trondheim, Morgan had had to move south-eastwards and away from it, so as to hold off the enemy who were pressing strongly up from the south. The southern pincer on Trondheim had thus swung open, while the northern pincer (Carton de Wiart) had scarcely begun to close. At this juncture the situation might still have been saved and Trondheim might still have been captured if the third move, to which both these operations were subsidiary and on whose success their usefulness entirely depended, had been immediately executed, namely the direct assault from the sea. The troops (15 Brigade and others) stood ready to embark, and although two of their commanders, Hotblack and Berney-Ficklin, had been lost, a third officer, Paget, for whom the war was to hold a most distinguished career, had been immediately appointed. But now the Navy had second thoughts.

Admiral Sir Charles Forbes, commander of the Home Fleet, had been pressed by the Admiralty to consider forcing an entry into Trondheim harbour. He examined the project with care and was doubtful. His doubts proved infectious, and on April 18 both the Admiralty and the Chiefs of Staff began to question the wisdom of the operation. Germany had command of the air, a large number of capital ships would be hazarded, and even if the naval assault succeeded, our troops might be unable to land in the face of air attack. The garrison were said to be improving their defences, there had been serious newspaper leakages about what we meant to do, and there had been neither time nor opportunity for the careful inter-Service planning so essential for carrying out a complicated, dangerous and delicate combined operation. On the 19th the Chiefs of Staff and the Military Co-ordination Committee on which General Massy, the Commander-in-Chief of the Central Norway forces was representing the C.I.G.S., recommended instead of a direct naval assault a pincer movement from Namsos and Andalsnes. Their decision was endorsed by the Prime Minister on the following day.

The change of plan was particularly galling to Admiral of the Fleet Sir Roger Keyes, who had himself offered to lead a naval assault on Trondheim. On several occasions he tried to enlist Ironside's support, but Ironside had to tell him that this was a matter for the Admiralty.

April 20

The new situation brought about by the giving up of the main attack on Trondheim means a great deal more weight upon the two little ports of Namsos and Andalsnes. Weight which we never expected would come there. Now we must mount all the paraphernalia of a Base port to see that it [the force] doesn't fall down in front. These two little ports have done very well with their forceful commanders. Now it is a matter of getting Carton de Wiart into Trondheim as quickly as possible. I believe as a basis of thought that we ought to be able to take the place inside a month.

I made an appreciation of the situation which I have *especially* made on the pessimistic side because I don't wish the Cabinet to take too rosy a view of our chances, chiefly because of the air danger. All the better if we get through earlier. There are so many reports of the Germans reinforcing Trondheim by air that one cannot neglect them. But they must be woefully short of ammunition and guns, and many of the planes must have crashed on arrival. They are absolutely ruthless and will spare no effort to prevent us from getting a good port. Until we have a good port we cannot expect to have enough men to fight the Germans in the south.

The whole of Audet's first contingent [the French Chasseurs Alpins] got ashore at Namsos in the night without incident. We seem now to have the technique of waiting till dusk and then coming in and getting everything off in the night. . . .

Our Military Decontamination Committee only lasted till about midnight. Winston was fairly moderate in his criticisms of detail. I handed in my paper and that has gone on to the Prime Minister. Now that we have the C.-in-C. Scandinavia appointed [Major-General Massy] he will take on any movement of the troops and the direction of the moves ashore. That relieves us and I shall not be forced to spend my time explaining local movements. Now it is a question of what Sweden is going to do.

Mackesy seems to be moving a little.

We had a successful Chiefs of Staff and War Committee. Winston is very apt to paint a rosy picture in his enthusiasm. He forgets all the administrative snags that exist and is run away with by his own explanations. We have been very lucky in our landings. *Unberufen*, not one single transport has yet been hit and we have had not one single man hit. May that continue. We now have a stream of transports approaching Namsos and Andalsnes, with as many troops as can be brought into Scandinavia. Until Trondheim is captured we cannot maintain more than I have in sight and we must now devote all our energies to capturing it. . . .

A bad wire in from Carton de Wiart about bombing at Namsos. Winston rang me up and I went over to see him. We found that the French Admiral had had his ship hit and had gone off with his three empty transports taking the [British] A.A. cruiser with him. He thus left his men without any A.A. defence and had no right to take our cruiser away. Carton de Wiart said that "effect on French bad". Not too good a beginning for the famous Alpini.

We have handed over the command of the forces at Narvik to Lord Cork. . . . Mackesy has not proved a very bold leader. . . . He would not try a *coup de main* at Narvik at a moment when he knew that we wanted speed and boldness. . . . The Germans are terribly strong and have been preparing for years for all this. Can we make up the leeway we have lost in all these years of sloth?

April 21 (Sunday)

When I look back upon the eight months of war that we have had I wonder whether we are sane. First Belisha who simply thought of nothing but himself, and now the operations run by committees. I cannot see how a war can be run like that. Perhaps it will settle down, as we are essentially a courageous and sensible people. I think the clumsy war machine comes fundamentally from the distrust that is in, or has been put in, the minds of the civilians of the military man. Direction of affairs must never be allowed to drift into a military dictatorship. I thought from the very first that each morning's Cabinet was taken up with the description in detail of every little incident in the air and naval fighting. It was, and still is, despite its seriousness, like a lot of children playing a game of chances. One hopes each day that the Cabinet will get down to essentials and leave the work of war to be executed with some degree of chance [of success] by the staffs.

With the coming of serious operations we hear less talk of politics. We are in the war and seem to have slipped into it quite naturally, but absolutely unready. Now we must get on with it. But there still are people who talk about the unjust Versailles Treaty and how we could have avoided this war. It doesn't seem to me to be the Treaty but the people of Germany who made war inevitable. The people of Germany were defeated in the war of 1914–18, a terrible blow to their pride. Their pride expresses itself in an outward show of military greatness and love of power. No other people has it. They have shown it over and over again. After this last war [1914–18] their leaders set to work to prove to themselves and their people two facts:

(i) That they were defeated by treachery on the home front.
(ii) That they had been tricked into asking for a military armistice.

The average German never accepted the fact that the defeat—if it were one—or the Treaty was in any way permanent. The German leaders called it a period of armistice. They had done the same after Jena. They had a firm belief in their star and considered it impossible for a superior people like themselves to be held down by inferior people such as all other Europeans. The iniquity of the Treaty of Versailles was used as propaganda at home and abroad. One might almost say that had there been no treaty one would have had to have been invented.

It was the coming of the Nazi Party which made war both inevitable and possible. Conditions economically in Germany were such that the people were only too willing to accept a seeming offer of rescue and safety given by the vigorous Nazis. Instead of accepting some of their programme as they would have done in normal circumstances and with a normal political change, the German people rushed headlong at the new Party. And before they knew what had happened they found themselves in the grip of a tyranny, of an efficient tyranny, greater than anything ever before seen. There is no turning-back for Germans now. Then the Nazis played upon the spirits of the German people. Mass meetings, inspiring tunes and marches. Uniforms. Fiery speeches and promises. Propaganda used relentlessly in the Press and with the wireless. The Nazi organization did away with liberty as we know it and commenced upon the youth of the country. In the twenty-one years intervening between the two wars the Germans had produced a new generation after the model designed by the Nazis. A perfect machinery, the most perfect Governmental machine that has ever been set up.

The Nazis had the chance of studying the tenets and the results achieved by the Bolsheviks and the Fascists, and they had a much more amenable, disciplined and organizable population with which to deal.

I suppose two main thoughts have been uppermost in the Nazi ideas of government:

(i) Self-sufficiency. Especially in war.
(ii) *Lebensraum* for the development of the superior German people.

Napoleon tried to get self-sufficiency in France and failed. And the *Lebensraum* idea has developed from the idea of re-incorporating essentially German peoples inside the Reich to the absorption or subjection of all alien—and thus inferior—peoples.

The elimination of the Jews became essential both to get rid of an unamenable portion of the population and to get hold of the Jews' riches. There followed the disciplining of the various Churches, for they also impeded political efficiency.

The point which will only be solved at the end of this war is how much the Nazi spirit has permeated the people, and whether it will stand the test of defeat, if defeat should be its lot. Perhaps there are even many people in Germany who welcomed war in 1939 because it might mean release for them. An escape from paganism. How many will survive the war? The *Lebensraum* and the self-sufficiency has taken Germany into so many countries that one expects a new victim every morning.

Have we got the power to check this last one, or have the Germans stolen once more a march on us? Only time and a staunch spirit will tell.

CHAPTER XVIII

Norway: Defeat and Withdrawal

April 21 (continued)

About 8 a.m. I got the reports. A mixed bag.

At Namsos, the absence of the A.A. cruiser, taken away by the French Admiral, allowed the Germans to destroy Namsos railhead. Audet, the French General, seems to have got inland, but has been affected by the bombing. "He wishes Gamelin informed." A typical French remark which one must pass over as being made in stress. There is now nothing to be done but to try to recover the station and make a road L. of C. It means no more troops there.[1]

At Narvik we have a complete *non-possumus* from Mackesy, after a reconnaissance. . . . I should say that a limited objective of the town of Narvik should be possible under cover of the *Warspite* and other cruisers.

At Andalsnes we have had no trouble so far. Morgan has moved right down to Lillehammer [more than half-way to Oslo] and taken over a bit of the front line from the Norwegians. Effect said to be electrical. The flow into this end is still devilish slow. We are like two fencers playing for an opening. In a country like this it is very slow.

[1] Ironside meant that now the railway station had been destroyed, the troops already on the spot could be supplied, though with difficulty, but no more troops could be sent to help them because it would be impossible to supply them as well.

*The key to the whole thing is a base and we have lost one trick at
Namsos.* We must get A.A. stuff across and get the air to try and
keep these swine down. . . .

The S. of S. has just sent for Dill and I have given him a paper
of notes so that we can talk with one voice. . . . We have chosen
Festing with a couple of officers [to go with a mission to the Nor-
wegians]. He knows the country and can easily have interpreters
attached to him if necessary. Language is not essential. I hope that
we are not going to have divided counsels. I may have to stand
down if he thinks that Dill can run it better than I can.[1]

I have prepared a paper for the S. of S. to take to the War
Cabinet upon the situation. We had some hours' discussion, with
Dill in the room. We all agreed eventually. Now we have to get
this paper discussed and decided upon. It is then to be brought to a
Co-ordination Committee. It is then decided that I shall go
across early to-morrow morning to see Gamelin in order to dis-
cuss the military situation. Then we go on to the Supreme War
Council. . . .

We have had an important ship with motor transport and a
signal section torpedoed by a submarine. The first to go.[2]

> The direct assault on Trondheim having been abandoned,
> it was now planned to reinforce Carton de Wiart at Namsos
> with the whole of the 1st Light Division of the Chasseurs
> Alpins, block the railway running into Trondheim from the
> east, and thus encircle the Germans. The 15th British Brigade,
> hitherto earmarked for the assault on Trondheim, would join
> Morgan at Andalsnes, and General Paget was put in com-
> mand of the combined force. Morgan had already reached
> Lillehammer so as to stop the Germans reinforcing Trond-
> heim from their main base at Oslo.

[1] General Sir John Dill, hitherto commanding the First Corps in
France, had been brought back as Vice-Chief of the Imperial General
Staff to relieve Ironside of much of the committee and departmental
work. Major (as he then was) Francis Festing was to have a distinguished career in the Far East, and himself became C.I.G.S. in 1957.

[2] A ship with A.A. guns for Namsos was also torpedoed, so Namsos
was short of A.A. protection.

All such schemes depended on having enough bases and lines of communication, and these would certainly be heavily attacked from the air. Ironside meanwhile had crossed to France.

April 22

A lovely morning and we got into the green and yellow plane at 8 a.m. sharp. A head wind and we took almost two hours. Down to Vincennes where we found Gamelin at 10.30 a.m. I found him quite calm and as kindly as ever. I told him the situation and how we had a difficult time in getting our people ashore at little ports of little importance. He told me that Reynaud had been very difficult, getting very excited. He wasn't going to have another Finland. What were the British doing? Why did they not get on with it? Gamelin said: "I had to get very angry twice and told them that I couldn't continue commanding if things were not left to the British in their own sphere." He finally told them that sitting round a table thousands of miles away from the scene of action is to behave like "les stratégistes du Café de Commerce. Voilà ce que nous faisons içi." He finished up by telling me that we could employ the French troops where we wished and how we wished, so long as in the end we collected them under their General.

I then had a very cheery lunch at the H.Q. Mess and then to the Embassy where I found the P.M. and Winston. I told the P.M. that we had a free hand and that we could do what we liked militarily. That seemed to please him. He was very calm and smoking one of the Embassy cigars in great good humour. Winston very much interested in the Narvik affair. He wanted to divert troops there from all over the place. He is so like a child in many ways. He tires of a thing, and then wants to hear no more of it. He was mad to divert the Brigade from Narvik to Namsos and would hear of no reason. Now he is bored with the Namsos operation and is all for Narvik again. It is most extraordinary how mercurial he is. . . .

Then the Supreme War Council in the great room at the Quai D'Orsay. Reynaud started and made a long speech. Then followed by the P.M. Complete agreement to continue as fast as possible in Scandinavia. . . . Everyone on the French side of the bare table—some twenty—was taking copious notes—Generals, Admirals and Diplomats. Ismay tells me that he has to produce the minutes. They never produce anything after all their writing.

It was terribly hot in the room and it was with difficulty that I managed to get a window open. We were finally away at 6 p.m. to meet again tomorrow at 9.30.

April 23

Writing in the big Flamingo. I was awake very early, thinking of the operations.

We had a successful Conseil. . . . There was at first a sharp diversion of opinion over the case that Germany attacks Holland first without going for Belgium. This may also be imminent. We want to bomb in Germany immediately. The French did not. After a good deal of arguing it was decided that we should have our way, bombing troops, marshalling yards and all the oil refineries in the Ruhr.

We then had a long argument over the forces on the ground. If Belgium is long-sighted, she will see that the German occupation of Holland will turn her main positions and that she will be at the mercy of Germany at a later date. . . . Gamelin has a free hand to advance or not according to circumstances. He has not to approach one or either Government. So far so good. . . .

(Later)

Back in a Flamingo to find Oliver Stanley and Dill sitting very glum in the War Office. Stanley said that he had told the P.M. that the situation at Namsos was desperate before he left for Paris. He never told me he had said this and the P.M. never said this to me. The position was not in my opinion desperate. Then Winston had a wire from the Admiralty saying that the Germans had landed from ships behind Phillips' Brigade at Verdal and that Steinkjer had been bombed to pieces. No news of the French at Namsos whatever, and Carton de Wiart is talking about evacuation and has asked for ships to be ready. There are more troops ashore at Namsos than there are Germans at Trondheim, and there should be no question of any hurried evacuation being necessary. I cannot understand this at all.

I have told the C.-in-C., Massy, to get a staff officer ashore at Namsos to see what is really the position. . . .We have made an effort to get forward and have apparently not been able to get there in time to stem the German advance, which goes very quickly. Also, the Swedes have allowed a train to go through to Narvik with medical stores and food.[1] This is against all that they should have allowed, and we have protested but cannot expect to do more than that.

I find people talking about "desperate situations" and of "evacuation" as if it had to be carried out in a minute. Too many damned strategists who all have a finger in the pie, all amateurs who change from minute to minute and are either very optimistic or very pessimistic. Very difficult to make war under such circumstances. We must get back to allowing the soldiers to make decisions. . . .

Things ended up as a long day. We had a Chiefs of Staff Committee at 8.45 p.m. and went straight on to a Contamination Committee, which we left at 11.30 p.m. A real stupid wrangle about stupid little tactics. Every plan is taken and torn to pieces by a lot of civilian amateurs. We simply cannot get on with the work at all. We are always explaining stupid detail. How can a staff function?

April 24

There is no doubt in my mind that any effort at taking Trondheim within ten days does not exist unless it can be done by the Navy by direct assault. There is no possibility of doing this. Also, the situation of the poor old Norwegians on their Oslo front, so-called, is very poor. They have gone back a long way and show no signs of being able to stand at all. Whether we shall be able to check the retreat with British troops or not I do not know, but I think it doubtful.

What it means is that the Germans will get more than probably Trondheim and all that that means in submarines, safely housed

[1] And, as was later discovered, troops.

in the deep fiord. Almost worse than the Zeebrugge show in the last war. Pretty serious.

The Germans can pour in more men to Oslo than we possibly can at Andalsnes. A poor lookout for any operations in this part of the world.[1]

April 25

We finished up with a Chiefs of Staff Committee at 5 p.m. and then the P.M. in the chair of the Co-ordination Committee at 7 p.m. These tried to examine Massy's plan in detail, which they were incapable of doing, since none of them could realize the conditions. All of them kept saying "I cannot think why they don't carry out demolitions." "How does the enemy get on so fast?" "We must prepare for evacuation. Cut our losses." Poor Oliver Stanley was very down at heart. He gets very tired and at the moment his mind is on evacuation and on nothing else.

The wretched Norwegians are withdrawing as fast as they can and last night we had a desperate telegram saying that they had been promised the capture of Trondheim and nothing had come. There would be a *débâcle* if we did not tell them what our intentions were. I am afraid that they have no arms and no will to fight like the Finns had. The poor C.-in-C. expects us to do a miracle.

The Namsos force is still there and the French have not done very much in getting out to see what is in front of them. I am afraid that they expected to land under better conditions and have gone a bit sour on us. Winston evidently thought that the Cabinet required bucking up, for he delivered an oration pointing out the way in which we had entered into Norway. It certainly had the effect of heartening up poor Sam Hoare, who was in the depths of despair. The P.M. is really very wonderful. A stout man.

Heavy snowstorms at Narvik. The results of the bombardment by the Navy are disappointing. I think that Mackesy is not doing very much in the way of pushing. . . .

[1] With the Germans in occupation of the good port of Oslo, their rate of reinforcement was also much greater than ours in the poor port of Namsos.

A disturbing wire that the Germans have pushed the Norwegians back on the eastern railway line to a place called Tynset, which is well up to Stören. If they succeed in getting only a little further, and I see no signs of the Norwegians being able to hold them up at all, then we cannot stop the relief of Trondheim. We cannot then get much further from Andalsnes and must limit our effort there.

Winston was a bit wild at the Cabinet, trying to command the troops in the field and railing at us for not having carried out demolitions on the front held by the Norwegians. . . .

I feel that if we are forced to evacuate, we must make a very short plan, get it agreed to in principle, and then have no further discussion in detail by this wretched Co-ordination Committee. The P.M. is quite agreeable to this . . . but is forced to sit on the Committee himself to prevent Winston from running off the rails.

It looks more and more likely that we will have to contemplate some evacuation of our troops. It may well mean the loss of a lot of equipment. Even Narvik seems a little further away owing to the bad weather.

At Namsos Carton de Wiart had pushed forward through deep snow and German air attacks, and by April 19 was fifty miles from Trondheim. The Germans had then sent troops from Trondheim by way of the inner fiord, there was heavy fighting on his western flank during the 21st, and his force was compelled to return to Namsos, where the Chasseur Brigade had stayed put. Carton de Wiart then decided that there was nothing for it but evacuation.

At Andalsnes, where General Paget was now in overall command, Morgan had joined up with the Norwegians at Lillehammer, more than half-way down the railway line to Oslo, where they were heavily engaged by Germans from the capital. On the 24th he was reinforced by the leading battalion of 15 Brigade, originally intended for the sea-assault on Trondheim. Here also there was deep snow (the thaw was just beginning), and as none of our troops were able to run on skis, Morgan arranged with the Norwegian commander that the British should fight near the road and the Norwegians on the high ground on our flanks. But the Norwegians, completely exhausted, fell back and moved to the rear. Morgan was constantly outflanked, and he also had to retreat. A valiant attempt had been made to provide our forces with protection from the air. A squadron of Gladiators flew from the *Glorious* on April 24 and landed on a frozen lake forty miles from Andalsnes. But an English newspaper published the news of their arrival, they were promptly bombed, and soon could fly no more.

April 26

We had another damnable evening [last night]. At 5 p.m. we were assembled as the Chiefs of Staff in the Admiralty War Room to consider the reconstitution of a main naval blow at Trondheim. This was a modified version of what the Navy had said took up the whole Fleet and was not worth it. Now, when the evacuation of Norway looks more than probable, it is put on as a desperate measure. Another change of plan. Men like Winston never think of the tail, which whisks about so violently behind the head they push so gaily into new adventures.

I told the Chiefs of Staff that I must take the proposed plan away and consider it with Massy, who was running the operations, and that we must assemble again. At 9 p.m. Here I put my points which were:

(i) Unless we did a main naval attack on Trondheim the early evacuation of Norway was essential. No alternative.

(ii) We must therefore order all the ingredients and prepare to carry it out.

(iii) The possibility of carrying out the attack depended upon whether we can stabilize the position to the south on the Andalsnes–Dombas front. Here the Germans have practically driven the Norwegians out of the way and are very nearly on the point of relieving Trondheim.

(iv) That if we evacuate Norway without having made a great

283

effort we shall be carrying out a move which helps the Germans.

(v) We have a lot of troops in sight and shall not have used them.

(vi) Political effect disastrous.

We were still talking and making our recommendations to the War Cabinet, when in walked Winston and said he wanted to hear what we were deciding. He had spoken to the Prime Minister who had agreed that all preparations should be made. I said that my Secretary of State had been informed of nothing, that he couldn't be informed for some time as he was away. That we had to deal with the French over all troops that were in France. I then told the S. of S. by telephone and he listened for some time and eventually said, "It makes it all very difficult." That didn't help very much after all.

Back to the War Office to bed at midnight.

Winston wants to make some change. He says that he is not going merely to attend a Co-ordination Committee and give his opinion, to be weighed with other opinions.

We simply cannot make war like this. It is too clumsy to have any success against a resolute enemy like the Germans.

We had a meeting of Chiefs of Staff at 9 a.m. [this morning] and the Co-ordination Committee at 10 a.m. There was no argument and the whole thing was over by 11.30 a.m. We recommended not to do a Trondheim operation owing to the scale of air attack which would come against us and to the scale of air defence that will be necessary afterwards if successful—80 high-angle guns and 160 low-angle—and this was accepted.

We were to push on with the Narvik operation quietly and carefully with the troops we have directed on them—the 1st Chasseur Division plus the Foreign Legion, two Battalions and four Battalions of Poles. The French 2nd Chasseur Division to go to the Clyde and there be available if necessary.

I have now issued the orders for the eventual evacuation of the Central Norway Force on a military basis, not to be hampered by a political consideration. We begin with Namsos. All the

Ministers were duly impressed with the gravity of the decision
and they had no arguments of a controversial nature. Rather a
welcome change. Now I hope that we shall have the machinery
working better.

I have never seen such relief on Ministers' faces as I saw. They
all, including the P.M., began making up stories they could tell
the public and make out that our stroke against Trondheim was to
put the Germans off Narvik. I daresay they will make a story that
will pass muster. Meanwhile we have the very difficult operation
of evacuation. Luckily, the amount we have engaged is small. It
will not be easy unless we have more luck than we have had so
far. It may teach us a lesson that you cannot make lightning
changes.

The thing that troubles me is that we have not taken the
French into account, nor called a Supreme War Council to consent to it. I don't know how we get over that.

As I thought, trouble is beginning. I went off down to the
aerodrome to fly over to France to acquaint Gamelin with the
decision when a message came that Gamelin would fly over to
England. I met General Mittelhausser at Hendon and told him.
He was flabbergasted and poured out a long story that we should
lose everything, including the iron-ore in Sweden, because the
Swedes would give in to all the Germans' demands. . . .

Mittelhausser and Gamelin are going to see the Ambassador
to-night and ask to see the Prime Minister. They naturally feel
that we have not carried out the orders of the Supreme War
Council and they may well say that we are not to have any of the
troops of the French contingent for Narvik. And they will be in
their rights if they do. I think we have done wrong in not calling
the Supreme War Council. I wonder if we shall now get any
counter-orders. Nothing has been done yet to evacuate, and the
Generals are studying the question of evacuation. We shall be
hard put to it if the P.M. gives in over the decision that the
Co-ordination Committee came to.

The P.M. rang me up and asked me to see Gamelin before
9.30 p.m. when he proposed to meet him, to find out what was in
his mind. This I did at the Embassy, having a spot of dinner with

Corbin and all the assembled officers. He seemed tired and disconcerted. He thought that the British Government was mad to think of evacuation. He even talked of holding on to the mountains in a *tête de pont*—but what for he could not say. I suppose a matter of prestige. We ought to be dealing with realities not imponderables.

Then we saw the P.M. at 9 p.m. and the French at 9.30 p.m. till 11 p.m. Then we propounded our cases. The French: morale. Ours: practical tactics. It was finally decided to get Reynaud over for a Supreme War Council and that we should sit down and examine the details of any project the French might like to put up. A rotten sort of day. I am tired of conferences and *projets* and all the gamut of nonsenses we go through.

April 27

Gamelin remained yesterday very calm all through the conference in 10 Downing Street. The other General, Mittelhausser, said nothing at all. I should have expected both to have been more excited.

Late at night before going to bed, Massy came in from the Admiralty, where he has been working out the scheme for the evacuation. His present idea is to clear out within the next few days with Paget. That can be done fairly easily, he thinks. But that is quite impossible politically, and we must stay and fight a bit, holding on to Namsos for some time longer.

If we do not hurry up and take Narvik we shall have exactly the same thing happening there. The whole question is a stabilization of the air and nothing more.

We had a conference with the French from 10 till 1 p.m. The usual *projet* from off the map. Offering French troops that have not even left France. We found nothing in it that was practical in the existing circumstances.

Paget and Massy are more or less agreed that we can stay a few days, and no more, based on Andalsnes. It means that if we move out [on the] night of 1st/2nd May we may get clear with little loss. Otherwise we shall have to hold on, augment our force and make more to be evacuated. That is the military opinion. . . .

At 1 p.m. I was summoned to the Cabinet to say what had happened in our conversations with Gamelin. I found a somewhat dismayed and anxious Cabinet. Both Halifax and Winston looked particularly harassed. I told them of the *projets* made by Gamelin and also of the conversation I had had with Massy in between the conferences. Massy has given as his opinion that there is a very good chance of getting the force out if we take it out the night of the 1st/2nd May. If we do not do that, we must put more troops in and fight it out. Then I said that Hogg [the Royal Engineer officer on the Q. staff], the man who went out to see the Base installation and its condition, had reported that—with no diminution of the air menace—it was not an operation of war to keep a force in mid-Norway. Massy calculates about a week.

So I have given it as my definite opinion that we must come out on 1st/2nd May if we wish to come out in an orderly way.

Winston demurred to evacuation and began to mumble about the British being allowed to disperse in the mountains to help the Norwegians to carry on guerrilla warfare. That it was better to condemn the force ashore to fight to the end. I could not find any military reason for doing this. It was all political.[1]

We had a Supreme War Council with Reynaud and Daladier and after the matter had been disclosed to them, it was agreed that we should evacuate when it was militarily necessary. [Reynaud] said that we had entered the country making a technical mistake. It was impossible to remain in Scandinavia under the menace of the air. I could not get the S. of S. to make the P.M. put it to the French that the matter was urgent to evacuate, and it was left to me to break it to Gamelin that the news was bad, and to-morrow morning to tell him that the War Cabinet has ordered evacuation. It was only after Massy and myself had appeared in front of the War Cabinet that we could get them to agree to evacuation at once.

Now it is to be night of 30 April/1 May and we hope to get all Paget's Andalsnes troops away in one night. Most of Namsos also, and the remainder the next night with a bombardment of the

[1] On this day the Military Co-ordination Committee agreed to the evacuation of the Andalsnes and Namsos forces.

entrance to the Trondheim Fiord. The War Cabinet were all very downcast and were thinking more of public opinion than of the military disaster of being driven into the sea. It was curious to see Winston acquiescing quickly. The P.M. came to a decision very quickly. I admire him more and more.

> It had been agreed that Narvik should be captured as speedily as possible. By the beginning of May three battalions of the Chasseurs Alpins, two battalions of the French Foreign Legion, four Polish battalions, and some 3,500 Norwegians would be available.

April 28

This business [of Narvik] is going to be pretty stiff in anti-aircraft guns, and the maintenance of large parties under heavy air attack is impossible. Small ones are different.

What we have to do now is:

  (i) Make a properly defended Naval Base at Narvik.
 (ii) Establish fighter aircraft in the Narvik area.
(iii) Fill the area south of Narvik at Bodö and Mosjoën with detachments. Maintain them from the sea.
 (iv) Carry out a systematic destruction of all the bridges and viaducts on the roads and railways running from Namsos to Mosjoën and northwards.

It will require a man to control this effort with the Navy and it must all be done quickly. It needs these parties to be mobile with motor bicycles and sidecars perhaps. Just small enough to need no large maintenance. Wireless to communicate with us, or Narvik, as the case may be. . . .

We went over to Winston's office about the command at Narvik. We have decided to send out Auchinleck with his staff at once and that the command shall pass when he gets there. . . . We have no time to lose. Luckily the French Divisional Commander has arrived at Narvik and he should be able to get a move on. . . . I hope we have the time to compete with this Narvik business. A very quick entry by Germans through Sweden would make things very difficult for us.

April 29

I had a bad time in the night. At midnight the French Admiral rang up to say that he had heard that the French troops were withdrawing in a couple of nights. He was horrified and he was sure that General Gamelin had not this impression. I told him that the orders were being issued by Massy, that I doubted whether any British officer would have rung up Gamelin in the same way. I told him to get hold of Lelong [the French Military Attaché in London] and to tell him to speak to me. Lelong rang up and he came down to the War Office. We rang up the officer on duty at Massy's Corps, a very young G.S.O.(I). I found that my orders issued about the occupation of various points on the fiords to the north of Namsos had not been obeyed . . . [Ironside went to Massy's house and tackled him]. Back to the War Office about 3 a.m. and into bed for a couple of hours sleep. . . .

Oliver Stanley told me after lunch that the P.M. had said that Winston had demanded the right to preside at the Committee of the Chiefs of Staff. That if there was time for their recommendations to be put to the Co-ordination Committee they would be so put, but that Winston had then the right to go straight to the P.M. to get a decision. This makes Winston in fact Defence Minister without the responsibility, which remains in the hands of the Service Ministers. Oliver Stanley was not prepared to accept this condition.

April 30

Once more, yesterday evening, I was astonished at the P.M. and Winston in the way they asked about the position of every company surrounding Narvik. What were they? To which regiment they belonged? Why did we think they were there? It seemed so very futile and showed that they were playing with futilities. I have no idea how we are to liberate ourselves from this. Perhaps, if the war becomes a little more general and when they are tired of playing with tin soldiers on a map, we may get on with our work. Oliver Stanley says that I must not get impatient because they are all so desperately interested. . . .

Bombing is particularly bad at Andalsnes and has now started at Namsos. Until we get fighters ashore at Narvik we shall be at a disadvantage. Narvik itself seems to be liquidating. The Germans have begun burning the town and look to be withdrawing to the Swedish railway. They will certainly destroy the railway before going over into Swedish territory. Will they be interned there by the Swedes?

The King [of Norway] and his Ministers and nine millions in gold have been embarked upon a British ship and are now on their way to Tromsö [in the far north beyond Narvik].

On May 1 the Prime Minister issued a Note which made new arrangements for dealing with Defence. Mr. Churchill would continue to preside over meetings of the Military Co-ordination Committee when the Prime Minister was not himself in the chair. But he was now also given authority to convene and preside over the meetings of the Chiefs of Staff Committee, and was made responsible for giving them guidance and advice *on behalf* of the Military Co-ordination Committee. At the same time General Ismay was appointed as his staff officer and representative, in which capacity the General became a full member of the Chiefs of Staff Committee. The Chiefs of Staff in this collective capacity were thus to a great extent made responsible to Mr. Churchill.

April 30 (continued)

I spent four hours doing conferences, and Dill another four hours. We simply waste our time. What will it be like when Winston has conferences running well on past midnight? Perhaps it will not come to that if Winston becomes Prime Minister. . . . The general opinion seems to be that the Government will fall over this Norwegian affair. I suppose it is natural that an unsuccessful Ministry always falls in war. Perhaps Labour will come in if Chamberlain goes. . . . Anyway, you cannot make war with all these Committees. It simply doesn't lead to any decision or constancy.

May 1

The new Co-ordination Committee is to be presided over by
Winston and is to become a real thing. . . . If we can manœuvre
properly we may get more unity of thought. I hope so.

I had a long talk with the S. of S. about the new Chiefs of Staff
Committee which is [also] to be presided over by Winston. I told
him how discursive the daily reports are that we read at the War
Cabinet. Hours wasted in discussing details. He said that that was
the P.M.'s method of running the Cabinet. I told him that it
couldn't be done when we had more than one campaign on our
hands. He agreed to that. I then told him that the War Office staff
was not being used properly, as it was continually explaining
details. It [the Cabinet] never laid down a principle, heard a short
report upon the course of events and kept off all details.

I told him that instead of considering problems as they arose,
the course of the conversation carried on by the Cabinet produced
bright ideas. These bright ideas were then put into principles, or
acted as such. They had never been thought of before or examined
either politically or militarily.

We are thrown militarily upon the defensive and I can see no
chance of our ever being able to get back to the initiative for a
year or perhaps more. We haven't got the equipment to equip
our men any faster. It is all coming back to roost, our neglect in
time of peace.

May 2

A thick fog last night on the Norwegian coast and all embarkation has been held up in consequence because the ships cannot come in. This must make hopeless confusion amongst the
wretched troops. I calculate some 3,000 British troops to embark
including most of the 15th Brigade. It might give a certain amount
of relief according to the way the Germans come on behind the
rearguard. . . .

We seem to be closing in on Narvik.

By 9 a.m. we heard that Paget was on board a war-vessel and
that all the men were on.

Now that Namsos was on the point of being lost, it was imperative to stop the Germans moving up the coast and relieving their garrison at Narvik before we had captured it ourselves. Ironside accordingly wanted his only ski-troops, the Chasseurs Alpins, to retire, not by sea, but slowly up the road to the north, *via* Grong and Mosjoën, being supplied from the several small ports on the Norwegian coast, delaying the enemy as long as possible and eventually joining the British at Narvik. The French General considered that his skiers would be lost and that the plan was impractical, and they were accordingly evacuated from Namsos with the rest of the Allied troops, who were all mechanized. The Germans, however, found the road to Narvik anything but impractical and followed it with speed. This was to lead to complications and to further efforts by the British.

May 2 (continued)

The Germans are reporting that we are evacuating. They followed Paget up pretty quickly. The troops had to march the last seventeen miles to get away as their train was smashed up. Paget seems to have put up a good show.

Now it is a matter of getting off the men at Namsos. I am afraid that the French will not walk up the road to Mosjoën. . . .

We had a peaceable Chiefs of Staff meeting and Cabinet too. So far Winston has not troubled us very much. He delivered a long tirade and then said that we had been right in recommending that we did not put ashore a large army in Norway. He forgets what he felt so passionately a week or so ago.

May 3

A wire in this morning to say that Namsos was completely evacuated this morning. Over 6,000 people out in the night. It was the fog which saved them. Not enough to stop the ships coming in but enough to stop the bombing. I must say I am glad to get them away. . . . You want more than a shade of luck for an improvised campaign.

The papers are all taking the thing well. Any failure must have criticism, and when all is said and done this Scandinavian business never had a chance owing to the following reasons:

  (i) The lack of trained troops in England.
 (ii) Political changes of strategy.
(iii) The great ascendancy of the German air.

Perhaps it has taught us a lesson that we shall not forget and that is so far to the good. Perhaps the most important thing is the over-hauling of the machinery by which the strategy is run. We shall not make any more mistakes here unless Winston is allowed a free run for his enthusiasm. . . .

The convoy from Namsos has been bombed going out to sea and the French destroyer *Bison* was hit. I hope there were not too many men aboard. If we had been able to persuade the French to send a considerable body of men up by road to Mosjoën we might have reduced their party considerably. . . .

We start meetings with Winston to-day. I hear that there is a first-class row commencing in the House and that there is a strong movement on foot to get rid of the P.M. Naturally the only man who can succeed is Winston and he is too unstable, though he has the genius to bring the war to an end.

Now I see very little chance of any initiative during 1940 and we must wait to see if the German will try to finish the war this year. I expect that he will and that he will try conclusions with the Army in Holland and Belgium. We must look to a bad time this summer, if we are right about the Germans wishing to come to conclusions this year.

Holding on to Narvik. Fixing ourselves there and harrying the Germans. It is a long way for us—800 miles from Scapa to Narvik so as to avoid the submarines and the air—and until we can get our aeroplanes established at Bardu [north of Narvik] we shall have a bad time holding them off.

May 4

I had Mittelhausser in to see me (for five minutes) and he stayed two hours. All discussion on the map as to what we could do in the narrow strip of Norway running up from Namsos to Narvik.

I failed to get the French to retire up the road and have had to put in a party[1] at Mosjoën. The French General [Audet] has said that his men would be lost if they went up there. I am quite convinced that the Germans will be up it very shortly—to our eternal disgrace.

I shall be interested to hear why a force of 3,000 mobile French Alpine troops stayed at Namsos inert without budging a foot, even to make the ordinary daily reconnaissances that mere curiosity would demand. They must have been demoralized.

The convoy got away with the loss of two destroyers, a French and a British, the *Bison* and the *Afridi*. Lucky that we did not have more.

I am told that the Government is not likely to have too bad a time on Tuesday next when they have the debate on Scandinavia. I hope they won't.

We had yesterday for two hours our first meeting with Winston as the Chairman of the Co-ordination Committee, and we found him very tired and sleepy and we hardly did anything at all. He took quietly what we said without demur. The lull after the storm. A relief that we had got out of Namsos. Several people came up and congratulated me on the show. I wondered if they knew all the facts. We were lucky. . . .

I am to go up to Scotland to see the troops that have come back and to tell them to keep their heads up and not to think they have done badly.

I am wondering whether the next [German] coup will be delayed by trying to relieve Narvik, or whether Hitler will abandon Narvik to its fate. We have now got it on paper that any descent by Germany upon the Dutch islands will be regarded as an invasion of the country and our Air Force will act at once. It has been a long and heated argument to get this allowed both with the Government and the French. Now we shall do it and bring bombing home to the Germans.

On April 28 General Auchinleck had been appointed to

[1] This was a British Force under Colonel Gubbins of five independent companies and a few extras.

take command at Narvik and was due to arrive there on May 12. So far, no attempt had been made to seize the place.

May 5 (Sunday)

There is a certain amount of havering going on over Narvik. The advance is pretty slow, chiefly because the French troops are so heavily loaded. I wish that I could have got Auchinleck there before, but the Operations people here prayed for more time. It seemed to me more important to get the *man* there. I know that that would have been my desire were I in Auchinleck's place. To get there and take charge.

Winston seems to me to be a little weighed down by the cares of being solely responsible for Narvik. He wants it taken and yet doesn't dare to give any direct order to Cork. Apparently the 8th is the date for pushing in the battleship. Will the Germans be able to do any bombing? . . .

We spent the whole morning on the Chiefs of Staff Committee debating the sending of some executive telegrams. Such fumbling and altering. Then we heard that the coming debate in the House is likely to be a severe one and that military strategy and tactics are going to be discussed. So we sent a message to the P.M. telling him of our fears. Poor devil. Adding to his troubles. Most of the Ministers are away for the Sunday and they are all employed making up the speeches which they will have to make to excuse their operations. A miserable state of affairs. If we don't get out of this appalling rut in which the machinery for making war has got, we cannot make any quick decisions. The machine simply will not do it. . . .

We are on the defensive and the Germans have the initiative. He can do what he likes. Where will he go next? I begin to think that he will make a concentrated attack upon us. Our shipping and our industry, and perhaps finally a landing from the air or on the coast. If this is so, we must set to and get down to brass tacks. First, I must get a good C.-in-C. in charge. Then I must get the troops organized in fast columns. I must have trial runs to exercise them. And we must have the closest liaison between the Civil Defence people, the Air, and the watchers both of the Air and the

Navy. This struggle may develop during June, July and August of this summer and may be the crisis of our existence. I think that we ought to be able to compete with it. But it will require organization and great courage and determination.

On May 6 the Military Co-ordination Committee considered a Chiefs of Staff report about capturing Narvik. The Instructions handed to General Auchinleck were confirmed, and it was agreed that we should secure and maintain a base in Northern Norway from which to deny iron-ore to Germany passing through Narvik, harass her supplies through Lulea by air attack, and keep part of Norway for the Norwegian King and Government.

May 7 [Edinburgh, after seeing the troops from Andalsnes and Namsos at Glasgow]

There is a mention in the papers that the Bosches have taken Mosjoën. I can hardly believe it possible. Gubbins should have left on the morning of the 5th after delays. He ought to be there during the night of the 6th. If not, he might delay till the night of the 7th, which may be too late. It will be damnable if the Germans do manage to move up to Mosjoën. I shall be eternally disgraced. I have rung up the War Office to know.

Nobody knew anything and it was not till 10 p.m. that I could find out that our parties had not landed at Mosjoën and that they might not even land to-night. I feel that we have muddled things in every way. Always too late. Changing plans and nobody directing. The Navy overworked, and very little time at night to get our people ashore.

To bed very upset at the thought of our incompetence. We are not a machine fitted to make war upon a scale of improvisation. You cannot do that against the Germans.

May 8

The latest news is that Holland is to be invaded. Apparently communication has been cut off for all the night. I wonder. Then we start bombing in Germany and that may be the beginning of the indiscriminate bombing that we have all foretold. This summer is certainly going to be something very stiff, and we must be prepared to face more knocks till we can emerge. I have no doubts of the end.

May 9

Down to London again [from Scotland]. I found the War Office in a buzz. Oliver Stanley says that the Government will go. . . .

Narvik goes none too well. Cork has wired that all the military officers have advised against a direct landing. Operations are terribly slow with the thaw coming, but there ought to be enough troops to deal with the Germans. There seems to be a lack of determination which has persisted since the beginning. The troops are faced with enemy in fortified positions and they do not appear to be able to face it. Auchinleck doesn't arrive till the 11th. He ought to have been there before and I ought to have insisted upon his going. . . . The establishment of aerodromes near Narvik is very slow indeed. We want some stout hearts here and determination.

Gubbins has arrived at Mosjoën, thank goodness. Only just in time perhaps. Always confusion and delay in these improvised operations. Unavoidable, I suppose. It now depends upon the guts that Gubbins has. He ought to be good.

Bombing is pretty stiff at Narvik. The Dutch are now hourly expecting to be attacked.

The debates in the House of Commons ended with the resignation of Mr. Chamberlain on May 10, and with Mr. Winston Churchill becoming Prime Minister. On the same day the Germans invaded Holland, Belgium and Luxembourg. Narvik was taken on May 28 by French, Polish and Norwegian troops, supported by the Royal Navy, the British being diverted to oppose the Germans advancing from Trondheim.

Six days before, the Chiefs of Staff recommended that we should evacuate Narvik as soon as it was captured. In due course, the Cabinet and the Supreme War Council agreed.

□□ The evacuation was successfully completed on the night of June 7, 1940.

The Norwegian campaign was a defeat for the Allies, but it was not an unmixed advantage for Germany. She secured her iron-ore, without which her campaigns of 1941 and 1942 might never have been fought, and she also protected her northern flank. But her naval losses were very severe, and she could not at first use her victory to raid the British sea lanes. Britain merely shifted her blockade-line through 90° to Iceland. At Dunkirk the German Navy was far too crippled to interfere, and when it came to "Sea Lion", the invasion of England in the summer of 1940, the naval staff had to tell the Army that their plan was too ambitious, and on too wide a front. Finally, the occupation of Norway caused a considerable and permanent dispersion of the German Army. As General Jodl remarked in 1945: "It tied down 300,000 men in order to protect our conquests, and these remained useless for the remainder of the war."

PART FOUR

THE BATTLE OF FRANCE

CHAPTER XIX

The German Break-Through

May 10

At 4 a.m. the invasion of Holland and Belgium took place. The French and British Armies have started into Belgium, but they were not at any great short notice. That means a certain amount of delay. The Dutch attaché came across with their official plan and a request that we send fighter squadrons to the Dutch aerodromes. He seemed quite surprised that we weren't doing it immediately. Such is the way of the weak neutral.

We were summoned at 7 a.m. to the Admiralty to a Chiefs of Staff meeting. I had great difficulty in getting in from Whitehall and then we sat for half an hour listening to rumours that were coming in, and they began telephoning to the French. Then I got away and could not get out again. All the night watchmen away and the day's men not there. Door double and treble locked. I walked up to one of the windows and opened it and climbed out. So much for security.

As far as the Army is concerned the plan is under the French and I don't know whether they have put it into full vigour. So far by nearly 8 a.m. no British ports have been bombed though Calais has received it.

Now we go to war with the old Cabinet or a change. We had a Cabinet Meeting at 8 a.m. The P.M. at once began asking where the Germans had landed and seemed quite surprised to know that everything was uncertain. Winston said he would show the

Cabinet the "homing A.A. fuze". It wouldn't take a minute. And we then had a description of what it was. We are impossible. . . .

We are not likely to get much news about the whole situation for some time. Meanwhile we still have this measly Cabinet which doesn't know if it is on its head or its heels. I hear also that Reynaud was intending to change Gamelin for Weygand. . . .

Winston has arranged three Military Co-ordination Meetings. War by Committees. There will have been nine to-day if we attend them all.

The mines in the Rhine [Operation "Royal Marine"] go off to-night.

May 11

Winston is now Prime Minister and was not able to come to our Conference at 10.30 p.m. . . . Chamberlain made a most moving speech on the B.B.C. last night. He is a most upright man and my admiration for him has got greater during the eight months I have been working with the Cabinet.

The news this morning seems to be good as far as the advance into Belgium is concerned. The air fighting has been very severe indeed. . . . The Dutch seem to have fought a bit better round the aerodromes at The Hague. . . . [The Germans] are attacking opposite Liège and the French are in contact in the south of Luxembourg. . . .

By the middle of the day one could get a better idea of the German advance. They are evidently trying to isolate Liège and have been able to penetrate in as far as Tongres with their parachutists. The big aerodrome at Rotterdam is still in German hands and we are rebombing it. Elsewhere the Dutch have cleaned up the parachutists. But the Germans are coming on slowly. It ought to mean that we get time to fortify the Dyle properly and to get some depth in. A long battle is going to ensue and then we shall have all the German heavy artillery coming in and pounding us. We have nothing like the amount he has to put in the line, nor have the French. Can we get the wire up in time? It will mean a race for time, and we cannot get in any of the necessary pill-boxes.

But we shall have saved the Belgian Army. On the whole the advantage is with us. A really hard fight all this summer.

Surely we must have a Labour man in charge of the Ministry of Supply? That seems essential to get the work out of the munition workers. . . .

During the next twenty-four hours I expect that the Germans will get hold of the whole of [Holland]. We shall only have debris coming into our lines at Antwerp. We cannot send troops into Fortress Holland. The usual request has arrived for troops with plenty of hand grenades.

In the afternoon we heard that the [German] Heavy Armoured Division was coming through Tongres and I am wondering if we shall be on the Dyle in time. D.V. The next few days will be critical days indeed and the fate of the Empire may well rest on the men now fighting in France. I wonder if the people know how serious things are? They have been kept in the dark for so long that they would be angry if they knew.

No signs of Winston's Cabinet yet. Just at a very critical moment. We want all the strength of the Labour benches to pull us through. The early part of the war has been so quiet that the people have been deluded into believing that it would remain like that. . . .

The Hague looks to be nearing its end. A couple of days and the whole place will be in German hands. They do get their men to fight. We don't seem to be able to do so. I wish I were fighting instead of making war in an office. That is the luck of the business and I must just keep at it. I can do no more for the moment.

May 12

The position in the Netherlands gets steadily worse. The Germans have now reached the northern and eastern shores of the Zuyder Zee and are embarking for the Fortress Holland. We are sending a battalion of somewhat untrained Guards over to The Hague to try to help clean up the situation. The big aerodrome at Rotterdam is still in the hands of the Germans who hold Moerdijk bridge [over the Maas estuary].

We are getting into position on the Dyle and the Belgians are falling back on us. At the moment the Germans have the Maastricht main bridge and two bridges over the Albert Canal, which the Dutch and Belgians failed to blow. The Belgians have reported that "their bridges were not blown up owing to a Colonel having been decapitated by a shell". The usual lack of preparation and confusion.

Now there is a general howl for aircraft from everybody and everywhere. The German preponderance is going to have a great effect upon the coming battle. I expect this in forty-eight hours or so, and the fate of the Empire depends upon it. I am afraid that we do not engage it under the best conditions owing to our deficiency in the air. We must fight it out and hope for the best. I am not optimistic owing to the air situation. . . .

No signs of the new Cabinet. They are all busy getting their seals. One cannot hope for an immediate change. It is all very serious and I do not think that the people have been kept informed of the serious condition of affairs.

The bombing of the Ruhr is being pressed by the Air Force, but we are opposing it at the moment. The arguments are that we don't want retaliation at the moment, for it will mean keeping fighters in England. Our fighters in France have had a hard time of it and the German bombers are not fighting well, and the extra fighters in France may well tip the scale in our favour. We are sure to have intensive air action while we are forming up on the Dyle and during the great battle that is now beginning. If the battle is lost, the bombing of the Ruhr means nothing at all to the fate of the Empire.

We have just heard that Rotterdam is still in a very precarious condition. . . . The Maastricht bridge has been badly damaged, thank goodness.

I said goodbye to the old Secretary of State [Oliver Stanley]. He looked very tired and worn-out. He talked of getting something in the Army. I then had a talk with Anthony Eden [who had been appointed Secretary of State for War in Mr. Churchill's new Administration]. He is not taking over at a very easy time and he seemed strong enough in character at the moment. I im-

Ironside and Gort presented with the Grand Cross of the
Legion of Honour at G.H.Q., France

Ironside receiving the accolade at the presentation of the
Grand Cross of the Legion of Honour

General Ironside, Mr. Winston Churchill, General Gamelin, General Gort and General Georges

pressed upon him the extremely critical situation owing to the German air situation at the moment. He also understood about the Ruhr.

On the night of May 12 General Gamelin rang up to say that all bridges over the river Meuse had been blown up.

May 13

The Germans have landed a lot more men by plane at Rotterdam and the situation appears to have got worse there. Meanwhile the Dutch are being hard pressed on the east, just south of the Zuyder Zee.

We had a meeting with the P.M. up to after 1 a.m. this morning. He took a general review of the situation and gave us a stiff telling-off over the loss of Mosjoën [in Norway]. I could not but admit that it wasn't a happy story. We debated the question of the bombing of the Ruhr and it has now been put on for the 14th unless counter-ordered. . . .

We have the usual squeals from the Belgians and Dutch asking for fighter support. [General] Needham [of the British Mission to Belgium] says that he thinks both Overstraten and the King of the Belgians are in a highly "temperamental" state and will require very careful handling to prevent a position of non-co-operation....

I spent the whole morning on Conferences and meetings, which made it impossible to get on with one's work. Very little accomplished. I have told Eden, who quite agrees, and perhaps he may be able to make some change.

There is yet no sign of the Germans having done anything except move forward their mechanized columns under cover of intense air activity. None of their infantry columns have shown up. We cannot tell whether the Germans are intending a main thrust against the centre of Belgium *via* the hole they have made at Maastricht and the Belgian–Dutch border, or against Mézières [about ten miles north-west of Sedan] with the object of turning the left of the Maginot Line. A third objective may be that they are merely getting possession of Holland so as to establish bases for a main attack on Great Britain, driving in the Belgian advanced troops behind our line from Namur to Antwerp. This latter is very probable, in which case we should have sufficient time to dig ourselves in on our present line. How much we can depend upon the Belgians to take their part in the defence of this line I don't know. Whether we shall be able to establish a real defence line, I don't know. If the wretched Belgians had only taken our advice and had made a real line of defence things might have been better. . . .

A War Cabinet at 6.30 p.m., Attlee, Greenwood and Alexander[1] are definitely better than the men we had before. . . . We debated the Ruhr bombing once again and it was put off once more, much to the disgust of the Chief of the Air Staff. I wrote a paper setting out the pros and cons which caused the delay. I told the Cabinet that I thought the battle that could decide the Empire was beginning. That we must do all we could to make that battle a good one. We should know soon whether the Bosche meant business. He couldn't remain opposite us with mechanical forces. They must keep moving and would have to retire or be backed up [by infantry]. The C.A.S. thought that the Bosches were putting up a show to allow them to seize Holland, from whence to deliver a great attack by air against us in Great Britain. I have sent a wire across to Gamelin asking him for his opinion.

May 14

The situation seems to be becoming clearer. The attack from Namur southwards to Mézières is the strongest. There are three Panzer divisions and twelve Infantry divisions in action. The Germans got across the Meuse at Houx, near Dinant, and in three places south of Givet and north of Sedan. In the north the B.E.F. has not been strongly engaged and every hour allows us to get down into position. The Dutch are nearly finished and will not hold very much longer. Our battalion at The Hague cannot do much to clear the situation. I hope we shall get them out without fuss.

---

[1] Mr. Attlee was Lord Privy Seal, Mr. Arthur Greenwood was Minister without Portfolio, and Mr. A. V. Alexander, later Lord Alexander of Hillsborough, was First Lord of the Admiralty in Mr. Churchill's War Cabinet.

We have still held up the bombing attack on the Ruhr. The wretched C.A.S. is trying to hold up his heavy bombers for this coup. Meanwhile the Germans are putting in all their bombers. He is obsessed with the idea that the Germans are only making a holding attack against the armies whilst preparing to have a go at England. So much for the elasticity of the Air Force. Now it cannot deal with the Army situation and then switch to the defence of England.

We have made a strong appeal to the U.S.A. to allow us to buy war material out of their stocks. The short-term policy is the only one to think of now, as it seems evident that Hitler is trying to win the war this year. I don't think that we can expect much out of the Americans. They won't do for us what they refused to do for the Finns.

A report in says that the French tanks have been fighting well and have proved themselves a match for the German tanks. We have only the Infantry tank for counter-attack.

Air situation remains difficult. The Germans are all out with their bombing all over the field of battle. I am sure that they have used up more of their bombing force than the R.A.F. think.

We are to get 900 Bosche prisoners captured by the Dutch. They must more or less all be these parachutists. I shall be interested to see if they are as young and as fanatical as they are said to be. . . .

The Egyptian Ambassador has just telephoned to say that the Italians have given him the notice that they promised they would about Italy coming in. They are just about to take the plunge. It looks very like it at last. This looks like our final trouble. We have been discussing the giving of Italy a blow the minute she comes in, by bombing Milan and Turin or by making a naval attack against the Italian coast. This latter can only be of the tip-and-run class of operation and we do not favour it in the least.

One wonders what will happen to Malta. The people cannot well be evacuated and they are certain to suffer heavily in a bombardment. We ought to be able to evacuate the people from Gibraltar to Morocco, and the refuges in the Rock should be of the greatest use when the moment arrives.

Critical days indeed. My mind still goes back to the main responsibility of Baldwin and the minor responsibility of Milne and Massingberd.

Reynaud has wired Winston direct asking him for ten squadrons of fighters. His wire is a little hysterical, saying that there are no lines of defence comparable with those that the Germans have broken between Sedan and Paris. Gamelin says that he was "surprised". He mentioned that the tanks must have been amphibious and very much stronger than anything the French have got. I cannot help thinking that the French troops must have given way in the first rush of the Germans. The gap is a bad one and the French are worried. We are getting somebody from the Mission to go down to Georges' H.Q. to find out what the real situation is. They may have more information.

These calls for the air will continue until we have little left, but this battle may be decisive of the whole war and it is impossible to neglect a call such as this from the French.

The final effort in the evening was that the counter-attack at Sedan stopped the German attack and bombing continues upon the Germans trying to burst through. Prisoners say that they are completely exhausted after five days without respite. Gamelin and Georges have all gone up to have a look and we could get nothing out of the H.Q.'s. Winston was very excited over his telegram from Reynaud and had a meeting at 6.30 of the Cabinet, with the Chiefs of Staff at 5.30, and then he ordered another meeting of the Chiefs of Staff and Service Ministers at 11.30 p.m. All when we couldn't take any decisions.

May 15

This morning at 8 a.m., just as I was talking to Gort, the P.M. rang up and told me that he had been talking to Reynaud [on the telephone], who was thoroughly demoralized. He had said that the battle was lost. The road to Paris was open.[1] Couldn't we send more troops? Winston told him to keep calm, that these

[1] The German axis of attack seemed to be in a south-west direction, aimed at the French capital. The French, having committed their reserves, had nothing to interpose.

incidents happened in a war. We have no extra demands from
Gamelin or Georges, both of whom were calm, though they
both considered the situation serious. I told him this. Apparently
the French are giving back at Namur and may bend back to
Charleroi, still keeping a hold on us at Wavre. I shouldn't be at
all surprised if the line was back again upon the French frontier
before long.

The Germans are using mechanized troops with very few
infantry columns. The German tanks are very good and I think
that there can be no doubt that the French have been caught
unawares and that they have not fought well. That happened
in the last war. Drastic steps had to be taken to put things
right.

Winston told Reynaud that even if the French gave in we
should fight on alone. He was quite calm and very firm.

Italy now seems certain to come in against us. Very soon too.
. . . Winston has asked the President of the U.S.A. to become non-
belligerent and to supply us out of stock—with forty destroyers
amongst other things.

Then the Cabinet decided unanimously to bomb the Ruhr. It
starts to-night. An announcement in the papers that the aerodromes of Holland would soon be completely in the hands of the
Nazis and England would soon feel the weight of the bombing
on her own body. We shall have had a start anyway. One never
saw the necessity for courage and determination more [than] at
this moment. It will be interesting seeing how the various
people react. . . . We at least have a Cabinet with some courage
now.

I never saw anything so light up as the faces of the R.A.F. when
they heard that they were to be allowed to bomb the oil-refineries
in the Ruhr. It did one good to see it. They have built their big
bombers for this work and they have been keyed up for the work
ever since the war began. Now they have got the chance. I am
wondering what the result in the way of reprisals is going to be.
Shall we get it as soon as to-morrow night in return? It may be
a diversion from the bombing in France. They may be too
employed there to turn off from their targets.

The war is coming nearer and nearer to us and it makes one think all the more. We are living in a new phase of history the course of which no man can foresee. Nobody believed that we should be engaged in war, certainly not in a death struggle so soon. We made no preparations, even for war industry to be developed, and we cannot now catch up. It is too late. The year may see us beaten, but it cannot bring us to the defeat of Germany, unless it is by economic means.

I have a sort of feeling in the back of my head that if Italy comes in, and this seems pretty certain, she will be the Achilles heel of the Axis. . . .

May 16

As the morning wore on the extent of the French break between Hirson and Mézières became evident. The Germans are in as far as Neuchatel–Marle, and getting near Laon. Gamelin is said to have some armoured troops there and a battle is expected.[1]

The great feature of the battle is the great hordes of bombers going about escorted by fighters. They have dominated the field of battle completely and demoralized the French. It is a matter now whether Gamelin and Georges can stabilize things or not. Nothing could be more serious.

We havered a lot about sending more fighters over to France. Having refused point-blank yesterday, we have now decided upon sending four squadrons. As is usual in crises, the reinforcements are being dragged out under the demands of the subordinate commanders. I recommended that we should send all we could—up to ten squadrons. It was a battle that might lay France low and we must not stand out.

A withdrawal is now being ordered from our present line in France to conform to the break in the French. Winston was most incensed and decided to go to France at once to see if he could hearten these French up. They are quite evidently not fighting well at all.

I went over to the Admiralty and had a cup of coffee with

[1] It was at this battle that General de Gaulle commanded an armoured division with much distinction.

Winston who had Lloyd George to lunch. L. G. looked very pink in the face with his long white hair. Railing against Baldwin, who he said ought to be hanged. Chamberlain quite unfit to be P.M. He said he was sorry for Winston, who bore none of the responsibility for our condition. We had a meeting under Chamberlain about Italy and then I spent a couple of hours at the flat lying down and reading.

The news is quieter, but the French have done equally badly in Beveland. The General has failed utterly. The men demoralized after very little fighting. An Admiral pulling them together. Gamelin says that there was a *"défaillance"* amongst several divisions due to Communism and fifth column. The rest are fighting well. A bad lookout for us I am afraid. I hope that Winston has put that right.

On the morning of the 16th the French H.Q. were obviously demoralized, for General Gamelin, reporting on the telephone, used the expression *"tout est perdu"*, but Mr. Churchill, who saw the French leaders in Paris that afternoon (the famous occasion on which he watched the archives being burnt in the garden of the Quai d'Orsay), did not appear to think the situation so absolutely desperate, for he sent the following telegram to London:

I shall be glad if the Cabinet could meet immediately to consider following. Situation grave in the last degree. Furious German thrust through Sedan finds French Armies ill-grouped, many in north, others in Alsace. At least four days required to bring twenty divisions to cover Paris and strike at the flanks of the bulge, which is now fifty kilometres wide.

Three armoured divisions with two or three infantry divisions have advanced through gap and large masses hurrying forward behind them. Two great dangers therefore threaten. First that B.E.F. will be largely left in the air to make a difficult disengagement and retreat to the old line. Secondly, that the German thrust will wear down the French resistance before it can be fully gathered.

311

⊡⊟ Orders given to defend Paris at all costs, but archives of the Quai d'Orsay already burning in the garden. I consider the next two, three or four days decisive for Paris and probably for the French Army. Therefore the question we must face is whether we can give further aid in fighters above four squadrons, for which the French are very grateful, and whether a larger part of our long-range heavy bombers should be employed to-morrow and the following nights upon the German masses crossing the Meuse and flowing into the Bulge. Even so results cannot be guaranteed; but the French resistance may be broken up as rapidly as that of Poland unless this Battle of the Bulge is won. I personally feel that we should send squadrons of fighters demanded [i.e. six more] to-morrow and, concentrating all available French and British aviation, dominate the air above the Bulge for the next two or three days, not for any local purpose, but to give the last chance to the French Army to rally its bravery and strength. It would not be good historically if their requests were denied and their ruin resulted. Also night bombardment by a strong force of heavy bombers can no doubt be arranged. It looks as if the enemy was by now fully extended both in the air and tanks.

We must not underrate the increasing difficulties of his advance if strongly counter-attacked. I imagine that if all fails here we could still shift what is left of our own striking force to assist the B.E.F. should it be forced to withdraw. I again emphasize the mortal gravity of the hour, and express my opinion as above. Kindly inform me what you will do. Dill agrees. I must have answer by midnight to encourage the French. Telephone to Ismay at Embassy in Hindustani.

The Cabinet authorized the despatch of the six extra squadrons, and Ironside, who had copied into his diary the entire text of this famous telegram, thus commented: "A Cabinet meeting to consider Winston's telegram. We were

right in wanting our bombing put on to the human
targets coming up from Germany. The bombing of the
Ruhr may have done 'some good, but we now have to
leave it."

Commenting on this telegram later, Ironside wrote: "It
was thus a week before we in England had any details as to
what had happened. This wire showed the gravity of the
B.E.F.'s position. If the French Army was collapsing, how
should we rescue the B.E.F. from the debris? It was felt that
the French H.Q. did not realize that the B.E.F. was completely mechanized and would therefore move for longer
distances than the French divisions, handicapped as they were
with horsed first-line transport."

May 17

Winston back and with a very gloomy report. He was able to
buck the French up a bit. He said that Reynaud was better than
Daladier. We have now sent over the equivalent of ten squadrons
of fighters in the last few days and an effort is being made to clear
the air. At the moment, the French are not fighting and are hopelessly demoralized by the bombing. It will take four or five days
to organize the defence of Paris and to put in the necessary
counter-attacks. These days will be critical.

I found that Greenwood [a member of the Cabinet] was inclined to say "these bloody gallant Allies". I told him that we had
depended upon the French Army. That we had made no Army
and that therefore it was not right to say "these bloody Allies". It
was for them to say that of us.

Gort seems in good heart on the telephone, but there are several
disturbing features, the worst being the withdrawal of the French
on our right. General Billotte is now at Douai trying to arrange a
counter-attack from the north. Reports are in that the enemy
armoured fighting vehicles are in Bohain and were moving up on
Cambrai. The main thrust is moving from Laon on Soissons. The
gap broadening every minute.

If Billotte cannot stop this broadening to the north we shall
find ourselves cut from our lines of communication in Amiens.

That means that we shall be trying to evacuate the B.E.F. from Dunkirk, Calais and Boulogne. An impossible proposition.[1]

We are now on the Brussels Canal and will be on the Dendre to-night (17th), Scheldt (18th) and our old line (19th). Then it is a question of getting back along our L. of C. and eventually to cover Havre and Rouen along the Seine in conjunction with the defence of Paris. If we achieve that, then there is a possibility of our being able to evacuate from the south-west ports including Cherbourg and Brest.

Winston had an interview with Kennedy [U.S.A. Ambassador], who handed him an answer from Roosevelt. He said that he would do all that he humanly could to help us. But there seemed so little that he could do in his own state of defence. His heart was with us.

I wonder if we have told the people in this country how serious things are. It won't do to have them suddenly waking up to a disaster.

There was no panic in the Cabinet, but they were all clear as to the serious nature of the crisis. Attlee said very little. Chamberlain looked worn and ill but undismayed. Winston very red-eyed and more like an old boar in a corner than anything else. Alexander seemed the most alive and capable of the new lot. Eden seemed to be all right and there is nothing much he can do.

All rests upon what the Air can do. We may even have to send more fighters to France. All the heavy bombers are now on to the German columns coming through the gap.[2] The policy of the human bodies rather than targets further back, which we have always maintained was the right thing. If we can stay the rot in the French Army, all will be well. There is nothing else we can do.

---

[1] Impossible, that is to say, to evacuate the B.E.F. with its equipment, as these ports were not capable of handling and loading the heavy vehicles and stores.

On this day Ironside proposed to the Admiralty that all small vessels should be collected and organized with a view to evacuating the men of the B.E.F. if the worst should happen.

[2] Many bombers were shot down while attacking the Meuse crossings in daylight.

152.

we stand faced by a completely Nazified Europe. What does that mean to Gt. Britain and the British Empire? What chance have we in reality of continuing the struggle by ourselves with the French knocked out? Could we maintain the Air struggle? Could we get enough machines to continue? Could we keep our industry going under Nazi bombardment from so close as Holland and the Channel ports? Could we get enough of the B.E.F. men & equipment back to England to ensure security against air invasion?

Very grave days indeed.

It seems hard to think that we are up against the crashing of the Empire. And yet we are most surely. Nothing could be more certain. What is the use of any recrimination as to whose fault it was? We have lived in a fool's paradise. Largely depending upon the strength of the French Army. And this Army has crashed or very nearly crashed. The turning point in history. Our own fault. And yet could any State under democratic rule have competed with a Nazi military preparation for war? I don't see how it could.

What we want now is fighting. Fighting for our lives. The struggle is now. There is no use holding anything up for a problematical continuance of the war if France collapses.

9.15 p.m. No more news from the French. Georges is reported to be master of himself and to be trying to compete with his break. All our fighters and all our bombers are on to the bad areas. We cannot control the battle in any way from here. It's a French battle.

At the moment it looks like the greatest military disaster in all history. It is time the miracle of the Marne came forward. Perhaps we don't deserve it.

315

The Air Staff now realize how the great battle has begun. They have ignored the question of the Army so far, acting very much by themselves.

Italy looks very like coming in.

Things at 12.30 p.m. could not well be worse. I have had in the Quarter-Master-General to tell him of the possibilities. I cannot see any of the B.E.F. equipment coming out of Calais, Dunkirk and Boulogne. We simply must get the line back to something reasonable to cover our communications. Otherwise there is no hope of any evacuation, not to speak of collecting any of the Belgian Army.

At the moment, streams of Belgian refugees are demanding to come over from Belgium from Zeebrugge and Ostend, and we cannot evacuate these people at the same time as block the ports. All our blockships are ready at Dover and take thirty-six hours to put into operation. For the moment, the Belgians are holding well because they are not being attacked, but I hear reports that an attack on Louvain is being staged to-morrow.

At the moment things are very black indeed and we stand faced by a completely Nazified Europe. What does that mean to Great Britain and the British Empire? What chance have we in reality of continuing the struggle by ourselves with the French knocked out? Could we maintain the Air struggle? Could we get enough machines to continue? Could we keep our industry going under Nazi bombardment from so close as Holland and the Channel ports? Could we get enough of the B.E.F. men and equipment back to England to ensure security against air invasion?

Very grave days indeed.

It seems hard to think that we are up against the crashing of the Empire. And yet we are most surely. Nothing could be more certain. What is the use of any recrimination as to whose fault it was? We have lived in a fool's paradise. Largely depending upon the strength of the French Army. And this Army has crashed or very nearly crashed. The turning point in history. Our own faults. And yet could any State under democratic rule have competed with a Nazi military preparation for war? I don't see how it could.

What we want now is fighting. Fighting for our lives. The struggle is now. There is no use holding anything up for a problematical continuance of the war if France collapses.

9.15 p.m. No more news from the French. Georges is reported to be master of himself and to be trying to compete with his break. All our fighters and all our bombers are on to the bad areas. We cannot control the battle in any way from here. It is a French battle.

At the moment it looks like the greatest military disaster in all history. It is time the miracle of the Marne came forward. Perhaps we don't deserve it.

Italy is now very near coming in. They say that the 21st is the date. There have been so many dates that this may at last be the right one.

May 18

The line has stabilized itself a little, less air fighting and less bombing. Evidently the Bosches are now making up their mind whether to go on with the attack, probably forcing a way to Amiens, or to have a big bombing attack against England.

Last night we successfully blew up and set alight the oil installations in Hamburg and Bremen. A pilot said that over Hamburg he could read a book at 10,000 feet. They also touched up the Ruhr again, finding very little A.A. defence in guns and lights. They have evidently all been moved forward.

One wonders what effect we have had over the battle by this bombing far into Germany. I hope it will have some more than mere annoyance. It is the first time that the Germans have had any taste of bombing in their own territory. . . .

The Cabinet had as near an altercation as I have seen over Aircraft Production. Beaverbrook, the new Minister, came in and asked for more control of the R.A.F. storage units. These are the units where the planes are prepared for issue to the squadrons. After a lot of argument it was acknowledged by the R.A.F. that there was an inflow of 1,000 to the storage units, and an outflow of 650. This had been going on for six months. What it really means is that there must be 2,000-odd machines awaiting completion because of various reasons. When one looked at Beaverbrook's ugly face, grown more ugly with the years, and heard him give his report after two days in his Ministry, it made one wonder if the R.A.F. were efficient in their administration. The faces of the Air Staff were pretty horrified.

The B.E.F. seems to have withdrawn to the Dendre without being hurried in any way. Gort seems in very good heart. He got away all his Infantry tanks which had come up to put in a counter-attack. They are slow-going creatures.

I am wondering whether the French are putting in enough stuff round Cambrai to prevent the German forces from cutting our communications.

May 19

I quite expected some bombing in return for our's last night, but apparently the Germans aren't ready yet, though they will be. Some German tanks have arrived even as far as Albert and nobody seems able to stop them. After all one can understand that, for only guns and tanks can take them on.

My chief fear is that we shall not be able to get the B.E.F. out. The Belgians are in a worse way than we are. Who is going to feed them if they come out of Belgium I don't know. It will be difficult enough for us. Our L. of C. is shifted north through Abbeville and Arras, but getting back is a matter of days. The long German columns must be pushing forward at top speed and it is a matter of perhaps hours whether we can get down and join up our right flank with any French that come up. One doesn't wake up to a good morning.

We had a better Cabinet this morning. All very serious and not much useless talk. I told them of the danger which existed to the B.E.F. through the cutting of their communications. I did not think that the French had enough troops available to stop the thrust now coming against Peronne and Amiens. I am quite sure that the French will always think more of Paris than anything else. I spoke to Gort and told him that he must arrange with his tactical trains to get some large proportion of his reserves down into the area Douai–Béthune–Arras so as to have something there.

If the worst comes to the worst the B.E.F. must be prepared to turn south and cut itself through to the Abbeville–Amiens line and eventually to the Seine to cover Havre.[1] What is to happen to the Belgians I really don't know. They have the longest wheel to make and are very unwilling to evacuate Belgium completely. I daresay that they will never get out at all. In any case we must think of the B.E.F. whose feeding is becoming very difficult already.

The [1st] Armoured Division[2] will not commence landing at Havre till to-night. They may be very useful for the extrication of the B.E.F. in the last resort.

I am told that the French staff are very despondent. I don't know what they can do more than they are doing. But I am quite sure that the German main columns will be coming up pretty soon towards this big gap in the Douai–Amiens area. I can find little out about the way the French are fighting. Perhaps the arrival of Weygand may make some difference in their morale.

On May 18 Reynaud had taken over the Ministry of National Defence from Daladier and had recalled General Weygand from Beyrout to replace General Gamelin. Weygand, who was 73, assumed command on May 20. At the same time, Reynaud invited Marshal Pétain to join his Ministry.

Before he was superseded, Gamelin drafted orders for a counter-attack from the south by divisions withdrawn from other parts of the line, but Weygand cancelled them, saying that he must investigate the situation for himself. Three days were thus lost while he tried to find out what was happening.

"I was strongly of opinion", wrote Ironside later, "that only a strong push towards Amiens could extract the Allied troops now enveloped by the strong turning-movement of the Panzers which had broken through at Sedan. I asked for permission to see Gort at once and, if he agreed to the manœuvre being possible, to strike with his whole force

[1] Editors' italics.
[2] The only armoured division in the British Isles at this time.

south towards Amiens, with a view to taking position along the Somme. I was certain that there would be a great gap between the tail of the Panzers and [the] head of any supporting troops coming up. I proposed, if Gort agreed, to give him the order to disengage the B.E.F. and carry out that manœuvre."

May 19 (continued)

Sunday evening, after many Cabinet meetings, it was decided that I was to go over to see Gort with what was practically an order to be prepared to draw southwards on his L. of C. It meant abandoning the Belgians. Anyway, I think the Cabinet was justified in issuing the order.

I caught a special train at 9 p.m. and [arrived at] Boulogne at 2 a.m. Gort's H.Q. at Wahagnies at 6 a.m.

"I told the C.-in-C.", Ironside wrote later, "that in my opinion only an attack with all his force, backed if it was possible by the French troops near him, in the direction of Amiens would release the B.E.F. from their present encirclement. Did he agree? Did he think it a possible solution? If he did, I was ready to give him an order to proceed at once. I would then proceed to get the French troops near him to conform. After some thought, Lord Gort did not agree. I asked him to try, but the C.-in-C. said no, he could not agree."

Gort's reasons have been described in the official histories. Seven of his nine divisions were in close contact on the Scheldt, and even if they could be disengaged, their withdrawal would open a gap on his left between himself and the Belgians through which the enemy would be bound to penetrate. Strong enemy columns were also moving round his right flank between Arras and the Somme, and only enough ammunition remained for one more battle. What then should be done? Gort had still two divisions in hand. If he could not break through to the Somme, he could at least narrow the gap, and Weygand, perhaps, would also attack

Refugees leaving Louvain

Troops fighting their way back to Dunkirk

Imperial War Museum

Troops being evacuated from Dunkirk by S.S. *Guineau*

Imperial War Museum

General Ironside, C.-in-C. Home Forces, inspecting troops

it from the south. But first of all it was necessary to get
orders from the French.

"I then asked Lord Gort", Ironside continues, "under
whose orders he was now acting. The answer was General
Billotte, who had a headquarters under the Vimy Ridge near
Lens. Billotte had given the B.E.F. no orders for some eight
days, nor had Gort complained to the Cabinet or to me. I
asked for the Chief of the General Staff (General Pownall) to
be allowed to come with me to visit Billotte."

What then happened is best described in Ironside's diary.

May 20

We arranged to get the 50th Division and 5th Division down
towards Arras. Also the 44th Division on our extreme left to be
relieved by the Belgians. This would make a beginning towards
facing the gap in the south. I then went down to Béthune to find
General Billotte, the C.-in-C. of the Armies in the North. The
road's an indescribable mass of refugees, both Belgian and French,
moving down in every kind of conveyance. Poor women pushing
perambulators, horsed wagons with all the family and its goods
in it. Belgian units all going along aimlessly. Poor devils. It was a
horrible sight and it blocked the roads, which was the main
difficulty. I then found Billotte and Blanchard at Lens (1st Army),
all in a state of complete depression. No plan, no thought of a
plan. Ready to be slaughtered. Defeated at the head without
casualties. *Très fatigués* and nothing doing.

I lost my temper and shook Billotte by the button of his tunic.
The man is completely beaten. I got him to agree [to a plan] and
Blanchard [Commander of the French First Army] accepted to
take Cambrai. There is absolutely nothing in front of them. They
remain quivering behind the water-line north of Cambrai while
the fate of France is in the balance. Gort told me when I got back
to his Headquarters that they would never attack.

Ironside wrote after the war that he told Billotte " 'You
must make a plan. Attack at once to the south with all your
forces on Amiens.' Billotte drew himself up to attention

x   321

saying that he would make an immediate plan to attack and I left him to do it."

May 20 (continued)

I spoke to Weygand on the phone, told him that there was no resolution here and that there was no co-ordination. I told him that Billotte should be relieved. I think that the French will never play under a British command, so that there is no use suggesting co-ordination by us. Weygand said that he was coming up to-morrow.

Thus all seemed arranged and Ironside returned to London. From the north, Gort, with the French First Army on his left, would attack to the south of Arras. From there to the Somme lay a gap of only twenty-five miles. Only two roads ran through it lengthwise, and on these the whole enemy force depended. Under Weygand's new plan, which was substantially the same as Gamelin's, the French Seventh Army would close it from the south.

"It is important", wrote Ironside afterwards, "to realize the position of our B.E.F. at the moment when the German blow took place on the 10th May 1940. Lord Gort was completely under the French command. His force consisted of nine divisions. He had the right of appeal against any orders he received. But matters were not simple if he wished to exercise such a right. In theory he was under the direct command of the French Generalissimo, but in actual fact he was under the command of General Billotte (in command of the Northern Armies) and Billotte was under General Georges, who was under General Gamelin. He was therefore far beneath the authority to which any appeal could be made and have any effect. No one thought much about such an appeal and all hoped that it would never be put into effect. If it were it would certainly slow up any operations if it did not destroy them.

"Doubts had certainly arisen in the British Military minds as to the French Command. Was it quick enough to bring

◻◻ off any counter-attack against the expected German attack ?
What was needed was accurate reports of enemy attacks
along the whole front, and instant placing of reserves to
meet these attacks and then, when the enemy's plan was
clear, instant counter-attacks to mend any breaks which had
occurred. It means an immediate alert in all commands from
the Generalissimo downwards and a general movement of
all commanders forward to their command posts. Not a
minute could be lost in repairing breaches in the line. The
Generalissimo who was going to act on the defence had to
be more agile in thought than did a Generalissimo who was
pushing forward an attack."

CHAPTER XX

Prelude to Dunkirk

IN ATTACKING through the Ardennes and thence on a narrow front along the Franco–Belgian frontier, the Germans ran a great risk to obtain a great result. To this attack they had committed a third of their infantry and no fewer than seven of their ten armoured divisions.

Supported by dive-bombers and headed by the armour, this onslaught drove in the Belgian covering-troops and the French cavalry, quickly reached the Meuse, and then made a lengthy and rapid advance north-westwards against no opposition. On the long, straight roads and at defiles such as the town of Luxemburg and the Meuse crossings, the tanks and vehicles offered good targets to the air, but the main allied bomber forces failed to strike them in time. Worse was to come. As the columns advanced they exposed two vulnerable flanks about a hundred miles long and with only thirty miles between them. These could have been cut from north and south, but the French soldiers, only trained and taught to fight in previously prepared positions, were baffled when they met the Germans in the open, and their tanks, which were as good and numerous as the enemy's, were for the most part spread out along the whole line in support of the infantry, instead of being concentrated, like the Germans', in armoured formations. And so they had little to punch with.

324

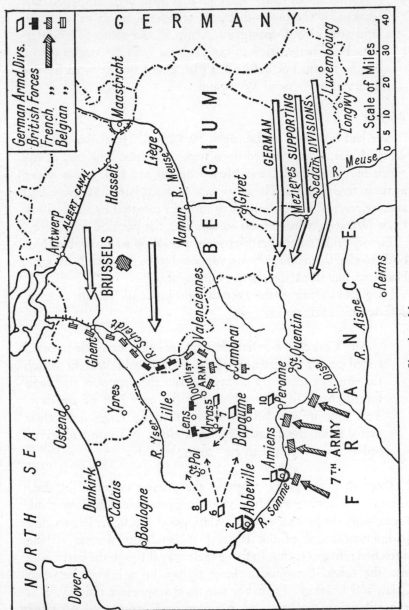

Situation, May 21, 1940.

General Gamelin, who at first had been surprised and shaken by the break-through, recovered much of his poise, and was now forming an Army in the south to counter-attack the penetration in conjunction with the armies cut off in the north, but before his plan could be executed he was relieved by General Weygand.

May 21

We had bombing in the night [at Calais]. Hotel Excelsior, in which I was, was straddled by a stick of bombs. The end of my room blown up and I was blown up off my bed. I was asleep again in five minutes. The aeroplane an hour late at St. Engelbert and we reached Hendon in forty minutes escorted by six fighters. I saw Winston, who persists in thinking the position no worse.

Enemy tanks entered Amiens and passed on to Abbeville. Nobody to stop them and they are supposed to be going to Boulogne. How can one think the thing is not serious?

I begin to despair of the French fighting at all. The great army defeated by a few tanks.

Mr. Churchill's belief that the position was "no worse.' rested on his experience of the First World War in which the enemy had nearly always outrun their supplies and been forced to a halt after advancing for only five or six days. This time it was different. The German tanks took their petrol from the French filling-stations. No one had given orders for the petrol to be "immobilized".

Towards evening we stopped the enemy columns in their advance on Boulogne. They went to ground in a hollow road. I can only hope the results were good enough. Brownrigg [Adjutant-General of the B.E.F.] at Boulogne reports all the wretched refugees trying to force their way through the barricades into the town. Parachutists have blown up a bridge between Calais and Dunkirk. Probably the most important railway. It is impossible now to distinguish between the German men dropped and the refugees.

Obviously it is impossible to go towards the coast with the
B.E.F. It has perhaps another four days' food and no more.
Situation desperate. Nothing done by the French Command.
The cruel thing is that the B.E.F. has never been asked for a
fight.

In the evening Winston saw us at midnight. He is off to Paris
in the morning to meet Weygand and Reynaud. Weygand has
gone back in a destroyer to Cherbourg. Personally I think we
cannot extricate the B.E.F. Only hope a march south-west. Have
they the time? Have they the food? God help the B.E.F. Brought
to this state by the incompetence of the French Command.

> Ironside was sure that if the B.E.F. had cut themselves
> loose from the Belgians and struck southwards through the
> gap between the German armour and the more slow-moving
> infantry columns, the enemy would have been surprised, the
> Somme could have been reached, and much British equip-
> ment would have been saved. As already explained, the
> German penetration was only twenty-five miles wide, and
> there were but two good roads from east to west for all its
> reinforcements and supplies. A short Allied advance from
> north and south would have cut off the German armoured
> columns, and even a small advance of half the width would
> have harassed them.
>
> Weygand's plan, similar except in emphasis to Gamelin's,
> was to attack the penetration at its narrowest point between
> Arras and the Somme valley with the French First Army, the
> Belgians and the B.E.F. from the north, and with the French
> Seventh Army from the south. He discussed his plan with
> King Leopold and with General Billotte on this same day,
> May 21. Lord Gort, tardily invited to attend, could not
> arrive until after Weygand had left, and Billotte, the General
> charged with the execution of the manœuvre, was to meet
> his death in a motor accident on the way back to his head-
> quarters. "There was now", comments the official historian,
> "no French commander with the Northern Armies who
> knew at first hand ... General Weygand's plan for a counter-

offensive. . . . There was now no one to co-ordinate French, British and Belgian actions."

Misfortune also befell the counter-attack at Arras which Ironside and Gort had planned on the 20th. The 5th and 50th British Divisions had duly advanced, and although only the leading battalion of each division was in fact engaged, they penetrated twelve miles inside the enemy's area. But the promised attack by the First French Army on their left failed to materialize, no attack started from the French Seventh Army in the south, and the British found themselves in a dangerous salient. Ironside thus closed his diary for this fateful day: "No communication as I went to bed at 1.0 a.m. I don't think the people have any idea of the disaster approaching!"

May 22 (London)

Winston came back from Paris about 6.30 p.m. and we had a Cabinet at 7.30 p.m. He was almost in buoyant spirits, having been impressed by Weygand. Said that he looked like a man of fifty. But when it came down to things it was still all *projets* The B.E.F. has lost a chance of extricating itself and is very short of food and ammunition. I am trying to square up this end to clear the Channel ports for Gort.

In Paris, the Prime Minister had had a conference with Reynaud and Weygand. Weygand had discussed his plan, with which Mr. Churchill had found himself in agreement. At the conclusion of this conference Mr. Churchill sent the following telegram to Lord Gort:

The conclusions which were reached between Reynaud, Weygand and ourselves are summarized below. They accord exactly with general directions you have received from War Office [conveyed to Lord Gort by Ironside on May 20] . . . It was agreed:

1. That the Belgian Army should withdraw to the line of the Yser and stand there, the sluices being opened.

□□   2. That the British Army and the French First Army
should attack south-west towards Bapaume and
Cambrai at the earliest moment, certainly to-morrow,
with about eight divisions, and with the Belgian
Cavalry Corps on the right of the British.[1]

3. That as this battle is vital to both Armies and the
British communications depend upon freeing Amiens,
the British Air Force should give the utmost help,
both by day and by night, while it is going on.

4. That the new French Army Group which is advancing upon Amiens and forming a line along the
Somme should strike northwards and join hands with
the British divisions who are attacking southwards in
the general direction of Bapaume.

It was hoped that the British would provide two, and the
First French Army six, divisions for the eight divisions which
were to attack from the north, and this would have been an
ideal plan if it had been issued and acted on earlier. But it was
now almost too late, and it would certainly be too late by the
time subordinate commanders had given their orders and
positioned their troops. The gap between the German armour
and its supporting formations was gradually closing. Bombing had delayed the arrival of the French Army Group (in
fact only an Army) in the south. Nearly the whole of the
B.E.F. was in contact with the enemy and would be difficult
to disengage, while Billotte, commander of the First Group
of Armies in the north, and the only Frenchman who knew
Weygand's plan, was dead. No successor was appointed for
some days, and orders arrived late.

The German armoured columns were now sweeping towards the sea and northwards up the coast. Troops had been
hastily sent from the United Kingdom to garrison Boulogne
and Calais. Included in the Calais garrison were the last

---

[1] This did not seem impossible, as reconnoitring light French forces
had already slipped through the gap between the German armour and
infantry, and reached Cambrai and Bapaume.

Regular troops left in England. They belonged to the Armoured Division, as did the Tank Regiment. Their task was to protect the flank of Dunkirk on the west by opposing any German Panzers coming in from the direction of Boulogne. A Colonel of the Royal Engineers also accompanied them with orders to arrange that all canals on that flank should have their sluices opened and be filled with water.

May 23

Things are not good. Boulogne was isolated by German tanks this morning at 8 a.m. and I have only just got my three battalions of motorized infantry and the Tank Regiment into Calais in time.

I am now pushing in the Canadians under their Divisional Commander [General] McNaughton. He may be able to do a little to open up the communications to St. Omer, but it doesn't look much as if he could. Meanwhile the B.E.F. is short of food and ammunition. Damned bad.

General Weygand now announced that the attack which should have been launched on May 23 would take place on the 26th, explaining that on the earlier date the French divisions coming up from the south had been delayed by their horsed transport and by German bombing of their strategical trains. Apparently ignoring General Blanchard, Billotte's successor, he asked the B.E.F. to co-operate by attacking towards Bapaume. Gort replied that his nine divisions were spread out on a front of sixty miles, and that the Germans were already on their right rear. With his left hand he was holding the Belgians. He could not stretch himself any further to the right, and in any case he only had ammunition for one more battle. He suggested that the attack from the north should be carried out by the French First Army. The diary for May 23 continues:

May 23 (continued)

The French are not pushing from the south as much as they ought to be and I don't know if Weygand will be able to galvanize them into action. We have messed this up properly.

4 *p.m.* Boulogne has definitely gone. The Germans entered the French fort north of the town and have taken the guns and have now prevented any chance of ships coming into the port. So goes all the people in Boulogne, including the two Guards battalions there. A rotten ending indeed.

I had a picture of the whole situation which shows all the German armoured divisions in action. Four of them are certainly running up north towards St. Omer and Calais.

We have sent complete discretion to Gort to move his Army as he likes to try to save it. The French are doing nothing with their First Army and I don't think that Gort has any connection with Blanchard, who has replaced Billotte. Gort is very nearly surrounded and there is just the possibility that he may be able to withdraw through Ypres to Dunkirk. I have directed some food there for him. That may help if he attempt to withdraw. I cannot see that we have much hope of getting any of the B.E.F. out. The only chance is that Weygand's manœuvre will be carried out. We have lost faith in the French power of attack. Whether it will come again is impossible for a foreigner to say. Only a Frenchman can incite them to advance.[1]

May 24

We have managed to get up some food and ammunition to Gort through Dunkirk and I think that it is possible through Ostend also. That has eased the situation considerably, though the main thing is that Gort still finds no co-ordination of the operations. . . . The whole thing now depends upon getting a man who can get the French to fight. We spent a bad time last night deciding upon the putting in of more troops into Boulogne or the taking of them out. Eventually we extracted what remained with some loss. A most gallant show on the part of the Navy.

[1] When the French divisions from the south arrived, they were spread out defensively along the Somme, instead of being concentrated for attack. It appeared that they had no intention of attacking but were trying to prevent the Germans from advancing on Paris.

3 *p.m.* McNaughton, the Canadian General, who went over to spy out the Dunkirk–Calais position, found Fagalde, the French Corps Commander, in Dunkirk. He has been appointed C.-in-C. in the North. His first order was to our people in Calais to stand fast. A good sign. The first order of co-ordination which has been given by the French Command in the North for ten days. Let us hope it is the beginning.

The German mobile columns have definitely been halted for some reason or other. Rather similar to the halt they made before. It is quite certain that there is very little movement about. They must have got quite a lot of petrol at Boulogne.

May 25

Things get worse. Gort has withdrawn from Arras and is now along the La Bassée Canal. This stops any chance there is—if there ever was one—of shutting the gap between Peronne and Arras. The French were complaining bitterly last night, but showed no signs of getting forward from Peronne, and Gort seems to have exercised his right to withdraw. Recriminations matter little in a moment like this. I do not think that Weygand's plan ever had any chance of success, because it depended upon the attack coming up from the south over the Somme. This it has shown no signs of doing. Still, it was a plan, even if the means available or the quality of the troops were insufficient.

Why Gort has done this I don't know. He has never told us that he was going to do it or even when he had done it. He has used his discretion and may now make a fight of it, which is something.

The final *débâcle* cannot be long delayed and it is difficult to see how we can help. It cannot mean the evacuation of more than a minute portion of the B.E.F. and the abandonment of all the equipment of which we are so short in this country. Horrible days to have to live through.

I wish I could have seen the dire destruction of all these damned armoured divisions which have done all the trouble. They have taken years to make and train and they have carried out their purpose.

The question now is what we shall do. We shall have the most appalling pressure to send an Army over to France to keep things going and we shall have the people here shouting for protection against invasion. What proportion we shall come to in the end is difficult to say. We must lay down a minimum for Home Defence. Then a small B.E.F. as a token. We shall have lost practically all our trained soldiers by the next few days—unless a miracle appears to help us.

I am now concentrating upon the Home Defence. The Cabinet are still wondering what they will do about appointing a Commander-in-Chief. . . . They want a change to some man well known in England. They are considering my appointment. I have said I am prepared to do anything they want. Obviously, when one considers how the Germans have worked out their plans for conquest of all the other countries, they must have considered how to get at us. Parachutists, troop-carrying aeroplanes, tanks in flat-bottomed boats and the like. Given perhaps foggy weather they might get a footing. The essence of the problem is information and instant action. Delay is fatal. Attack every body of men seen, irrespective of loss. Only extreme energy from the top will allow us to deal with this menace. . . .

3.30 *p.m.* There seems to be some sort of "accord" between Gort and Blanchard to attack south on a broader front. One wonders if they can get going now in the position they are. It is what ought to have been done before.

We are in the position of being asked to act intelligently without knowing what is going on. Gort may well have sent details which have not come, or even sent an officer in a plane who has been shot down.

I had Lelong [the French Military Attaché] in and he acknowledged that the R.A.F. had done the most wonderful work shooting down the German bombers almost as they liked. I am inclined to think that the German supply of pilots has begun to feel the strain considerably. It may well be that the decision will lie in the supply of pilots.

What would have happened if the French had built an armoured force for the price of the money expended on the Maginot

Line?[1] It would not have appealed to the popular idea in France of defending the sacred soil of France. Also the use of the manpower of France was something the French understood. It would have become a question of land-fleets. You had to have a superior fleet or it would not be able to function. All that is useless conjecture. We have to deal with the situation as it is. We cannot make any Panzer divisions. It is too late. We must deal with them with guns. The one thing necessary is for the French Commands to revivify their men. I am glad to hear that the 2-pounder anti-tank gun has proved itself most efficient. It has dealt with the German big tanks. We have definite reports to this effect. This is all right in positions, but it cannot chase after the tank, which merely turns off and comes in at another angle, making it necessary to hold a biggish perimeter.

May 26

A memorable day. We have at last given orders for the B.E.F. to withdraw to the coast with a view to making an attempt to get out. It will be a matter of getting as many men out as possible with very little equipment.[2] They will want a lot of putting right when they are landed and will want to be reconstituted.

Anyway, after much havering and protests by the French that they were attacking from the south[3]—all of which was obviously untrue—we are free to go if we can. Weygand's magnificent directives have been of no avail. The French soldiers are terrorized,

[1] When touring the Maginot Line early in 1940 Gamelin told Ironside he regretted the money spent on the Maginot Line, and that if he had had his way a large armoured force and a strong air force would have been substituted, with only field fortifications along the frontiers.
[2] Ironside said privately at this time that he thought we should be lucky to evacuate 30,000 men. This was before we knew that Hitler had halted the German armoured advance which threatened to cut the B.E.F. off from Dunkirk.
[3] The French reported all-day advances that they alleged had been made to towns and villages north of the Somme, apparently with the object of drawing us southwards. In fact, no advances took place.

especially the heads of the large formations. They cannot think or operate. A sad business.

On the night of the 25th Ironside proposed to the Prime Minister that he should leave the post of C.I.G.S. and become Commander-in-Chief, Home Forces. Mr. Churchill agreed, saying that the defence of Great Britain was vital to the Empire.

Then I was told that I had to take over the command in England and organize that. I am to be made a Field-Marshal later. Not at once, because the public may think that I am being given a sop and turned out. An honour for me and a new and most important job, one much more to my liking than C.I.G.S. in every way.

The next few months may show whether we can stand in England by ourselves. All a matter of the Air Force. If we can keep that in being all is well. And to keep that in being we must keep the industry in being. With night bombing can we keep in being all these factories or indeed get the workers to go on with production? As we have always said, this wretched bombing business develops into a barging match, each side going for the industry of the other. Day bombing has become more or less too costly and so the fighters will not have a chance. We have not got the "homing" device fitted to fighters yet in order to tackle a bomber in the dark. They have some sort of a machine ready, but very imperfect.

It is conceivable that the Germans may try to reduce this country by air-attack alone. That invasion will only follow on air superiority. The position is serious.

On May 27 the announcement was made that General Ironside had succeeded Sir Walter Kirke as Commander-in-Chief, Home Forces, and that General Dill had succeeded General Ironside as C.I.G.S.

PART FIVE

HOME DEFENCE

CHAPTER XXI

Calais and Dunkirk

ON MAY 27, 1940, Ironside became Commander-in-Chief of the Home Forces of Great Britain. The battle in France had impressed on him the great difficulties which confront a military commander who is on the defensive. A General about to attack can choose, unknown to his opponent, not only his objective and the place and the time of his onslaught, but by feints and false information can mislead his enemy and make him disperse and weaken his forces. At the same time the attacker concentrates his own army for the main blow. He will try to deliver this as a surprise. He can prepare everything well ahead, his plans are cut and dried, and they will require little or no alteration throughout the struggle.

A defending commander, on the other hand, is largely unaware of the attacker's plans. He cannot tell where the crucial stroke will fall. He must guard all his vital points against both ground and air-borne attack. A measure of dispersion over a large area will be necessary, but he must not unduly weaken his reserves, for they will be his only means of influencing the battle. He must be constantly on the alert to avoid surprise. He must not be misled by feint attacks, and when the main stroke is identified, he must counter-attack at once. His opportunity may be fleeting. He must therefore be skilful in placing his reserves and he must retaliate at the

339

□□ right place and at the right time. He can have no cut-and-dried plan and he must largely improvise. He may have to decide and issue his orders on the instant. He must possess imagination, intuition, powers of deduction and agility of mind.

Such was the reasoning which governed Ironside's planning for the defence of the United Kingdom and the vital areas of London and the industrial Midlands. He expected that the German onslaught would come in four stages: first, indiscriminate and widespread bombing to break down public morale; then concentrated air attacks on ports and shipping to cripple the Royal and the Merchant Navies and cut off supplies from abroad; then an intensive attack on the Air Force and its supporting industry to gain air supremacy; and lastly an invasion both from the skies and the sea. Parachutists would seize airfields and natural landing-spaces for troop-carrying planes, and attack our beach defences in rear. Thus assisted, the main invaders, composed of hard-hitting and fast-moving tanks and infantry, would arrive by sea.

The most vulnerable area of our coastline was at first thought to be between the Wash and Folkestone, but as the Germans advanced in Northern France, this "danger area" was extended to any port on the southern coastline which lay within two hundred miles of a German-occupied aerodrome.

To oppose this threat (and on May 29 the Chiefs of Staff informed him that, in their view, a full-scale attack on England was imminent) Ironside had theoretically at his disposal 15 infantry divisions, 1 armoured division, 57 Home Defence battalions, and the Local Defence Volunteers, first raised in mid-May and soon to be re-christened the Home Guard. The evacuation from Dunkirk provided him with some trained men but with no equipment. He had very little artillery, since nearly all the new 25-pounders and anti-tank guns had been lost in France. The armoured division had a few light tanks. Numbers, equipment, mobility and training were generally so defective that few units were fit for offensive operations, and a large part of the Army had accordingly to be committed to static defence; but as these weaknesses were made good, more and more formations were withdrawn into reserve for counter-attack.

His general plan was to have a "crust" along the beaches to defeat minor enterprises and to pass back information; blocks and stop-lines further inland to prevent armoured penetration; small fast-moving units to deal with parachutists and airborne troops; and a general reserve north and west of London for counter-attacks towards East Anglia or the South Coast.

Added to all this were many duties in the civilian sphere. Ironside was not only Commander-in-Chief of the Home Forces, and as such responsible for the military protection of the United Kingdom, but he was also Chairman of a new body, the Home Defence Executive, and was charged among other matters with the security of our communications, the preparation of demolition plans, and the suppression of the Fifth Column. This last, though it seemed otherwise at the time, was almost non-existent.

May 27

The news in the morning is bad. We have got off 25,000 men from Dunkirk. Just the men and no equipment of any sort. I met Eastwood [Commander of the 4th Division in France] on the steps of the War Office. He had come over last night and described things as very bad. He did not expect any of the B.E.F. to get off at all. Certainly no equipment. The French Command has failed completely and our Army has been placed in an impossible position. Not even given a chance to fight for its life. The next few nights will be very critical indeed. We cannot count on more than the bodies of the men. . . .

I packed up all my goods and here [Kneller Hall, Twickenham] I am at one more job. I always seem to get the tail-end of things to pull them together. Kneller Hall [is] the most awful Victorian country-house. Very different to being in London. A lovely summer's day with green grass all round us and a comfortable little mess that has been made up a few days ago. Kirke said goodbye and went off. He has been placed on retired pay and was very sorry to go, poor chap. . . . He has done a lot, but has been hampered by people not taking the defence of England seriously. Now they do, which will make it much more easy for me. It is always better to take over something on the up-grade.

I have been into the general situation:

(i) Enemy aliens. They must be cleared out of the coast area at once.

(ii) All [units] must be filled up with men and material at once.

(iii) The petrol situation is not good. There is far too much petrol in the coast areas, most of it unguarded.

(iv) There is unrestricted movements at week-ends in the coast areas, offering the Germans any amount of transport for the taking.

(v) There must be much more realization of the serious nature of the position in England.

(vi) There is a very scratch staff here in the Home Forces.

(vii) The Civil Departments are all very slow in their methods and do not realize the value of time in military operations.

I am to have a meeting to-morrow afternoon of the Defence Committee [i.e. the Home Defence Executive] and I am going to get things on the move. I shall have much more authority than poor Walter Kirke had and people cannot withstand our demands. I am glad to see that the "parashooters", as they are now called, are going well. Not only will they be a body of good stout people, but they will be able now to get us a good deal of information that has been denied to us so far. . . .

I have decided to form troops of three motor cars with Brens in them, commanded by a young Tank Corps officer, and to christen them Ironsides. They will be given to each division to the tune of three troops.

I have a few moments in which to take stock of my time as C.I.G.S. Intensely interesting, but marred by too many committees and too much explanation to all and sundry. Military decisions delayed, or criticized and weakened, before they can be executed. One's own decision feels weakened by the amount of talk to which it is subjected. It is bad enough to have three Chiefs of Staff to settle something, but when their hard-earned decision is subject to committee rulings, the running of war is well-nigh impossible. . . .

The real vice of the military position was its complete subjugation to civilian control, almost in detail. The Cabinet assumed a predominant position in the direction of military affairs and kept the military leaders so much on the run that they never had time to think and plan. We were always hurrying along with explanations and justifications of what we wanted. Too many cooks at the boiling of the broth. Anyway, as far as I am concerned, there is an end of that phase. I never had to work so hard in my life before, and never had the sense of futility so strongly before.

Now I start another phase. I must confess that it is much more in my line than the other. I am now in command and am not hampered by a machine that was made for peace conditions and was not fit to function in war. I wonder how much more the civil side will fall into my hands.

May 28

11 *a.m.* News just in that the Belgian line has broken and that they are suing for an armistice.[1] This means that it is more than ever difficult to get anything of the B.E.F. off from France. I am glad that I haven't the anxiety of the evacuation. I am sorry for poor Dill.

A horrible tragedy for British arms.

5 *p.m.* Up to London to a meeting of the [Home] Defence Executive at the Horse Guards. Not too bad. The state of the armament is catastrophic. I hope that it will get better in a week or two. Hope we get the week or two.

Finlayson told me that we had a bad night last night for the B.E.F. Three hospital ships sunk with all their wounded. We got off some 10,000 and no more. The Belgians' going has made a bad hole. I am afraid less and less chance of many of the B.E.F. Damned sad. Local Defence Volunteers going well. I must get

[1] The Belgian Army surrendered to the Germans in the early hours of May 28.

343

them armed with Molotoff cocktails[1] in all the villages of England. The only way to deal with a tank.

Although Ironside wrote that the Home Defence Executive was "not too bad", he in fact found fifty people in the room—ten ministers each with four assistants. He decided that this "debating society" was no way in which to get quick decisions and that a much smaller executive with Sir Findlater Stewart as Chairman, the Civil Defence Officer, Wing Commander Hodsoll, from the Home Office, and the C.-in-C.'s representative, Colonel Macleod, should form the new Executive, with power to co-opt representatives from Ministries as necessary.

May 29

We had dinner [on May 28] in the Wellington Hotel [in Tunbridge Wells] with Auckland Geddes [Regional Commissioner for South-East England]. A cheery evening and we swopped stories. Every now and again I thought of the B.E.F. and Jack Gort. I shan't see him again. A gallant man. Little we thought a couple of weeks ago that this would be the end of the B.E.F.

Anyway, we shall get these L.D.V.s going. Static defence in every village by blocks, and information going out from there. And thousands of Molotoff cocktails thrown down from the windows of houses. That might well settle tank columns. We just want the courage of the men. Nothing else matters. No defence is any good if the men behind it leave it and run away. The old L.D.V.s won't do that.

An interesting day all round Kent. The troops in fine form and very keen. They are all settling down in deadly earnest. The main thing we want is mobility. This we shall get in about a week—some 400 of these little armoured cars in groups of three to be called "Ironsides".

I dined with Winston in the evening with him and his wife alone. He was in great form. He showed me Louis Spears' letter

[1] Home-made incendiaries, consisting of a bottle filled with petrol, fitted with an improvised fuse or wick. First used by the Finns against the Russians.

344

that had come in from Paris. There is a good deal of defeatist attitude amongst the French. Weygand is a good hard conscientious worker. Georges is purely "negative" and does not function very much.

Very little chance of the real B.E.F. coming off. They have now sunk three ships in Dunkirk harbour and so there is very little more chance of getting any units off. Jack Gort has sent a very fine message to the King. I was only wondering whether I should have done as well as him had fate taken me to the command of the B.E.F., as it looked as if it would at the beginning of the war. One must never quarrel with fate.

May 30

Still the most gorgeous weather. It is good to be out of London on these days.

We are gradually getting order out of chaos. Paget, my Chief of Staff, is a very able man, besides being a cheery one. One [who] would never be downhearted.

Winston said to me last night, "We all depend upon you because you don't lose your head in a crisis and have shown that during the last few months." He also repeated the fact that I was going to be made a Field-Marshal in a few days. That will give me a good deal of added authority. . . .

I shall get a great deal out of these L.D.V.s. It will differ according to the man who is in charge. I put down the following:

1. Static defence of village by blocks to prevent armoured columns moving
2. Information from bicycle patrols issuing from the village.
3. Molotoff cocktails to deal with tanks from the windows of houses.

If we can get this going we ought to make easy movement through the country impossible and so avoid [repeating] the spectacle of France having her guts torn out without any effort being made to deal with the aggressor. All the troops cowering behind a water obstacle and facing nothing. Not fighting, but waiting while their very entrails were being torn out. A pitiable sight.

I have been wondering whether a general curfew would be a good thing. We are getting very near the moment. . . .

If the Germans ever attempt a landing here they will put the utmost energy into establishing what might be called a "bridge-head" in England. All our energies must be put into stopping this. No waiting for more troops to come up. Our mobile forces must attack at once regardless of losses and nip the landing in the bud. We cannot inculcate that idea too much into everybody concerned. . . .

A string of visitors. Dowding, the C.-in-C. Fighter Command, is a curious old thing. Very pessimistic about the use of his fighters to try to extricate the B.E.F. He does not understand that the men we are extricating are very valuable, even if we did not take the sentimental side of abandoning the B.E.F. into account. He told me that the output of Spitfires is 40 a month and of Hurricanes 40 a week. We cannot speed that up much now. . . .

3 p.m. Later we heard that 40,000 men were off last night, which puts a completely different complexion upon the picture of 4,000 as they gave me at first. It is wonderful what you can do with any number of small boats.

Our great handicap in this country is the lack of any kind of tank. If the Germans get their tanks ashore they will be much more difficult to round up. Once a column is ashore they will push on with the utmost brutality. I hope to have a good many of these 6-pdr. and 12-pdr. guns mounted on light lorries. They may not be tanks, but they may get a shot and knock the gentlemen out. Our people must act just as the Germans do and go straight in and attack whatever the casualties. Gradually perhaps I shall get some tanks.

What will the German do now? Will he turn on the French, or will he have a go at us in this country? The soft spot is un-doubtedly the French. They wouldn't take much finishing off. To get control of England would finish the war completely, but I fancy that he will make his preparations most carefully before he tackles us. That must take him time, even if he has begun his preparations already. After all, he may well try to finish us off by air-attack alone. He evidently wants to finish it straight away. . . . I should say that there will be a respite for the Germans to lick their mechanical sores and then the avalanche. . . .

Last thing at night, a call from Dill who is going over with Winston to see Weygand. They are calling for more divisions, more Air, more anti-tank, more anti-air. I told Dill that it would probably take the essential equipment of one or perhaps two divisions to make up the Canadians to their full strength, if they are to go to France. That is a most serious thing to contemplate. Personally, I think that the Germans are more likely to finish up the French than to go straight for us. They usually finish what they have put their hand to. At the moment I do not think we are in any immediate danger—14 days. My chief desire is now armoured cars. When I can have those I shall be very much better off. They should deal with motor-boat landings. With infantry in buses we should be able to deal with the parachutists.

May 31

Apparently, people are pleased to hear of 75% of the men from the B.E.F. coming back with their rifles. In all the rush of trying to get down to the boats, the tendency to throw off all weight is irresistible. I can only hope that we are taking heavy toll of the Germans. With all the bombing going on we ought to be killing a good number. It will all take them time to reorganize and get going again. I also wonder if the French are fighting, too, to get away. I see that the C.-in-C. of the First Army has been captured somewhere near Steenvoorde. . . .

Fifth Column reports coming in from everywhere. A man with an arm-band on and a swastika pulled up near an important aerodrome in the Southern Command. Important telegraph poles marked, suspicious men moving at night all over the country. We have the right of search and I have put piquets on all over the place to-night. Perhaps we shall catch some swine.

At 4.30 p.m. I went up to see the King and found him in very good form. He told me that two of the Corps Commanders, Adam and Brooke, were off and that Gort was coming off to-

night. That they had 160,000 men odd off. He said that they
hoped to get off the remainder to-night. Some 11,000 French had
come off. I told him how things were going, that we were very
short and that equipment was wanting everywhere.

June 1

What we want is the static defence in the towns and villages
and the mobile columns working in between. . . . We cannot
make the whole place a fortress, but we can probably canalize the
routes of attack. . . . My own view is that we want for the defence
of England two things:

(a) *A static defence*

To cover vulnerable points, and the L.D.V.s for the re-
striction of movement.

(b) *A mobile defence*

Largely motor columns, with the special "Ironsides",
followed by sufficient infantry in lorries. All these columns
must be small. They should not be organized on a divisional
basis at all. Such an organization is too clumsy.

June 2

Conferences yesterday and to-day in London. I begin to see
light in our organization. It is the terrible lack of equipment
which keeps us behind.

More and more people are coming in from the B.E.F. I saw the
Divisional Commander of the 50th Division who tells me that we
haven't more than 2,000 men on shore. The rest are French. Many
of the French fighting very well. It is most extraordinary what we
have been able to get off. I would never have believed it possible.
Of course no equipment, but the bodies of the trained men are
precious. . . .

I had Wingate, of Palestine fame, in to see me. He wants to
start the same sort of organization he had in Palestine here in
England. I am all for it. You cannot run this defence of England
on stereotyped lines. We want resolute men, well-led, to act immediately. The clumsy division is a thing of the past and I have
already got them divided up into Brigade Groups of all arms. . . .

Still the most glorious weather. It is too damnable that we have a war on. Let us once get the B.E.F. out and we would like downpours of rain. That will hold up the Bosches in getting their stuff across. They have had the most surprising luck.

The King has given a well-deserved G.C.B. to Gort. A sign that he has brought his Army in with honour. I still cannot understand how it is that the Bosches have allowed us to get the B.E.F. off in this way. It is almost fantastic that we have been able to do it in the face of all the bombing and gunning. It brings me to the fact that the Bosches may equally well be able to land men in England despite the bombing. Had the Germans had any Navy they might have upset our embarkation. What have their submarines been doing?

The German armour had halted within twelve miles of Dunkirk, when there was practically nothing between them and the town, and when the complete destruction of the B.E.F. seemed to be within their grasp.

The order to halt, as we now know, was first given by General von Runstedt, under whose command the German Fourth Army had been placed. Hitler confirmed the order on the following day, May 24. The following reasons, among others, have since been advanced as to why these orders were issued:

1. The British attack at Arras had alarmed Runstedt, who feared another attack on his rear from the same place and also from the French in the south. He halted his tanks until the situation was clarified.

2. The German armour had run almost continuously for one hundred and fifty miles, without time for rest or maintenance. Half the tanks were out of action. Both men and machines urgently needed time for restoration.

3. The country in front of the tanks was marshy and crisscrossed with ditches and streams; and sluice gates were being opened in an attempt to flood it. The armour might suffer heavy casualties in crossing it.

4. The French and British troops appeared to be bottled-up at Dunkirk with their backs to the sea and with little chance of escape, and could be mopped up at leisure.

5. The Germans may have regarded the destruction of the main French Armies in the south as their chief task. It would be a mistake to employ the tank force on a minor task in which it might suffer heavily.

6. Goering was jealous for the reputation of his Air Force, and wanted a large share of the credit for defeating the Allies. He is said to have requested Hitler to be allowed to finish off the B.E.F. at Dunkirk.

7. Hitler may have banked on Great Britain agreeing to peace terms after the fall of France. He may have thought that the destruction of the B.E.F. would endanger such negotiations.

Any or all of these reasons may have accounted for the failure of the German armour to advance to the kill.

June 3

There can be no doubt that Italy is now getting ready to join Germany. France will be the victim. I don't think that we can stop it. We shall be hanging on to the eastern end of the Mediterranean with all our might. It is what I anticipated, and why I tried to get the Supply people to develop industry in Palestine. All my efforts failed because none of the people concerned would contemplate the loss of the western end of the Mediterranean. Nor would they contemplate the arming of the Jews. Wavell will become one of the most important people in the Empire. . . .

Winston has decided to send two divisions to France. I have designated the 52nd Division, the Canadians, and then a reconstituted 3rd Division later. None of the senior officers think that even the 52nd Division will get to France at all. Certainly no more.

Anyway, we now have all the B.E.F., so that we have more men here. They are to have a short leave and then begin again.

Winston has ordered eight Regular battalions home from the
Middle East to be replaced by Indian battalions, and eight battalions from India. That will give us something here with which
to play. But I would have preferred very much not to have taken
the battalions from the Middle East. . . . I think that Gort ought
to go out to India at once. It is essential to hold the East firmly
whatever happens here. . . .

I believe that it has been decided to send to France two Territorial Divisions to add to the 51st already there with the Armoured
Division. Brooke is, I believe, to go to command the Corps. He
seemed very distraught over the thought and considered that the
Terrier divisions would never stand up to the bombing. Not very
good hearing. But we ought not to send the Canadians for reasons
that are political, as well as the fact that we want them in this
country.

It is really very sad to think that we cannot use our Territorial
Army after nine months of training. It is the lack of training of
the officers and N.C.O.s that has made the standard so low. We
must back France and send out something. Will France stand up
long enough to allow us to get them out?

June 4

Dowding rang me up from the Fighter Command to say that
he had had a good day with the Cabinet. He had told them the
state of his Fighter Squadrons and had been assured that he would
not be further depleted. He was now reorganizing back to their
own squadrons, and within a month he expected to be as strong
as ever he was. He sounded very much less lugubrious than he
was. He is very much inclined to regard himself as completely
outside the operations in France, which is quite impossible. . . .

I appeared in front of the Cabinet and gave them an account of
what we have been doing towards meeting an invasion. Anthony
Eden told me afterwards that they were all very happy that I was
there, and felt that something was being done. . . .

Only seasoned troops seem able to stand up to this combination of Armoured Fighting Vehicles and air bombardment. Once
they have been through it they have a contempt for it. In the last

war the shelling got intense very slowly and troops were able to get acclimatized gradually. This time the bombing fell upon them at once and the French failed utterly. Our men stood it much better and gave a good account of themselves.

The casualties have been some 30,000 in all and amongst the senior officers very small indeed. None of the senior commanders, and yet they were all in the thick of the fighting. The bombs bursting in the sand of the sand-dunes had very little effect indeed. I must say that I never credited the fact that we should get so many bodies off. Now they are useful, but the equipment is lacking. Shall we ever get the time to get them ready to fight. . . .

More than ever do I feel that we must get men who can fight. The namby-pamby people that have grown up in late years are not to be trusted in this emergency. Character and guts. That is what is wanted. Not all brains. . . .

I came back from London feeling very hopeless about the prospects of the French. I don't believe that they will stand. Their black troops will never stand up to the bombing. They didn't to the heavy shelling in the last war.

This eternal preaching of the defensive and the taking cover behind tank obstacles has been the curse of our tactics. The saying that we were never again to have "the bloody massacres of the Somme" has deluded the people. Nobody has been educated to the horrors of modern war. I don't believe the people understand it yet. We must brutalize the whole population to stand up to this menace. If they don't stand staunch, it means the loss of the Empire at the least. We can do it. No weakness to be allowed anywhere. We must be ruthless with weakness. No thought for the person. All for the show.

June 5

Dunkirk is over and finished with. A most extraordinary effort —335,000 evacuated. One can hardly understand how the Germans allowed it to happen. I expect that they could not bring up enough stuff to prevent it. . . .

A great effort [the stand at Calais] which I hope we shall never forget. It would have been impossible to have used Dunkirk as a

CALAIS

The Rifle Brigade
The 60th Rifles
The Queen Victoria Rifles
The Tank Corps
The Soldiers of France

Their Name Liveth for Evermore!

Reproduced by kind permission of " The Daily Mirror."

Cartoon pasted by Ironside into his diary above the passage beginning:
"A great effort [the stand at Calais]."

point from which to evacuate the B.E.F. and the 1st French Army without this stand. The most famous regiments in the Army. They fought it out to the end. When I sent them into Calais I was sure that they would do their duty and they did it. A fitting finish to their history. Requiescant. The historic name of Calais should be written once more on British hearts.

One wonders how many survived.

338,226 British and Allied troops were in fact evacuated from Dunkirk. 2,300 guns, 7,000 tons of ammunition, 90,000 rifles, 8,000 Bren guns, 400 anti-tank rifles and 120,000 vehicles were lost.

Despite exhaustive enquiries it has proved impossible to discover the casualty figures for the operations at Calais.

CHAPTER XXII

Invasion of England?

June 6

Up by train to York. . . . I had a good meeting with the L.D.V. people, who are mad keen, but want co-ordination very badly. . . . We saw all kinds of B.E.F. men going off on leave. All very sunburnt and cheery. They will have a good effect upon the people in England. They will make them realize that there is a war on and that we have to fight to keep what we have got. I am sure that they will bring a healthy spirit into things. A curious incident. The withdrawal of an army with the destruction of all its equipment. Something quite unknown in history. Brought about by the incompetence of the French Command. Apathy from the top. What an extraordinary thing to have to do to give up all your armament. But it was the only thing to do with the French not fighting and not even trying to fight. A disaster in our present state of equipment, but one which has been faced as the only practical possibility. The French Command still not realizing and dealing with *"projets"*. We now have the men of the B.E.F. in the country and after seventy-two hours' leave they will be back forming in their divisions. They will be of the greatest value in every way. . . .

June 7

I had lunch with Neville Chamberlain at 10 Downing Street. . . . I thought that Chamberlain looked very fresh and debonair.

He is just moving from Downing Street. I was told that the Labour Party had been trying to get Chamberlain out of the Cabinet completely and that they were all trying to bring to his person the responsibility for not having the necessary armaments. They are all to blame. . . .

I don't like the look of the German attack on the Somme. They have managed to get across the river in many places. I doubt if the show will stand. Our 51st Division seems very isolated down there by itself. I am told that we now get peremptory demands for more air and more troops from Weygand and Reynaud. All rather of the defeatist order. If they do not stand, France is finished for good, and then we shall be hard put to it to keep our end up with the lack of equipment we have in this country. . . .

I must now go up to the Eastern Counties and have a look at what they are doing there. I think I shall get away my diaries and send them over to Canada. There is no use in their remaining in Hingham to be overrun.

June 8

It is extraordinary how the shuttle moves backwards and forwards. Now the P.M. has given "priority" to the re-equipment of the B.E.F. for France. Naturally, while they are in this country they are available for operations. We shall get no more equipment for the troops in this country.

Meanwhile we have had an appreciation made out of what the Bosche effort might be against us. The first effort will be an air one against our Air Industry, aerodromes and Air Force generally. The R.A.F. say that we may expect 4,800 tons of bombs a day. This is a total calculated upon the initial carrying capacity of the planes available.

The initial effort of the Bosches against our Navy will be to mine our Fleet into its bases, then to attempt a diversion to draw off our naval forces.

As regards air-borne expeditions, the Bosches have sufficient aircraft to transport 9,750 lightly equipped men in one flight. The number of flights per day will vary from $1\frac{1}{2}$ per day for East Anglia to 3 for Kent. Taking into account air opposition and

ground opposition, it is thought that the numbers can be calculated upon a basis of 10,000 for East Anglia and 20,000 for Kent.
These only after a large measure of air superiority had been
achieved. Sea-planes and gliders may add to these numbers. Such
air-borne expeditions will be followed by sea-borne expeditions
pushed forward with the utmost brutality.

This is a dismal enough picture as regards numbers and takes
little account of weather and opposition from the Navy and Air
Force. Probably it can be very much reduced. . . .

Things are not going well on the Somme. I saw Pownall, who
had just come back from France. He told me that exactly the
same thing had happened on the Somme. The Germans had
broken through even past the Bresle and looked like getting to
Rouen. He found exactly the same thing happening as happened
in the north. The French General, Altmeyer, had been told by
Weygand to stay put and was doing so, omitting to give any
orders of any sort or kind. They are unable to compete with these
breaks-through. They just allow their guts to be eaten out. One
continues to wonder what would have been the result if the
French had spent the money they spent on the Maginot Line upon
good mobile columns and aviation. The fact remains that no
democratic nation could ever hope to compete with a nation
which has developed its war effort as the Nazis have. You must
also become a Nazi nation in order to survive. We must find
some means of surviving and then dealing with the German
nation. . . .

I have written an exhortation for all senior officers to be handed
out to everyone in England. I wrote it straight down as I felt it
and I hope that it will get people out of their lethargy:

> General Headquarters,
> Home Forces
> 11th June 1940

The war has come closer to us owing to the German occupation of North-East France. This fact should be turned to advantage because the British people are at their best when faced
with danger. We are now faced with danger. The attitude that

357

there is little we can do against the invincible German war machine must be stamped out with the utmost brutality. This attitude seems to have arisen through the theory of economic warfare without fighting. There could be no such false theory as this. We are fighting for all we hold dear, liberty and the right to live as we wish to live, and if we do not fight we shall certainly lose the privileges we have enjoyed and developed so long. Is there any Britisher who really wishes to be subordinated to such a rule as has been started by the Nazi leaders? I am sure there is not. Would life be worth living under such circumstances? Is there any Britisher who wishes to hand down such an inheritance to his descendants? Again, I am sure there is not. What are we then to do? We must train and prepare in deadly earnest. We must turn that preparation to the best account by fighting in deadly earnest, as did Cromwell's Ironsides, for what they considered their rights. There must be no weakling amongst the military leaders, just as there must be none amongst the rank and file. The day has only a certain number of hours in it and we must work as if there were only too few available. The time has gone for quiet and ease and the comfortable routine of peace. All military leaders must exact the utmost from their subordinates. In the defence of our country the principle of instant attack against any enemy landing on our shores, either from the air or from the sea, must be inculcated into all ranks. There must be no question of cowering behind an obstacle, waiting to be attacked. The enemy must be located instantly, isolated, and attacked before he can gather strength. When he comes, he can but be lightly equipped during his initial assaults. Then is the time to deal with him with the utmost determination and self-sacrifice. Any leader who fails to act at once is failing in his duty. Let each leader and each man go out with Cromwell's words in his mind: "It's no longer disputing, but out instantly all you can."

Edmund Ironside.

General.

Commander-in-Chief, Home Forces.

June 9

Another blazing hot day. Hitler is having very good weather
for his attacks on the Somme. . . . By reducing the efficiency of
our Air Force and Navy he will make any attack upon this country
by actual invasion a more feasible proposition.

The invasion will be of two kinds:

> (i) Air-borne.
> (ii) Sea-borne.

Air-borne attack may take place at many places and from any
direction. It may begin by parachutists, to be followed by troop-
carrying planes. Such attack may come very quickly, but it must
be limited in strength, both by reason of numbers and of weight.
It is impossible to block all possible landing-places for troop-
carriers, and parachutists cannot be prevented from landing. But
they can be subjected to very heavy casualties before they reach
the ground. The answer to such attacks is extreme mobility and
instant action for their extermination, combined with a good local
defence to supply information, and a check to movement from
the centre of the main landing.

Such attacks will be employed in conjunction with sea-borne
landings to cause dispersion and to upset our command. They may
be extremely annoying if the commanders do not keep their heads.
But in themselves such attacks will not be decisive.

Sea-borne attacks will be of a much more serious nature. It is
possible to make surprise landings, however vigilant are our air
and sea patrols. They may be carried out at many points, thus
confusing the commander in his judgment as to which are feint
attacks and which the real ones. All may be intended as attempts
to gain a footing, with a view to exploiting any success gained.
Several landings will tend to confuse the defending commander
and make him disperse his troops and so prevent him from crush-
ing a landing at its conception.

The enemy now has very definite advantages over his pre-
decessors. He now has the use of many fast motor-boats and
special craft for landing that he has been preparing for many
years. He has the choice of many landing-places and he has the

advantage of combining his sea-borne attack with air-borne attacks.

There still remains the difficulty for the enemy that a sea-borne expedition is a risky affair. Unless it has luck it may come to hopeless grief, through failing to achieve surprise, through bad weather, or through lack of experience in preparation. The balance of chance that the landing may be successful and so expanded is always a fine one. The number of landing places available, beaches, coves, piers and small harbours, is very large. We are forced to disperse our troops to oppose the actual landing owing to the existence of so many landing-places, and in our case, we are forced to disperse still further owing to the lack of training and equipment of our troops. We dare not hold back and concentrate, both because our troops are not fit to attack, and in many cases can only be trusted to act defensively, and because we dare not give the enemy any elbow-room. Our country is a small one and armoured troops can penetrate at a prodigious speed.

Added to these forms of attack the enemy has proved himself an adept at employing internal forces, now known as the 5th Column. Even in England we have disruptive influences, Fascists and Bolsheviks, besides a large number of alien elements introduced as refugees. Do what we can we have not been able to discover the Headquarters—if such exists—of any alien 5th Column. . . .

My main fear is the penetration by armoured fighting vehicles. I am very lacking in gun-power and I can see no immediate prospect of reinforcement at the moment. I have called into being every available gun that I can find and I have mounted them both as static and as mobile units. I can do no more at the moment.

I have the greatest belief in the strength of the L.D.V.'s given only a little time for organization. We have an inexhaustible supply of experience and courage in the country. I hope that the leadership will be all right.

5 *p.m.* Just as I had arranged a trip down to Reading, Portsmouth and Salisbury I found myself summoned to attend a conference with the P.M. upon Home Defence. No details as to what for.

June 10

The 51st Division and a couple of French divisions are now withdrawing on Havre. Exactly the same thing has happened on the Seine as happened in the north. The German armoured columns burst through and took Rouen with practically nothing. Weygand ordered everybody to stand still and then does nothing to hold up the armoured columns. Now we shall have to evacuate again. The French Command is ridiculous. . . .

We had our Home Defence Meeting. Winston asking a lot of questions and wasting time. I handed in my report upon progress and we escaped after two hours of somewhat futile discussion. . . . Chamberlain struck me this morning as a man with great courage. But he seemed thunderstruck that we had come to the pitch we have reached. He seemed lost as to how it had come about. . . .

Half our troubles as regards Supply of Material has come from the fact that we have no Master-General of Ordnance. The Army cannot get its demands fulfilled by the Ministry of Supply. The user has had little say in what he requires. The other reason is the absence of the Labour Party from the Cabinet. I am told that Supply has been speeded up as much as 60% in many essential articles. So we have wasted eight months of precious time not realizing that the war was serious. Perhaps I ought to have insisted more as C.I.G.S. With Belisha the insistence was of no good whatever. It was probably too late with Oliver Stanley. Naturally, the Labour Party would not co-operate with Chamberlain for political reasons and so they never came in to help with all their influence. Now we are in this parlous mess, made so much worse by the loss of all our equipment in France with the B.E.F. This loss looks like being continued with the withdrawal of the 51st Division, and the loss of a lot of stores at Havre and Nantes and St. Nazaire.

June 11

Italy came in against us yesterday afternoon. A great many brave words in the papers accompanied by "a stab in the back" accusation. The U.S.A. has said that she is going full speed ahead in the delivery of munitions to the Allies. Roosevelt denounces Mussolini. That is so far as it has all gone. The results are incalculable. Can Italy do enough in the short time available? Will her men fight? The Air Force and the Navy are efficient. . . . Italy may well be the weak point in the Nazi strategy. Everyone has a contempt for the Italians, even the Germans. I suppose we come back to the Shah's saying of "*Au fond, tout le monde est égoïste*".

June 12

The news this morning is that France is withdrawing to the Marne. Paris will be in the front line before very long. The next thing will be that the northern end of the Maginot Line will cave in. . . .

I am sure that the Nazis are convinced that they can defeat us before October, and we must brace ourselves up to meet their methodical offensive. Guts and discipline is what we want. We shall come to conscription of everything and a dictatorship in the end. Winston with a very small executive. . . . We have now got down to dividing the country into lines of defence. They must largely be lines of posts, defended villages and river lines. They are in all directions because one can never tell where the enemy may come from. He will try landings in many places and will exploit any successful one very quickly. I find the Navy still very confident despite their lack of success in detecting enemy action. As the weather gets worse we shall be safer from the sea-borne attack.

I went and inspected Northolt Aerodrome to see the defences. They are good, but have just been taken in hand. The sad thing about the R.A.F. is that they have some 2,000 unarmed men on such an aerodrome. The R.A.F. personnel consists of some good artificers and many servants and underlings. Only 100 armed with rifles. Too late now to do much training. The proper way to protect big aerodromes is by armoured cars and a good all-round wire.

I then went on with Dowding to see the Operations Room at Fighter Command. An underground H.Q. with hundreds of men and women plotting the course of all aeroplanes as signalled by the R.D.F.s[1] along the coast. It seems to be very efficient. But the fighters can only deal with things by day.

While there I heard that the 51st Division Headquarters had laid down their arms at St. Valerie. Some 5,000 men are off. Another division, the last of the B.E.F., destroyed in a few days. We seem to be fated. Are we going on shipping people to France to be caught and stripped off their equipment?

. . . My diaries, 60 volumes, have gone off to the Canadian Headquarters to be sent to Major Lindsey in Canada. I think I have done the right thing in getting rid of them.

June 13

We are now going to turn the cavalry from the divisions of the B.E.F. into the "Ironsides". They have no equipment and are somewhat at a loose end. They are the best troops in this country and will be fitted to attack. . . .

War Office have released to me the 8th Tank Battalion at Tidworth with fifty "I" tanks of old pattern and seventy light tanks. I have fixed up flats on the railway for them and they should be brought quickly wherever we want them. I am collecting a mobile reserve, if it is not taken away from me at once.

One's hopes go up and down as one collects something, and then has it taken away from one. The Reserve must be able to attack. If it cannot, it is not fit to be a reserve and had better be laid out statically, which is most uneconomical militarily. It is all a race for time to get something organized before we are attacked. . . .

Rearmament of B.E.F. goes faster than it was. I shall be able to get these divisions moved into their proper positions very soon. I am calling for a report each evening of the state of the six cavalry regiments being rearmed with armoured cars. That is what we want for dealing with both air and sea-landings. Infantry are no good for attack without them.

June 14

Up to see the Prime Minister. I saw him at 11 a.m. and very fit

[1] Radio Direction Finders.

and well. He has been over yesterday to see Reynaud at Tours, and back again in the same day. He told me that Reynaud had been all for asking for an armistice, but that he had argued them out of it. He said that Hitler wished to go to Paris and there dictate terms to the French Government and all the others in Europe. Then he hoped the place would be bare and that there would be no one else there. That the French Government had already gone to Bordeaux.

He then read me a letter from Corbin, the French Ambassador, saying that I had said the French were not fighting. I have only said this in the Cabinet, so that the reports must have been made by a Cabinet Minister.

Then he tackled me about my answer to the War Office upon their paper giving me the scale of offensive by the Germans of five divisions. He was indignant and said that the Navy could stop that. I thought to myself that with France out of it we might well have more than that coming against us.

Then back to Kneller Hall, where I heard that our people who have landed in France are coming back again. This meant that France had practically given in. We then found that Paris had been evacuated and was a city of the dead, all the doors and windows shut and only the gendarmes remaining. The French withdrawing on either side. Then we heard that the Generals had no more control over the men who were retreating out of control. . . .

We are working away and pouring out the equipment as fast as we can and every day makes a difference to us. It takes a week's output of Brens to equip a division. Slow enough.

The U.S.A. seems to be sending off the stuff to us and it may come in time. Shall we have any of our ports open in three months time? A great struggle for the existence of the Empire. . . . We are rapidly getting the local defence in order. It is the arming of the whole population. Exactly the same thing as happened in 1803–1805 when Napoleon was menacing this country. Power will pass more and more into the hands of the Home Forces Command. The biggest Command of any. I am lucky to have it and hope I shall keep it for a bit until I have it in order.

June 15

Paris has escaped being bombed, as Brussels did, by being declared an open town. Who would ever have pictured this at the beginning of the war? Such was the terror of bombing that the French would rather retain their capital intact. The Maginot Line must fall fairly soon through being attacked in rear, and then I don't know what the French can do to hold on. Even if the Reynaud Government disappears into Africa another will spring up in France ready to negotiate with the Germans. Even if it is only the defeated Generals who negotiate, someone will make an armistice with the Germans. . . .

My influence in the coming days may be very great if I am intended to exercise that influence. And I keep turning over in my mind how I can best fit myself for this. For my own self, what happens I do not mind much. I have lived my life and I can only pray that I can help the people in their struggle by using my energy and experience. Guidance may be given one for this purpose if it is intended that we shall be saved. My outlook on life altered very much from the moment that I had finished my command at the Staff College in 1926, when I was 46 years old. Everything seemed in front of me and I was full of personal ambition. That disappeared gradually under Milne and Massingberd for the ten years that ensued. I began to realize that I was no longer the man that was going forward rapidly to do things. Neither of these two men wanted me and I began to lose confidence in myself—or rather in my future. Gradually I realized that time was slipping away and I don't think I ever lost interest in what I was doing. But I began to feel an irritation that I was in no way responsible for the organization and training of the Army. Then suddenly I was faced with the war and its direction as C.I.G.S. I had no time to do anything but keep my head above water.

Now I am trying to piece together an Army in the most terrible crisis that has ever faced the British Empire. Please God I shall not be found wanting in my share of the responsibility.

I was looking through some memoirs of Sir George Arthur and found to my surprise Kitchener's remark in 1915 about the Statesmen:

"Did they remember, when they went headlong into a war like this, that they were without an army, and without any preparations to equip one?"

Cambon's remark about the Italians paints them the same:

"Nos bons amis, les Italiens, attendent avec impatience le moment pour voler au secours des vainqueurs."

June 17

Reynaud has gone, leaving Pétain as President of the Council and Weygand as Vice-President. There are Flandin, and Bonnet and company, and the Peace Party, so what Churchill feared has come to pass. The soldiers will make an Armistice soon, for I see that some of the Maginot Line has been given up and even the Rhine has been passed by the Germans. I am afraid that it is the end of France. What terms can she expect to receive? A Fascist State won't suit the revolutionary Frenchman for long. How will the Germans ensure such a state of affairs? It must be by an army of occupation. Our chief concern is what will happen to the French Fleet. If that comes into the hands of the Germans we shall have a difficult war to wage. The combined French and Italian Fleets will make things impossible for us in the Mediterranean. . . .

I have decided to start in with making all the Town Councils and Borough Councils to do work. It is stupid to have all their employees doing repair work on the roads, and cutting hedges and grass when we want pill-boxes made. I must decentralize, but getting out instructions alone takes time. And all the troops are moving into their positions from where they were assembled. So few people can be spared to make reconnaissances.

How soon will the Germans be able to start their attacks? They will be very stupid if they delay much longer.

. . . With all our units reforming, rearming and moving into their new areas, we are in a pretty good confusion. I calculate that it will be nearly towards the end of the week that we can say that we are in position. It was unavoidable with all these troops and materials coming back from the front. They were all put in place very hurriedly and the men of the B.E.F. were allowed to go on leave—in some cases 72 hours, which was a long time in the circumstances.

. . . There is no doubt that Winston has any amount of courage and experience. Thrown with his back to the wall, he may lose some of his lack of balance. He is quite undismayed by the state of affairs. . . .

The evening papers gave us the news that Pétain had said the French Army could do no more, and with a broken heart he had turned to make terms with the Germans. That must have been a terrible thing for an old Marshal of 84 to do. . . . The French Air Force seems to have disposed of itself by flying over to this country or to Africa to join us. What of the Fleet? I could get no information to-night whatever. It must not get into German hands. That would be a disaster. The next few days will tell us what is to happen.

June 19

A Defence meeting in the morning. Winston in good form and gingering people up. His energy is unabated. Several interesting bits of information. Brest was taken by a half-dozen motor-cycles and cars. Almost incredible. I don't know if the naval parties got away. I suppose that with so much of the population away mobilized there were no "guts" left in any of the towns and villages of the interior. . . .

June 20

I ran up to Cambridge in the evening. Passed through all the 52nd Division moving up. Nothing but Lowland Scots talk everywhere. It must have surprised the people of Cambridgeshire.

I dined in Corpus Christi with Will Spens. A real old Fifeshire accent. A most efficient Regional Commissioner. I had a long talk with him. He told me that there were many intellectuals who were already defeatists. I cannot imagine such a mentality. His own attitude was that he hoped the Government was not continuing out of pride or fear of telling the House that there was no chance. I told him that the war had not yet begun. That the history of Napoleon was being repeated and that we need have no fear it we had stout hearts. That I knew we could defeat the Germans given stout hearts. He agreed.

He then tackled me about the people "staying put" in case of an invasion. He had it on his conscience that we were arranging sabotage behind the lines if the Germans succeeded in landing. He wanted it stopped. A most upright attitude, I thought, but treating the Germans as if they were civilized beings. . . .

The whole of the day I made a reconnaissance from King's Lynn to Cromer, looking at the troops and their work. They are working, and guns and wire are being put up on all the likely points. Work will never end. It ought to have been begun months ago.

The great failure is to realize that all the nodal points inland must be fitted with blockhouses to cover big solid blocks. To restrict all movement in the country and so prevent enemy columns rushing about the country.

June 21

I slept the night at Hingham and then continued the reconnaissance [of] all the coast from Cromer to Southwold. An immense amount of work being done. An immense amount to be done still. Decentralization to all the lesser commanders. All civilian contractors should be put to the work at this critical moment. No frills are necessary. The bottle-neck is the allotment of the work by the military. They are so apt to make a fuss about an intricate reconnaissance, and then never get any work done.

June 22

Hitler arranged his armistice meeting in the same train as the French used in 1918. He actually sat in Foch's chair. I suppose that it was irresistible to him as a conqueror. Poor Pétain. What a finish to a Marshal's life at 84. So many people thought that he had been put in as a soldier to continue the fight, whereas he had been chosen to get the best terms he could. . . . Probably too much money spent upon the Maginot Line, which appealed to the Frenchman's imagination. We are now engaged in putting up minor Maginot lines along the coast, but I have impressed upon the Corps Commanders that they are only meant as delaying lines, and are meant to give the mobile columns a chance of coming up to the threatened points. What we lack now chiefly are anti-tank guns. I am wondering whether we shall get the 75s [from the U.S.A.] over in time to get them into position at all the nodal points in the country.

The tactical problem is such a difficult one with no idea where the enemy may come from, either from the sea or the air. A clever enemy may be able to join up the two efforts very quickly. We want so much time to get our preparations ready, and time is the one thing the Germans are not likely to give us. The complete blank wall of Intelligence is still in front of us, and we can get no information about the preparations being made the other side.

I have impressed upon the Government that they ought to be ready with offensive operations if we can see a reasonable chance of upsetting their efforts at invasion. To sit immobile here is the worst thing to do. . . . It is the weakness of waiting for an attack that preys upon people's minds. Waiting for an attack which may come in so many places. Even the stoutest heart begins to wonder whether he can meet all the eventualities he pictures to himself. I felt it myself as I went round the endless coastline of East Anglia yesterday. Still, we can meet these swine with stout hearts if we mean to defeat them. Right is on our side. . . .

We are still a week-ending Cabinet. This evening I have not been able to get on to half the people I wanted to get on to. I am sure that the Nazi machine works full time at week-ends. I have been held up over the getting of Town Councils and Borough Councils to work in with the military over necessary work. So many of them are already doing so, but the wretched central authority, the Home Office, does not seem to be able to get out the Instructions. We are still very unmilitary.

June 23

It has been raining all night. Much needed. The French have signed the Armistice. Hunziger told the Germans that France expected honourable terms. So ends France in under two months. A dreadful disaster for a great nation. Shall we be the same? The

Battle of Britain begins. No one can say how much of France the Germans will be able to use for an attack on us. . . .

Curious that Spens should ask me whether the Government was continuing the fight from motives of pride or fear of telling Parliament. Can a great nation give in on a threat? Unheard of. The struggle may well come to a point when both sides are exhausted, and it is the little extra courage which turns the scale. Personally, if I didn't think we could still go on successfully I should still fight. . . .

I think that we may say that whatever sized Army we had had in France in May 1940—after nine months of war—the result would have been the same. The French Army failed and involved out little Army in the ruin. We should have lost more equipment and that is all. We might have had our Supply in better order. We are suffering for that. We shall never get the time to recover that. . . .

June 24

Off at 3 p.m. Sunday and to Spalding. . . . Then on to Boston. . . . Then to Skegness, where I put up at the County Hotel. The place is a mass of amusement parks and now quite dead. The Navy have some 4,000 technical recruits with 1,000 rifles in one of Butlin's camps. I found an Admiral in charge. Very keen that I should inspect his men. The idea was to evacuate his school to somewhere in Wales, as they are now in the front line so to speak. We had a very quiet night and I moved off in the morning to Grimsby, where I found an R.E. school. Here again a lot of recruits without rifles. A good type of man, mostly volunteers.

I also found an Admiral Cowan, now serving as a Captain, with his brother Sir Walter Cowan, who had retired as a full Admiral, serving under his brother as a Commander. . . . Then to Lincoln, where Lord Liverpool had got together the heads of the L.D.V.s, all old Generals and Colonels. . . . Then Nottingham to see the Regional Commissioner, Lord Trent. A most capable man. He is the fourth Commissioner who . . . says that the Home Office will not decentralize. . . .

Back at 11 p.m. and to bed. I was lying asleep when my telephone-bell rang and I was told by Bevir, one of the Prime Minister's secretaries, that I might be wanted to speak in ten minutes or so. This about 1 a.m. . . .

June 25

Up to the meeting of the Chiefs of Staff and then to the Cabinet to explain about Home Defence. Dill told me that what I had been wanted for was to go out at 6 a.m. in a flying-boat to Casablanca to see Nogués. Eventually, they decided to send Gort with Duff-Cooper. They are trying to get all the French Empire to continue the struggle. I knew him [Nogués] so well that Dill thought I ought to go. The Cabinet would not risk my being away, for which I was thankful.

On this day, June 25, "General Ironside", in Mr. Churchill's words, "exposed his plans to the Chiefs of Staff. On the whole", and again the words are Mr. Churchill's, "they stood approved".

His plan of defence was as follows:

1. An extended crust of defence along the probable invasion beaches to beat off minor enterprises, to keep a watch for, and to report immediately, German invasion attempts, and to break up, delay, and canalize penetrations. These defence troops were to fight where they stood, to gain time for support by mobile reserves who would put in immediate counter-attacks.

2. Blocks manned by L.D.V.s at all defiles and nodal points, to stop or delay German armoured columns that had broken through. The other task of the L.D.V.s was to harry any penetration. To stop the movement of enemy tanks every type of tank obstacle was devised, concrete and other forms of road blocks were put up, and anti-tank ditches were dug. The L.D.V.s were armed with Molotoff cocktails and with other devices for attacking tanks.

3. Defence lines built to cover London and the industrial Midlands. These were:

(1) A G.H.Q. stop line extending in the south from Bristol to Maidstone, and in the east from Maidstone through Cambridge to the Wash and thence to Richmond in Yorkshire.

(2) Corps and Divisional stop lines between the G.H.Q. line and the coast.

4. A general reserve of three infantry divisions and an armoured division, centrally placed to deal with a major break-through.

5. Small mobile local reserves to deal with paratroop landings and minor break-throughs.

These dispositions ensured defence in depth and, as far as resources permitted, provided troops for counter-attacks.

At first the defence was necessarily mainly static, owing to lack of equipment and vehicles, and the untrained state of many formations. As more equipment and vehicles became available (much civilian transport being requisitioned), and as the troops became better trained, a more offensive form of defence became possible, and was duly instituted.

June 26

Pétain is now trying to stop Nogués in Morocco and Mittelhausser in Syria from continuing the war. The Fleet seems to be doubtful still. . . .

This position under the War Office is not satisfactory. They continually, in their efforts, skim the cream off the jug for Overseas operations, Northern Ireland and the Azores. I never know when things will not be taken away from me at any moment. I know that they are available in England if the show starts, but it is unsettling to have one's reserve taken away without any notice. If the remainder of the troops were of any standard of training it wouldn't matter, but they are not even half-armed and are certainly half-trained. My attempts to get something ready of offensive value have not been very successful. Always a lack of material. Every day is of use to us. . . . .

I had a goodish day with the Chief of the Air Staff. I have got more control over the bombers than I had and we ought to get them on [to their targets] more quickly. Newall was much better than usual. Then I saw Eden and Dill. I am being bombarded with letters from people saying that this and that place is not defended, and that the quality of the troops is bad here and there. I know that it is, and can do nothing to alter it. Our equipment is ludicrously deficient and the War Office knows it. Only about 30% of our complement of guns.

June 28

Down in the evening to Folkestone, where I met [General] Thorne and worked along the coast *via* Hythe to Rye. Work is going on apace, but we are woefully short on the ground. We cannot put all the men into the "crust" of defence on the beaches. We may be attacked at so many points and must have a reserve that can be moved about to meet both the sea landings and the air landings. I think there is no doubt that the Germans might effect a landing at any point and with little warning. Our defences are advancing, but terribly slowly in view of the imminence of the attack and the resources available to the Germans. Every portion of the coast at which I look seems weaker than the other and the troops less trained and more unhandy. . . . In the morning I continued along the coast to Brighton. Work is progressing well. Thorne is a very good Commander and full of the right kind of heart and energy.

They are beginning to worry at the War Office, and both I and Paget are being continually sent for to see people. Paget to see the P.M. and I to see the Secretary of State and the Chiefs of Staff. I also find that the paper which is being poured out by the War Office is terrific. It is hampering efficiency in every way. You cannot make war with a pen.

Everybody is getting nervous and is beginning to scent the invasion coming. Just what Hitler wants to make us believe. Feint attacks or attacks which may be turned into main attacks if they are at all successful. I had an example to-day of the 3rd Division being taken in War Office reserve, put back to me again, and sent back to War Office. Shilly-shallying and doubt. The politicians will not leave the soldiers alone.

June 29

I spent an unsatisfactory day with the Chiefs of Staff. They are not clear in their minds as to what they want as to our defence. At one time they say that we must defeat the enemy on the beaches when he lands, and that we must hold a sufficient reserve. That the teaching of the war is that we mustn't hold lines. The whole thing is very difficult and I have given them my views:

(i) The coastline is terrific in length and we may be attacked at any point of it, owing to the fact that the Germans may start from Norway, the Baltic, Holland, Belgium or France. They may even take Ireland first and so extend the possibility of landing still further to the west. The veil of secrecy in Germany is complete. Very few preparations had been made to prepare beaches and possible landing-points, and work is still very incomplete.

(ii) Air landings can take place anywhere in the United Kingdom or Ireland with even less warning than in the case of sea-borne landings. With the means at Germany's disposal, large forces—up to 20,000—can be transported by air.

(iii) The forces we have available in the United Kingdom are both untrained and armed insufficiently, especially in tanks and guns and anti-tank weapons.

And so we have decided to hold the coast as a "crust". Work is proceeding fast on anti-tank obstacles at beaches, wire and pill-boxes. The idea is to inflict all the losses we can, and to attack at once with our mobile forces at the beaches or at any point to which they have penetrated. For this we have what local reserves we have, and two [G.H.Q.] reserves each of a mobile division and an armoured division.

We are also creating a local static defence of armed riflemen using blocks and pill-boxes all over the country.

Every day gets our preparations better and our troops better

armed. If the Germans intend to attack—and everything seems to
point to the fact that they will—it is a race between their preparations and ours. They are much better prepared than we are, and
we are improvising all the time.

We have the Navy and the Air Force, neither of which can
guarantee us against a landing, though they can limit the alimenta-
tion of such landings as have taken place.

With luck they may not surprise us.

We are forced to disperse. They can concentrate on any point
or points they have chosen. All the main points are therefore in
the Germans' favour, so long as they can be assured of good
weather. . . .

June 30

A lovely day. Eastwood, commanding the 4th Division, came
over with me to the Isle of Wight. There we were met by the
Brigadier of the 12th Brigade, Beak.

As we went over we saw a big French battleship and six
destroyers lying outside Portsmouth. They all went inside the
harbour and later we saw a lot of French sailors ashore. After all,
we have got some of the French Fleet here safely.

Beak is the most extraordinary man. He has a V.C., a D.S.O.
and two M.C.s, all gained in the last war. He has just been pro-
moted, having commanded the South Lancs Regiment so far in
this war. He gives one a feeling of great energy and fire, and all
the officers and men know that they have a good man over them.
His clean-shaven face and sparkling eyes make him more like a
professional man than a soldier. He had only been a few days in
the Isle of Wight and already he had the place and its peculiarities
at his fingers' ends. Eastwood, the Divisional Commander, had
also been only a few days in command of his division.

Beak is just 49 and certainly doesn't look it.

The Isle of Wight is well insured, much more so than most other
places in England. I hope that we shall be able to reduce the
garrison when some more defences have been built.

We actually had lunch in J. B. Priestley's house. He had done
up an old manor and had some good pictures. The garden was

walled and must have been very pretty in spring. Now very much dried up.

Very few people in the island except the residents. Very little bathing and nothing but old people to be seen sitting about.

Coming back I picked up a lot of week-end traffic from Hindhead going back to London. All hurrying along and a lot of people parked on the side of the road. I have asked the civil people to send out a message telling people that it is against the law to do this. They make an obstruction. One could have seen how these people careering back home would have got in the way of troops if they had persisted in moving with them. . . .

Many of the commanders in the late B.E.F. are now suffering from the effects of what they went through and are often too anxious. They know what may come and are perhaps doubtful over the state of their troops both in training and discipline. Anyway, they are tried men and the best we can get now.

CHAPTER XXIII

Retirement

July 1

We seem to have passed through June and this looks like the decisive month now coming, if the Bosches have made up their minds to come for us. They cannot allow us to go on bombing them as we are doing without doing something to stop us. They should have finished with France during this month and re-organized their forces. They have no Press and no public opinion and no chance of expressing themselves in any way. So we never hear what effect our bombing has on either the people or the material. . . .

The weather still remains very fine, worse luck. We could do with storms.

July 2

It is extraordinary how we get circumstantial reports of 5th Column and yet we have never been able to get anything worth having. One is persuaded that it hardly exists.[1] And yet there is signalling going on all over the place and we cannot get any evidence. A German wife of an R.A.F. man, who has been in domestic service in the Admiral's house at Portsmouth, was run in for trying to get hold of blueprints. She got 10 years and the man 14 years.

[1] In fact, in spite of the reports and rumours, there was scarcely any 5th Column in this country.

I saw Winston in the morning at 10 Downing Street. He is in terrific form. Guns and ammunition coming in, and Beaverbrook has been able to push on the R.A.F. output to an extraordinary extent. There must have been something wrong somewhere for such energy to be expended now.

We are now into our new quarters at St. Paul's School. I think we shall be better here than at Kneller. Much nearer London and a good many minutes saved in the journeying back and forwards.

It may be interesting to compare the German plan for the invasion of Great Britain, Operation "Sea-Lion", with Ironside's measurement of the situation.

The Germans lost valuable time. In early June we were at our weakest and most disorganized, and a few well-trained divisions might have brought them victory. They let the whole month go by, hoping no doubt that the collapse of France would lead the British Government to treat. It was not until July that they began serious planning.

The German High Command at first proposed to embark their troops from ports stretching from Holland to Bayonne in the Bay of Biscay, and land them on a very broad front from Ramsgate in Kent to Lyme Bay on the border of

	FIRST PLAN	SECOND PLAN
First Wave	13 divisions with a large proportion of tanks and A.A. Artillery	9 divisions ditto
Second Wave	6 armoured and 3 motorized divisions	divisions— (4 armoured 2 motorized 2 infantry)
Third Wave	9 infantry divisions	6 infantry divisions
Fourth Wave	8 infantry divisions	To be allotted later
	THIRTY-NINE DIVISIONS	TWENTY-THREE DIVISIONS PLUS (?)

378

□□ Dorset and Devon, but the Navy protested that they could neither transport nor protect so large a force, and this first plan was scaled down. A first wave of thirteen divisions would start from ports between Ostend and Cherbourg, and land on a much narrower front from Folkestone to Brighton. Still later, it was decided to reduce the first wave from thirteen divisions to nine.

Two parachute divisions would also land on the Downs behind Dover and Brighton, and capture both places. In the second, i.e. reduced Plan, Brighton was abandoned in favour of Folkestone, with a single dropping-area north-west of that town.

The first German objective was to establish a bridgehead fifteen miles deep on the Dover–Brighton front. The second objective was a line running from the Thames Estuary via the North Downs to Portsmouth. While this was being consolidated, smaller forces would cut off London from the west and capture bridges over the Thames in preparation for an advance to the third objective, namely a line running from Watford to Swindon.

In addition, German forces in Norway and elsewhere would prepare to land between Edinburgh and Newcastle upon Tyne, between the Wash and Harwich, and from Wexford to Dungarvan in Eire. These would all be part of a deception plan, and no actual landings would take place.

The troops began training, there were massive preparations, and the Navy started to collect transport. But even on this reduced scale, the invasion would not be ready until mid-September, and no account seems to have been taken of the danger of equinoctial gales. All, moreover, depended on getting and keeping air superiority. Hitler laid down that the first task of the Luftwaffe was to destroy the British Air Force, operations to begin about August 5. In the event, air superiority was not achieved and the R.A.F. was not destroyed, partly because Goering was not whole-heartedly behind the plans. He hoped to reduce Britain by air-power alone, and he switched a part of his force on to other targets.

On the British side, the Army now consisted of twenty-divisions, of which less than half were even reasonably equipped, and only two were armoured. Most of this Force was concentrated in East Anglia, Kent and Sussex, with reserves both north and south of the Thames. What was called "the G.H.Q. Stop-Line", namely a line of natural and artificial anti-tank obstacles, defended by pill-boxes, and manned chiefly by the Home Guard or L.D.V.s, ran, as has been explained, from Bristol to Maidstone and then north through Cambridge to Yorkshire, thus enclosing in an inverted "L" the most vital areas of the United Kingdom, namely London and the industrial Midlands, and forming a barrier, though this was not of course realized at the time, against the second and third German objectives. Ironside's dispositions for the military defence of England, for the conception was mainly his, and the enemy plans for invasion, are illustrated on the accompanying map.

July 4

The main landings in this country will undoubtedly be carried out in Kent and East Anglia. All other operations, which may be landings in the Shetlands, Yorkshire, the South Coast, Devon and Cornwall, and Ireland, will be diversions to get us to move away our main reserves. We have only these two Corps [in reserve], each of a division and an armoured division, which are available and these must be kept for the north and south of the Thames. It all shows what a disadvantage we exist under in having to remain on the defensive against an enemy who has unlimited means at his disposal and unlimited material. We want a good many months before we can possibly be ready to put the troops we have called up into action. They are untrained and unequipped.

July 5

Everything seems to point to the Germans starting something from Norway and the Baltic against Iceland, the Shetlands or perhaps Scotland. I have only the troops necessary for the barest defence there and cannot send any of my reserve up to the north,

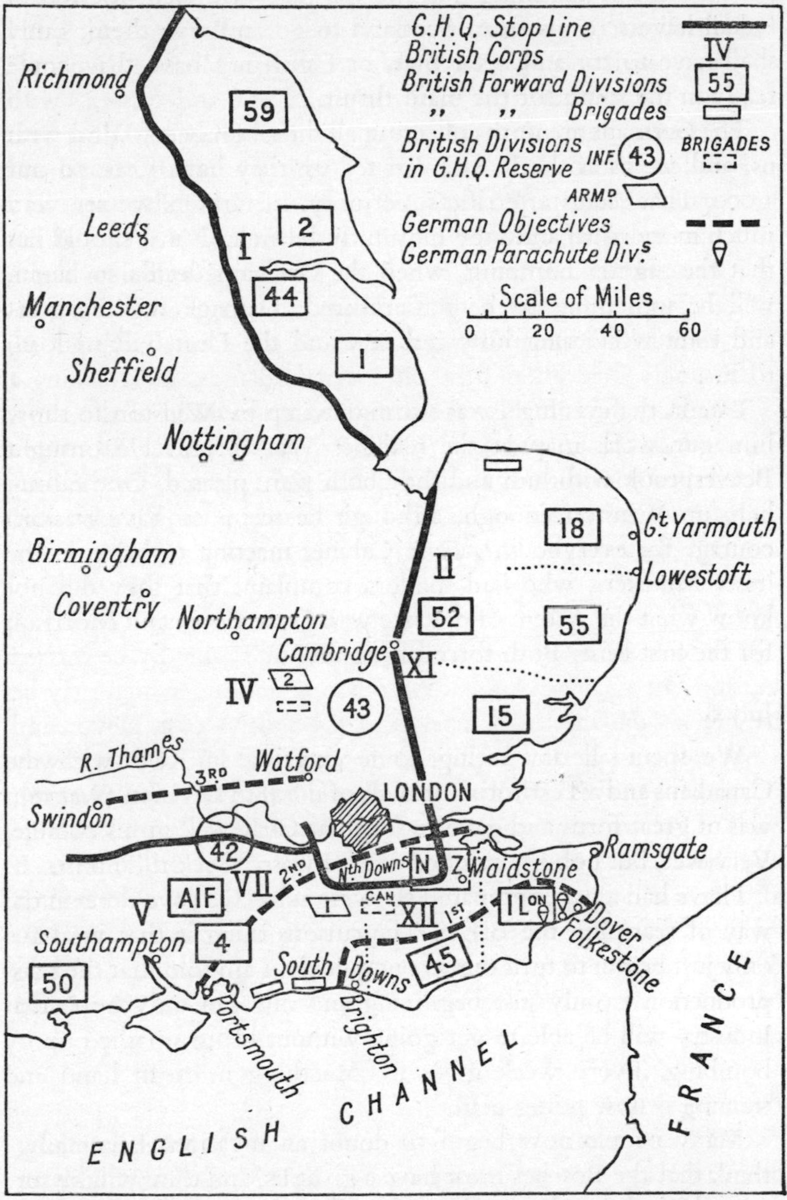

G.H.Q. Stop Line
British Corps
IV
British Forward Divisions
55
,, ,, Brigades
British Divisions in G.H.Q. Reserve
INF.
43
BRIGADES
ARMD
German Objectives
German Parachute Divs
Scale of Miles
0 20 40 60
Richmond
59
Leeds
2
I
44
Manchester
Sheffield
1
Nottingham
18
Gt Yarmouth
Lowestoft
Birmingham
II
Coventry
Northampton
52
55
Cambridge
XI
IV
2
43
15
R. Thames
3RD
Watford
LONDON
Swindon
42
Ramsgate
N
Z
Maidstone
2ND
Nth Downs
VII
AIF
V
1
CAN
XII
1ST
1 LON
Dover
Folkestone
Southampton
4
45
50
South Downs
Portsmouth
Brighton
ENGLISH CHANNEL
FRANCE

Ironside's dispositions and German "Sea Lion" Plan, July 1940.

tor that will be the thing that the Germans will want me to do. I shall have screams from Scotland to go and save them, but I shall have to try and resist that, or I shall not have the people ready in the south for the main thrust. . . .

The Germans are now collecting all their bombers to deal with us, and, as far as the R.A.F. can tell us, they have 5,000 to our 1,000. That seems a terrific superiority. In fighters we are very much more equal and they may turn the scale. But, I should say that the nightly bombing, when the Germans decide to begin, will be something to be remembered. Damage will be great and I am wondering how Industry and the Fleet will stick up to it. . . .

Late in the evening I was summoned up by Winston to show him our work map in the Cabinet War Room. He brought Beaverbrook with him and they both were pleased. One cannot help up Winston enough, although he seems to have enough courage for everybody. . . . A Cabinet meeting to bring in the lesser Ministers, who had made a complaint that they did not know what the system of defence was. I saw Bevin and Morrison for the first time. Both forceful people.

July 6

We spent all day seeing some exercises in Kent with the Canadians and a Territorial Brigade of the 48th Division. Winston was in great form and gave us lunch at Chartwell in his cottage. Very wet, but nobody minded at all. I wasn't back till 9 p.m. . . .

I have had a paper prepared showing what we have done in the way of rearming the B.E.F. The curious thing is that we have only just begun to turn things out quickly. I am told that the mass production is only just beginning and one can only hope that Industry will be able to get going without being smashed up by bombing. Every week gives us something more in hand and training is now going better.

Many people now begin to doubt an invasion. Personally I think that the Bosches must have a go at us, and they will be sure to make a determined effort when they do. I wish I knew how their food and material position was progressing. I cannot help being sure that there will be a famine in Europe this winter and that must affect their calculations.

July 8

Up to London in the morning to the Chiefs of Staff. We arranged that I should not try to fight the battle from London. I told the Chiefs of Staff that I ought not to be in the position of being called continually to London to see various people like the Prime Minister. I should have to have an armoured car anyway and one didn't want even with that to be continually on tap. Odd people, like Lord Hankey, are continually sending for Paget to interview him about something or other. We should not be at the beck and call of odd people. . . .

It is our business to evolve the best kind of Army for Home Defence, with a proportion ready to serve abroad offensively. Our fortifications are getting better every day. Our L.D.V. are being steadily armed and we could soon reduce the number of mobile troops that are being used for a static rôle. It is all a matter of time. We are working against time.

July 9

My morning that I thought likely [for invasion] has come and gone without incident. Three Dutch Naval officers came over from Holland in a small boat. They all said that the Germans were all talking about the 11th as "Der Tag". The Dutch are treating the Germans as if they didn't exist. If any Germans come into a hotel or bar all the Dutchmen go out. This annoys the Germans very much. There can be no doubt that vast preparations in the way of air and sea invasion are being made. . . .

The Prime Minister has sent down an order, or what is practically an order, to withdraw two divisions from the beach-line. I have sent in to say that I can withdraw one in a few days. He has his son-in-law, now Captain Sandys, on his staff and he uses him as a go-between with my staff. It is difficult to tackle Winston when he is in one of his go-getter humours. I have so many factors to take into account:

(i) The state of the beach defences.

(ii) The state of the training of the troops in reserve.

(iii) The state of the mobility of these troops.

(iv) The availability of some troops for beach defences.

A vicious circle. To use troops in training for beach defence stops their training. This prejudices the future.

July 11

Damp warm morning. Another day gone without the predicted invasion. All the more for our work.

I find a great many fingers in the Home Defence pie. I allow them to work away so long as they do not overstep the mark. It is natural that things should be scrutinized closely as everybody is in this show. . . .

The Norwegian ports are full of Germans, who are now being sent into Sweden quite openly, and there is no doubt that an expedition of from two to three divisions is in a high state of readiness there. Other indications are nothing like so strong in Holland, Belgium and France.[1]

July 12

Dinner at Lady Maureen Stanley's. She confided to me that there was a "whispering campaign" going on about me. I told her that I was quite prepared to disappear into my garden if people thought it necessary. She implored me to be careful in what I said. I told her that I never went out anywhere and never discussed military matters outside my own staff.

July 13

It is curious how one goes to bed wondering whether there will be an attack early the next morning. As we have done all we can in the way of preparation, it doesn't worry me much. I merely give thanks that we have another day of preparation and issue of defence material.

The attack upon us by air is intensifying. Chiefly against aerodromes, ports, shipping and aircraft factories. But so far the attack

[1] The activities in Norway were a part of the Germans' deception plan. The actual invasion force was a well-kept secret.

has been badly directed and not carried out in great strength. The R.A.F. say that that is what happened before the German attack in France. Desultory bombing and then one morning a very heavy attack on everything. It may be coming again. The seemingly desultory bombing may be a method of testing our defences. Certainly the Germans have never been up against such a good fighter defence, such A.A. fire, and such a warning system. I am inclined to think that Germany will try to wear down our air defence before she tries any invasion. It seems the natural thing to do. . . .

I find a general idea that the Germans will not now attack us. A false hope, I am afraid. They daren't not do something. They will begin with some three or four days' intensive bombing, and then air landings with parachutists, followed by sea landings according to the weather. All carried out in very different places so as to upset us and get our troops rushing about the country. If our men will attack *à fond*, all is well. But they are so dreadfully untrained that we cannot depend upon them to go in successfully.

July 14

A long day. We were off at 8 a.m. and motored to Chesham, where we found [General] Nosworthy in Lord Chesham's house. A beautiful place overlooking a trout stream. Nosworthy has his Corps in fine order and is an efficient leader, full of enthusiasm and confidence. Then on to the 2nd Armoured Division, commanded by a Tank Corps officer called Tilly. This has now been newly re-armed and was in good condition. I found Latham commanding the Support Group, which included two Royal Horse Artillery Batteries—my old troop "I" battery one of them—armed with brand-new 25 pdrs. The two Yeomanry Regiments are now commanded by Regular Cavalry officers and have a high state of efficiency. I felt much more happy after seeing such a good show.

Then to Coventry, where I found much had been done to protect the city and to make it into a tank-proof island. A most efficient A.A. colonel called Sakry. Then lunch in Birmingham, where I saw the L.D.V. leaders and the Regional Commissioner, Lord Dudley. And finally the Lord Mayor.

To sleep at Kenilworth. Here I found a tank unit that had come in from the west. Very short of material, but organized in a useful mobile column for tank-hunting or parachutist catching. The men were all working in their black working suits and were billeted all over the town. Very workmanlike men and very smart.

July 16

The morning at Corsham, where I was glad to see an immense amount of defence work had been done since I was last there. Lunch at Wilton with [Alan] Brooke, the Corps Commander, and then the Australians in the afternoon. They are very raw and untrained, but are beginning to get in trim. Things will go quickly when they have their equipment. They mean to fight if called upon to do so. As usual, discipline a little lax. Home about 7 p.m.

Three days' hard work at inspecting. Things are much better and every day makes a difference. . . . I noticed no "defeatism" at all. What there is, is now amongst certain intellectuals.

July 17

We have reached another morning without any active operations by the Bosches. It does not seem that he can go on allowing us to bomb him so badly without much return from him. There are tentative statements in the papers about a "peace ultimatum" but nothing very definite. Winston's speech in the House the other day[1] ought to have dissipated any hopes of our people having become intimidated like the French. Winston minced no words. I wonder if the Bosches think that their present bombardment is better than it is. Will they increase it in violence as they find we continue firm? I am sure that any honest effort at peace will find a following here in England, but we all know that we cannot trust the Bosches at all. . . . But the show is warming up one way or another. We have had 17 days in July which I would never have expected to get.

[1] July 14, world broadcast, in the course of which the Prime Minister said . . . "We would rather see London laid in ruins and ashes than that it should be tamely and abjectly enslaved."

July 18

I had lunch with Lord Marley, lately a Marine called Aman. He wants me to talk to some of the Labour Party and to explain to them what is going on. I shall have to ask to be allowed to do this. All M.P.s are so keen to do something that they ought to know what is going on. The soldiers are blamed for crimes that are committed by Government, and I am personally blamed for a great deal that is beyond my control. And yet one is tied absolutely by the veto put upon talking by soldiers.

July 19

We must begin to get a Home Army organized at once. We cannot use all the Field Army for operations of pure defence in England.

I have started with the principle that we want the following forces:

   (i) A coast defence and its immediate reserves.
   (ii) Striking columns.
   (iii) [Anti-] parachute columns.

We still have an immense amount of work to do to get the coast defences in order, but we are well on the way towards it. When that is finished we can arrange the local reserves. . . .

I was summoned to see the Secretary of State at 2.45 p.m. and told that I was to be replaced by Alan Brooke as C.-in-C. Home Forces. Eden told me that the Cabinet wished to have someone with late experience of the war. I told Eden that he needn't worry and that I was quite prepared to be released. I had done my best. In order that the matter should be placed on a good footing, I was to be made a Field-Marshal.

And so my military career comes to an end in the middle of a great war. I have had 41 years and one month's service, and have reached the very top. I can't complain. Cabinets have to make decisions in times of stress. I don't suppose that Winston liked doing it, for he is always loyal to his friends.

EPILOGUE

An Extract from Ironside's Diary

August 18, 1940

I HAVE BEEN PONDERING over this war in the last few weeks, and it astonishes me more and more that Chamberlain had the courage to declare war on Germany. He certainly didn't want to do so. Had he any clear idea of the military strength of the Germans? I am sure that he hadn't. He didn't think that the British Empire could be assailed, and he had a firm belief in the French Army. He would not have acknowledged that he was banking on the French Army to give us time to get ready. But that was what he was doing. He also had no idea of the length of time that it took to make all the material required for a modern army. He did not know that you had to train after you had the equipment. He was completely unmilitary. He didn't realize that the military leaders had had no experience in leading large armies. Company commanders had been dealing with 20 and 30 men in a company instead of 250, and all the technical troops were short. I am sure that the Cabinet did not ask the War Office if they thought they were ready for war. I didn't take over C.I.G.S. until the day war was declared. I am sure that the Cabinet did not ask any soldier's advice. Mine certainly never was asked. None of them reckoned that the French Army was largely served by horsed transport and that their Air Force was very inferior in both bombers and fighters. We could not replace this deficiency in the Air Force.

Did Chamberlain realize that we had allowed the Empire to get dangerously weak? I am sure that he didn't. Did he realize that we were in for a political struggle in which we were staking the Empire? I am sure that he didn't. He was a typical British business-man and couldn't realize that the Empire was in danger. He didn't realize that Hitler was out to down us. He couldn't believe it. His courage was certainly there, but I wonder if he realized all the mistakes that he and his party had made in the years since it became certain that Germany was preparing for war?

We have the two contending ideas: Naziism and Democracy. Can they live together? Perhaps he thought that because Bol-shevism had failed to spread, Naziism would fail also.

We did not study Hitler and his methods. We hoped that he was ordinary. And yet we had his words:

"If I were going to attack an opponent I should act quite differ-ently from Mussolini: I should negotiate for months beforehand and make lengthy preparations, but—as I have always done throughout my life—I should suddenly, like a flash of lightning in the night, hurl myself upon the enemy."

. . . I have no reason to believe that we are being depressed by this air attack. We seem to be glorying in the exploits of the R.A.F. We are all convinced that we shall win air superiority one of these days. We may be expecting help from our blockade, but the idea of merely waiting till the blockade does its work—which certainly prevailed at the beginning of the war—has now definitely gone.

France was defeated by terror and not by the slaughter of numbers of her soldiers. The mobile columns, having broken through, simply eat out the guts of the country, and this they did in France. They rushed into the towns shooting at everybody, shooting refugees, women and children indiscriminately. Rouen and Brest, great cities, were captured by a few armoured cars. We have avoided this by arming and training the L.D.V.s. The population cannot be terrorized as the French were. I shan't forget Billotte at Lens saying to me, "Nous crevons derrière des ob-stacles." Hitler created a terror and a belief in his infallibility. He won his victory without suffering many casualties in his own Army. How did Hitler do this? Mainly through discipline and also by preparation of armed forces fit to fight in co-operation.

He did this at express speed during long years, and we would not believe that he was serious. And we did not understand that it took a long time to prepare all the material necessary for armed forces. We allowed Hitler a desperately long start both in material and in training. How good is this discipline? How long will it last under Nazi conditions? This can only be answered if we can answer the question as to whether our Government can produce the stead-fast purpose necessary to keep up the civil morale. In Winston Churchill we have a man capable of keeping up the courage of the people. Thank God for that. I know no one else amongst our political leaders who can do it. We can willingly sink ourselves in the good of all. The Germans are being forced to sink themselves in the cause of Naziism, the creed of Hitler. There can be no doubt which will win in the end. I think that we must acknowledge that during the first few months of the war we had not the proper leadership. Not through lack of courage, but through lack of understanding.

APPENDICES

I

A PAPER ADDRESSED BY IRONSIDE TO THE C.I.G.S.

*Notes on Higher Organization to ensure Better
Preparation of the Army for War*[1]

Dec. 4, 1937

I HAVE been concerned for many years, and more particularly since taking over the Eastern Command, with the absence of a tactical doctrine, lack of uniformity of training, and uncertainty as to organization in the Army at home. I consider these evils are chiefly due to the present position of the C.I.G.S.

Under existing arrangements the C.I.G.S. is charged with advice to the Secretary of State and the Government on the military policy for the Defence of the Empire; with plans for war and peace (D.M.O. and I.); with the organization and equipment of the Army to carry out that policy (D.S.D.); and with the direction of Training of the Army (D.M.T.).

Besides the above the C.I.G.S. has other duties such as President of the Selection Board, all of which take up a considerable amount of time. Not only is the above too heavy a burden for one man, but also the duties require differing qualities which are seldom found in one man. Some require the grasp of policy for a mass of detail and the presentation of that policy lucidly to the Government, and its discussion with the C.I.D. and elsewhere. Others require experience in Command, and a day-to-day study of tactical methods, and the power of impressing the doctrine so developed on the Army as a whole. In other words, the C.I.G.S. is expected to be a perfect Staff Officer and a perfect Commander,

[1] See page 39.

without having the time to be either properly. The preparation and implementation of certain material may be delegated by him to Directors, but in case of matters concerning the fighting troops, both Regular and T.A., more especially in training, the actual direction being in the hands of Commanders-in-Chief, such complete delegation is not possible.

I feel very strongly that under the present system there has been, and is, a lack of clear policy and of single-minded direction in training, with the consequence that the Army is drifting uncertainly, and cannot be expected to answer uniformly to the helm. Further, this lack of uniformity in training has militated against prompt decisions as to organizations required or equipment needed. At present each Commander-in-Chief is training and experimenting largely on his own ideas, and I consider that unless they are given an official lead, not even co-operation between them will produce the necessary homogeneity.

I therefore consider that a separate officer is required to be responsible for the preparation of the Army for war. I suggest he might be called Inspector-General, and that normally he should be the Commander-in-Chief designate for the Field Troops. He would be the best placed to understand its handling, and the relative capabilities of its various parts and commanders. I would recommend that this officer should not be a member of the Army Council or of the War Office staff, to ensure his not being immersed in administrative detail. His duty would be to forge the instrument decided on by the Army Council, and to advise the latter on changes which his experience deems necessary. He should, of course, have access to, and be liable to be called upon for advice by, members of the Council.

It is not the place in this preliminary paper to discuss in detail the division of duties between the C.I.G.S. and this Inspector-General, or to suggest in detail the staff which the I.G. should require. But I submit they should be generally upon the following lines:

Duties of the C.I.G.S.

(*a*) Advice to the Secretary of State and the Government on

Imperial Military Policy, and the apportionment of the military resources to the various parts of the Empire.

(*b*) War Plans and Intelligence.

(*c*) Implementation of Organization and Equipment.

Duties of I.G.

(*a*) All Military Training including Schools, Colleges and promotion examinations.

(*b*) Tactical doctrine.

(*c*) Advice on Organization and Equipment.

I suggest that the I.G. might be Chairman of the Selection Board and the Staff Selection Board, as he is in daily personal touch with officers of all ranks. In order to carry out his orders for preparing the Army for war, it is essential that he be instructed through the C.I.G.S. as to the Government's policy on the purposes for which the Army is required.

The C.I.G.S. would still require the assistance of D.M.O. and I. and D.S.D., though it is possible with his reduced responsibilities the D.S.D. could also act as D.C.I.C.S.

I do not consider it would be advisable for the I.G. to be charged also with the Command and Administration of a Command, certainly not one of such size and complexity as the Eastern Command. Assuming that he is thus independent, I consider he would require two Chief Assistants to carry out the duties of D.M.T. and the other duties suggested for him. For purposes of discussion we might call them Deputy Inspector-General and D.M.T.

If the I.G. is to be considered C.-in-C. designate in war, his headquarters should form the nucleus of G.H.Q. in war. While D.M.T. would require to stay at his post on mobilization, the D.I.G. could be either the C.G.S. or B.C.G.S. designate.

"In my mind", wrote Ironside some years later, "there was no doubt that the Army of 1914 had been given a Tactical Doctrine which was clearly understood. As we stood at the end of 1937 we had no such Doctrine. We had no plan even for the assembling of an army to go to France in case of war with Germany.

"The maddest thing of all was that the R.A.F. had carved out for itself a special character. They made no effort to join in any war doctrine, much less a doctrine in tactics with either Army or Navy.

"*I thought it a most dangerous situation.*"

2

IRONSIDE'S LETTER TO GORT
September 28, 1939[1]

I AM not absolutely happy over the question of the occupation of the Scheldt in case of necessity. Gamelin understands that it is impossible for the British Army to find itself on the Scheldt, with its back to the sea and only 35 miles from it in the original position from GHENT to AUDENARDE. He further writes:

"One must, however, have in mind that the Scheldt has an incontestable value as an obstacle in its lower reaches.

"This river allows us to give depth forward to our frontier defence, a depth which we cannot gain towards our rear, owing to the proximity of the urban mass of LILLE, ROUBAIX, TOUR-COING. But, in any case, it is understood that the decision will not be taken except in conjunction with the situation at the moment, with the time at our disposal and with the conditions under which the Belgian Army withdraws. . . .

"If events permit us to advance to the Scheldt the British left will not extend past the COURTRAI Canal at BOSSUYT."

This means that your left will be thrown forward considerably in advance of your frontier defence that you will be asked to occupy before Belgium comes into the war.

I think you should get quite clear from Georges:

(i) What French troops are to continue the defence of the

[1] See page 113.

Scheldt towards AUDENARDE–GHENT–DUTCH Frontier? Where are they in the stage before Belgium comes in?

(ii) Will your command cease at your left at BOSSUYT or will you have any French troops under your command on your left?

(iii) Has any project been studied for the defence of the BOSSUYT–COURTRAI Canal by French troops if by any chance they cannot swing round right on to the Scheldt? Either because time has been miscalculated or air action prevents their moving?

(iv) If you move forward to the Scheldt, where will your right rest? Will it be as before at MAULDE?

If this project of moving up on to the Scheldt from BOSSUYT to GHENT and the DUTCH Frontier seems to you a firm project and that it is not a pious hope, you should have this in mind in making your front position on the Franco–Belgian frontier and any position behind it. These positions then become rear positions to the front line on the Scheldt.

We cannot get the Belgians to agree to any conversations or reconnaissances and so your projects for occupying the Scheldt must remain paper ones. Can we help you in any kind of maps or reports from the W.O. as regards this country along the Scheldt?

You may be able to get them better from the French together with the nature of the old fortifications at TOURNAI.

3
NOTES OF C.I.G.S.'S VISIT TO B.E.F.
November 29, to December 2, 1939

Defences in Area occupied by B.E.F.[1]

1. *Situation affecting Defence Measures*

(*a*) 1 Corps consisting of 1 and 2 Divisions was hurried into the line on the 4th October 1939. 2 Corps of 3 and 4 Divisions did not come up till ten days later.

[1] See page 167.

Corps took over the existing defence works in the area from the French. These works were entirely linear and consisted of:

(i) An A.Tk.Ditch along the front more or less continuous.
(ii) A single line of concrete block-houses enfilading the A.Tk. obstacle.
(iii) A partially constructed wire obstacle along the front. The development of a position in depth to strengthen this front line of defence was put in hand at once.

(*b*) According to General Gamelin's appreciation a German attack might have been expected any time up to the 15th November. The divisions were therefore disposed tactically to meet such an attack, and not with a view to work on defences.

The most probable lines of attack were carefully studied and the defences in those areas given priority.

These sectors are:

(i) Astride road TOURNAI–DOUAI in the direction of ORCHIES.
(ii) Road TOURNAI–LILLE turning South towards ELSQUIN into good tank country.
(iii) Front TURCOING–HALLUIN where there is important high ground and no natural tank obstacle.

(*c*) *I think it may be taken that the tension relaxed about the end of October. Up to then the troops were employed upon making what strong points they could and in getting themselves under cover close to the line so that they could come into action at once. They were, in fact, on short notice for attack. The number of organized working days that the B.E.F. has had under no tension of attack can be taken as thirty.*

(*d*) An advance to the line of the SCHELDT and, later, also to the Dyle had to be taken into consideration and stores earmarked and loaded for the defences of these two lines when reached. Orders for material were placed from the 8th October. Orders were given that all new work was to be carefully concealed. This, apparently, has been so successful that much of the work has escaped notice by visitors. It should be remembered that such defensive positions now no longer consist of continuous lines of trenches with communication trenches from rear to front. But of lines of A.Tk obstacles with strong points commanding them and small works in between.

2. *Labour Available*

Troops available for work on defences:

(*a*) From the 4th October 1 and 2 Divisions and 1 Corps Tps. From the 18th October 3 and 4 Divisions and 2 Corps Tps. 1, 2 and 3 Divisions each on a 12,000 yard front with 9 Bns., smaller in number than the last war ($\frac{3}{4}$ of a Bn. per 1,000 yds).

In 1914 to 1918 a 6,000 to 7,000 yard front was considered wide with 12 Bn. Divisions and 200 more men in a Bn. (2 Bns. per 1,000 yds). These include 14 R.E. Field Companies.

(*b*) 4th Division in G.H.Q. reserve has been working on 2 rear positions right across the B.E.F. front.

(*c*) 5th Division will be available for work early in December.

(*d*) "X" Force (Brig. Minnis) 12 Engineer Companies fully assembled by the 25th October and 2 Labour Groups by the 14th November after collecting machinery and stores, are now just beginning concrete work at full blast. Its transport Company is now arriving.

(*e*) Colonel Bertschi (Commander of the Defence Sector of Lille) has 2 companies of concrete workers and 5 labour companies at work in the B.E.F. sector.

3. *Pill-boxes planned and constructed*

(*a*) Standard designs have been prepared for concreting blockhouses. By this means twice as many of these blockhouses will be constructed. Our weapons are different from the French, so we have to design pill-boxes to take both our and the French weapons, for we may be relieved at any moment by French troops.

(*b*) According to French calculations we require some six pillboxes per kilometre of front in the front positions alone. We have thirty-six kilometres of active front, ten kilometres of house front and twenty kilometres of river line. For this we require roughly:

Two hundred and sixteen pill-boxes in the active front, sixty in the river front.

For this work we should have sufficient men and material, now present. No calculation can be made for the rear areas, but it should at least be equal to this. For this rear area we require more men and more machines for mixing and filling. These we are now collecting and sending over.

(*c*) Both Corps have completed the strengthening of houses as strong-points up to the number of thirty-five. Some of these have been commenced as pill-boxes inside the house and others have the material close at hand.

(*d*) I Corps have now got *fifty-one* concrete pill-boxes completed on their front and twenty-six under construction. The sites for one hundred and thirty-three pill-boxes have been selected.

A large number of the sites have been cleared and material is being collected.

Two hundred tons of cement is being handled each day on the 1st Division front. No figures available for the 2nd Division.

(*e*) II Corps (which may be taken to be fourteen days behind I Corps in work owing to taking over later) have *fifty-three* concrete pill-boxes completed on their front and have *seven* under construction.

The sites for *one hundred and five* pill-boxes have been selected. A large number of sites have been cleared and material is being collected.

4. *Other Work*

(*a*) Preparations for demolition on the rear position. This was not done by the French, and has been done by us since our arrival.

(*b*) Preparations for inundations on our right flank and in our centre.

(*c*) Layout for a complete buried-cable system by mechanical diggers. These can do half a mile a day. There are four diggers at work and four more are coming out.

(*d*) Trenches built for the period in which the attack was expected. These often fill up with water, but this water will be pumped out when the trenches are needed for use. All trenches cannot be continually pumped dry now. Pumps are available on the spot.

(*e*) Artillery positions. Hundreds of tons of material have been used.

(*f*) A large amount of labour has been needed on roads—two hundred and forty tons of metal per division each day.

(*g*) An increasing amount of work will be needed on aerodromes.

(*h*) Putting up barbed-wire obstacles. Only a limited amount (three hundred tons) of wire has been released because a reserve must be kept in view of an advance to the SCHELDT or DYLE. G.H.Q. has asked for eight thousand tons of wire in twelve months. Plans for a complete system of wiring are ready and could be carried out in twenty-four to forty-eight hours when the order was given. Wiring is easy and quick to do and is not a limiting factor in strong defences.

(*i*) Revetting and digging. It is only just possible to keep pace with essential revetting behind the digging machines.

(*j*) Anti-tank obstacles. 1,350 yards completed last week by about eighteen mechanical diggers.

4

COPY OF C.I.G.S.'S TELEGRAM TO S. OF S.
Sent from France on November 30, 1939[1]

THE position of the equipment available for ten divisions is in my opinion most depressing, but in view of the insistence of the French and of the necessity for taking a greater share in the land defence in France it seems to me essential that we have a force of

[1] See page 169.

ten divisions in France by the end of February equipped to the best of our ability. But the Cabinet should realize that the German Army if it attacks will do so fully equipped with modern weapons. And in view of their well-known tactics the shortage of anti-tank and light anti-aircraft weapons is very serious. These must be made up as soon as possible. A minimum of six more anti-tank Regiments (making a total of ten) each comprising twenty-four 2-pr. and twelve 18-prs. older pattern with platforms and tracer ammunition should in my opinion be sent out with the new Divisions.

As regards light A.A. guns, in view of the German tactics in Poland I regard a scale of forty per cent., including reserves, as most dangerous and the allocation of these guns to B.E.F. should be given first priority. Cannot the R.A.F. be forced to disgorge some Hispano guns in our extremity? They could be put in a simple mounting. The 3.7-inch A.A. guns should be increased by March to fifty per cent. of establishment, i.e. to a hundred and twenty.

The S.A.A. situation given in para 8 is not definite, but ammunition is the life blood of all our rifles and automatics and any shortage, which never occurred in the last war, puts an end to all fighting.

As regards tanks, no offensive or counter-offensive operation is possible with a shortage of Infantry tanks of sixty per cent. (not counting any reserves) and the Cabinet should realize this.

The medium and heavy artillery ammunition is deplorable, making offensive operations impossible.

The French should be made to give a firm promise for the delivery of the 25-mm. anti-tank gun up to the quota of twenty-seven per division on their arrival in France, making sure that they include tracer ammunition, which they did not in the past.

The Cabinet must clearly understand that divisions armed on such a reduced scale have not the same fighting value even in defence as those which are fully equipped. Moreover, a force not properly found in arms, ammunition and transport cannot take part in offensive action.

5

LIST OF PERSONALITIES REFERRED TO IN THE TEXT
many of whom may not be familiar to readers

ALEXANDER, Rt. Hon. Albert Victor, (later Viscount Alexander of Hillsborough). 1885-. First Lord of the Admiralty 1940-45, 1945-46. Leader of Labour Peers in House of Lords 1955 onwards.

AMERY, Rt. Hon. Leopold Stennett, M.P. 1873-1955. Secretary of State for India and Burma 1940-55.

BEAK, Major-General Daniel Marcus William, V.C. 1891-. Commanded 1st Battalion, South Lancs Regt. 1939-40. G.O.C. Malta 1942.

BERNEY-FICKLIN, Major-General (as he became) Horatio Pettus Mackintosh. 1892-. Commander 15th Infantry Brigade.

BEVIN, Rt. Hon. Ernest. 1881-1951. Chairman T.U.C. 1937. Minister of Labour and National Service 1940-45.

BROWN, Engineer Vice-Admiral Sir Harold Arthur. 1878-. Director-General Munitions Production, Army Council, War Office 1936-39. Director-General of Munitions Productions, Ministry of Supply 1939-41.

BROWNRIGG, Lieutenant-General Sir W. Douglass. 1886-1946. Served Gallipoli and Mesopotamia. Commander 51st (Highland) Division T.A. Military Secretary 1938-39. Director-General, Territorial Army 1939. Adjutant-General to B.E.F. 1939-40.

BURGIN, Rt. Hon. Leslie. 1887-1945. Minister of Transport 1937-39. Ministry of Supply 1939-40.

CARTON DE WIART, Lieutenant-General Sir Adrian, V.C. 1880-. Served South Africa; East Africa; First World War. Retired 1924. Served Second World War. British Military Mission with Polish Army. Commanded Central Norwegian Expeditionary Force 1940, etc.

CHATFIELD, Admiral of the Fleet Lord Alfred Ernle Montacute. 1873-. First Sea Lord and Chief of Naval Staff 1933-38. Minister for Co-ordination of Defence 1939-40.

CORBIN, André Charles. 1881-. French Ambassador to London 1933-40.

CORK AND ORRERY, William Henry Dudley Boyle, Earl of. 1873-. Admiral of the Fleet 1938.

COWAN, Admiral Sir Walter Henry. 1871-1956. Retired 1931. Served with Commandos 1939-45.

DALADIER, Edouard. 1884-. Prime Minister in French Government, and Minister of National Defence 1938-40. Minister of War and of Foreign Affairs March-June 1940.

DE GAULLE, Général. 1890-. Commanded French armoured division, 1940, which made successful counter-attack on Germans in the Argonne, May 1940.

DEVERELL, Field-Marshal Sir Cyril John. 1874-1947. C.I.G.S. 1936-37. Served in India and First World War, commanding 3rd Division 1916-19.

DILL, Field-Marshal Sir John Greer. 1881-1944. Served South Africa; First World War. D.M.O. & I. 1934-36. G.O.C. in C. Aldershot Command 1937-39. Commander 1st Army corps B.E.F. 1939-40. V.C.I.G.S. 1940. C.I.G.S. 1940-41. Head of British Joint Staff Mission, Washington 1941-44.

DOWDING, Air Chief Marshal Hugh Caswall Tremenheere, 1st Baron. 1882-. Air Officer Commanding in Chief, Fighter Command 1936-40.

DUDLEY, William Humble Eric Ward, Earl of. 1894-. Regional Commissioner for Civil Defence, Midland Region.

EASTWOOD, Lieutenant-General Sir T. Ralph. 1890-1959. Commandant Royal Military College 1938-39. Commander 4th Division 1940. Director-General Home Guard 1940-41. Governor and Commander-in-Chief, Gibraltar 1944-47.

EVANS, Major-General Roger. 1886-. Commander 1st Armoured Division 1938-40.

FISHER, Colonel (later Major-General) Donald Rutherford Dacre. 1890-. General Staff, War Office 1939. Director General Army Regiments 1942-46.

FORBES, Admiral of the Fleet Sir Charles Morton. 1880-1960. Commander-in-Chief Home Fleet 1938-40.

FORBES-ADAM, General Sir Ronald. 1885-. Served First World War. D.D.M.O. 1936. C.R.A. 1st Division 1936-37. Commandant Staff College, Camberley 1937. D.C.I.G.S. 1938-39. Commanded Third Army Corps 1939-40. G.O.C. in C. Northern Command 1940-41. Adjutant-General to the War Office 1941-46.

FORTINGTON, Harold Augustus. 1890-1944. Director-General, Progress and Statistics, War Office 1939-40.

GAMELIN, Général Maurice. 1872-1958. Chief of Operations Department G.Q.G. 1914-15. Chief of Staff to General Joffre 1916. C.-in-C. French Forces in the Middle East 1925-28. C.-in-C. French Land Forces, and Supreme Commander of Allied Armies in France 1939-40.

GAMMELL, Lieutenant-General Sir James Andrew Harcourt. 1892-. Commanded 4th Infantry Brigade 1938-40. Later Chief of Staff to Supreme Allied Commander, Mediterranean Theatre 1944.

GEDDES, Rt. Hon. Auckland Campbell, 1st Baron. 1879-1954. Regional Commissioner for S.E. and N.W. Regions 1939-42.

GEORGES, Général, C.-in-C. North-East sector of France, from Switzerland to the sea. Was wounded when escorting the King of Yugoslavia who was assassinated at Marseilles in 1934.

GORDON-FINLAYSON, General Sir Robert. 1881-1956. Commander 3rd Division 1934-36. C.-in-C. British troops in Egypt 1938-39. Adjutant-General, War Office 1939-40. C.-in-C. Western Command 1940-41.

GREENWOOD, Rt. Hon. Arthur. 1880-1954. Deputy Leader of Labour Party 1935. Member of War Cabinet, Minister without Portfolio 1940-42.

GRIGG, Rt. Hon. Sir Percy James. 1890-. Permanent Under-Secretary of State for War 1939-42. Secretary of State for War 1942-45.

GUBBINS, Major-General Sir Colin McVean. 1896-. Commander Special Force, Norway 1940.

HALIFAX, Edward Frederick Lindley Wood, 1st Earl of. 1881-1959. Secretary of State for Foreign Affairs 1938-40. British Ambassador at Washington 1940-46.

HANKEY, Maurice Pascal Alers, 1st Baron. 1877-. Secretary of Committee for Imperial Defence 1912-38. Minister without Portfolio in War Cabinet 1939-40.

HENDERSON, Rt. Hon. Sir Nevile. 1882-1942. British Ambassador at Berlin 1937-39.

HOARE, Rt. Hon. Sir Samuel (later Lord TEMPLEWOOD). 1880-1959. Foreign Secretary 1935. First Lord of the Admiralty 1936-37. Secretary of State for Home Affairs 1937-39. British Ambassador to Spain 1940-44.

HODSOLL, Wing-Commander Sir John. 1894-. Inspector-General Air Raid Precautions, 1938-48. Chief Civil Defence Adviser to NATO 1954-61.

HOGG, Brigadier D. McA. 1888-. Brigadier I/C Administration A.A. Command 1938-40. Major-General I/C Administration Northern Command 1941.

HORE-BELISHA, Leslie, 1st Baron of DEVONPORT (1954). 1893-1957. Minister of Transport 1934-37. Secretary of State for War and President of Army Council 1937-40.

HORTHY DE NAGYBENYA, Admiral Nicholas. 1868-1957. Regent of the Kingdom of Hungary 1920-44.

HOTBLACK, Major-General Frederick Elliott. 1887-. Military Attaché Berlin 1935-37. General Staff, War Office 1937-39. General Staff, B.E.F. 1939. Commander Division 1939-40.

HOWARD-VYSE, Major-General Sir Richard Granville Hylton. 1883-. Head of Military Mission with French High Command 1939-40.

ISMAY, General Hastings Lionel, 1st Baron. 1887-. Secretary, Committee of Imperial Defence 1938. Chief of Staff to Minister of Defence 1940-45.

JOUBERT DE LA FERTÉ, Air Chief Marshal Sir Philip Bennet. Assistant Chief of Air Staff. Officer Commanding in Chief, Coastal Command 1941-43.

KENNEDY, Joseph Patrick. 1888-. U.S. Ambassador to London 1937-41.

KENNEDY, Major-General Sir John. 1893-. Director of Plans 1938-39. C.R.A., 52nd Division 1940. B.G.S. 1940. D.M.O. 1940-43. Assistant C.I.G.S.(Ops. & Int.) 1943-45.

KEYES, Admiral of the Fleet Roger John Brownlow, 1st baron of ZEEBRUGGE and of DOVER (1943). 1872-1945. Retired 1935. M.P. 1934-43. Replaced on active list 1940. Special Liaison Officer to King Leopold of Belgium 1940. Director of Combined Operations 1940-41.

KING-SALTER, Major E. J. C., later Lieutenant-Colonel Rifle Brigade, was originally Military Attaché at Helsingfors, Finland.

KIRKE, General Sir Walter Mervyn St. George. 1877-1949. Served First World War. Director-General, Territorial Army 1936-39. Inspector-General of Home Defences 1939. C.-in-C. Home Forces 1939-40.

LAMMIE, Colonel (temp. Major-General) George. 1891-1946. Commander 147 Infantry Brigade 1940-41. Director of Quartering, War Office 1941-44.

LATHAM, Brigadier Francis. 1883-1958. Commander Sub-Area 1940-43.

LLOYD, General Sir Henry Charles. 1891-. Commander 2nd Division, B.E.F. 1939-40. Chief of General Staff, Home Forces 1941-42.

LINDSELL, Lieutenant-General Sir Wilfrid Gordon. 1884-. Served First World War. C.R.A. 4th Division 1937-38. Major-General in charge of Administration, Southern Command 1938-1939. Quartermaster-General of B.E.F. 1939-40. Lieutenant-General in charge of Administration in Middle East 1942-43.

LIVERPOOL, Arthur William de Brito Savile Foljambe, 5th Earl of. 1870-1941.

McNAUGHTON, General the Hon. Andrew George Latta. 1887-. Commander 1st Canadian Division 1939-40. G.O.C. VII Corps 1940. G.O.C. in C. First Canadian Army 1942-43.

MACKESY, Major-General Pierse Joseph. 1883-1956. Commander of Land Forces in Narvik area 1940.

MAISKY, Ivan Mikhailovich. 1884-. Soviet Ambassador to London 1932-43.

MAITLAND, Lieutenant-Colonel Frederick Lewis Makgill Crichton. 1878-. Gordon Highlanders.

MANNERHEIM, Field Marshal. 1867-1951. Served in the Russian Imperial Army, but in 1917 escaped to Finland. Organized a Finnish army, and was C.-in-C. Finnish Forces 1939-40.

MASSY, Major- (later Lieutenant-) General Hugh Royds Stokes. 1884-. D.C.I.G.S. 1939-40. Commander Central Norway Force 1940. Corps Commander 1940-41.

MILNE, Field-Marshal Lord George Francis. 1866-1948. C.I.G.S. 1926-33. Served in Sudan; South Africa; First World War.

MONTGOMERY-MASSINGBERD, Field-Marshal Sir Archibald. 1871-1947. C.I.G.S. 1933-36. Served South Africa; First World War.

MOORE-BRABAZON, John Theodore Cuthbert (later Lord BRABAZON OF TARA). 1884-. Minister of Transport 1940-41. Minister of Aircraft Production 1941-42.

MORGAN, Brigadier (later Major-General) Harold de Reimer. 1888-. Commanding 148 Brigade, Norway 1940. Commander 45th Division 1941-43.

MORRISON, Rt. Hon. Herbert Stanley (now Lord MORRISON OF LAMBETH). 1888-. Home Secretary, Minister of Home Security 1940-45.

NEEDHAM, Major-General Henry. 1876-. Retired 1935. Special appointments in Near East and Belgium 1939-40.

NEWALL, Marshal of the Royal Air Force (1940) Cyril Louis Norton,

1st baron of CLIFTON-UPON-DUNSMOOR (1946). 1886-. Chief of the Air Staff 1937-40. Governor-General and Commander-in-Chief of New Zealand 1941-46.

NOSWORTHY, Lieutenant-General Sir Francis Poitiers. 1887-. Corps Commander 1940.

PAGET, General Sir Bernard Charles Tolver. 1887-. Commandant Staff College 1938-39. Commander 18th Division and in Norway 1939-40. C.G.S. Home Forces 1940-41. C.-in-C. South Eastern Command 1941. C.-in-C. Home Forces 1941-43. C.-in-C. 21st Army Group 1943. C.-in-C. Middle East Forces 1944-46.

PAKENHAM-WALSH, Major-General Ridley P. 1888-. Engineer-in-Chief B.E.F. 1939-40.

PÉTAIN, Marshal Philippe. 1856-1951. The Hero of Verdun, 1916, in resisting German attacks on the fortress. C.-in-C. French Armies after Nivelle 1917-18. Chief of the French State, 1940-44.

PHILLIPS, Admiral Sir Tom Spencer Vaughan. 1888-1941. Vice-Chief of Naval Staff 1939-41 C.-in-C. Eastern Fleet 1941.

PHILLIPS, Major-General Charles George. 1889-. Commander British Troops, Namsos, Norway 1940 (under General Carton de Wiart).

POUND, Admiral of the Fleet Sir DUDLEY. 1877-1943. C.-in-C. Mediterranean 1936-39. First Sea Lord and Chief of Naval Staff 1939-43.

POWNALL, Lieutenant-General Sir Henry. 1887-1961. D.M.O. & I. 1938-39. C.G.S., B.E.F. 1939-40. Inspector-General Home Guard 1940. V.C.I.G.S. 1941. C.-in-C. Far East 1941-42. C. of S. "ABDA" Command, Far East 1942. G.O.C. Ceylon 1942-43. C. of S. to Supreme Allied Commander, S.E.A.C. 1943-44.

RAWLINSON, Lord Henry Seymour. 1864-1925. Commanded 4th Corps—4th Army in First World War and Forces in N. Russia in 1919. Subsequently Commander-in-Chief of the Army in India.

REYNAUD, Paul. 1878-. Finance Minister in French Government 1938-40. Prime Minister, Minister of Foreign Affairs and of National Defence 1940.

ROSEWAY, Sir David. 1890-. Private Secretary to the following Secretaries of State for War (1936-40): Mr. A. Duff-Cooper; Mr. Leslie Hore-Belisha; Mr. Oliver Stanley; Mr. Anthony Eden. Subsequently Deputy Under-Secretary of State, War Office 1944-55.

RUNCIMAN, Walter, 1st Viscount of DOXFORD. 1870-1949. President of the Board of Trade 1931-37. Head of Mission to Czechoslovakia 1939. Lord President of the Council 1938-39.

SANDYS, Rt. Hon. Duncan. 1908. Commissioned in T.A. 1937. Served in Expeditionary Force to Norway 1940. Lieutenant-Colonel 1941.

SIMON, Sir John Allsebrook (later Viscount). 1873-1954. Secretary of State for Foreign Affairs 1931-35. Chancellor of the Exchequer 1937-40.

SLESSOR, Marshal of the Royal Air Force Sir John Cotesworth. 1897-. Director of Plans, Air Ministry 1937-41.

SPENS, Sir Will. 1882-. Regional Commissioner for Civil Defence, Eastern Region 1939-45. Master of Corpus Christi College, Cambridge 1947-52.

STANLEY, Rt. Hon. Oliver Frederick George. 1896-1950. President of the Board of Trade 1937-40. Secretary of State for War 1940.

STERN, Lieutenant-Colonel Sir Albert. 1878-. Chairman, Special Vehicle Development Committee, Ministry of Supply 1939-43. Member of Tank Board 1941.

STEWART, Sir Samuel Findlater. 1879-1960. Permanent Under-Secretary of State for India 1930-42. Special Duties, May 1940.

STRANG, William, Lord of STONESFIELD (1954). 1893-. Councillor at Moscow Embassy 1932. Assistant Under-Secretary of State in Foreign Office 1939-43.

SWAYNE, Lieutenant-General Sir John George des Reaux. 1890-. Head of British Military Mission to French G.Q.G. (General Georges) 1939-40. G.O.C. 4th Division 1940-42. Chief of General Staff, Home Forces 1942.

SWINTON, Major-General Sir Ernest. 1868-1951. Official "Eye-Witness" in First World War. Had much to do with the invention of the tank. Author of *The Green Curve*, etc. Colonel-Commandant Royal Tank Corps 1934-38. Ministry of Supply 1939-40.

TAYLOR, General Sir Maurice Grove. 1881-1960. Deputy Master General of the Ordnance 1938-39. Senior Military Adviser to the Ministry of Supply 1939-41.

TILLY, Major-General Justice Crosland. 1888-1941. Commander 1st Tank Brigade 1938, and 2nd Armoured Division 1940.

TRENT, John Campbell Boot, 2nd Baron. 1889-1956. Regional Commissioner for Civil Defence, North Midland Region 1939-45.

VENNING, General Sir Walter King. 1882-. Director of Movements and Quartering (War Office) 1934-38. Quartermaster-General War Office 1939-42.

VON RUNDSTEDT, General Gerd. 1875-1953. Commanded the German Armoured Divisions in the break through in the Ardennes and the drive to the coast.

WALEY-COHEN, Sir Robert. 1877-1952. Managing Director Shell Transport & Trading Co. Ltd.: Petroleum Adviser to the Army Council.

WARRENDER, Victor Alexander George Anthony (later Lord BRUNTIS-FIELD). 1899-. Financial Secretary, War Office. 1935-40.

WEYGAND, Général Maxime. 1867-. Chief of Staff to Général Foch 1914-23. High Commissioner in Syria 1923-24. Commander-in-Chief of the French Forces in the Eastern Mediterranean 1939-1940. Commander-in-Chief French Land Forces May-June 1940. Minister of National Defence to Marshal Pétain June-September 1940.

WHITWORTH, Admiral Sir William Jock. 1884-. Vice-Admiral Commanding Battle Cruiser Squadron 1939-41. Second Sea Lord 1941-44.

WIGRAM, Vice-Admiral Ernest. 1877-1944. Retired 1931.

WOOD, Rt. Hon. Sir Kingsley. 1881-1943. Postmaster-General 1931-35. Minister of Health 1935-38. Secretary of State for Air 1938-40. Thereafter Chancellor of the Exchequer.

WOOLTON, Frederick James Marquis, First Earl of, 1883-. Director-General of Equipment and Stores, Ministry of Supply, 1939-40. Minister of Food 1940-43.

INDEX

Aalesund: 262

Abbeville: 318, 326

Abyssinia: 16, 25, 41, 45, 223

Admiralty: 100, 115, 141, 263, 271, 279, 283, 301, 310; "very light-hearted" about 1938 situation, 48; Churchill returns to, 91; never asked to "show what it is doing", 134; no knowledge of Army instructions for Narvik attack, 254; doubts on Trondheim naval attack plan, 271; asked to organize boats for B.E.F. evacuation, 314

Africa: *see under* North Africa, East Africa, etc.

Afridi, H.M.S.: loss of, 294

Air Conference: 125

Air Force: *see under* Royal Air Force; also French, German Air Force, etc. and individual leaders

Air Ministry: 47, 141, 142, 144, 189; "very light-hearted" about 1938 situation, 48; disbelief in passive defence, 58; plans for Air Striking Force in France, 84, 86; bomber plans, 140; Ironside wants Army Air Arm, 141; no plan for opposing air attacks on Army, 141; refuse machines to Army, 144; struggle over co-operation with Army, 159

Air Raid Precautions: 71, 103

Alamein: 130

Albania: 72, 192

Albert (France): 318

Albert Canal: 149, 151, 152, 154; main Belgian defence line, 150, 206; Allies ignorant of defences, 241; Allies wish to reconnoitre, 241; intact bridges over, 304

Aldershot Command: 46, 84, 86, 91, 160

Alexander, A. V.: First Lord of the Admiralty, 306, 314

Alexander, General: 122

Alexandria: 66

Alsace: 199

Altmark: Navy liberates prisoners from, 219; and Norwegian neutrality, 246

Altmeyer, General: 357

Amery, L. S.: 92, 193

Amiens: 85, 166, 313, 317, 318, 319, 321, 326

Amsterdam: 149

Andalsnes: 262, 264, 272, 276, 281, 286; landing at, 266, 267, 270; pincer movement on Trondheim planned from, 271; 15th British Brigade to join Morgan at, 277; Paget in overall command, 282; need to stabilize Andalsnes-Dombas front, 283; troops from in Glasgow, 296

Anderson, Sir John: 70

Anglo-German Naval Agreement: denounced by Hitler, 73

Anti-aircraft defence of Britain: 103; six A.A. divisions contemplated, 58; neglect of, 60; Ironside's concern over, 109; slow A.A. gun production, 127; London defence anxieties, 128; Sweden refuses Bofors guns, 128, 129

Antwerp: 133, 150, 151, 154, 303; Namur-Antwerp line, 233, 306

Archangel: 14, 187

Archangel, 1918-19 (Ironside): 14

Ardennes: 118, 120, 149, 150, 205

409

mobilization request refused, 89;
mobilization ordered, 91; Ironside
C.I.G.S., 93; war plans for, 103,
108; Army Service Corps, 106;
Middle East build-up, 112; in
France, *see* British Expeditionary
Force (B.E.F.); R.A.F. strengthened
at expense of, 122; artillery, 126;
delay over ammunition, 129; need
for Air Arm, 139-43; and Plan D,
148-54, 166; conflict with R.A.F.
over Air Arm, 144, 159; Pioneer
Corps formed, 155; chain of command, 157; Hore-Belisha cancels
Ironside's orders, 161; little action
compared with R.A.F. and Navy,
188; gun shortage, 216; in Norway,
see under Norway, *and under* names
of places; expansion and training,
241; Ironside criticizes training,
242-3; attack before 1941 impossible, 243; Middle East battalions replaced, 351; 51st Division in
France, 351; battalions in India for
U.K., 351; calm command needed
to repel invasion, 359; demands on
Supply Ministry unfulfilled, 361;
51st Division withdraws on Havre,
361; 51st Division lays down arms
at St. Valerie, 363; size and disposition, 380

British Empire: 65, 115, 391, 393;
major war 1919-1928 unlikely, 20;
Coast Defence costs, 22; Franco
victory bad for the, 53; vulnerable
to German-Italian air attack, 66;
Mediterranean route essential to,
66; dangers of unpreparedness, 69;
not to be risked over Czechoslovakia, 70; no plans for, 103;
Ironside's plans, 103-5; likely effects
of Italian hostility, 108, 112;
Weizmann claims Zionism good
for, 135; status of Ireland, 235;
fate may rest with troops in
France, 303, 304; fateful battle for,
beginning, 306; "up against the
crashing of the Empire", 315;

defence of Britain vital to, 335;
Wavell's position in, 350; staunch-
ness needed to save, 352; great
struggle for existence of, 364, 365;
weakness in Chamberlain's day,
388, 389

British Expeditionary Force: 344,
345; organization, 24; no men
or money for, 57; Hore-Belisha's
enquiries into, 37; varying views
on need for, 37, 38, 41, 42-3, 55,
58, 60; decision to send to France,
73; Ironside expects to be C.-in-C.,
74, 76, 91, 92; as goodwill gesture
to France, 79; Lindsell as Quarter-
Master General, 79; plans for, 84-5;
Gort to command, 94; under
French orders, 100; Ironside's plan
for, 103, 104, 105; equipment
deficiencies, 106; numbers, 107;
French to have fighter aircraft
from, 120; Ironside tours front,
122-4; and Plan D, 148-54, 166;
existence unknown to many French
troops, 155; troops in Saar to meet
French, 155; very small Force, 158;
Gamelin wants larger, 162-3, 172;
Hore-Belisha visits, 164, 166; dis-
satisfaction with defences of, 164-8;
defence work done, 395-9; reactions to Hore-Belisha's resignation, 194, 195, 198; alerted, 205;
wanted by French to enter Belgium,
205, 206-7; 5th Regular Division
for Norway, 210; enters Belgium,
301; not strongly engaged, 306;
only has infantry tanks for counter-
attack, 307; new position, 310;
Churchill sees dangers facing, 311,
312, 313; evacuation plans, 314;
withdraws to Dendre, 318; communications danger, 318, 329; plans
for move to Abbeville-Amiens line,
319; Ironside and Gort differ over
Amiens attack, 320, 327; under
Billotte, 321; no orders for in
eight days, 321; Belgians to relieve
44th Division, 321; food, ammuni-

propaganda of, 114; size of Western Front Army, 115; Belgian fear of, 116; possible advance through Low Countries, 144, 145, 146, 279, 294; and Plan D, 148-56; alleged East Anglia raiding force, 160; and the Balkans, 170, 171, 174; Allied need to disperse forces of, 176, 190; iron-ore supplies for, 181, 182, 184-5, 216, 229, 297; likely effects of Allied Scandinavian plans on, 184, 185, 187, 189; plans for invading Low Countries captured, 204; Sweden fears Russia more than, 210; Baltic shipping of, 211; estimate of grand strategy of, 211; must know Allied plans in Scandinavia, 217; may attack Gällivare, 222; Russian agreement with purely economic, 223; urges Finnish armistice, 224; strong position of, 226; Allied plan to mine waterways of, *see* Operation Royal Marine; puts out rumours of attack, 240; Scandinavian plans of, 245-6, 248-9; has the initiative, 295; bombing of, 317; may reduce Britain by air alone, 335, 349; Italy joins with, 350, 361, 362; advantages for attacking Britain, 359-60, 375-6; French armistice with, 367, 369; military strength of, 388-90

Ghent: 154, 394

Gibraltar: 69, 76, 307: Straits, 45, 171; Ironside Governor of, 52, 53; unsafe from air attack, 66; difficulty of combining Governorship with C.-in-C., Mediterranean, 68; defences strengthened, 72; Ironside leaves, 75

Givet: 150, 306

Glasgow: 296

Glorious, H.M.S.: 283

Goering, Hermann: 57, 233, 240, 350; meets Ironside at German manœuvres, 28, 29, 30, 31

Gort, Field-Marshal Viscount: 69, 71, 76, 89, 91, 106, 116, 157, 163, 204,

242, 243, 333, 344, 351; Military Secretary, 26; upset by Hore-Belisha, 33, 34; C.I.G.S., 38, 39, 40; lectures, 55; no grasp of situation, 59, 60; wants Ironside as C.-in-C., Middle East, 64, 68; reviews Allied plans, 79; Ironside's views of, 83, 87; C.-in-C., British Expeditionary Force, 94; Ironside's letter to, on Scheldt occupation, 113, 394-5; at Vincennes, 148, 150; objects to orders through Army Council, 161; "Pill-Box Row" and, 164-8; Hore-Belisha's resignation and Gort, 195, 196, 198; Legion of Honour, 198, 199; difference with Ironside over instructions, 318, 319-20; no orders to in eight days, 321; B.E.F. chain of command, 322; difficulties of B.E.F., 327, 328, 330-1; withdraws from Arras, 332; message to King, 345; leaves France, 347; G.C.B. from King, 349; with Duff Cooper in Casablanca, 371

Great Britain: 158, 172, 370; strong 1918, weak 1939, 19; Cabinet changes, 24; no Army policy, 40; Italy and, 45; Ironside foresees demands on, 49; sends Runciman to Prague, 58; conscription in, 72; promises Expeditionary Force to France, 73, 126; confirms Polish treaty, 89; ultimatum to Germany, 91; Army plans for, 103; prepares for three-year war, 106; German propaganda about, 114; "peace mentality" of Government, 128; Plan D would keep enemy fighters from, 152; Government and Ruhr bombing, 146; must be defended, 155; mobilization figures, 162, 163; war strategy, 174, 175-6, 194; misunderstood by Hitler, 177; Belgium wants support of, 205; chance of taking initiative, 212; Russia opposes Scandinavian plans of, 223; Norway and Sweden in-

Index

peace with Britain, 350; dictates French terms, 364, 368; orders Luftwaffe to destroy R.A.F., 379; methods, 389, 390

Hoare, Sir Samuel: 71, 281; and Army Air Arm plan, 140; "no military conception", 144

Hochwald: 200, 201

Hodsoll, Wing-Commander: 344

Holkham: 198

Holland: 109, 111, 115, 118, 120, 132, 150, 151, 152, 154, 156, 206, 293, 302, 307, 315, 374, 378, 383, 384, 394, 395; no agreed plan if Germans invade, 145; French expect invasion of, 146; Allies consider action over, 148; Dutch defence plan, 149; German invasion plan captured, 204; Allies ignorant of Dutch plans, 233; no Allied aid to through Belgium unless invited, 236, 237; invasion of likely, 249, 296, 297; possible German moves against, 242, 279, 294; invasion of, 301, 305; failure to blow bridges, 304; Dutch hard pressed S. of Zuyder Zee, 305; cannot continue for long, 306; Nazis bomb aerodromes, 309

Home Defence Executive: 343; Ironside Chairman, 341, 342; reduced in size, 344

Home Office: 344, 369, 370

Home Forces: Ironside C.-in-C., 335, 339; forces available, 340-1; Brooke as C.-in-C., 387

Homing Fuze: 302

Hong Kong: 41, 103

Hore-Belisha, Leslie: 35, 36, 58, 69, 70, 71, 78, 92, 100, 116, 125, 127, 132, 133, 134, 136, 140, 141, 144, 157, 164, 177, 361, 399; War Minister, 23; Ironside's views on, 24, 33, 34, 273; improves Army service conditions, 25, 26, 36; Deverall criticizes, 34; first meets Ironside, 36-7; appoints Gort C.I.G.S., 38, 39, 40; lacks Army

plan, 43, 85; offers Ironside Gibraltar Governorship, 52, 53; changes Army officer strength, 55; recruitment methods, 56; introduces conscription, 72, 83; Territorial policy, 73; offers Ironside Inspector-General, Overseas Forces post, 74; sees Ironside, 76, 77, 80; ignorance of Poland, 83; unprepared for Cabinet questions, 89; advised to mobilize, 89; informed of Polish bombing, 91; appoints Ironside C.I.G.S., 93; Gort made C.-in-C., British Expeditionary Force, 94; and Army Council, 101; military ignorance, jealousy of Churchill, 105, 116, 125, 144; friction with Ironside over issuing orders, 160-1; in "Pill-Box Row", 164-8; views on action in Scandinavia, 192; resignation, 194, 195, 196, 197, 198; abolishes Master-General of the Ordnance, 242

Horthy, Admiral: 52

Hotblack, Major-General: 107, 266, 268, 270

Houx: 306

Hungary: 50, 64

Hunt, Frazier: 239

Huntziger, General: 232, 369

Hurricane fighter: 346

Hythe: 373

Iceland: 380

Imperial Defence, Committee of: 69, 83, 161

India: military authorities, 74, 75; Hitler and, 111; troops, 85, 103, 105, 134, 136, 351

Information, Ministry of: 239, 240

Iraq: 105, 115; Britain to rearm, 22; Hitler and, 111

Ireland: 235, 374, 380

Ironside, Field-Marshal Lord: 304, 307, 308, 309, 310, 326; early life, 13; author, *Archangel, 1918-19*, 14; career to 1936, 13-15; G.O.C., Eastern Command, 15; diaries of,

422

Mons: 108, 154

Montgomery, General: 123, 167

Moore-Brabazon, Lt.-Colonel: 140, 143

Morgan, Brigadier: 264, 266, 267, 277; contacts Norwegians, 269; at Andalsnes, 270; at Lillehammer, 276, 282; retreats, 283

Morocco: 307, 372

Moscow: 77

Moselle: 231, 233

Mosjoën: 288, 292, 293, 294, 296, 297, 305

Mussolini, Benito: 64, 84, 103, 389; and Abyssinia, N. Africa, 16; at German manœuvres, 28; Churchill's views on, 45; abets Hitler in annexing Austria, 49; with Hitler at Munich, 65; refuses arms to Allies, 128; Roosevelt denounces, 362

Namsos: 288, 289; Ironside urged to land force at, 253; Co-ordination Committee discuss, 255; Carton de Wiart at, 256, 263, 264, 266, 270, 282; half Narvik troops diverted to, 257, 258, 260; troops arrive without commander, 259; pincer movement from on Trondheim, 271; bombing, 272; railhead destruction, 276; A.A. protection needed, 277; position desperate, 279; Allied troops in, 280, 281; evacuation, 282, 284, 286, 287, 292; behaviour of French troops at, 294; troops from in Glasgow, 296

Namur: 125, 133, 149, 151, 152, 154, 309; Namur-Antwerp Line, 233, 306

Nantes: 361

Napoleon I: 275, 364, 367

Narvik: 173, 193, 237, 261, 262, 263, 280, 285, 286, 291, 293, 295; iron-ore port for Germany, 181, 182; best port for Allied aid to Finland, 182, 184-6, 188; landing planned, 187, 189, 190; hasty ore traffic

stoppage inadvisable, 194-5; Cabinet's views, 196, 209, 210; aid to Finland through, 215, 219, 224-8; Allied intentions known, 221; mine-laying plans to aid Allied entry, 222, 238; Narvik-Lulea railway problems, 223, 225, 228, 267; Expedition abandoned, 228; Cabinet conditions for Narvik occupation, 245; mines laid, 247, 248; Germans land, 248, 249, 250; British plan to capture, 250, 251, 252; Navy attacks, 252, 256; diversion to Namsos proposed, 253, 257, 258; convoy sails, 254; Instructions for, 254-5; misgivings over operation, 259, 260; difficulties, 265, 266, 267, 281, 282; differences between Army and Navy commanders, 269, 270; Lord Cork takes command of forces at, 273; prospects of taking, 276; operation to go on, 284, 288; Auchinleck to command, 288, 295, 296, 297; Germans burn, 290; need to stop Germans relieving, 292; Hitler and, 294; Allies capture, 297; Allies evacuate, 298

Nazis: 309, 362, 389, 390; in Austria, Czechoslovakia, 16; demand Sudetenland autonomy, 57; tyranny, 274; aims, 275; Nazified Europe, 315; democracy and Nazism, 357

Needham, General: 305

Neuchatel: 310

Newall, Air Chief Marshal Sir Cyril: 117, 140, 146, 253, 373; on Chiefs of Stagg Committee, 100, 101, 188; French seek air aid from, at Vincennes, 120; at Vincennes Conference, 148, 150; wants to keep Germany from Belgian airfields, 150, 151; wants Ruhr bombed, 156, 306, 307

Newcastle upon Tyne: 379

New Zealand: 41, 103, 105

Ninove: 133

Noguès, General: 102; in Casablanca,

371; Pétain against his continuing to fight Germans, 372

North Africa, French: 72, 365

North Downs: 379

North Sea: 248, 251, 263

Northern Ireland: 372

Northolt Aerodrome: defences at, 362

Norway: 189, 214, 243, 244, 256, 262, 374, 379, 380, 382; plan to mine territorial waters of, 181, 184, 196, 230, 238, 247, 248; cherishes neutrality, 182, 186, 187; possible German occupation of South, 187; effects of Allied action in, 192, 193; still allows German access to ore, 209; air defence inadequate, 212; neutrality unaffected by Petsamo landing plan, 213; Narvik plan may bring Norway into War, 216; no consent to Allied landings, 219, 225; protests over *Altmark* incident, 219; British hesitation over landing without permission, 221, 223, 224, 226, 238, 245; no British intention to fight through, 228; Germans consider occupying, 245-6; Germans invade, 248-9; resistance in, 249; seeks British aid, 260, 261, 281; Norwegians retreat against Germans, 280; Norwegian forces, 288, 297; King and Government, 290, 296; Allied defeat in, 298

Norwegian Expedition: *see under* names of places and leaders

Nosworthy, General: 385

Nottingham: 370

Operation "Royal Marine" (Rhine mine-laying): 230, 243, 244, 246, 302

Operation "Sea-Lion" (invasion of Britain): too ambitious for German Navy, 298; plans for, 378-9; map, 381

Orchies: 396

Orkneys: 161

Oslo: 192, 223, 247, 248, 249, 256, 276, 277, 281, 282

Ostend: 331, 379

Overstraten, van: 241, 242, 305

Paget, General: 270, 277, 282, 286, 287, 291, 292, 345, 373, 383

Pakenham-Walsh, General: 165, 167

Palestine: 24, 45, 105, 108, 348, 350; Ironside visits, 65; suggests changes, 69; Basra-Palestine overland route plans, 103; Mounted Division "sneaked out" to, 112; "Maginot Line" in, 131; idea of Jewish units from, 131; possible factories in, 132; Weizmann and Zionism, 135, 137

Paris: 101, 114, 116, 231, 246, 311, 327, 345; general reserve around, 118, 150; Supreme War Council in, 173, 186, 215, 216; decisive time for, 312; defence of, 313, 314, 318, 331n1, 362; evacuated, 364; declared an open town, 365

Peronne: 318, 332

Pétain, Marshal: President of the Council, 366; makes terms with Germans, 367; armistice meeting with Hitler, 368; tries to stop continuance of War in French Empire, 372

Petibon, Colonel: 117

Petsamo: 193, 214, 215

Pfaffenhofen: 200

Phillips, Admiral Sir Tom: 253, 263

Phillips, Brigadier: 257, 264, 279

Plan D: 148-54, 166

Poland: 52, 64, 72, 111, 124, 146, 148, 177, 221, 226, 400; Russo-German partition of, 16, 97, 182; "a possible Spain", 44; Chamberlain guarantees, 72, 77, 225; Hitler denounces Non-Aggression Pact with, 73; Ironside's mission instructions to, 76-8; Danzig plan, 76; Polish view of German plans, 80; rearmament efforts, 81, 82; Hore-Belisha's ignorance of, 83; Churchill foresees fate of, 83; French lies to, 85; Russo-German Non-Aggression Pact and, 89, 182; Warsaw, Cracow bombed, 90, 91; seeks British aid, 97; Germans invade, 97; Air Force wiped out, 114; lessons to Allies from campaign in, 117; effects of British guarantee to, 216, 227; Allied diplomatic defeat in, 223; speedy collapse of, 225, 312; troops from in Scandinavia, 288, 297

Portsmouth: 360, 377, 379
Portugal: 267
Pound, Admiral: 100, 101, 188, 253, 254, 262
Pownall, Lt.-General Sir Henry: 49, 50, 57, 89, 91, 321, 357
Poznania: 78, 80, 92
Prague: Hitler's objective after Austria, 50; Runciman mission to, 58
Press, the: 217, 220, 228, 292, 309; influence on Cabinet, 145; "Belisha Scandal", 195; angered by Ironside's interview in *Daily Express*, 240; and "stupidity of the brasshats", 243; leakage of plans through, 271, 283
Prétalat, General: 200
Priorities Committee: 101, 128

Quai D'Orsay: 216, 278: archives burned, 311, 312

Ramsgate: 378
Rawlinson, Lord: 14
Reading: 360
Recuin, General: 201
Red Sea: 25
Reichenau, General von: with Ironside at German manœuvres, 26; "brotherhood with England, but only for two years", 27, 177
Renown, H.M.S.: 258
Reynaud, Paul: 236, 237, 243, 286, 313, 327, 365; criticizes British mobilization, 162, 163, 164; French

Prime Minister, 231, 233; paper on winning the War, 234-5; criticizes Chamberlain, 234; wants War direction revised, 235; at Supreme War Council, 237-8, 250, 278; in England, 249; difficult over Norway, 278; intends to change Gamelin for Weygand, 302, 319; wants fighter aircraft, troops, 308, 356; says battle is lost, 308; better than Daladier, 313; takes over Defence Ministry, 319; Pétain joins ministry, 319; conference with Churchill, 328; Churchill dissuades from armistice, 364; goes, 366

Rheims: 158
Rhine: 124, 151, 156; German defences on, 199; mines in, *see* Operation "Royal Marine"; Germans pass, 366
Ribbentrop, von: 89
Richards, Emma Maria: 13
Richmond, Yorks.: 372
Richtman, General: 27
Roosevelt, President: Churchill seeks aid from; 40; denounces Mussolini, 362
Rosen, Baron: 220, 221
Rosyth: 128, 248, 261
Rotterdam: 149, 302, 303, 304, 305
Roubaix: 394
Rouen: 314, 357, 361, 389
Roumania: 45, 82, 84, 85, 105
Royal Air Force: 103, 104, 114, 118, 122, 134, 141, 263, 357, 385, 389, 400; in 1918 strong, in 1939 weak, 19; slow expansion, 42; little Imperial defence by, 43; getting all money, 47; and U.K. defence, 48; disbelieves in passive defence, 58; no co-operation with Army, 60, 394; and indiscriminate bombing, 80, 142, 146, 296, 297; under War Cabinet, 100; oppose Ironside's plans, 104, 109; hardly used in first month of War, 113; Gamelin wants aid from, 120, 155;

wants more action in Balkans, 169;
1930 defence plans of, 232; re-
places Gamelin, 302, 319, 326; is
asked to relieve Billotte, 322; new
plan similar to Gamelin's, 322;
Arras-Somme gap attack plan, 327,
328, 329, 330; discussions with
King Leopold and Billotte, 327;
directions of no effect, 334; wants
more British troops, planes, 356;
as Vice-President of the Council,
366

Whitworth, Admiral: 259

Wiart, Major-General Carton de:
81, 266, 267, 271, 272: commands
Namsos and Trondheim troops,
255; ordered to Namsos, 256, 261;
arrival difficulties, 262; lands, 263,
264, 270; to be reinforced, 277;
German attacks compel evacuation, 279, 282

Wight, Isle of: 375

Wigram, Admiral: 99

Wilton: 386

Wingate, Colonel: 348

Wood, Sir Kingsley: 100, 140, 141,
144, 147

World War, First: 48, 130, 230;
Salonika Expedition, 105, 106;
German defeat in, 273; Zeebrugge,
281

Yorkshire: 380

Ypres: 331

Zuyder Zee: 303, 305